D1630279

Performance Politics and the British Voter

What matters most to voters when they choose their leaders? This book suggests that performance politics is at the heart of contemporary democracy, with voters forming judgments about how well competing parties and leaders perform on important issues. Given the high stakes and uncertainty involved, voters rely heavily on partisan cues and party leader images as guides to electoral choice. However, the authors argue that the issue agenda of British politics has changed markedly in recent years. A cluster of concerns about crime, immigration and terrorism now mix with perennial economic and public service issues. Since voters and parties often share the same positions on these issues, political competition focuses on who can do the best job. This book shows that a model emphasizing flexible partisan attachments, party leader images and judgments of party competence on key issues can explain electoral choice in Britain and elsewhere.

HAROLD D. CLARKE is Ashbel Smith Professor in the School of Economic, Political and Policy Sciences at the University of Texas at Dallas and Director of the Social and Economic Sciences Division of the National Science Foundation.

DAVID SANDERS is Professor of Government at the University of Essex.

MARIANNE C. STEWART is Professor of Political Science in the School of Economic, Political and Policy Sciences at the University of Texas at Dallas.

PAUL F. WHITELEY is Professor of Government at the University of Essex.

Performance Politics and the British Voter

HAROLD D. CLARKE

DAVID SANDERS

MARIANNE C. STEWART

PAUL F. WHITELEY

CAMBRIDGE
UNIVERSITY PRESS

CAMBRIDGE UNIVERSITY PRESS
Cambridge, New York, Melbourne, Madrid, Cape Town, Singapore,
São Paulo, Delhi

Cambridge University Press
The Edinburgh Building, Cambridge CB2 8RU, UK

Published in the United States of America by Cambridge University Press, New York

www.cambridge.org
Information on this title: www.cambridge.org/9780521697286

First published 2009

Printed in the United Kingdom at the University Press, Cambridge

A catalogue record for this publication is available from the British Library

Library of Congress Cataloguing in Publication data
Performance politics and the British voter / Harold D. Clarke ... [et al.].
   p.   cm.
Includes bibliographical references and index.
ISBN 978-0-521-87444-1 (hardback)   1. Voting–Great Britain.
2. Elections–Great Britain.   3. Political parties–Great Britain–Public opinion.
4. Great Britain–Politics and government–1945–   5. Public opinion–Great Britain.
I. Clarke, Harold D.   II. Title.
JN956.P47 2009
324.941–dc22   2009017296

ISBN 978-0-521-87444-1 hardback
ISBN 978-0-521-69728-6 paperback

Contents

Figures

Tables

Acknowledgments

National election studies long have been major infrastructure projects in political science. The British Election Study (BES) has been conducted at the time of every general election since 1964. Starting in 2001, we have been privileged to be BES principal investigators. The core analyses in *Performance Politics and the British Voter* are based on survey data gathered in the 2005 study. When conducting the BES and related projects, we have benefited from the advice and assistance of a large number of organizations and individuals. We are pleased to have this opportunity to acknowledge their help.

First is the Economic and Social Research Council (the ESRC). The ESRC funded both the 2001 and 2005 BES, as well as the Dynamics of Democracy surveys conducted in Paul Whiteley's Participation and Democracy programme. The latter surveys provided us with monthly portraits of British public opinion between January 2000 and December 2002. The ESRC also funded national surveys in March, April–May and October 2003 to gather information on the dynamics of British public opinion about the Iraq War early in the history of that controversial conflict. We particularly appreciate the interest in our research expressed by ESRC officers, Gary Williams and Jennifer Edwards. Gary's enthusiasm for, and advocacy of, the BES has done much to invigorate research on voting, elections and public opinion in Britain.

Thanks are due also to Sam Younger and the UK Electoral Commission. The Commission helped to fund the 2005 study. These funds enabled us to include extra question batteries, and to expand the Scottish and Welsh booster samples. In addition, we thank BBC *Newsnight* and other media outlets for providing Sanders and Whiteley with opportunities to discuss the 2005 election with national and regional audiences. These opportunities helped us to disseminate information about BES findings to a large public audience in a timely way.

We thank the National Science Foundation (US) for its support for a now lengthy series of monthly surveys that interface with the BES. The first of these surveys (the Dynamics of Party Support (DPS) project) covered the 1992–9 period, and the second (the Government Performance and Valence Politics (GPVP) Project), the 2004–8 period. Together with the Democracy and Participation project surveys, the NSF-funded research has enabled us to assemble a seventeen-year portrait of British public opinion. In the mid-1990s former NSF Political Science programme officer, Frank Scioli, reacted positively when we first suggested that researchers needed to capture inter-election shifts in public opinion that are crucial for explaining electoral choice. Importantly, he also believed us when we told him that we would not 'break the bank' – the requisite research could be done effectively at low cost. Most recently, we secured NSF funding for the 'Internet Surveys and National Election Studies' conference organized jointly with Skip Lupia, Jon Krosnick and the American National Election Study (ANES). Again, Frank – with new administrative duties at the NSF's cyber-infrastructure initiative – was keenly interested in our ideas. We greatly appreciate his support.

Monies provided by University of Texas at Dallas (UTD) to Harold Clarke and Marianne Stewart helped to fund surveys and supported graduate student research assistants. UTD also helped Clarke and Stewart to travel to the University of Essex and other locales in Britain to work with Sanders and Whiteley on the BES and the related projects mentioned above. We especially wish to thank UTD Provost Hobson Wildenthal for his continuing interest in our research and his willingness to facilitate our efforts. At the University of Essex, Jane Daldry, Lennie Lillepuu, Carole Parmenter and other members of the administrative staff in the Department of Government have done much to enable David Sanders to participate in the project while fulfilling his duties as Department Head and joint editor of the *British Journal of Political Science*.

As BES principal investigators, we have benefited from the support of many members of the academic community. The BES Advisory Board has been especially helpful. Members of the 2005 Board include John Bartle, Paolo Bellucci, André Blais, Rosie Campbell, Ivor Crewe, Russell Dalton, David Denver, Cees van der Eijk, Mark Franklin, Rachel Gibson, Richard Johnston, Ron Johnston, Anthony King, Lawrence LeDuc, Michael Lewis-Beck, Ian McAllister, William

Miller, Tony Mughan, Iain Watson, Chris Wlezien and Sam Younger. We appreciate Board members meeting with us to share ideas on how to design the study to maximize its utility for a diverse user community. Ron Johnston's contribution is especially noteworthy. Besides offering advice and insights, Ron provided a wealth of constituency- and sub-constituency-level data that researchers can use to locate BES respondents in their social environments. Like all BES data, these contextual variables are available for downloading from the project website: www.essex.ac.uk/bes.

We were very fortunate to secure the services of the National Centre for Social Research (Natcen) to conduct the 2005 pre- and post-election in-person surveys. Project Director Katarina Thomson, Senior Researcher Mark Johnson, and others at Natcen were terrific. Everything went exactly as promised in their 'reverse site visit' with us at Wivenhoe House in summer 2004. Katarina and her colleagues were always available to answer our questions, very high-quality data were delivered 'on time', response rates were increased by nearly 10 per cent on 2001, and a comprehensive end-of-project technical report was provided. We sincerely appreciate the work of Katarina and others at Natcen.

We accord equally high praise to YouGov, the firm that conducted the 2005 Rolling Campaign Panel Survey (RCPS). As described in Chapter 1, the RCPS component in the 2005 BES was designed as a mode experiment to gauge the quality of internet data. Results strongly indicate that Internet surveys can be cost-effective vehicles for investigating the dynamics of British public opinion and the forces affecting electoral choice. The success of the 2005 RCPS owes much to the work done by YouGov and its Project Director, Joe Twyman. Like their counterparts at Natcen, Joe and his team delivered high-quality data in a very timely way. YouGov also has conducted the 2004–8 NSF-sponsored monthly surveys and, again, the work consistently has been top-flight. Thanks so much.

As principal investigators of the BES, we were very fortunate to have top-flight research assistants. Kristi Winters, University of Essex, served as Research Director for the 2005 project. Kristi's efforts in the validated vote exercise – a job that involved numerous visits to London and to local sheriff's offices in several Scottish constituencies – were most valuable. We also appreciate her expert organization of the BES consultation exercises, the 2005 EPOP conference and the

2007 'Internet Surveys and National Election Studies' conference. In addition, we thank Paul Tran, University of Texas at Dallas, for coding thousands of responses to open-ended questions on the monthly GPVP surveys. Recently, David Smith has begun to shoulder this burden. David also helped to prepare the tables for this book. Thanks David.

Over the years, we have been fortunate to have colleagues whose stimulating ideas have shaped, and are shaping, research in our field. In addition to members of the Advisory Board, we wish to thank Jim Alt, Ian Budge, Ray Duch, Geoff Evans, Jim Gibson, Jim Granato, Anthony Heath, Simon Jackman, Rob Johns, Skip Lupia, Tony King, Allan Kornberg, Jon Krosnick, Allan McCutcheon, William Mishler, Jon Pammett, Peter Schmidt, Norman Schofield, Tom Scotto, Jim Stimson, Paul Sniderman, Lynn Vavreck and Guy Whitten. We also thank Phil Cowley, David Denver and Justin Fisher for their efforts on behalf of the Elections, Public Opinion and Parties (EPOP) group, and Justin and Chris Wlezien for their work editing EPOP's new journal, *JEPOP*. Chris, David, Justin and Phil have done much to make EPOP a vibrant research community.

Our editors, Carrie Cheek and John Haslam, at Cambridge University Press also deserve our thanks. Their interest in this book, and their patience while it was being written, are greatly appreciated.

Performance Politics and the British Voter has been an enjoyable collaborative effort. Periodic meetings at the University of Essex have pushed the project forward and, occasionally(!) pushed the authors to consider the need for refreshment. Seeking such at Wivenhoe House Bar, the Rose and Crown quayside, or the garden at the Sun in Dedham (better food than the Marlborough) has been our practice – one that we highly recommend. The synergies of intellectual sustenance and a pint of Broadside should not be underestimated.

Harold D. Clarke
David Sanders
Marianne C. Stewart
Paul F. Whiteley
Wivenhoe House

1 | *Performance politics and the British voter*

In December 1981, Charles Frost was a worried man. The small engineering company that he owned and ran was suffering severely from a decline in export orders, largely as a result of the high value of sterling against other currencies. He was already laying off some of his workers and he was not sure whether the company, which his father started in 1951, would survive another year. He was particularly disappointed with Margaret Thatcher's Conservative government. Mrs Thatcher had promised to pursue a rigorous 'tight money' policy that would squeeze inflation out of the British economy and restore its international competitive position. As he contemplated a difficult winter, Frost could not help feeling that she had somehow lost her way. The trust that he had placed in her economic and political judgment was ebbing fast. Perhaps her confident pronouncements about the virtues of monetarism were little more than hot air. He grew even more alarmed in April 1982 when Thatcher despatched a large naval task force to deal with the Argentine invasion of the Falkland Islands. How could the objectives of such a force possibly succeed when most of the Third World, and much of the developed world, appeared to sympathize with Argentina's claims to sovereignty over the islands? Frost was as surprised as anyone when, by the summer of 1982, it was clear that British forces had achieved a rapid and overwhelming victory in the conflict. There were also signs that the British economy was beginning to respond positively to the dose of monetarist medicine that had been administered by Thatcher's chancellor Geoffrey Howe.

Frost's reaction to these developments had important implications for the way that he thought about politics over the next decade. Thatcher and her cabinet colleagues really did have extraordinarily good political judgment. If there were problems that government needed to solve – whether they related to the economy, to foreign policy, or to other matters – then it was the Conservatives who were likely to solve them. The prime minister and her colleagues had that perhaps all too rare virtue of competence; they were 'a safe pair of hands' and could get the job done. Frost had no compunction in voting Conservative in 1983 and 1987. Even after Thatcher's departure in November 1990, Frost's loyalty to the party remained. Confident in its continuing ability to deal with the most serious problems affecting the country, Frost again voted Conservative in April 1992.

Frost's daughter, Isabella, turned eighteen in late 1994. She had been aware for the two previous years that her father's confidence in the Conservatives had been waning. Although she did not really understand the details, she knew that 'the ERM crisis' of September 1992 had somehow been a watershed. Her father frequently made comments about the decline in the Conservatives' economic judgment, about the leadership's failure to deal with its increasingly disruptive Euro-sceptic rebels, and about the haze of financial and moral 'sleaze' that now hung over the party.

Isabella was not particularly interested in politics but she was quite taken with the new Labour leader, Tony Blair. Just at the moment that the Conservatives appeared to have lost their reputation for savvy decision-making and competent administration, Labour seemed to have found a leader who combined responsiveness and trust (virtues Isabella valued highly) with sound political judgment.

In May 1997, both Isabella and her father voted for New Labour. They remained pleased with their choice for some time. Charles' business prospered and Isabella's income as a newly minted fast-track civil servant rose progressively. Blair's chancellor, Gordon Brown, ran the economy efficiently and effectively. Labour had promised to remain within the Conservatives' planned public spending limits for their first two years in office, and they delivered fully on that promise. Labour's early decision to give the power of setting interest rates to the Bank of England provided the framework for an extended period of macro-economic stability. Blair sent British forces to Bosnia and to Kosovo, and on both occasions the interventions seemed to assist in pacifying local tensions. Blair also continued to move forward with the Northern Ireland peace process that had started under John Major, working with the Irish government to reduce the risks of republican and loyalist terrorism. These domestic and international policy successes reinforced Charles' and Isabella's convictions that Labour had

what was needed to run the country. In 2001, their decision to \
Labour again was an easy one.

Things then started to go awry. The two Frosts had shared in the
increased fear of terrorism that followed the attack on the World
Trade Center in New York on 11 September 2001. Nonetheless, they
had approved of Tony Blair's resolute response; they were favourably
impressed by his insistence that al-Qaeda represented a challenge to
Western democracy that required a united response. They also recognized the difficult policy choice that Blair and his government had
to make in deciding whether to support the US-led invasion of Iraq
in March 2003. Indeed, they admired Blair for his courage in taking
a bold and difficult decision. They thought it was in keeping with
his character as a leader of sound judgment who was prepared to
make hard choices. Charles Frost was reminded of Thatcher's coura-
geous decision two decades earlier to send British forces to the South
Atlantic to recapture the Falklands. He could see the parallels even
more clearly as the coalition forces toppled Saddam Hussein's regime
with remarkable speed, and plans were rapidly put in place for a constitutional convention whose members would be elected by the Iraqi
people. For Frost senior, Blair's gamble in backing the American president, George W. Bush, wholeheartedly appeared to be paying off.
Once again, Blair had demonstrated his capacity for making wise policy decisions in difficult and uncertain circumstances. He was clearly
a man to be supported.

However, as the conflict evolved into a protracted occupation, first
Isabella and then her father became more equivocal about the wisdom
of Blair's decision to go to war. The first blow was the coalition's failure to find any of Saddam's 'weapons of mass destruction', the threat
of which had provided the legal justification for the invasion. The second was increasing recognition that the evidence on which the threat
had been based was fragmentary and contentious. The third was the
worsening security position in Iraq and the associated consequence
that the invasion appeared to have generated additional support for
al-Qaeda terrorism there and, indeed, around the world.

As the occupation continued with no end in sight throughout 2004
and early 2005, the Frosts' confidence in Blair's political judgment –
and in that of his government – progressively weakened. Although
they still recognized the solidity of Chancellor Brown's economic
judgment, they came to doubt Labour's competence to make sound

decisions in other policy areas. For Charles, the economic stability that Brown and Labour had provided since 1997 was enough
to keep him loyal to Labour in the May 2005 general election. For
Isabella, who was more concerned with the increased terrorist threat
that the war and occupation had engendered, Blair's failing political
judgment was sufficient to prompt a switch in party preference. The
decision was not easy – indeed, at one point she considered not voting at all. However, she ultimately decided to support the Liberal
Democrats. They were the only party that had consistently opposed
the war on both ethical and practical grounds since the supposed
threat from Saddam's weapons of mass destruction had become a
serious political issue in the autumn of 2002.

The Frosts' story, in microcosm, reflects the main themes of this
book. Their changing political views over the quarter century between
1980 and 2005 reflected their changing perceptions of the decision-
making competence of the main political parties and their leaders. At
any point in time, their preferences were strongly influenced by their
perceptions of the capacity of the rival parties – the putative alternative governments of the day – to solve the major policy problems
facing the country. The Frosts, in short, were interested in *performance*, and when they made their assessments of the likely performance
of various parties, they paid close attention to the qualities of the
party leaders. For Charles, Margaret Thatcher's resolute leadership in
the Falklands campaign combined with her chancellor's management
of the economy were enough to convince him that the Conservatives
were the *competent* party. His view remained unchanged until
September 1992, when the Major government was obliged, in humiliating circumstances, to remove sterling from the European Exchange
Rate Mechanism.

By 1997, both Charles and his daughter were convinced that Labour
and, especially, Tony Blair now offered the best prospect of providing the sound political judgment that effective government requires.
Charles and Isabella's continuing conviction that Labour was best
able to address major problems confronting the country led both of
them to vote Labour again in 2001, a conviction, notwithstanding his
doubts, that remained with Charles through to 2005. New Labour's
record on the economy and the funding it generated for important
public services such as healthcare and education were just too strong
to deny. However, for Isabella, Tony Blair's failure to understand the

damaging consequences of his gamble in supporting George Bush in Iraq demonstrated that the Labour leader had lost the capacity for wise judgment that had characterized his earlier years, first as opposition leader, and then as prime minister. In her mind, Blair's image had been irreparably tarnished and she was no longer prepared to support him or his party.

But, if perceptions of *competence* mattered in all of these changes in preference, there was one example where competence perceptions were not quite so important. In deciding to vote for the Liberal Democrats in 2005, Isabella was moving away from a calculation about *performance*. She knew from the opinion polls that there was little prospect of the Liberal Democrats forming a government after the general election. However, having *rejected* Labour on competence grounds, she voted *for* the Liberal Democrats because they adopted a *position* that was very close to her own on the issue that mattered most to her, the war in Iraq.

All of the calculations that Charles and Isabella were making reflect two distinct, but related, forms of *voter rationality*. Calculations about judgment, competence and performance – about which party and which leader are best able to address the problems of the day – are well described by the *valence* model of electoral choice. In this account, large majorities of voters agree about what government should provide – a strong economy characterized by low rates of inflation and unemployment, a panoply of well-funded and well-functioning public services in key areas such as healthcare, education, housing and transportation, a clean and healthy environment, protection from criminals and terrorists, and a secure, stable international order – but they disagree about which party is best able to achieve these consensual policy goals. People vote for the party that they think is most likely to deliver the mix of policy outcomes that are widely seen as 'good things'.[1]

When making their choices, voters rely heavily on their party identifications and their images of the party leaders. In a world where political stakes are high and uncertainty abounds, partisan attachments and leader images serve as cost-effective heuristic devices or cognitive shortcuts that enable voters to judge the delivery capabilities of rival political parties. Open to new information, voters revise their party identifications and leader images in light of ongoing performance evaluations.

⌈The second form of rationality⌉, evident in Isabella Frost's decision
to support the Liberal Democrats, derives from the *spatial* model of
electoral choice. According to this model, the issues that matter in politics are 'pro–con' ones that divide the electorate.⌐Voters and parties
adopt *positions* on these issues. People then vote for the party that is
closest to them on the issue or set of issues that matter most to them.⌐
In Isabella's case, Labour and the Conservatives both supported the
war but the Liberal Democrats opposed it. She had already decided
on *valence* grounds that she could no longer vote for Labour. In her
mind, Blair had misled the British public about Iraq and the results
had been nothing short of disastrous. In turn, this led her to mistrust the Labour leader and to lose faith in his party's general policy-
making capability. Then, she made a *positional* calculation to vote
Liberal Democrat because they were the party closest to her on what
she believed to be the most important issue of the day.

In making her decision, Isabella had arrived at the same point as
her friend, Annie. Both abandoned Labour in 2005. But Annie had
made her decision differently. The youngest daughter of long-time
Labour activists who had marched in CND rallies in the 1960s and
an erstwhile Labour identifier and party member herself, Annie had
been strongly opposed to the Iraq War from the outset. For Annie,
like her parents, launching a war was not an acceptable means of conflict resolution. It was immoral to make a pre-emptive military strike
that risked the lives of thousands of innocent people. After demonstrating against the war to no avail, she angrily tore up her Labour
membership card and sought an anti-war alternative. Whether the
Blair-led Labour government could win the war, let alone secure the
peace, was irrelevant.

After listening to Isabella, Annie thought about voting Liberal
Democrat in 2005. It was true, as Isabella argued, that Mr Kennedy
and his party had been consistent opponents of the war. But, it was
equally true that they had no chance of winning. They might capture a few more seats, but that was it. Other anti-war parties like the
Greens or Respect were also sure losers. Voting for them was simply a
waste of time. Since there was no viable anti-war party, Annie decided
to stay home on election day. Unconvinced that she had a duty to vote
regardless of the choices on offer, she wondered whether there might
be other ways to make her voice heard on major issues. There surely
had to be more to British democracy than just parties and elections.

The aims of the book

This book has two principal aims. One aim is to describe and explain major developments in British electoral politics that occurred between 1997 and 2005, and in particular the loss of popular support that Labour experienced between 2001 and 2005. As Figure 1.1 shows, although the Conservatives failed to gain much electoral ground in 2005 – increasing their UK vote share by less than 1%, Labour suffered a substantial loss, falling from 40.7% to 35.2%. In contrast, the Liberal Democrats made gains, moving upward from 18.3% to 22%. And, although the combined nationalist (SNP plus Plaid Cymru) vote was slightly down, the total share for all 'other' parties reached 10.4%, the highest on record. In accounting for these changes in party fortunes, we pay particular attention to the way in which the attack on the World Trade Center in September 2001 transformed the issue agenda of British politics. We also examine the pivotal role the Iraq War played in damaging Tony Blair's image and Labour's electoral fortunes.

Another feature of our analysis involves factors affecting electoral turnout. As Figure 1.2 indicates, the 2005 election was characterized by

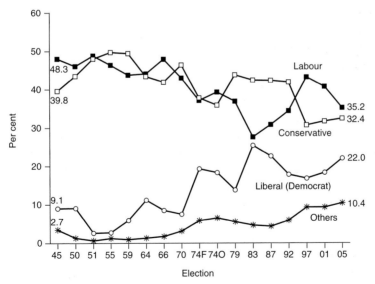

Figure 1.1 Vote shares, United Kingdom, 1945–2005 general elections (*Source*: Kavanagh and Butler, 2005: Appendix 1)

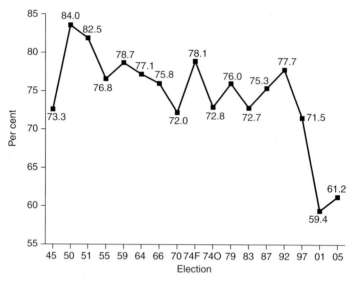

Figure 1.2 Voting turnout, United Kingdom, 1945–2005 general elections (*Source*: Kavanagh and Butler, 2005: Appendix 1)

a very modest recovery in turnout (1.8%) after the sharp declines that occurred in 1997 and especially in 2001. In 2005, turnout remained down over 16% compared to what it had been in 1992. Despite a closer 'horse race' between Labour and the Conservatives, many people – especially young people – did not go the polls. We explore why some people decided not to cast a ballot, and investigate whether nonvoters are turning to other political activities or abandoning politics altogether. We also place the British findings in comparative perspective by examining patterns of electoral turnout and other forms of political participation in several European democracies.

Our second aim is more ambitious. In *Political Choice in Britain* (Clarke *et al.*, 2004b), we demonstrated that explanations rooted in individual rationality provide far more compelling accounts of voting behaviour and the dynamics of British electoral politics than do explanations based on social forces associated with membership in groups defined by characteristics such as ethnicity, gender or social class. We also demonstrated that *valence* calculations about the performance capabilities of rival parties have provided a more powerful statistical explanation of British voting behaviour over the past fifty years than *positional* calculations based on positions on specific issues or more general ideological dimensions. In this book, the theory of valence politics is developed in three main ways. First, we specify more precisely what valence calculations entail. Second, we investigate sources of valence judgments to establish *why* people conclude that one party rather than another is better able to deliver effective performance on key valence issues. Third, we argue that valence judgments can help to explain more than just party choice. Valence considerations also affect people's turnout decisions and how they evaluate the practice of democracy in contemporary Britain.

The New Labour story

Labour's victory in the May 1997 general election silenced years of debate about the party's future. After eighteen years in the political wilderness, years when Labour was viewed by many people as incapable of governing, there was a new determination among the party's activists and MPs that the New Labour government must demonstrate – and must be allowed to demonstrate – its ability to govern Britain effectively. That determination paid off. Throughout the 1997 parliament, with the brief exception of the September 2000 fuel crisis, Labour's and Tony Blair's opinion poll ratings consistently outdistanced those of their rivals. The Blair government behaved prudently in managing the economy; ambitiously in increasing expenditure on education and health; boldly in introducing constitutional reforms in terms of Scottish and Welsh devolution and the Human Rights Act 1998; and courageously (and successfully) in its military commitments in Bosnia and Kosovo. Labour received its due reward in June 2001 with a second landslide election victory. Then, on 5 May 2005 – in the first British general election held in the post 9/11 era – the party won a historically unprecedented, third consecutive parliamentary majority.

Unlike 1997 and 2001, the 2005 election was not 'a sure thing'. When the campaign began, Labour and the Conservatives were running 'neck and neck' in the polls. Labour was ahead, but its lead was slim and often within the statistical margin of error. There was serious media speculation about the possibility of a hung parliament. The enthusiasm that had accompanied New Labour's rise to power eight years earlier was noticeably absent. The economy remained healthy, but the mix of salient issues in 2005 was very different from what it had been in 1997 and 2001. To make matters more difficult, Blair was much maligned by friends and foes alike for his insistence that Britain join the United States in what many judged to be an ill-advised military adventure in Iraq. In the event, Labour emerged victorious, although its extremely mediocre vote share (35.2%) and reduced percentage of seats in Parliament (55% compared to 63%) gave the party faithful little cause for celebration. The bloom had clearly faded from New Labour's rose and yet the party managed to hold on to power. Why and how did this happen?

The credit and debit sides of the equation are not especially difficult to assemble. To its credit, Labour had continued to manage Britain's economy very effectively. Inflation and unemployment remained low by historical standards, and the economy had grown year on year throughout Labour's first two terms in office, the longest period of continuous economic growth on record. Although government borrowing was relatively high, Chancellor Brown had successfully operated within his 'golden rule' of ensuring that government revenues and expenditures were in balance over the course of the economic cycle. Moreover, this balance had been achieved at the same time as spending on health and education had increased substantially.

Labour's achievements in the first of these fields – the economy – were duly recognized by the electorate. As we report in subsequent chapters, Labour was widely seen as the party best able to manage the country's economic affairs. Also, although Labour did not receive especially high grades from the electorate as a whole for its stewardship of the health system, education and other public services, among those who gave priority to those issues, the party had a clear edge over its rivals. By constantly reminding voters of its successes on the economy and public services, Labour's advantage on these issues grew over the course of the 2005 election campaign.

Advantaged on some, but by no means all, important issues, Labour's key strengths in the run-up to the 2005 election were its continuing superiority on two key valence considerations of party identification and leader evaluations. In *Political Choice in Britain* (Clarke *et al.*, 2004b), we demonstrated that party identification, or partisanship as it is often called, has dynamic properties. It is not an 'unmoved mover' in the storied 'funnel of causality' (Campbell *et al.*, 1960) leading to the vote. Rather, to echo Fiorina's (1981) felicitous phrase, party identification can be usefully seen as a 'running tally' of assessments of the performance of parties and their leaders. We also demonstrated that partisanship and leader evaluations exert powerful effects on party choice.

Figure 1.3 shows how the distribution of party identification changed between 1964 and 2005. As illustrated, in both 1997 and 2001, Labour had significantly more partisans than did the Conservatives or the Liberal Democrats. Labour averaged in the mid-forties, the Conservatives in the mid-twenties, and the Liberal Democrats were just below the teens. Even in 2005, when opinion polls indicated that Labour was more vulnerable to a Conservative challenge, Labour's cohort of identifiers (37%) was still considerably larger than that of the Conservatives (26%) or the Liberal Democrats (13%). Such a large partisan advantage normally, but not invariably, translates into electoral victory (Clarke, Kornberg and Scotto, 2009).

Party leader images were another story. ⌐As argued above, leader images matter because voters use them as cues to make decisions about the overall capabilities of parties to govern.⌐ Figure 1.4 reports the 'like–dislike' scores of the leaders of the three main parties in

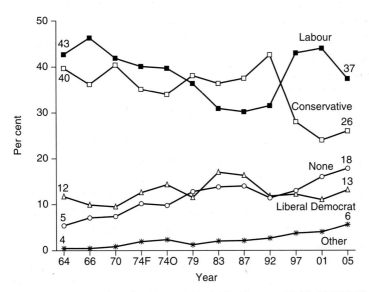

Figure 1.3 Party identification, 1964–2005 (*Source*: 1964–2005 BES post-election surveys)

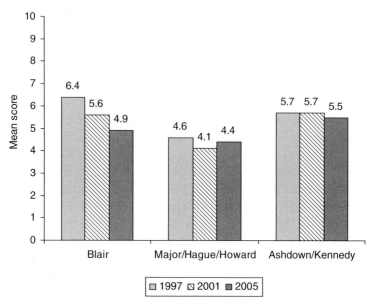

Figure 1.4 Feelings about party leaders, 1997, 2001, 2005 (*Source*: 1997, 2001, 2005 BES post-election surveys)

1997, 2001 and 2005. In Chapter 5, we document that these scores are good proxies for voters' overall assessments of the qualities of rival leaders. Tony Blair was very popular in 1997. He clearly out-distanced his rivals, with an average rating that was almost two points ahead of John Major (6.4 vs. 4.6 on a 0–10 point scale). In 2001, Blair's average score had fallen nearly a full point (to 5.6), and Liberal Democrat leader Charles Kennedy received a slightly higher rating (5.7). However, Blair's only realistic competition was the then Conservative leader, William Hague, who registered a disastrous average of 4.1 on the scale. In 2005, Blair's average rating (4.9) had fallen again. Although Blair now was well behind Kennedy (who averaged 5.5), he remained well ahead of his Conservative challenger, Michael Howard (4.4).

The 'like–dislike' figures for Blair and his Conservative rivals provide an important clue about Labour's continuing success between 1997 and 2005. During this period, the Conservatives were the only party other than Labour that could realistically hope to form a government. Yet, although Blair's ratings fell progressively after 1997, the alternative leaders proffered by the Conservatives consistently failed to present an image that resonated positively with most voters.[7] The Conservatives were undoubtedly adept at electing leaders who appealed to the party faithful. Indeed, their leadership election rules actively promoted such choices. But the party was clearly unable to choose a leader who could rival Blair in his appeal to the electorate as a whole. To be sure, Blair was not warmly received in 2005, but he was helped by the Conservatives who repeatedly exercised the bad political habit of selecting leaders who were actively disliked by many voters.

The credit side of Labour's balance sheet in 2005, then, was weaker than in 2001, but relatively strong in comparison with that of their principal rival – the Conservatives. What about Labour's debits? It has become a cliché to observe that 'the world changed' as a result of 9/11. However, like many clichés, this one has an element of truth. There is no doubt that 9/11 had a dramatic effect on the issue agenda of British politics. As discussed in Chapter 3, concomitant with growing prosperity, the economy had faded as an issue in the late 1990s, leaving the health system, education and other public services, as well as Britain's position in the EU, as the most salient concerns. However, after September 2001, there was an upward step-shift in the priority accorded to a new set of issues focused on crime, terrorism and asylum/immigration. Although these issues were not traditional Labour priorities, Tony Blair's astuteness allowed him to ride the crest of this new political tide with little difficulty. His determination to address the global terrorist threat resonated well with a British public that was increasingly concerned with its own security, both at home and abroad.

Blair's – and Labour's – real problems began with the invasion of Iraq in March 2003. Iraqi dictator Saddam Hussein had promised that invading Iraq would 'open the gates of hell' for the Western powers. As the rapid removal of Saddam's regime degenerated into a quagmire of continuing terrorist insurgency and mounting sectarian violence punctuated by widely publicized acts of barbaric savagery, it became graphically clear that, although the 'gates' had not yet opened for the West, they had certainly done so for many innocent Iraqis. Indeed, for many observers, rather than providing a lesson that 'rogue states' could expect severe punishment if they tolerated terrorists on their soil, the war's main consequence had been to strengthen support for al-Qaeda and its global terrorist network.

The failure of the Bush–Blair 'coalition of the willing' to bring any-thing resembling a satisfactory outcome to the Iraq crisis inevitably increased people's doubts about the wisdom of the invasion. This had knock-on consequences for public confidence in Tony Blair and, ulti-mately, for Labour's popularity. In subsequent chapters, we estimate models that indicate that the war cost Labour substantial support in 2005. Some of the effect was direct, but much was indirect, working through the aforementioned erosion of Blair's image. In different cir-cumstances, this could have cost Labour the election. That it did not is testimony, in part, to what Labour got right (the economy, the deliv-ery of public services); in part, to the failure of the Conservatives to choose a convincing leader who could present the party as a realistic alternative government to Labour; and in part, to the un-engineered bias in the way the electoral system translated votes into parliamentary seats. This bias worked powerfully in Labour's favour, enabling the party to secure a comfortable sixty-six-seat majority in the Commons with only slightly over 35% of the popular vote (Whiteley, 2005).

Developments in Scotland and Wales constituted an important addendum to the national picture. In deference to nationalist pres-sures, soon after coming to office in 1997 Blair had moved to create a devolved parliament in Scotland and a devolved assembly in Wales. With members chosen using mixed electoral systems that included proportional representation, these new assemblies witnessed the emergence of more flexible and variegated patterns of party govern-ment than those in place at Westminster. Prior to 1997, Scotland and Wales had been regarded as Labour strongholds. In 1997, Labour secured 46% of the vote in Scotland and 54% in Wales. By 2005, these shares had fallen to 40% and 43%, respectively. The Liberal Democrats were a major beneficiary. Between 1997 and 2005, they increased their vote share by six points in Wales and by fully thirteen points in Scotland. Given the sizes of the Welsh and Scottish elector-ates, these changes were insufficient to undermine Labour's domin-ance at Westminster. Nonetheless, they were important indications of growing vulnerability. Labour dominance in the 'celtic fringe' could no longer be taken for granted.

In 2005, Labour still enjoyed substantial support through-out Britain, based largely on perceptions that it had delivered on the economy and on public services. However, Blair's inability to envisage how the indirect consequences of devolution might weaken his party's support in Scotland and Wales, combined with his failure to think through the consequences of his support for British participation in the Iraq War, presented the image of a leader who was not as capable as he had appeared in 1997. The electorate did not desert Labour en masse in 2005. But ⌐enough voters withdrew their support to give serious cause for concern. Indeed, within weeks after the 2005 election, Blair was obliged to confirm publicly that he would step down as prime minister before the next election. He had played a key role in three consecutive Labour victories, but now he was very much 'damaged stock' and had to go. The scene was set for his replacement, in June 2007, by Gordon Brown, a change designed to give Labour the opportunity to renew itself before confronting the electoral challenge posed by a David Cameron-led Conservative Party.

Developing the theory of valence politics

In the world of valence politics, voters make choices primarily on the basis of their evaluations of rival parties' likely ability to deliver policy outcomes in issue areas characterized by broad consensus (Stokes, 1963, 1992). A classic example of a valence issue is the economy. Economic well-being is fundamental; virtually everyone wants a healthy economy, characterized by a felicitous combination of vigorous, sustainable growth, coupled with low rates of unemployment and inflation. Similarly, the vast majority of people want to live in a safe society – one that is not blighted by crime against individuals or property, or vulnerable to terrorism and other threats to personal and national security. Again, almost everyone wants a broad array of adequately funded, well-functioning public services in areas such as education, health, transport and environmental protection.

Valence issues typically dominate the political agendas of Britain and other mature democracies, and such issues are important in emerging democracies as well. Although the mix of ⌐valence issues⌐varies over time, their continuing salience works to focus political debate on 'who can do the job' rather than on 'what the job should be'. Political discourse is dominated by discussion of which party and which leader are best able to deliver policy outcomes consistent with consensually agreed upon goals.

The main rival account of voter and party behaviour within the rationality framework derives from the spatial model pioneered by Anthony Downs (1957). The major assumption underpinning spatial models is that 'position issues' are the dominant factors in explaining electoral choice. Unlike valence issues, in the case of position issues there is widespread disagreement among both voters and parties on the desirability of different policy goals. For example, for many years the Conservatives differed from both Labour and the Liberal Democrats on the desirability of cutting taxes, even if this would necessitate cuts in public services. Similarly, whereas Labour and the Conservatives supported the invasion of Iraq in 2003, the Liberal Democrats and minor parties such as the Greens and Respect opposed it, reflecting widespread disagreement about how to respond to the threat of 'rogue states' and international terrorism in the wake of 9/11. A third example relates to parties' contrasting positions on the need for greater European integration: the Liberal Democrats broadly support it; Labour is generally ambivalent but broadly supportive; and the Conservatives, with some minority dissent, are largely against it.

In Downs' spatial framework, 'de gustibus non est disputandum' is the order of the day. Voters have fixed preferences on various position issues, and they attempt to 'maximize their utilities' by supporting a party that is closest to them in a 'policy space' defined by one or more such issues. As spatial models have evolved, the ancillary assumptions have been modified in various ways (see, for example, Adams *et al.*, 2005; Merrill and Grofman, 1999; Rabinowitz and Macdonald, 1989). However, the core idea in these models has remained the same: prominent position issues are what matter for the choices made by utility-maximizing voters whose preferences are taken as given.

Until recently, most academic theorizing about, and empirical analysis of, the factors affecting electoral choice have tended to emphasize position issues and associated spatial models of party competition. In contrast, with the notable exception of the voluminous literature on 'economic voting' (e.g. Dorussen and Taylor, 2002; Duch and Stevenson, 2008; Lewis-Beck, 1988; Norpoth *et al.*, 1991; van der Brug *et al.*, 2007), less attention has been devoted to valence issues, despite the central role that they have played in the issue agendas of successive general elections. In this book, we develop the theory of valence politics, building on the pioneering critique of spatial models provided by Donald Stokes (1963, 1992) and recent work that attempts to add valence components to spatial models (e.g. Schofield, 2005).

Both positional (or spatial) and valence (or performance) theories of voting behaviour can be seen as specific cases of a more general utility-maximization model. The key idea is that the expected utility a person gets from voting for a particular party is a combination of two things: the utility derived from being *closer* to that party on a given set of important issues (the positional/spatial component); and an assessment of the probability that the party can *deliver* effective performance in relation to that issue set (the valence/performance component). If voters assess the *delivery* probabilities of two different parties as identical, then they will decide between the parties on purely *positional* grounds. If they assess the spatial positions of the two parties as identical, then they will decide between them on purely *valence* grounds. If parties' delivery probabilities are identical and positions are identical, voters will be indifferent and, *ceteris paribus*, they will abstain.

The clear implication is that, within this general framework, rational voters can, *in principle*, be exclusively 'spatial' in their calculations, exclusively 'valenced', or a combination of the two. An important part of our argument is that, *empirically*, it is the valence part of the calculation that tends to predominate. The reason is simple – the issues that matter for most people most of the time are valence issues and parties, like voters, have the same preferences on these issues. Since all actors have the same preferences, political debate focuses on 'who' and 'how', not 'what'.

A secondary aspect of this part of our study concerns the way in which people process political information. Over the past half century voting studies have repeatedly shown that many voters are uninterested in and largely ignorant about politics (e.g. Berelson *et al.*, 1954; Campbell *et al.*, 1960). Moreover, many lack coherent ideological frameworks that would help them to make sense of specific political issues and particular events. In Converse's (1964) language, they lack 'tightly constrained belief systems' that would provide the architectonics for sound political judgment.

Absent an adequate supply of factual knowledge and the intellectual tools to evaluate it, how can voters possibly make what could be difficult decisions about how best to advance and protect their interests? Recent research in political psychology and experimental economics helps to answer this question by indicating that many voters are 'cognitive misers' who use *heuristics* – information cues or cognitive shortcuts – to make political decisions. The use of heuristics means that people can avoid the costs of gathering and processing large amounts of complicated and often contradictory information in order to understand issues and events in a complex and uncertain world (Conlisk, 1996; Lupia and McCubbins, 1998; Lupia *et al.*, 2000; Popkin, 1991; Sniderman *et al.* 1991). We argue that partisan attachments and leader images are two of the most important heuristics that voters use when making electoral choices.

We also explore other sources of valence judgments. We identify three key sources: people's *direct experiences* of what government does (or fails to do); their *evaluations* of government performance in delivering an array of policy outcomes; and their *emotional reactions* to these outcomes. Our analyses examine these experiences, evaluations and emotions in three key policy areas of public services (health and education); the economy; and public security. We demonstrate that all three have powerful effects on the way that people arrive at their valence judgments – their assessments of the competence of rival political parties. We show that, in general, positive experiences, emotions and evaluations are associated with positive judgments about the governing party, and negative experiences, emotions and evaluations are associated with positive judgments about opposition parties.

The final aspect of our efforts to extend the theory of valence politics relates to the *consequences* of valence judgments. We have already hypothesized that people's assessments of rival parties' likely performance will strongly affect their choices between or among them. However, valence judgments have two other significant consequences. First, following the logic of the utility-maximization model sketched earlier, we hypothesize that valence judgments will influence voter turnout. As observed above, rational voters will abstain when they believe that rival parties are equally likely (or unlikely) to deliver on their policy goals and the voters are equally close to (or distant from) the parties in the relevant policy space. In a world where voters and parties have the same ideal points, estimated delivery probabilities will dominate the turnout decision.

This line of reasoning suggests that the explanatory power of valence judgments extends beyond party choice per se. These judgments can help to explain not only why people choose one party rather than another, but also why some people choose not to vote at all. We incorporate this idea into our empirical analysis by developing a model that views the decision to choose between parties and the decision whether to vote as being part of a single calculation. This approach allows both for the possibility that some people will cast a ballot for the party they think is most likely to deliver generally agreed policy outcomes, and for the simultaneous possibility that other people will decide not to cast a ballot because they believe that no party is better placed than any other to deliver those outcomes.

The second way in which we explore additional consequences of valence judgments relates to the democratic process more generally. Over the past decade, many observers have expressed concern about declining levels of political engagement in Western mass publics. Turnout has fallen in a number of countries, including Britain (Wattenberg, 2000), and younger people in particular seem to exhibit lower levels of interest in politics than used to be the case. It is possible that these rising levels of disengagement could be related to the perceived inability of conventional democratic politics to deliver the outcomes that people need and want. To the extent that citizens think that none of the established political parties can properly solve the key policy problems that their country faces, their confidence in democratic institutions is weakened and their commitment to the democratic process is reduced.

We consider this possibility by examining the impact of valence judgments on people's attitudes towards Britain's principal national political institutions, their degree of satisfaction with the democratic process, and their sense of civic duty and feelings of political efficacy. We find that several types of valence judgments exert strong effects on these attitudes and dispositions. Put simply, performance matters. People who have confidence in the ability of the major parties to solve the pressing problems of the day exhibit high levels of support for Britain's democratic regime and a strong sense of political obligation towards it. In contrast, those who think that none of the parties has much to contribute exhibit low levels of both regime support and civic obligation. Taken together, these findings suggest that if there is an incipient 'crisis of political engagement' in contemporary Britain, then its solution lies largely in the hands of the parties and the politicians themselves. By performing – by finding solutions to critical policy problems – they not only help themselves as vote-seeking, would-be officeholders; they also contribute to the health of British democracy.

Data and measures

The 2005 British Election Study (BES) was designed to achieve a judicious blend of continuity and innovation – to ensure the long-run comparability of the time-series of BES studies that began in 1964, and to enable analysts to study the explanatory power of competing theoretical models of electoral choice. The design of the 2005 BES, outlined in Figure 1.5, has two main components. The first, shown in the top half of the figure, was an in-person, national probability, panel survey. Respondents (N = 3,589) were interviewed over a six-week period before the start of the official campaign. Then, these people were re-interviewed beginning immediately after the election. Because of panel attrition – some Wave 1 respondents were unavailable for a Wave 2 interview – a 'top-up' group was added to the post-election sample to ensure a representative post-election cross-section of the British electorate, thereby maximizing comparability with BES surveys conducted before 2001 that employed post-election surveys only. The pre-campaign/post-election panel has 2,959 respondents, and the post-election survey with the top-up component has 4,161 respondents.

The second component of the design, displayed in the lower half of Figure 1.5, was a multi-wave national internet panel survey. This

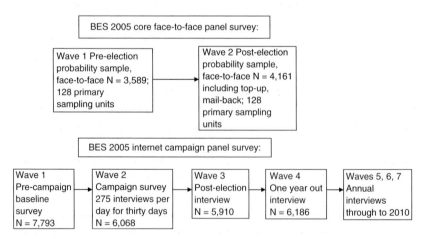

Figure 1.5 Survey design, the 2005 British Election Study

survey began with 7,793 respondents who were interviewed in the month before the official campaign began. Then, a rolling campaign survey was conducted (see Johnston and Brady, 2002). Every day during the campaign, random samples of approximately 256 pre-campaign respondents were invited to do a second survey. The total achieved sample size of the campaign wave was 6,068. Immediately after the election, 5,910 of the pre-campaign respondents participated in a third survey. This multi-wave rolling campaign panel survey (RCPS) permits detailed analyses of the dynamics of key political attitudes during the election campaign. In addition, because the same set of respondents will be re-interviewed periodically through to the general election in 2009/10, the survey ultimately will facilitate fine-grained analyses of forces affecting stability and change in party support over a period spanning two general elections.

To assess why people voted the way they did in May 2005 – and why some chose not to vote at all – the main dataset that we employ is based on the pre/post, face-to-face 2005 British Election Study survey (total N = 4,791). This dataset contains a large number of variables needed to investigate the explanatory power of competing models of electoral choice. We can study in detail the extent to which vote decisions are predicated on valence judgments and other considerations, while applying controls for a wide variety of socio-demographic characteristics. When making over-time comparisons, we employ data from the 2001 and earlier British Election Studies.

To analyse the short-term dynamics of the official election campaign, we use the rolling campaign panel survey (total N = 7,793). As discussed above, the three-wave panel includes a pre-campaign base-line wave, a rolling campaign wave with an average achieved sample of 209 cases per day (N = 6,068), and an immediate post-election survey of all respondents participating in the pre-campaign or campaign wave (N = 5,910). We have conducted extensive statistical tests comparing the properties of the internet panel data and the in-person probability sample. Results of these tests (Sanders *et al.*, 2007) demonstrate that the Internet and in-person data have very similar distributions on key variables and yield virtually identical parameter estimates for a wide range of comparable models of party choice and turnout. The 'stylized facts' produced by analyses of the two data sets are virtually identical. Without being told beforehand, one would not know one survey from the other. This strong result indicates that the internet data can be employed with confidence to study models of the dynamics of public opinion and party preference.

To analyse the inter-election dynamics of party support in the period leading up to the 2005 general election, we use monthly survey data (total $N = 47,333$) gathered in the Participation and Democracy in Britain (PDB) project and the Government Performance, Valence Judgements and the Dynamics of Party Support (GPVP) project. These studies conducted consecutive, identical, monthly surveys, initially by telephone (from July 2000 to October 2003) and subsequently by internet (from April 2004 to April 2005). The latter project has continued until the present, and we use data gathered in it in Chapter 4 to study the evolution of public attitudes towards the Iraq War and their impact on feelings about Tony Blair. The data also are used in Chapter 7 to study factors affecting voting turnout in comparison with other forms of political participation.

Similar to the BES surveys, the PDB and GPVP inter-election surveys contain a large number of questions designed to measure valence judgments in various policy areas. The PDB and GPVP surveys have added value because some of their question sets relating to leaders, economic evaluations and partisanship have been asked on an almost continuous monthly basis since January 1992. We combine this longer run of survey data with MORI data from the early 1980s on the public's issue priorities to produce an aggregate-level dataset to study the evolution of party support patterns in Britain over the past quarter century.

Finally, we employ data from the 2002 wave of the European Social Survey (ESS) to place British data on turnout and other types of political participation in comparative perspective. The 2002 ESS, with comparable survey data gathered in Britain and other European countries, is ideal for studying the extent to which factors driving various forms of political participation are common across Britain and a broad range of European democracies, old and new alike. In addition, the wide spatial variation in the data enables us to study the impact of contextual factors that affect political participation in Britain, but remain constant when one is analysing only British data.

The plan of the book

In Chapter 2, we develop the theory of valence politics, placing particular emphasis on the way in which valence should be conceptualized and specified. The chapter begins, for expository reasons, by introducing basic assumptions of the rival *spatial* model. The key point is that people think about politics in terms of how to optimize what is valuable to them. This 'subjective optimization process' involves people evaluating their proximity to the parties in a one-dimensional, left–right ideological space or a low-dimensional issue space (e.g. Downs, 1957; Merrill and Grofman, 1999). We then consider two major critiques of the classic Downsian model. The first simply modifies Downs' ideas, suggesting that some voters may be less interested in the magnitude of the distance between themselves and a given party, and more interested in whether or not the party is on the 'correct' side of some presumed 'mid point' of the relevant ideological or issue space (Rabinowitz and Macdonald, 1989). The second, more fundamental, critique, articulated by Stokes (1963, 1992), is that Downs' core assumptions are incorrect. Contrary to what those adopting a Downsian perspective assume, the relevant policy space is not necessarily uni-dimensional or of low dimensionality; the dimensions of the policy space are not fixed over time (parties actively seek to affect the dimensions of the policy space in order to fight the election on issues where they believe they have an advantage); and voters and parties may not, as Downs assumes, have a point of common reference as to what the key issues actually are. Stokes contends that, although all issues potentially have both a spatial and a valence component, it is primarily on the basis of their valence aspects that voters choose between (or among) political parties.

As noted earlier, the theory of valence politics employs a rational choice perspective – broadly conceived. The theory of valence politics endows voters with agency, not omniscience. Voters think about how best to achieve their goals, but they are not the perfectly well-informed calculating machines envisaged by neo-classical economists and other purveyors of mainline rational choice theories. Moreover, although position issues occasionally achieve salience, Stokes was correct to conclude that valence issues typically dominate the political agenda. As a result, valence considerations normally play a more prominent role than spatial ones in the determination of vote choice. In most elections, voters and parties share the same preferences on key issues. Accordingly, voters must decide on the basis of who is most likely do the best job. This can be a tough call. Lacking an abundant supply of relevant information about what competing parties will and can do if elected, voters supplement party performance judgments with heuristics – primarily the cues provided by leader images and partisan attachments – when making their electoral choices.

These results also have important implications for party strategy. In a world dominated by valence considerations, office-seeking parties and party leaders focus on two key themes. First, they seek to demonstrate *general managerial competence* – which they can do, even in opposition, by achieving success in local or regional government, by decisive intra-party management, or by conspicuous performance in the House of Commons itself. Second, aspirant office-seekers can focus their campaigning efforts on *raising the salience* of those issues that voters believe they are best able to handle (Budge and Farlie, 1983).

Chapter 3 considers the *effects* of valence thinking on party support during the 'long campaign', which effectively began immediately after the 2001 general election. It also considers some of the *sources* of valence thinking during the same period. We investigate these topics using data gathered in the PDB and GPVP monthly surveys. These data are particularly helpful for exploring how the post-9/11 issue agenda differed, and continues to differ, from the agenda at the time of the 2001 general election. After 9/11, the classic valence issues of the economy, healthcare and education were supplemented (not replaced) by a new set of valence issues focusing on crime, asylum seekers/immigration and terrorism. These 'new issues' form a closely inter-connected cluster in the public mind. Analyses reveal that government performance evaluations and emotional reactions in the three highest-salience policy areas – public services, internal security and the economy – have powerful effects on party preferences. Regarding the sources of valence thinking, direct personal experience has consistently strong effects on performance evaluations and emotional reactions and, hence, on party choice. This finding testifies that valence judgments, although undoubtedly influenced by media coverage of economic, political and social events and conditions, are also rooted in people's everyday experiences.

The overall story of the consequences of long campaign is one that we have already anticipated. In the run-up to the 2005 election, Labour had a number of key 'fundamentals' in place. A sizable plurality of voters were Labour identifiers; the economy was sound; the government had performed reasonably well on public service delivery and internal security; and Blair, although his image was tarnished, was clearly preferred to his Conservative rival. But, a new issue agenda was in place, and it was unknown how this agenda would play in the electoral arena. Also, it remained to be seen whether the Iraq War would further damage the prime minister and his party.

Public reactions to the war and their consequences are explored in Chapter 4. The chapter begins by tracing the evolution of public opinion on the possibility of war with Iraq from the autumn of 2002 until the autumn of 2003. Survey data show that the British public was divided about invading Iraq, with support increasing quickly and substantially when the invasion began in March 2003. However, by October of that year enthusiasm had waned substantially. As the conflict continued through 2004 and 2005, Iraq increasingly took on the properties of a valence issue, with a consensus emerging that it had been a big mistake, and the likelihood of success was minimal.

Chapter 4 also investigates the ability of rival morality, cost–benefit and general heuristic models to explain why some people approved of the war and others disapproved. Related analyses indicate that there were sizable gender differences in attitudes towards the war, and that these were largely due to women being more likely than men to believe that there was no compelling moral case for the conflict, that there were significant collective and personal costs, that benefits were dubious and probability of success was low. The chapter concludes by studying the aggregate- and individual-level effects of attitudes towards the war on Tony Blair's standing with the electorate. It is evident that as the war dragged on it inflicted substantial damage on his job approval ratings and like–dislike scores. By tarnishing Blair's image in the public mind, the war indirectly eroded Labour support in the ensuing 2005 general election.

Chapter 5 analyses the ability of rival models to account for party choice and turnout. The chapter begins by mapping the values of key predictor variables such as government performance evaluations, party identification, party preferences on important issues, party leader images, and party–issue proximities at the time of the 2005 election. Then, binomial and multinomial logit models are employed to assess the explanatory power of competing models of party choice. Echoing results reported in *Political Choice in Britain* (Clarke *et al.*, 2004b), the valence politics model dominates its rivals, although other models also make contributions to explanation. These findings are confirmed by analyses using a mixed logit model that enables us to consider the varying choice sets presented to the English, Scottish and Welsh electorates.

We also use the mixed logit model to investigate the effect of information availability and processing capacity – political sophistication – on the impact of party leader images on party choice. The analyses show that sophistication has a curvilinear effect on how leader images influence the vote. As sophistication grows, the impact of leader image first increases, and then decreases. Although theoretically intriguing, this model does not outperform a simpler model that specifies simple linear effects for political sophistication, or one that ignores differences in voter sophistication altogether. We believe that the parsimony and simplicity of the latter, basic, model are very attractive features. The explanatory superiority of analyses that take variations in voter sophistication into account is not demonstrated.

Chapter 5 concludes by analysing voter turnout from two perspectives. First, we estimate a composite turnout model using validated vote as the dependent variable. This model shows that in 2005, as in 2001, a general incentives model that incorporates the theoretical perspectives of rational choice and social psychology provides the basis for explaining why some people, but not others, choose to cast a ballot. However, this is not the end of the story. Specifying a general model in which nonvoting is an alternative along with the choices provided by competing parties reveals that valence politics variables such as party leader images and evaluations of party performance of important issues influence turnout as well as party choice. This finding suggests that the valence politics model is relevant for explaining all aspects of electoral choice.

In Chapter 6, we investigate how the 2005 campaign affected turnout and party choice. It once was conventional wisdom that British election campaigns did not matter. However, research conducted over the past decade has demonstrated that, in fact, campaigns can be influential. One set of analyses in Chapter 6 considers the impact of constituency-level campaigning conducted by local party activists and the effects of constituency-level party spending – what we call the 'ground war'. A second set of analyses focuses on the national campaign presented largely through the media – the 'air war'. The potential importance of these two dimensions of the campaign is suggested by the dynamics of party support between when parliament was dissolved and election day. The RCPS data and public opinion polls clearly show that the campaign was a disaster for the Conservatives. They went virtually straight downhill from day one. In contrast, Labour at least held its own and the Liberal Democrats made sizable gains as the election approached.

Many voters were undecided when the campaign began, and both the air war and the ground war influenced their decisions. Multilevel models reveal that contacting activities by local party activists and party spending in the constituencies generally worked as intended by helping parties to build support. Exploiting the dynamic properties of the daily RCPS data reveals the impact of national-level campaign events. Multilevel analyses show that widely publicized events, such as the campaign kickoff and the Rover car crisis, influenced the dynamics of turnout intentions. More generally, the analyses clearly indicate that sizable portions of the effects of major predictor variables in the party choice and turnout models occurred during the campaign. There also are hints that the tone of campaigns matters. The 2005 campaign was quite a nasty affair, with Conservative leader Michael Howard openly calling Tony Blair a liar over Iraq. For his part, Blair 'gave as good as he got', claiming that Mr Howard and his colleagues were obsessed with one issue – immigration. Racism was hinted at, but left unspoken. Trends in the RCPS data suggest that these negative exchanges worked to nullify the mobilization potential of the campaign.

Chapter 7 investigates turnout and its relationship to other forms of political participation in Britain in comparative perspective. The departure point is two observations. One is that turnout has declined in Britain and many other mature democracies over the past two decades. Another is that there are now steep age gradients in turnout and the belief that it is one's civic duty to vote. These observations have prompted some analysts to conjecture that substitution processes are at work. Younger people are not abandoning politics; rather, they are abandoning the ballot box in favour of other political activities. In addition to rallies, marches and demonstrations, young people are increasingly using 'market-place politics' – boycotts and buycotts of goods and services – to exercise political influence.

In an age of fair-trade coffee, fair-wage running shoes and green chic, the hypothesis intrigues, but we find little empirical support for it. With precious few exceptions, individual-level correlations between voting and other types of political activity are positive, not negative, in Britain and elsewhere. This is true for both younger and older age groups alike. Nor is substitution a significant aggregate-level phenomenon. At the country level, the ESS data testify that the correlation between turnout and non-electoral forms of participation is negative but weak and insignificant. What matters for buycotting, boycotting and other non-electoral activities is a country's wealth. The ESS data testify that these activities are very much the preserve of citizens in Britain and other wealthy northern European countries.

More generally, it is evident that political participation in Britain is in many ways quite typical of other European democracies. The structure of participation is similar in Britain and other European countries, as are the correlates of various activities. Age everywhere has the same curvilinear relationship with voting, being lowest among young people and the elderly. And, with the exception of protesting, young people everywhere tend to be less engaged in various forms of participation. These individual-level similarities do not gainsay the importance of contextual effects. Multilevel analyses indicate that a variety of contextual factors related to a country's electoral and party systems affect levels of turnout, party activity, volunteering and protesting.

Chapter 8 extends our investigation of valence politics to consider voters' orientations towards British democracy more generally. We consider two broad types of orientation: the way people think about themselves as political actors; and their perceptions of the British political system and its political institutions. Regarding individual political orientations, we focus on political interest, political efficacy and sense of civic duty. At the system level, we consider several aspects of regime support – trust in political institutions, attitudes towards parties and elections, and the extent of satisfaction with democracy. We develop a model that distinguishes among three types of valence judgment that citizens make: policy judgments (which involve the sort of judgments that are included in our analysis of party choice in Chapter 5); incumbent versus opposition partisanship (which provides a summary measure of retrospective assessments of the performance of the governing party vis-à-vis the opposition); and generic judgments about the mainstream parties and their leaders.

We examine the power of these three types of valence judgment to explain individual and system orientations in comparison with rival explanations rooted in ideology and values, personal beliefs (attitudes towards personal responsibility), and social orientations (social trust). The analyses testify that individual orientations are affected by a complex mix of all of these factors. However, system orientations are most powerfully influenced by policy and generic valence judgments. Thus, valence considerations not only play a pivotal role in explaining electoral choice; they also help to explain how people think about the democratic system itself.

Chapter 9 draws together the various themes of the book. The key message is that valence calculations – citizens' evaluations of government and party performance – are central to democratic politics. The valence politics model does not formally encompass other models of party choice in a statistical sense, but it certainly dominates them. Spatial models are hardly 'embellishment and detail', but adding spatial variables to a valence politics model provides only modest gains in explanatory power. Composite models are statistically superior to pure valence politics models – but the margin is marginal.

Valence politics variables also influence turnout, indicating that valence considerations are at work in ways that have not been appreciated in most previous analyses of electoral choice. This is because treating party choice and turnout in separate analyses obscures how valence considerations influence electoral participation. In addition, the impact of these considerations extends to other forms of political participation, indicating that the ambit of valence politics extends well beyond the electoral arena. Evaluations of the performance of governing and opposition parties and their leaders are a driving force of citizen involvement in democratic politics.

Finally, it bears reiteration that valence considerations extend to support for political regimes and, we venture, to political communities. The promise of democracy, that politics is not only *by* the people, but also *for* the people, establishes a criterion by which citizens make political support decisions at all levels. Democratic politics is about delivering the goods and services that citizens need and want. The force of valence politics is rooted in the broad consensus about what those goods and services are. The result is that political support at all levels is a renewable resource.

2 | *The theory of valence politics*

In *Political Choice in Britain* (Clarke *et al.*, 2004b) we examined several rival models of electoral participation and party choice. One model involved the role of social class given its historic prominence in academic accounts of electoral behaviour in Britain (e.g. Butler and Stokes, 1969; Heath *et al.*, 1985; Pulzer, 1968). However, analyses revealed that social class now plays a relatively minor role in explaining party choice and, at least since the 1960s, the effects of class have been smaller than commonly assumed. The really powerful explanations of party choice are found in voter attitudes related to choice-based models of individual decision-making that see voters as active participants in a complex, dynamic and uncertain political process. These models contrast sharply with sociological accounts in which socio-economic forces and early socialization experiences drive people's political attitudes and behaviour.

Choice-based models of electoral behaviour are strongly informed by spatial and valence theories of political choice. The former theory has its origins in the work of Harold Hotelling (1929) and Duncan Black (1948, 1958), but was developed and popularized by Anthony Downs (1957). The latter theory derives from a seminal article by Donald Stokes (1963) which set out a comprehensive critique of spatial models. Spatial and valence models are closely related to each other, although this has not been fully recognized in the literature. This is partly because spatial models have received an enormous amount of attention from political scientists compared with valence models – their main theoretical rival.

Stated informally, spatial theory asserts that people vote for the party with which they *most* agree on the issues of the day. Issues that matter are ones on which voters have differing opinions, i.e. the issues have a 'pro–con' quality that divides the electorate. Taxation is the archetypal spatial issue, since some voters prefer to pay lower taxes even if this means cuts in public services, whereas others are willing to accept higher taxes if that produces better public services. Since the political parties take differing stances on what constitutes an optimal mix of taxation and public spending, the tax–spend trade-off is a classic spatial issue. In contrast, [valence theory asserts that people support the party best able to deliver on issues they care about and, crucially, these are issues over which there is virtually no dis-agreement. Everyone has the same preference.] The [economy is a clas-sic valence issue since the great majority of people prefer prosperity to stagnation, and so they will support the party which they think can best deliver economic 'good times'. Low rates of inflation and unemployment coupled with robust growth constitutes a consensu-ally winning combination.]

The empirical evidence both in our earlier book (2004b) and in the present one shows that [most voters focus their attention on how com-peting parties (will) handle valence issues.] These performance evalua-tions are a crucial component of a more general 'valence politics' model that does a better job of explaining electoral behaviour than does a standard Downsian spatial model. The aim of this chapter is to under-stand why this is the case, as well as to examine theoretical linkages between spatial and valence models. By way of overview, our explana-tion of the power of the valence model is based on two broad proposi-tions. The first proposition is that, in the complex and uncertain world of electoral politics, the requirements for reasoned choices set for voters by the valence model are much easier to meet than those imposed by the spatial model. As a result, voters find making choices using valence considerations attractive. The second is that the valence model makes it much harder for politicians (wittingly or unwittingly) to manipulate and mislead voters. Stated simply, the valence model dominates the spa-tial model because it facilitates reliable political choices.

This chapter begins with an exposition of the classic Downsian spatial model and some of its variants. Next, we offer a critique of these models and why the valence model is an attractive alternative. We then discuss the theoretical origins of valence reasoning and explain why voters are likely to rely on this model in the real world of electoral politics.

The spatial model of electoral competition

Downs' spatial model is rooted in neo-classical economics and assumes that individuals seek to maximize their utility when they vote for a political party or candidate. According to the theory, people vote for the party that they think will provide the highest utility income during the post-election period. It is a theory of prospective evaluations of political party aims. Using Downs' notation (1957: 39), the model can be written as follows:

If $E(U^A t + 1) - E(U^B t + 1) > 0$ then voter i chooses party A

If $E(U^A t + 1) - E(U^B t + 1) < 0$ then voter i chooses party B

If $E(U^A t + 1) - E(U^B t + 1) = 0$ then voter i abstains

where: $E(U^A t + 1)$ is the expected utility which voter i obtains from supporting party A, the incumbent party of government, during the post-election period $t + 1$. $E(U^B t + 1)$ is the expected utility from supporting competing party B. As Downs argues: 'the difference between these two expected utility incomes is the citizen's expected party differential. If it is positive, he votes for the incumbents; if it is negative, he votes for the opposition; if it is zero, he abstains' (1957: 39).

Thus, the theory offers an explanation of both electoral turnout and party choice. But, there is more. The theory provides an analysis of the dynamics of both voting and party competition. The simplest case is two-party competition in a one-dimensional issue space, which is commonly defined as the left–right continuum of electoral politics as it developed in many twentieth-century Western democracies. The core idea is that both voters and parties are distributed along this left–right dimension, and that voters will choose the party which is closest to them in the space. Thus:

$$E(U^A t + 1) = -[V_i - P_A]^2$$

where: V_i is voter i's preferred position on the left–right scale; P_A is party A's position on the left–right scale.

Given this,

if $-[V_i - P_A]^2 < -[V_i - P_B]^2$ then voter i chooses party A

if $-[V_i - P_A]^2 > -[V_i - P_B]^2$ then voter i chooses party B

if $-[V_i - P_A]^2 = -[V_i - P_B]^2$ then voter i abstains

If the distribution of voters along the left–right scale corresponds to a normal or other 'single-peaked' distribution, then the model produces an equilibrium outcome in which both parties converge to the median position on the scale. This is the well-known median voter theorem (Hotelling, 1929). Downs explains why this equilibrium occurs with an example in which the left–right dimension is measured along a 100-point scale:

If we place parties A and B initially at 25 and 75, they will converge rapidly upon the center. The possible loss of extremists will not deter their movement toward each other, because there are so few voters to be lost at the margins compared with the number to be gained in the middle. (1957: 118)

The loss of voters at the margins assumes extremist parties will enter the electoral arena and attract those voters. Absent such entry, the logic of utility maximization indicates that mainstream parties converging to the centre of the ideological continuum will retain the support of voters they leave behind.

As Stokes (1963) notes in his critique of the spatial model, it requires a number of underlying assumptions. They are:

Unidimensionality: electoral competition takes place on a single 'left–right' dimension (or at least a very small number of independent dimensions).

Fixed structure: the dimensions are fixed and parties will manoeuvre along them seeking to maximize votes.

Ordered structure: the dimension is ordered from low to high values, and voters and parties are located at various points along this dimension.

Common reference: the issue space is the same for parties as it is for voters. When parties take a position on an issue, the voters understand what it means and are able to compare it with their own views.

One may add another important assumption which Stokes took for granted:

Vote-maximizing parties and candidates: political parties and candidates are solely interested in winning elections, and they adopt policy positions to achieve this goal.

The spatial model has generated a great deal of theoretical analysis and a more limited, but still substantial, body of empirical research. The theoretical work has focused on elaborating the model by extending it in various ways to include multiple parties, to allow for probabilistic voting, and by relaxing the various assumptions (see, for example, Banks *et al.*, 2002; Calvert, 1985; Enelow and Hinich, 1984; Hinich, 1977; Kollman *et al.*, 1992; Mueller, 2003; Wittman, 1973). Empirical analyses have focused on testing different versions of the spatial model (e.g. Adams *et al.*, 2005; McKelvey and Ordeshook, 1990; Merrill and Grofman, 1999), or assessing whether the model can explain government policy making (Denzau and Grier, 1984; Pommerehne and Frey, 1976).

Criticisms of the spatial model

There have been two types of criticisms of the spatial model. One takes issue with specific aspects of the model, while retaining the basic framework, whereas the other rejects it completely. The first type of criticism really amounts to changing one or more of the assumptions and then working out what this means for the predictions. These might be described as incremental adjustments to the model designed to enhance its explanatory power by making it more realistic. The second is more radical and fundamentally challenges the model's core assumptions. This is the approach taken by Stokes (1963).

Considering incremental changes first, one approach has been to question the assumption that parties are only interested in winning elections and not in developing policies which reflect their own values. Wittman (1973, 1977) suggests that parties will pursue their own policy agendas as well as pursuing office, and he modifies the model accordingly. Kollman *et al.* (1992) propose that ideological considerations enter into party electoral strategies. Also, since parties have imperfect knowledge of voter preferences, their pursuit of the median voter is rather difficult. Glazer and Lohman (1999) contend that parties and candidates have their own preferences and use these to make public commitments to specific policies before the election takes place. This reduces the complexities of party strategy by placing some issues off-limits, since they have already been decided before electoral competition takes place. These various modifications change aspects of the Downsian model, but none of them eliminates the equilibrium results. However, they do make achieving equilibrium a more complex task.

Directional models of party competition represent a rather more significant change to the spatial model. In the Matthews (1979) work, voters choose among parties on the basis of direction in an issue space, rather than because of proximity. A party can move away from the status quo in one of two directions, and it is the movement which counts rather than the distance covered. This approach is justified on the grounds that it is much easier to judge whether a party moves from the status quo, thereby signalling a policy change, than it is to judge how far it moves. Thus, in a one-dimensional space, a party can move only to the left or the right, making the utility of the move +1 for voters who agree with the change, and –1 for voters who disagree with it. In a two-dimensional policy space, the calculation is more complicated, but again the direction of movement is what counts. This implies that voters might choose a party which is further away from them in the issue space compared with a rival, just because their chosen party is on *their* side of the issue when the rival is not.

Grofman (1985) makes two modifications to the original spatial model. He introduces the idea that voters discount party positions, since they are well aware that candidates do not always deliver fully on their promises. Promise does not equal performance. Second, like Matthews, Grofman argues that voters locate parties in relation to the status quo, rather than in relation to the distance along the left–right dimension. Since voters are not sure that parties will actually move to their declared location in the policy space when it comes to actually delivering on policies, the outcomes change. Discounting any movements announced by a party implies that electors assume that the party will travel only part of the way to its announced location. This change means that parties will not necessarily converge to the median.

The Rabinowitz and Macdonald model (1989; see also Macdonald and Rabinowitz, 1998) also relies on directional considerations. In their approach, both the direction and the distance between parties and voters in the space matter. The model assumes that most voters have a rather general preference in relation to specific issues, so that they support or oppose a policy change. At the same time, voters vary in the intensity with which they hold these preferences. Voters prefer the party which is closest in the issue space and, in this respect, their model is the same as the Downsian model. However, for Rabinowitz and Macdonald, direction also matters – voters prefer parties on the same side of the issue as themselves to parties on the opposite side of the issue. Voter utilities are a combination of both the intensity and direction of party positions in the space. Thus, when voters compare two parties, they will opt for one which is on the same side of the issue as themselves, even though it may be much further away from their own ideal point than a rival party. Direction trumps proximity. When two parties are on the same side of the issue as they are, then they will choose the one which is closest. A third possibility is that the two parties are on the same side as a voter and the same distance away. In this case, the voter will choose the party which is more intense in its preferences. So, in a Rabinowitz and Macdonald world, parties can take extremist positions and win public support.

Merrill and Grofman (1999) present what they describe as a unified model. This model combines both proximity and directional components. Voters use proximity to judge some parties while at the same time using direction to judge others, and a combination of the two for yet other parties. Merrill and Grofman hypothesize that voters are likely to judge incumbent parties using proximity considerations while judging opposition parties, which lack a track record in office, by means of directional considerations (Merrill and Grofman 1999: 41).

As this brief review suggests, there is a rich set of variations on the basic Downsian model, all of which represent incremental modifications to the original analysis. Voters remain distributed in an issue space, and parties compete for their voters by manoeuvring in that space. For all of these models, position issues define the relevant terrain of party competition and electoral choice.

In contrast, Stokes' critique is more radical – it calls into question not only Downs' model per se, but also the entire approach. His argument is as follows:

The ground over which the parties contend is not a space in the sense that Main Street or a transcontinental railroad is. Treating it as if it were introduces assumptions about the unidimensionality of the space, the stability of its structure, the existence of ordered dimensions and the common frame of reference of parties and the electorate that are only poorly supported by available evidence from real political systems. (Stokes, 1963: 369–70)

Thus, Stokes criticizes all four of the assumptions discussed earlier, and finds them all wanting.

Stokes rejects the uni-dimensionality assumption, arguing that, in fact, electoral competition takes place in multiple dimensions. These dimensions are largely independent of each other in the minds of voters. For example, he cites findings from the American National Election Studies (ANES) of the 1950s showing that public attitudes to welfare spending were largely independent of attitudes to foreign policy. This aspect of Stokes' analysis is supported by the work of his colleague Philip Converse whose seminal study 'The Nature of Belief Systems in Mass Publics' (1964) demonstrated that most voters lacked coherent beliefs about political issues. He found that correlations between responses to questions in ANES panel surveys over time could be best explained by what he described as a 'black and white' model. In this model, the public is divided into two very different groups in terms of their understandings of the political world. One group understands issues and the links between different policy areas, and answers survey questions consistently and coherently over time. These voters have highly structured beliefs. The second group has no real attitudes or consistent opinions on issues and answers survey questions more or less randomly on different occasions. The beliefs of people in this second group are inchoate. Converse argued that the latter group greatly outnumbered the former one, implying that a great majority of voters cannot meaningfully locate themselves on an overarching left–right issue scale, let alone identify the location of the political parties. The implication is that parties gain little by trying to find the median position, since most voters will not recognize it or their own location in the issue space.

One possible solution to this problem is to conceptualize party competition as occurring in a multi-dimensional issue space in which all independent issues are taken into account. Given this, voters need not structure their beliefs to any extent, although they will be required to have genuine opinions. In such a world, parties would seek out the multi-dimensional median voter, depending on the distribution of electors in the space. However, this particular solution faces a formidable problem. It is extremely unlikely that the parties can find the equilibrium in such a space because the conditions for its existence are so restrictive (Plott, 1967). It is quite likely that no equilibrium exists at all, so that parties will cycle around in the issue space seeking temporary advantage over their rivals (see Mueller, 2003: 230–40; Schofield, 1978, 1985). This state of affairs then feeds back into the electorate, since it makes it impossible for voters to determine where parties will be in the future, making the theory indeterminate.

One implication of a multi-dimensional issue space and the lack of coherent belief systems among voters is that it makes political manipulation much easier. Even in the case where voters do have well-defined preferences on specific issues, political leaders have a strong incentive to try to manipulate the political agenda, to make some issues more salient than others or to mislead voters about where they are located. This is the power of agenda-setting (McKelvey, 1976). In his discussion of political manipulation, Riker writes: 'in the long run, outcomes are the consequences not only of institutions and tastes, but also of the political skill and artistry of those who manipulate the agenda, formulate and reformulate questions, generate "fake" issues etc., in order to exploit the disequilibrium of tastes to their own advantage' (1980: 445).

Manipulation of this kind is easier if voters rely on party promises rather than party performance. In a Downsian world, it is not rational for individuals to support or oppose parties for their past performance per se since these represent 'sunk' costs, or outcomes that cannot be changed. The rational actor always looks to the future – this is where utilities come from. Rational voters have no interest in 'rewarding' or 'punishing' any party or politician for what they did in the past. The only use for retrospective judgments is as a guide to making prospective evaluations, i.e. to forming expectations about what will happen in the future.

This is a rather weak justification since retrospections only provide a reliable guide when things do not change, or changes can be forecast with considerable accuracy. However, in a world of strategically pervasive manipulation and large-scale uncertainty, things change all the time – often in difficult-to-forecast ways. When the future is difficult to forecast and politicians have incentives to prevaricate, political choice is difficult. This line of reasoning suggests why voters rely heavily on the cues provided by leader images and partisan attachments – a topic to which we return below.

The second assumption challenged by Stokes is that party competition takes place in a fixed space, with voters being anchored as parties manoeuvre for electoral advantage. This assumption has its origins in economic theory where consumer preferences are assumed to be exogenously determined, i.e. outside the scope of the theory

(Koutsoyiannis, 1975). However, a good deal of electoral competition involves parties trying to impose a preferred structure on the electoral contest, by framing choices in ways that work to their advantage. This is another aspect of political manipulation and has been described by Budge and Farlie (1977; see also Clarke *et al.*, 1992; Kiewiet, 1983) as the 'issue-salience' or 'issue-priority' model of party competition. In this analysis, the issue space itself is contested as parties try to impose their own definitions of what is important on the electorate. As Budge and Farlie explain:

How do parties approach voters? A common view is that they stage a 'great debate' in which government spokesmen defend their programmes on the important questions of the day, while the opposition criticise[s] them and argues that its own preferred policies are better. The actual evidence offers only limited endorsement for this view. Far from discussing details of their opponent's plans, parties tend in their public pronouncements to ignore them so far as possible, and to deflect popular attention to other policies which have not been mentioned by their rivals. (1977: 23)

Experimental studies indicate that parties' efforts to frame political debate are sensible – framing effects exert a powerful influence on decision-making in all types of choice situations (Kahneman and Tversky, 2000). There is a considerable amount of evidence indicating that the major British political parties design their campaigns with a close eye to the power of framing effects. For example, as discussed in Chapters 5 and 6, during the 2005 election campaign Labour concentrated on the economy, while the Conservatives emphasized crime, asylum seekers and security-related issues (see also Whiteley *et al.*, 2005). If this is how electoral competition operates in practice, then the idea of a shared issue space becomes problematic. Rather than comparing parties on the same issues, voters are being asked to judge them on different ones.

Stokes' challenge to the third assumption of spatial modelling – that an ordered distribution of opinion exists in relation to issues – gives rise to the valence model of party competition. In developing his argument, Stokes cites the example of the issue of corruption in the 1952 American presidential election – 'if we are to speak of a dimension at all, both parties and all voters were located at a single point – the position of virtue in government' (1963: 372). Valence issues, ones about which there is a wide consensus about what is desirable, challenge the idea that electors and therefore parties are *distributed* within a policy space. Clearly, if there is no spatial variation in the locations of parties and voters, then there is no spatial competition, and so for these consensus issues the spatial model actually becomes the valence model. In the world of valence politics, debate is about who is best able to deliver what everyone wants, rather than what should be delivered. 'Who can do it', not 'what should be done', is what matters.

The fourth element in Stokes' critique relates to common reference, or the idea that the policy space is the same for parties as it is for voters. He suggests that party spaces may differ from electoral spaces: 'we may, in fact, have as many perceived spaces as there are perceiving actors' (1963: 375). Thus, if the parties define the left–right dimension in terms of one set of issues and the electorate view them in terms of another, then the spaces may be non-comparable. Parties may shift to the centre on issues of concern to them, seeking to maximize support, only to find that the electorate does not recognize that any movement has taken place. This is because the voters are focusing on other issues – they are in spaces of their own.

In general, the strongest criticisms of the spatial model relate to the amount of information that electors are expected to acquire and process when they decide how to vote. The spatial model requires enormous amounts of information acquisition and processing. It requires electors to know the issue space, to understand where they and each of the parties are located, to be able to track movements by the parties, and to adjust their own electoral choices in light of these movements. In addition, the model pays little attention to uncertainty. As Grofman (1985) points out, voters should discount the utility income streams associated with each party, since they are uncertain about the likelihood of parties actually delivering on their commitments. Thus, a party which appears likely to lose an election should have its promises discounted by a large amount. Equally, a party which has shifted its policy positions recently should also be discounted by the voters, since the change adds to the uncertainty about its position in the future. If it can move once, it can move again. In addition, the possibility of political manipulation by party strategists adds further uncertainty, and requires additional information processing. A rational voter in the Downsian sense needs to take into account such manipulation when deciding which party to choose. All of these uncertainties need to be factored into a voter's decision-making calculus and, collectively, they impose considerable information-processing costs (Conlisk, 1996). Since information processing is at the heart of the critique of the spatial model, we consider this more fully next.

Information and the spatial model

A paradox apparent in Downs' work is that it is not actually rational for electors to spend time processing information about electoral politics. Rather, it is rational for them to be ignorant and uniformed. Downs himself was aware of this paradox when he wrote: 'it seems probable that for a great many citizens in a democracy, rational behaviour excludes any investment whatever in political information' (1957: 245). This 'paradox of information' follows from the well-known 'paradox of participation'. If it is not rational to vote because an individual cannot change the outcome of an election, then it is not worth learning about the choices on offer in that election either (Whiteley, 1995). In the absence of a coherent theory of information processing, the whole spatial model collapses.

Any worthwhile theory of electoral behaviour has to take seriously the question of information costs. One approach might be to use standard microeconomic analysis. This argues that individuals should collect information up to the point that the marginal benefits of that information equal the marginal costs of collecting it (Koutsoyiannis, 1975: 373; see also Conlisk, 1996). However, this fails for two reasons. First, it is not worth incurring any costs at all if the voter cannot influence the outcome of the election, making the marginal benefits of any extra information relevant to electoral choice zero. Second, even if this were not true, the standard cost–benefit analysis cannot be applied to information processing, since no one knows the value of information until it is actually acquired. If the costs have to be incurred before the marginal benefits can be assessed, then theory is indeterminate. Thus, standard microeconomic theory is not a promising avenue for resolving these difficulties.

For this reason, psychological models of information processing in elections recently have come to the fore. Over the past decade, much work on electoral choice has been devoted to the task of understanding how voters make sense of the political world, while at the same time avoiding the high costs of information processing required by

the spatial model. Popkin (1991) was the first to introduce the idea of
'low information' rationality (see also Lupia and McCubbins, 1998).
Popkin writes: 'The term low information rationality – popularly
known as "gut" reasoning – best describes the kind of practical thinking about government and politics in which people actually engage'
(1991: 7). He introduces the 'two-step' model of voter information
processing. The first step involves electors picking up messages from
party campaigns and from the media that are relevant to their voting
behaviour. When doing so, they use informational shortcuts to evaluate candidates by assessing their behaviour during the election campaign, their personal characteristics, and their views on groups which
the voter knows and cares about. The second stage involves electors
seeking to verify these messages using a trusted source, usually an
opinion leader of some type. The latter might be a personal friend, or
it might be a trusted newspaper columnist or media expert (Popkin,
1991: 45–9).

Popkin cites partisanship as an example of a low-information
cue. He disputes the Michigan interpretation of party identification
as an affective orientation towards a political party that is acquired
in early life and typically strengthens over the life-cycle (Campbell
et al., 1960; Converse, 1969). Rather, Popkin adopts Fiorina's (1981)
interpretation of partisanship as a 'running tally' of evaluations of
party performance over time. In this capacity, party identification is
an information-economizing device, or a heuristic, that helps electors
to judge the validity of campaign messages.

Sniderman and his colleagues also interpret partisanship as a cue
or heuristic device: 'Heuristics are judgemental shortcuts, efficient
ways to organize and simplify political choices, efficient in the double
sense of requiring relatively little information to execute, yet yielding
dependable answers even to complex problems of choice' (Sniderman
et al., 1991). They explore a number of different heuristics and
examine interactions between them and political sophistication and
prior political knowledge. For example, they suggest that relatively
unsophisticated voters who lack political knowledge are likely to use
an 'affect' heuristic. Such voters will decide what to do on the basis
of their feelings about candidates. Which candidate they like or dislike is key. This 'affect-driven' reasoning represents a huge saving in
information-processing costs (see also Marcus *et al.*, 2000; Neuman

et al., 2007). In contrast, sophisticated voters who know a lot about politics are much less likely to use affect-driven kinds of reasoning.

Regarding the prospective issue-based voting required by the spatial model, Sniderman *et al.*, (1991: 172) argue that: 'there is no evidence for this kind of voting among the poorly educated'. Rather, poorly educated voters are likely to 'decide whether the incumbent's performance is satisfactory … If his performance is satisfactory, [they will] support him' (1991: 176). In other words, these voters rely on valence factors because they are easy to use for people who know little about politics. Lodge and his colleagues (1995) reach a similar conclusion with their 'on-line' processing model of candidate evaluations. They argue that people do not recollect the policy positions adopted by candidates in the way required by the spatial model. Rather, they keep an unconscious record – a summary running tally – of the positive and negative messages associated with candidates, and then draw on these to make a choice on polling day. This running tally remains largely in voters' unconscious memories, while the details of policy positions are forgotten. Again, a candidate's past performance dominates the decision-making process, and future promises play a relatively minor role.

It is clear that the psychological literature addresses the problem of information-processing costs by emphasizing the importance of past policy delivery, rather than issue-based prospective evaluations. This is because it is much easier to judge parties in these terms rather in relation to future policy promises. Thus, the valence model, with its emphasis on performance, deals with the costs of information processing in a way in which the spatial model does not.

Overall, the spatial model fits rather badly with the work of political psychologists on low-information rationality. The model requires a great deal of information processing, in a context where individuals have little incentive to undertake it. It also fits rather badly with the use of affect heuristics, because it emphasizes cognitive calculations as the exclusive basis of choice. Equally, it largely ignores problems of political manipulation, in particular attempts by parties to set agendas and frame issues to their own advantage. Recent research on the psychology of electoral choice thus points in the direction of the valence model as a solution to these difficulties. We develop this model more fully in the next section.

The theory of valence politics

The valence model differs from the spatial model in many respects. The valence model pays little attention to spatial distances between voters and parties, because there is little or no spatial variation in opinions on valence issues. This follows from the point made earlier that (there typically are few differences among parties on policy goals when it comes to salient political issues such as the economy, health-care, education, crime and terrorism./ Similarly, when voters are asked for their views on these issues, overwhelming majorities will opt for economic prosperity, excellent public services, and national and personal security.) A related difference is that political debate involving valence issues focuses on delivery – who can do the job – whereas, the Downsian version of the spatial model assumes that delivery takes place automatically and, thus, conflates promise and performance. In addition, as we have already suggested, the valence model greatly reduces information-processing costs by emphasizing past performance and cues provided by partisanship and leader images, rather than future promises. Finally, the valence model helps to reduce political manipulation, again by focusing on outcomes that are known rather than on possibly insincere promises which may not be realized.

However, there are also similarities between the spatial and valence models. In reality, all political issues have both valence and spatial aspects. For example, the divisive issue of UK membership of the European Monetary Union, at first sight, appears to be a classic spatial issue with both voters and parties being distributed along a continuum varying from outright support to outright opposition. But, it has important valence characteristics as well. Voters strongly opposed to UK membership would vote for the UK Independence party (UKIP), if they were only concerned about issue proximity, since this party takes the strongest Euro-sceptic line. However, no UKIP candidates were elected to Westminster in 2005, and so the party is never likely to deliver on the desired policy goal. If opponents of UK membership take into account the delivery aspects of the policy, which is the central concern of the valence model, then they would support the Conservatives since that party has a real prospect of delivering. When issues are looked at in this way, it is difficult to think of a spatial issue which does not have a valence component.

By the same token, valence issues frequently have a spatial dimension. We suggest that economic prosperity is a classic valence issue, but over a broad range of outcomes, economic growth can be viewed as a spatial issue. Most people would prefer positive economic growth to no growth at all, but it is not at all clear that they would prefer double-digit growth to modest growth. This is because very vigorous growth may be accompanied by negative externalities. There may be tradeoffs involving disruption of the fabric of society and damage to the environment. Taking these possibilities into account, economic growth can be viewed in spatial terms. A similar point can be made about the delivery of public services. Everyone prefers good to bad public services, but this preference is not unlimited since good services involve higher public spending and therefore higher taxes. Public-service delivery is a valence issue, since people want better services, while at the same time being a spatial issue since, arguably, good services have to be paid for with higher taxation. This means that the theory of valence politics has to take into account spatial considerations, just as the theory of spatial politics must incorporate valence considerations. It is not inevitable that a particular issue will always be framed in valence or spatial terms, either by parties or voters.

Some work has been done on incorporating valence issues into spatial models of party competition. Ansolabehere and Snyder (2000) and Schofield (2003) add valence variables to their spatial models. These take the form of measures which attach a utility premium to one candidate rather than another. If one candidate is seen as being, for example, more honest and reliable than another, this valence premium will convey an advantage. Not surprisingly, the premium can make the difference to the outcome of the election, when candidates are close together in the issue space. Yet another approach is to add extra terms to a voter's utility function which is otherwise dominated by spatial variables. These additional variables represent non-policy components (e.g. Adams et al., 2005). These variables may capture the effects of valence issues or possibly 'Michigan-style' party identifications such as Adams et al. append to their spatial model.

These approaches face the key problem of not being able to explain the sources of valence evaluations. They are added to spatial models as an afterthought and are not integral to the theory that drives the model. Similarly, the Adams approach (2005) cannot explain the origins of non-spatial variables such as partisanship which are incorporated into voter's utility functions. What is needed is an analysis of the sources of valence judgments that starts from first principles rather than an approach that adds valence variables to a spatial model in an ad hoc manner. We consider this possibility next.

The sources of valence judgments

The starting point of an understanding of the sources of valence judgments is to recognize that only a limited number of issues that arise in elections are actually salient to voters. At any point in time, relatively few issues really matter to the extent of influencing the voting behaviour of large numbers of people. Traditionally, in Britain and other mature democracies, this core issue agenda has been heavily biased towards domestic matters, with the economy and public services having pride of place. Recently, these concerns have been joined by (not displaced by) a set of issues involving crime, immigration and terrorism. The appeal of these several issues is understandable because they are related to risks that have personal relevance. Taken together, they tap a complex of security concerns – cultural, economic, physical and social – to which voters attach high priority.

The idea that voters confine their attention to a limited number of issues in the larger set of issues arising in an election campaign is supported by Zaller's research on public opinion (Zaller, 1992; Zaller and Feldman, 1992; see also 2000 Alvarez and Brehm, 2002; Tourangeau *et al.*, 2000). According to Zaller's receive–accept–sample model, citizens carry a limited number of 'considerations' in their minds about political issues, which they can draw on when responding to a question posed by an interviewer in a public opinion survey. There are significant variations across the electorate in the number of considerations that people carry in their heads, and also how they use them to formulate a response to survey questions. Clearly, sophisticated voters – people with a lot of political knowledge and who are engaged by the electoral process – will have more considerations in their minds than those who are ignorant and disengaged.

Exactly the same type of process is likely to be at work when people decide how to vote. They will take into account a very limited number of issues, which are not necessarily a representative sample of all the ones in play in a particular election campaign. Zaller contends that many people have highly biased issue perceptions reflecting 'top of the head' considerations relating to their recent personal experience or to stories they have picked up from the media. This type of shifting agenda is one of the reasons why there can be significant opinion dynamics during election campaigns. The sample of issue considerations is influenced by political campaigns and parties' attempts to set the electoral agenda. The influence of the limited sample of issues on voting behaviour depends on a process of averaging across the considerations that voters have in mind. If they have an ambivalent attitude to an issue, which favours some aspects of it and opposes others, then the effect will depend on the overall net balance of attitudes. For example, they may like economic growth while at the same time dislike the environmental pollution that can accompany it. The impact of the economy as an issue that affects their voting behaviour will then depend on the running tally of these considerations (see also Lodge *et al.*, 1995).

Issue sampling effectively deals with problems of multi-dimensionality in an issue space, but it does so in a different way from that advanced by the Downsian spatial model. In the latter, the assumption is made that individuals bundle up many issues into an overall left–right dimension, implying that voters are politically sophisticated, with high levels of political knowledge, ample information-processing capacity, and Converse-like (1964) ideologically 'constrained' belief systems. In the present analysis, the issue space is small because the number of relevant issue considerations in the minds of voters is very limited. If voters tend to focus on a limited set of security-related issues, which they believe have strong potential to impinge on their everyday lives, such as the economy, crime, public services and terrorism, and ignore the rest, this greatly simplifies their decision-making task. More abstract issues, such as UK membership of the European Monetary Union, are likely to be ignored by all but an atypical minority, because they are remote from everyday experience and their implications are difficult to fathom. In contrast, the price of goods in shops, the state of local hospitals, the quality of education received by children and the amount of crime in the neighbourhood, have an immediacy that raises the salience of issues associated with these conditions. This is an important reason why a selection of these issues regularly is at the centre of electoral politics. Voters often have first-hand experience with some of conditions associated with a number of these issues, but information provided by other sources, such as the mass media, political parties, and friends and neighbours is also relevant.

Another way for voters to cope with the complexity of the choices they are being asked to make is to focus on the past rather than the future. This means that they will judge a governing party primarily by its record rather than by its promises. This does not eliminate prospective evaluations since opposition parties often do not have a contemporary track record in office which voters can judge. In these cases, voters will rely on promises or on proxy indicators of likely performance such as the perceived competence, responsiveness and trustworthiness of rival party leaders. In general, past performance will be preferred to future promises, because information about performance is more reliable. Despite this, voters are being asked to make judgments about the future when they cast their ballots. Downs was aware of this fact and argued that: 'it is more rational for him [the voter] to ground his voting decision on current events than purely on future ones' (1957: 40).

The focus on performance thus applies both to spatial and to valence issues. But the information-processing costs for dealing with valence issues are significantly less than for spatial issues. In both cases, voters have to decide if a party will deliver on its policy proposals. But for spatial issues, they have also to decide if a party is being honest about its objectives. Unlike the valence model where there is a consensus about goals, in the spatial model opinions about goals are distributed, perhaps widely, across the electorate. This fact creates a conflict of interest between the voters and parties, and generates incentives for the latter to dissemble about their objectives with 'cheap talk' or misleading information (Crawford and Sobel, 1982).

Parties are faced with the task of building support among a widely dispersed set of voters in the spatial model, which gives them an incentive to be ambiguous or deceptive about where they are actually located. Recent work on signalling games suggests that rational actors will ignore promises from agents who have different interests from their own (Camerer, 2003; Lupia and McCubbins, 1998). Although different interests abound in the case of spatial issues, interests are nearly all the same in the case of valence issues. This does not of course remove the incentive to mislead about future policy delivery. Parties can claim that they will fix a problem, such as unemployment or crime, without knowing how to do so, but if voters use past performance to evaluate such claims, then they are likely to identify deception more easily.

Another way of coping with complexity has already been mentioned – the use of heuristics as informational shortcuts. Instead of using complex cognitive calculations of the issue positions of the parties, voters can use party leader images as cues, and assess leaders in terms of traits such as competence, responsiveness and trustworthiness (Clarke *et al.*, 2004a). More simply, voters can ask: 'Do I like or dislike this particular party leader?' (Brady and Sniderman, 1985; Marcus *et al.*, 2000). In a world where political stakes are high and uncertainty abounds, looking for 'a safe pair of hands' to steer the ship of state makes eminently good sense. A rather similar device is the partisanship heuristic, where voters ask: 'what does my preferred party say about this?'. A voter who identifies with a party can use this to evaluate how parties will perform in office.

Yet another device, suggested by Sniderman *et al.* (1984), is the desert heuristic which is based on responsibility attributions. If voters think that the unemployed deserve help because their situation is not of their own making, then this will make increases in unemployment benefits popular. If, on the other hand, they think that unemployment is the fault of the individuals concerned, they will see such benefits as a waste of public money. In sum, heuristics provide readily grasped tools that enable voters to simplify complex choices – choices which they would otherwise have to make when faced with a multi-dimensional issue environment containing strategic parties and considerable uncertainty.

Some of the literature on heuristics suggests that voters are often able to make decisions using a variety of information shortcuts that are very close to those they would make after a full analysis of all the alternatives. In this view, 'low information' rationality is almost as effective as full rationality. This idea derives from laboratory experiments in which voters appear to act as though they are well informed, even in very sparse informational environments (Lupia and McCubbins, 1998). On the other hand, there are some researchers who think that decision-making without full information will lead to greater errors and more uncertainty (Alvarez and Brehm, 2002). If so, heuristics come with a cost of increased forecast errors. However, heuristic devices do help to reconcile the gap between the information-processing costs of a fully informed choice, and the fact that many people lack the incentive and the capacity to become adequately informed to make classically rational choices.

Conclusion: implications of the theory of valence politics

The preceding discussion has important implications for analysing electoral choice. Clearly, analyses of voting behaviour should pay attention to valence, spatial and demographic variables. The latter are included since factors like education may interact with the valence and spatial variables and mediate their effects. Valence effects are associated with issues, leadership evaluations and partisan attachments, the latter two being particularly easy heuristics to use for the politically unsophisticated and disengaged. Regarding issues, the prevalence of valence reasoning implies that voters will make retrospective evaluations rooted in the performance of governing and opposition parties in delivering on the issues which they care about. These issues will be relatively few in number and they will be about key security concerns. Some components of this valence issue agenda, such as the economy and public services, are longstanding, whereas others, such as crime, immigration and terrorism, are of more recent vintage. Occasionally, a more remote issue, such as the Iraq War, can play an important role, but again it is the valence aspects of the war that are likely to count for more than the spatial aspects. Thus, the key question is the success or failure of the war, rather than the 'for' or 'against' positions taken by the parties on the issue. If a war is judged a success, as in the case of the Falklands conflict of 1982, this will boost support for the party that took Britain to war, but if it is deemed a failure it can damage that party and its leader. An excellent recent example concerns how British public opinion on the Iraq War eroded confidence in Tony Blair. This is the subject of Chapter 4.

Although valence issues, leader images and partisanship are crucial for understanding electoral choice, spatial issues are not necessarily irrelevant. For example, in Britain there are clear differences between the major political parties on public spending and taxation. There is also the point that voters can often only evaluate opposition parties on their promises and most of these are designed to distance themselves from their rivals and consequently are often spatial in character. We might expect to see spatial reasoning play a more important role for politically sophisticated and educated voters because it is more difficult than valence reasoning. In contrast, leader and partisan heuristics may be less important for more sophisticated voters. These hypotheses imply the existence of interaction effects in models of electoral choice. We consider this possibility in Chapter 5. Overall, however, spatial reasoning is likely to play a smaller role than valence reasoning.

Other implications arise from the discussion of electoral behaviour presented above. One is that there will be a relationship between the competitiveness of the election and the willingness of individuals to cast a ballot. This follows from the fact that opinion polls provide relatively accurate and accessible information about an election outcome. If one party is well ahead of another in the polls, this informs people that their fellow citizens have solved their decision-making problem by choosing one party rather than another. Given this, some people are likely to accept this as the majority verdict, even when they do not agree with it, and save themselves the costs of voting. This is an attractive option for less interested and motivated citizens, who might otherwise cast a ballot if the election were more competitive. The mechanism here is not that individuals believe themselves to be pivotal in a close election, but rather that the expressions of party support by their fellow citizens create a disincentive to participate if the polls give one party a big lead over another. Voters may believe that they or, better, people like them, have political influence, but that influence is not unlimited. Faced with polling evidence that the race is not competitive, voters are tempted to conclude that the election is over and the majority have spoken. If they do decide to cast a ballot, it will be because other factors, most notably a sense of civic duty, motivate their participation.

Another implication of the discussion is that voters are always likely to give priority to valence issues over spatial issues. This follows from the greater uncertainty and extra information-processing costs associated with the latter compared with the former. Longstanding incumbent parties are likely to be evaluated almost entirely on valence grounds because they have a track record which is readily apparent. Opposition parties, which have recently been in office, also will be evaluated largely by valence issues, although in their case spatial issues will play a somewhat more important role than for incumbents, because of increased uncertainty. However, if opposition parties have been out of office for a long time (perhaps forever), then in so far as they are evaluated by issues at all, voters will be inclined to emphasize spatial issues. In such cases, valence indicators that are not based on issue perceptions such as leader images and partisanship heuristics also become attractive alternatives.

A third implication of the discussion arises when parties make very similar policy promises in their election manifestos; this implies that they are all located relatively close together in the issue space. This reduces the spatial information available for discriminating among parties, and this, in turn, will have the effect of deterring some people from turning out to vote. This would not be a problem if all parties could be judged on valence issues alone, but opposition parties which have been out of office for many years cannot be judged in this way. So, *ceteris paribus*, a paucity of spatial information, together with a lack of valence information, will tend to deter people from voting. On the other hand, a loss of both spatial and issue-based valence information will encourage individuals to use non-issue-based reasoning such as leadership and partisanship heuristics. And, these are cues that are applicable for choosing among all political parties, incumbent and opposition alike.

In retrospect, the enormous amount of attention political scientists have paid to the spatial model over the past half century is puzzling. Its mathematical tractability, enabled by a set of extremely restrictive and unrealistic assumptions, may explain its attractiveness. However, developments in the psychology of political reasoning increasingly suggest that the spatial model fails to provide an adequate general theory of voting. In reality, electoral choice is grounded mainly in valence reasoning, with spatial considerations playing a secondary role. In subsequent chapters, we examine empirical evidence for the claim that the theory of valence politics provides a parsimonious and powerful explanation of electoral choice.

3 | *Valence politics and the long campaign*

Modern election campaigns are lengthy affairs. In Britain, although official general-election campaigns typically last for approximately four weeks, the continuing long-term battle for the hearts and minds of voters resumes almost as soon as an election is over. Parties manoeuvre to ensure that the issues thought to favour them are salient on the issue agenda by devising media strategies aimed at securing the best possible coverage of their policy proposals and core values. They also work assiduously to project images of their leaders as capable, responsive and trustworthy. At the same time, events and developments – policy successes and failures, domestic scandals, international crises and other exogenous shocks – occur. Voters react by making judgments about parties, candidates and leaders on a continuing basis, that is, during the official 'short' campaigns in the month preceding a general election, as discussed in Chapter 6, as well as over the course of the inter-election cycle as a whole.

In this chapter, we show how important changes in the issue agenda after the 2001 general election affected voting in 2005. Two related events had a profound impact on public opinion during this period – the September 2001 terrorist attack on the World Trade Center and the March 2003 invasion of Iraq followed by the protracted, unresolved war in that country. These events changed the valence judgments of the British electorate in two important ways. First, they led to the development of a new set of issue priorities in the minds of voters, with traditional concerns about the economy and public services being overtaken by a 'new' agenda focused on internal and external security. Second, notwithstanding Labour's ongoing success in managing the economy, the interminable, bloody conflict in Iraq damaged Prime Minister Blair's reputation as a competent and trustworthy leader. Given the importance of the leader heuristic as a source of voters' valence judgments about parties, the damage inflicted on Blair's image had important consequences for the decline in Labour support that occurred between 2001 and 2005.)

The analysis of forces at work in the run-up to the 2005 election is not confined to the emergence and effects of the new security agenda. We also consider the role of personal experience in the formation of valence judgments. It has long been recognized that personal experience with the economy can have important effects – the so-called 'pocketbook effect' – on people's s evaluations of governing parties and their leaders. Using a new cross-sectional time-series dataset, in which an identical set of survey questions was administered to repeated representative samples of the British electorate every month between April 2004 and April 2005, we investigate the extent to which people's direct experience in two policy domains – public services and public security – affected their valence calculations. Analyses indicate that, just as direct experience of the economy affects people's evaluations of a government's overall economic performance, direct experience similarly affects valence judgments in other important policy domains.

The first section of the chapter uses aggregate monthly time series data to demonstrate the dramatic and, thus far, permanent way in which the issue agenda of British politics was reshaped by 9/11. The next section uses time series data for the period since New Labour came to power in May 1997 to show that Labour's fluctuating electoral popularity, especially since 2001, can be broadly explained by a combination of three factors: Blair's leadership image, Labour's continuing reputation for economic competence and the perceived failure of the government's policy towards Iraq. A key finding, which is repeated in the analyses presented in later chapters, is that a substantial part of Labour's declining fortunes after 2001 derived from increasing public disaffection with Tony Blair.

The remaining sections of the chapter analyse individual-level data gathered via repeated monthly surveys of the British electorate. The third section develops a series of models of party support using data collected almost every month between July 2000 and April 2005. The results show that, controlling for a range of standard demographic variables, support for the three major parties was conditioned by the images of the party leaders, partisan attachments, perceptions of the economy and attitudes towards Europe. Crucially, the repeated cross-sectional time-series research design allows us to document how, at the individual level, the Iraq War reduced Labour support in the two years before the 2005 election. The party support models are extremely stable over time, suggesting that the same general factors affect electoral support in more or less the same way at different stages of the electoral cycle.

The fourth section extends the party support analysis by using a richer set of measures that became available in the April 2004 survey, and subsequent monthly surveys. Party support models analysed in this section include several additional 'valence politics' variables – evaluations of and emotional responses to the economy, public services, and internal and external security, and opinions regarding important issues facing the country. Results show that all of these variables affect party support in consistent and predictable ways.

Finally, the fifth section analyses the role of personal experience in making political choices. As anticipated above, we investigate whether direct experiences with public services and policies, and whether those experiences are good or bad, constitute important sources of judgments that, in turn, guide the choices voters make among political parties. Analyses reveal that between April 2004 and April 2005 there was very little variation in people's direct experiences of five key policy areas: the NHS, the education system, asylum-seekers, crime, and measures to combat terrorism. However, direct experiences in these policy domains exerted consistent effects on evaluations of, and emotional reactions to, government performance in major policy areas which, in turn, fed through to the party choices that people made.

The changing issue agenda

As discussed in Chapter 2, parties tend to 'own' particular issues, and the issues that voters think are most important at any given time represent a crucial aspect of valence politics. In both 2001 and 2005, the BES post-election survey asked respondents an open-ended question about what they thought was the most important issue facing the country. The results, reported in Figure 3.1, are clear and instructive. In 2001, over 50% of the respondents prioritized the economy (9%) or public services such as the health service (29%) and education (12%). In sharp contrast, only 3% cited crime, and only 2% mentioned asylum seekers or immigration more generally. Foreign policy issues and terrorism were essentially off the radar screen. By 2005, the agenda

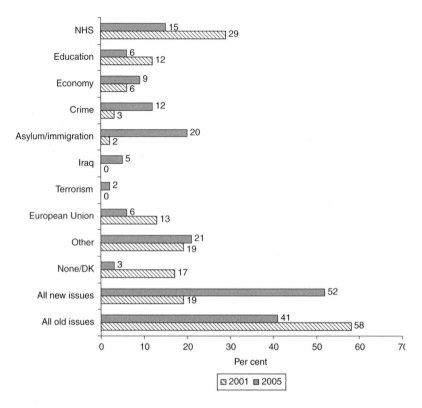

Figure 3.1 Most important issues facing the country, 2001 and 2005
(*Source:* 2001 and 2005 BES post-election surveys)

had changed dramatically. The percentage citing the health system
or education as the most important issue had dropped by almost a
half. This decrease in what we term 'older issues' was accompanied
by large increases in the numbers citing crime, asylum/immigration,
the Iraq War, or terrorism. Of the 2005 BES respondents, 39% mentioned one of these 'new' issues as their top priority, up almost eight-
fold since 2001. Altogether, slightly over half of the 2005 respondents
cited these or other new issues, whereas less than one-fifth did so in
2001. However, older issues did not disappear; just over two-fifths
referenced one of them, down from nearly three-fifths in 2001. A mix
of new and older issues jostled for attention as voters prepared to go
to the polls in 2005.

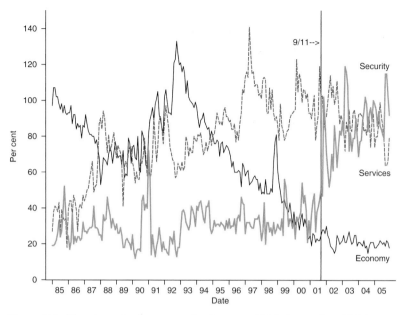

Figure 3.2 The changing issue agenda, January 1985–December 2005 (*Source:* 1985–2005 MORI monthly surveys)

Time series data allow us to determine when and why these changes in the issue agenda occurred. Since the mid-1980s, the MORI monthly polls have included an issue agenda question comparable to that asked by the BES. Unlike the BES, the MORI respondents are asked to cite the *three* most important issues facing the country, which means that the percentage citing any particular topic tends to be greater than what is recorded using the BES question. Figure 3.2 illustrates the changing pattern of issue priorities in the MORI surveys conducted between 1985 and 2005. The issues have been grouped into three clusters: the economy, public services and (internal and external) security.[1] Key features of the figure are obvious. First, until the early 1990s, the economy and public services vied with one another for top place as most important, with security issues running a poor third. Second, during the mid-1990s, services overtook the economy as the focus of voters' issue concerns, and the salience of the economy progressively declined. Third, beginning in September 2001, the importance of the security cluster quickly increased such that, from the middle of

2003, security was competing with services for the top issue priority position and the economy was lagging far behind.

The rise of security issues after 2001 was not simply a reflection of Britain's greater *overseas* involvement. Rather, breaking the 'security' issue cluster into its internal (crime/law and order, race) and external (defence) components reveals that both security priorities increased after 2001 (Figure 3.3). This, in turn, suggests that increasing concern with security matters after 2001 was a general development rather than a specific response to British involvement in Afghanistan and Iraq.

Why might the importance of economic issues have declined during the 1990s while that of security-related issues increased so dramatically after 2001? One possible answer to these questions is that both trends result from the changing issue agendas pursued by the political parties – since the early 1990s, the major parties have tended to de-emphasize the economy and, since 2001, to emphasize security. The problem with this explanation is that New Labour has

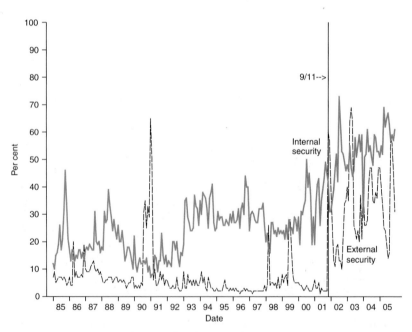

Figure 3.3 Dynamics of internal and external security issues, January 1985–December 2005 (*Source:* 1985–2005 MORI monthly surveys)

consistently campaigned strongly on its ability to deliver a healthy economy. Recognizing its reputation for competent management of the economy, the party has sought to focus the political agenda on economic issues.

A second possible explanation is that major shifts in the issue agenda derive primarily from framing effects of the mass media. Although this hypothesis is widely canvassed, there is no systematic British evidence to support it. Limited evidence suggests that people respond to what they read in newspapers and see on television, but studies indicate that the effects of media coverage are modest in comparison with those associated with changes in the 'real world'. This observation leads directly to a third explanation – one that we favour – that major changes in the issue agenda reflect changes in the electorate's objective environment.

Compelling evidence for this latter proposition can be seen with regard to two key economic indicators of unemployment and inflation. Figure 3.4 displays the relationship between the priority accorded unemployment as an issue (the percentage of MORI respondents who

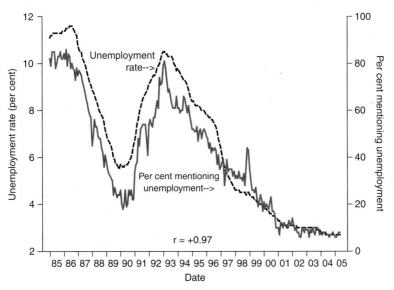

Figure 3.4 Relationship between unemployment as one of top three issues and the unemployment rate, 1985–2005 (*Source:* 1985–2005 monthly MORI surveys and Monthly Digest of Statistics)

cite unemployment as one of the three most important problems facing the country) and the unemployment rate (per cent of the working population unemployed in Great Britain, seasonally adjusted) between January 1985 and May 2005. Over this twenty-one-year period, the correlation (r) between the two series involving the issue priority and the actual level of unemployment is a very impressive +0.97.[2] The prevailing level of unemployment at any given point in time is reflected in the public's assessments of the importance of joblessness as an issue. Similarly, Figure 3.5 shows that the importance ascribed to inflation as an issue rises and falls with changes in the objective inflation rate. A correlation of +0.87 indicates that the dynamics of the two series are very closely associated. Thus, over the two decades preceding the 2005 general election, movements in the public's sense of economic issue priorities has closely paralleled changes in the country's economic circumstances.

The above findings raise the question of whether issue priorities and objective indicators of non-economic policy areas also track each other closely. Although objective monthly data on, for example, the

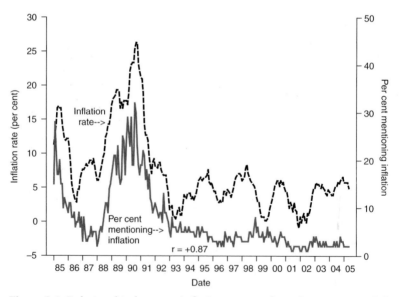

Figure 3.5 Relationship between inflation as one of top three issues and the inflation rate, 1985–2005 (*Source:* 1985–2005 monthly MORI surveys and Monthly Digest of Statistics)

magnitude of security threats or the quality of public-service provision are not available, there are several indirect, albeit frequently
government-revised, indicators that enable analogous, but cautious,
comparisons to be made.[3]

With these caveats in mind, Figures 3.6 to 3.8 compare the public's issue priorities in relation to crime and asylum/immigration with
available data on the incidence of violent crime and recorded demands
for asylum or immigration more generally. There is an ongoing
debate over whether crime rates are best measured by official statistics recorded by the police or by data gathered by the British Crime
Survey. The former is preferred by those who mistrust unchecked
self-reports of exposure to crime, where the latter is preferred by
those who emphasize the importance of crimes unreported to police.
Note, also, that over-time crime statistics are complicated by government tendencies to pass laws that illegalize more activities and, thus,
recorded crime tends to increase over time. Accordingly, we use *violent* crime as the least ambiguous of available crime statistics, and as
the measure most likely to elicit concern among the general public.
Since only annual objective data – for a limited number of years – are

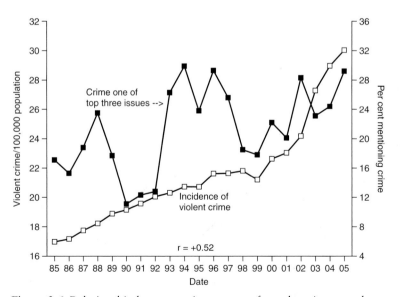

Figure 3.6 Relationship between crime as one of top three issues and
incidence of violent crime, 1985–2005 (*Source:* 1985–2005 MORI monthly
surveys and Home Office statistical bulletins)

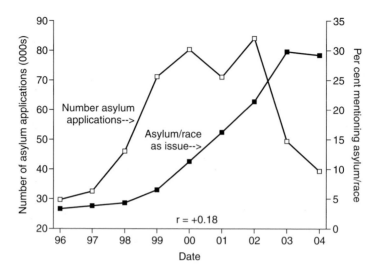

Figure 3.7 Relationship between asylum/immigration/race as one of top three issues and number of asylum applications, 1996–2004 (*Source: 1996–2004 MORI monthly surveys and Home Office statistical bulletins*)

available, we aggregate the monthly MORI issue-priority data to the annual level.

Figure 3.6 charts the relationship between recorded violent crime and people's view of crime as one of the three major issues facing the country between 1985 and 2005. As the figure illustrates, their relationship is not as strong as that between unemployment and inflation and their respective issue-priority measures. It also is clear from Figure 3.6 that both the objective and subjective measures generally trend upwards, with a step increase in the subjective series in the early 1990s and an accelerating trend in the objective one at the turn of the century. The overall correlation between the two series is a substantial +0.52 – which suggests that changes in violent crime are a major mover of the public's emphasis on public safety but that many other factors are at work.

Figures 3.7 and 3.8 compare published data with people's issue priorities involving the demand for asylum and immigration. The time periods displayed in the two figures are shorter than in previous graphs, reflecting the difficulty of assembling comparable longer-term time-series data from government sources. Figure 3.7

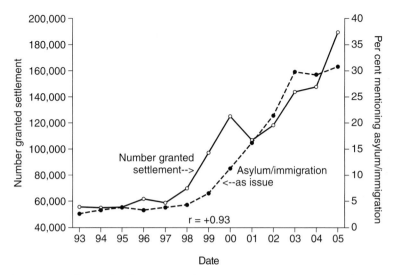

Figure 3.8 Relationship between asylum/immigration/race as one of top three issues and number of grants of settlement, 1993–2005 (*Source: 1993–2005 MORI monthly surveys and MPI Data Hub, available at: www.migrationinformation.org/datahub*)

shows the relationship between the annual number of asylum applications and the importance of asylum/immigration as an issue. Between 1993, when the series began, and 2002, both series increase sharply. However, the relationship then dissolves, with the recorded demand for asylum collapsing to levels not seen since the early 1990s, while public concern continues to climb. Given this divergence, it is not surprising that the correlation between the two series is very weak (0.18).

Figure 3.8 suggests a possible reason for why the relationship depicted in Figure 3.7 collapses after 2002. Although the number of asylum applications decreased after 2002, the overall number of immigrants granted settlement in the UK continued to climb. Paralleling this trend, public concern with the complex of issues associated with asylum, immigration and race mounted sharply. This, in turn, suggests that it is not the influx of asylum seekers per se that people are worried about; rather it is rapidly increasing immigration of all kinds. Although the coincidence of the two trends depicted in Figure 3.8 is not perfect, the correlation between them, +0.93, is extremely strong.

Clearly, mounting public concern with issues relating to asylum and immigration has been very closely associated with the rising numbers of immigrants granted permission to settle in the UK.

In sum, the data in Figures 3.4 through 3.8 suggest that, although people's issue priorities are not impervious to the agendas touted by political parties and the mass media, trends in these priorities are connected to developments and experiences in 'the real world out there'. In Britain, these connections have been very strong in the economic sphere. They are also substantial, if imperfect, with regard to two key components of what we term the 'new security agenda' – crime and asylum/immigration. In the next section, we develop the idea of this new agenda further and offer an account of why it strengthened so markedly after 2001.

Modelling the rise of the new security agenda

After the al-Qaeda attacks on New York and Washington in September 2001 (9/11), politicians, media and the public alike became increasingly concerned with national and personal security and the potential threats posed by criminals and terrorists. The upward, almost step-shift, impact of 9/11 can be seen clearly in Figure 3.9, which plots the underlying trend in the rise of the security agenda.[4] In addition, it is possible that the war in Iraq has further heightened people's concerns with security matters, over and above the effects of 9/11. It is also possible that the increased importance of the security agenda has been at least partially an artefact of the aforementioned declining salience of economic issues.

To investigate these alternatives, we specify an aggregate time-series model of the dynamics of mentions of security issues in the monthly MORI polls. The model is:

$$\text{SECURITY}_t = B_0 + B_1\text{SECURITY}_{t-1} + B_2\text{POST9/11}$$
$$+ B_3\text{IRAQ} + B_4\Delta\text{UN}_t + B_5\Delta\text{INF}_t + \varepsilon_t \qquad (3.1)$$

where: SECURITY_t represents the monthly percentage of MORI respondents who regard internal or external security, as defined previously, as one of the three most important issues facing the country; POST9/11 is a 0–1 dummy variable scored one after September 2001 (implying a permanent shift in the security series after 9/11); IRAQ is a 0–1 dummy variable scored one from April 2003 (implying a

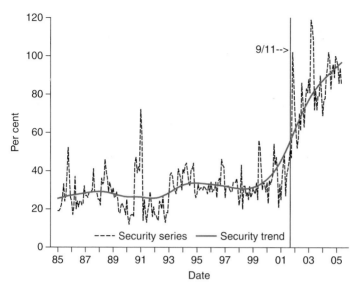

Figure 3.9 Trend in the dynamics of security issues, 1985–2005
(*Source:* 1985–2005 MORI monthly surveys)

further permanent shift); ΔUN_t and ΔINF_t are monthly changes in the unemployment and inflation rates, respectively, which are assumed to represent the objective importance of the economy; and ε_t is a stochastic error term ($\sim N(0, \sigma^2)$). Model parameters are estimated via OLS regression.

Model A in Table 3.1 reports the results of estimating Model 3.1 for the period February 1985 to May 2005. The variables for the occupation of Iraq and for unemployment and inflation fail to achieve statistical significance. These results clearly indicate, first, that there was *no* further upward step-shift in the security agenda as a result of the Iraq occupation, and second, that economic factors were *not* responsible for the changing salience of security issues. Critically, however, the post-9/11 dummy term is positive and highly significant. This effect is confirmed in Model B in Table 3.1, which reports the consequences of excluding the statistically insignificant variables in Model A. The significant regression coefficient for 9/11 ($\beta = 22.2$) testifies that the terrorist attack had the expected large initial impact on concern with security issues.[5] Also, the significant coefficient ($\beta = 0.59$) for the lagged endogenous variable in the model indicates that effects of 9/11

Table 3.1 *Time series regression analyses of the dynamics of the security issue agenda, January 1985–May 2005*

	Model A	Model B
Predictor variables	β	β
Security issue agenda $(t-1)$	0.57***	0.59***
9/11	22.51***	22.21
Iraq War	1.41	
Δunemployment rate	−6.18	
Δinflation rate	−1.65	
Constant	12.88***	12.69***
Adjusted R^2	0.85	0.86
AIC	1757.95	1748.22

Note: dependent variable (security issue agenda) is the percentage of MORI respondents identifying issues as one of the two most important problems facing the country.

*** –p ≤ 0.001; ** –p ≤ 0.01; * –p ≤ 0.05; one-tailed test.

Source: MORI monthly surveys and *Monthly Digest of Statistics.*

continued over time, gradually increasing the salience of the security agenda. By the end of 2001, it was well over forty percentage points greater than before September 2001. The growth continued and, circa April 2005, the percentage mentioning a security issue was fully 54% greater than prior to 9/11.

These results clearly indicate that the horrific terrorist attack transformed the British electorate's issue agenda. Before the attack, most people most of the time focused on some aspect of the economy or the provision of public services. Afterwards, these traditional concerns were joined by new worries about a complex of issues related to internal and external security. Later in this chapter we use individual-level data to document that the British public does indeed view this new security agenda as a single complex distinct from other issues. First, however, we use aggregate-level data to show how the changing security agenda affected support for New Labour in advance of the 2005 general election.

New Labour and the new issue agenda

Both later in this chapter and in subsequent ones, we develop a series of individual-level models of party support. Here, we provide a broad-brush, aggregate-level characterization of the dynamics of Labour support between 1997 and 2005. The analysis is rooted in a valence, or performance, account of electoral behaviour, as discussed in Chapters 1 and 2. There are three compelling reasons for restricting the analysis to a performance-based approach in this chapter, although later chapters explore the merits of alternative accounts of electoral choice. The first reason derives from our previous analysis of electoral behaviour in Britain that consistently found that variables reflecting valence considerations had the most powerful statistical effects on vote choice. The second reason is more practical. We are interested here in how changes in party support relate to changes in explanatory variables over time, including periods between elections. However, suitable continuous data, such as monthly data on non-valence variables, are not available and, accordingly, a study of their effects on the dynamics of party support is not possible.

A third reason for focusing on valence-based accounts is that available aggregate-level data on the well-known, alternative spatial model suggest that, between 2001 and 2005, voters saw both themselves and the parties as drawing closer to the ideological centre-ground. Table 3.2 reports the marginal distributions on an eleven-point 'tax versus spending' spatial scale. This scale correlates very highly with the analogous 'left–right' spatial scale, but it has the added advantage of eliciting a much higher item-response rate than the left–right scale. As shown, in 2001, both Labour (average score 5.0) and the Liberal Democrats (4.4) were generally perceived as being very close to where the average respondent perceived her/himself to be (4.5). The Conservatives were perceived as being much more in favour of tax reductions (by 1.9 points) than the average respondent.

By 2005, distances between voters and parties had narrowed. On average, voters considered themselves to be at exactly the same point on the tax/spend scale as both Labour and the Liberal Democrats (all 4.9). Even the Conservatives (6.0) were perceived as being only 1.1 points to the 'right' of the average voter. This

Table 3.2 *Average scores on increased taxes and services versus*
reduced taxes and services scales, 2001–5

	2001	2005
Average perception of:		
Labour position	5.0	4.9
Liberal Democrat position	4.4	4.9
Conservative position	6.4	6.0
Average self-placement	4.5	4.9
Number of points Labour to the left of average respondent	−0.5	0.0
Number of points Conservatives to the right of average respondent	2.9	1.1
Sum of absolute distances between respondent and each party	3.5	1.1

Note: Eleven-point (0–10) scales; a low score indicates a preference for higher taxation to improve services, and a high score indicates a preference for lower taxation and no improvement in services.
Source: 2001 and 2005 BES surveys.

general narrowing of spatial distances between parties has important implications for the possible explanatory power of the spatial and valence models. As argued in Chapter 2, when parties in a Downsian ideological space converge on the median voter position, there is nothing to differentiate among them but their valence attraction, i.e. their promised policy performance. Although the aggregate spatial results for 2005 do not represent a condition of complete spatial convergence, they nonetheless suggest a considerable narrowing of perceived ideological/policy distances between parties and between voters and parties. This, in turn, implies that during the 2001/5 period valence considerations should have had more powerful effects than spatial ones on party support. In this sense, therefore, a data-enforced focus on valence calculations fits well with prevailing political circumstances.

What, in practical terms, do we mean by valence judgments? In sum, the valence approach is rooted in two key claims. The first concerns overall *policy competence*. Voters support a party that they think is likely to best handle issues that they consider most important. In this regard, a key development of the mid-1990s was

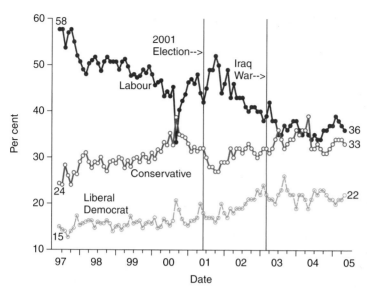

Figure 3.10 The dynamics of party support, June 1997–April 2005
(*Source:* 1997–2005 'Poll of Polls' monthly average vote intention percentages; Gallup, ICM, MORI and YouGov polls included in calculations

that Labour replaced the Conservatives in the public mind as the
party of economic management competence. The second claim
involves the *issue agenda*. Parties tend to have reputations both for
prioritizing, and for being better able to handle, particular issues.
For example, law and order, defence and the control of inflation
have traditionally been regarded as being 'owned' by right-of-centre
parties. In contrast, public service provision, the defence of civil liberties and job creation generally have been seen as being 'owned'
by parties of the left. The argument is that parties are likely to be
more successful if and when 'their' issues dominate the political
agenda.

The changing pattern of Labour support, as well as corresponding patterns of Conservative and Liberal Democrat support, which
we explain, are displayed in Figure 3.10. Although Labour support trended downward after its sweeping 1997 victory, the party
emerged from the 2001 election well ahead of its rivals. Its support
then declined progressively during 2002, rose slightly just before the
invasion of Iraq in March 2003, and then declined again thereafter.
Labour support recovered modestly in the months preceding the 2005

election, though even that recovery faltered just as the campaign was about to begin.

Conservative and Liberal Democrat patterns are almost mirror images of the Labour pattern, if in more muted form. Both parties enjoyed modest increases in support in the first half of the 2001–5 parliament, as Labour lost ground. Indeed, the Conservatives briefly overtook Labour in the summer of 2004 in the wake of Michael Howard's selection as party leader, but their revival had clearly petered out by the autumn of that year. Liberal Democrat fortunes also fluctuated, but the general trend was mildly positive, with the party making modest gains immediately before the 2005 election was called.

To study movements in Labour's vote intention share, we employ data across the entire period since the party was returned to power in May 1997. The valence-based account of the dynamics of Labour support uses both the 'policy competence' and the 'issue-agenda' aspects outlined above. We measure voters' evaluations of Labour's overall policy competence in two ways.[6] The first uses Tony Blair's ratings as 'best prime minister'.[7] As argued in Chapter 2, leader images constitute a key heuristic or cognitive shortcut for many voters. To avoid having to process large amounts of information involving competing parties, voters can make cost-effective summary judgments about them based on assessments of the qualities of party leaders.[8] In this regard, Figure 3.11 illustrates how Tony Blair's leadership ratings varied over the 1997–2005 period. The strong downward trend exhibited in the figure suggests that Blair's image, with some short-term perturbations, deteriorated substantially throughout his first two terms, although there were mild recoveries in the run-ups to the 2001 and 2005 elections, and a short-lived recovery when hostilities were initiated against Iraq in March 2003. If voters used their images of Blair as a guide for making judgments about Labour's overall competence, then his leader ratings should exert a strong and significant impact on Labour support.

A second variable employed to assess voters' overall policy competence assessments is a measure of their evaluations of the economic management capabilities of Labour versus the Conservatives. Even when voters do not designate the economy as their highest priority, the valence politics model claims that they are more likely to support

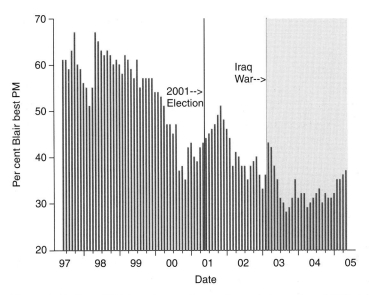

Figure 3.11 Tony Blair's ratings as best prime minister, June 1997–April 2005 (*Source:* 1997–2005 Gallup and GPVP monthly surveys)

a party deemed capable of sound economic management. Figure 3.12 displays the overall balance of judgments that Labour rather than the Conservatives has superior economic management skills across the 1997–2005 period. As shown, with the exception of the month of the petrol crisis (September 2000), Labour's positive image on the economy was sustained well past the 2001 election. However, Labour's economic edge over the Conservatives declined sharply in the latter half of 2002, and the Conservatives actually surpassed Labour in late 2003 and early 2004. Then, Labour's reputation for economic competence gradually recovered so that by the time the election campaign began, the party's lead over its chief rival was almost as big as it had been four years earlier. If the valence politics model is correct, then Labour's reputation for sound economic management should be positively related to its support in the electorate.

The *issue-agenda aspects* of valence enter into our model very straightforwardly. Figure 3.2 above described the changing emphasis that the electorate accorded to three general issue areas – economy, public services and security. There are a priori theoretical reasons to

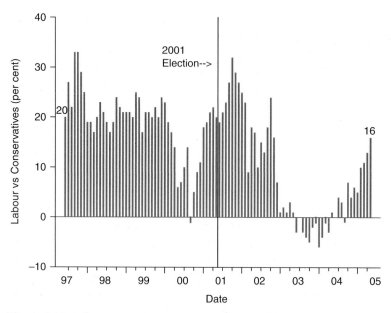

Figure 3.12 Labour versus Conservatives as party best able to manage the economy, June 1997–April 2005 (*Source:* 1997–2005 Gallup and GPVP monthly surveys)

suppose that changing priorities in all three areas could have affected Labour support. In terms of the *economy*, the party's record of maintaining low unemployment, low inflation and steady economic growth gave it a strong incentive for trying to ensure that economic concerns would rank highly on the electorate's issue agenda.[9] In this regard, it may be hypothesized that Labour support would be positively associated with the extent to which the economy is emphasized in voters' issue priorities. A similar argument applies in relation to *services*. Given Labour's traditional association with the welfare state and public service provision, and given its undisputed record after 1997 and especially after 2001, of increasing state spending on public services, it is likely that the party would benefit to the extent that voters prioritized the issue of public-service provision.

With regard to *security*, the situation is ambiguous. As noted above, 'law and order' and 'defence' traditionally have been regarded as issues on which the Conservatives have the strongest 'natural advantage'. However, successive home secretaries after 1997 strove to present

Labour as tough on crime and on threats to public security, and made repeated revisions to the legal frameworks for criminal justice and the prevention of terrorism. At the same time, Prime Minister Blair made it clear that his government was prepared to make difficult defence policy choices in Bosnia, Afghanistan and Iraq. These changes in Labour's approach, which to many observers have rendered it indistinguishable from the Conservatives on foreign policy and defence, make it difficult to determine whether a higher priority accorded to the security agenda should have helped or hindered Labour. We accordingly include a security agenda variable in our model but do not make an a priori prediction about the direction of its effect.

Other components of the Labour support model involve 'events'. We observed earlier that 9/11 had a profound effect on the security issue agenda. Precisely because that effect is included in the security agenda series, we do not need to make separate provision for it in our model. However, there are two other notable events that did appear to affect Labour support between 1997 and 2005. The first was the petrol crisis of September 2000. This crisis caused an abrupt fall in Labour support, although the effect was very short-lived and disappeared by the end of the year. We include a dummy variable in the model to control for the impact of this temporary reversal in Labour's fortunes.

The second event is of far greater substantive importance – the Iraq War and subsequent occupation. British forces joined a much larger US force in March 2003 to invade Iraq. The express intention was to remove Saddam Hussein from power, thereby eliminating the threat posed by weapons of mass destruction he allegedly possessed. After deposing Hussein, the occupying forces would install a functioning, democratically elected government that would be responsible for its own security as soon as possible. By the time of the 2005 election, no such government was operating and US/UK-led coalition forces remained in Iraq, supposedly to prevent bloody ethno/religious conflict from escalating into open civil war. As the highly publicized conflict continued, the inability of the coalition to 'win the peace' in Iraq caused some voters to re-appraise their views of Tony Blair and his government. The broad consensus among most observers is that the war had significantly eroded Labour's popularity by the time of the 2005 general election (e.g. Sanders, 2005). To capture this effect, we include a dummy variable for the Iraq War in the model.

There are different ways to incorporate the set of predictor variables described above in a model of the dynamics of party support. Here, we use an error correction specification. This is because the dependent variable – Labour support – and two of the key predictor variables – Blair's approval ratings and Labour economic management competence – form a co-integrating set. This means that they tend to move together over time; in effect, there is a long-run dynamic equilibrium relationship involving the three variables. Shocks to the Labour Party support system, from whatever source, are eroded over time by this co-integrating relationship. An attractive feature of co-integration models is that they allow estimation of the rate of adjustment back to equilibrium. This is particularly useful for estimating the effects of events, like the Iraq War. In summary, the specification is:

$$\Delta \text{LABOUR}_t = B_0 + B_1 \Delta \text{BLAIR}_t + B_2 \Delta \text{ECMAN}_t + B_3 \Delta \text{ECON}_t$$
$$+ B_4 \Delta \text{SERVICES}_t + B_5 \Delta \text{SECURITY}_t + B_6 \text{S2000}_t$$
$$+ B_7 \text{IRAQ}_t - \alpha(\text{LABOUR}_{t-1} - c_1 \text{BLAIR}_{t-1}$$
$$- c_2 \text{ECMAN}_{t-1}) + \varepsilon_t \qquad (3.2)$$

where: LABOUR is the monthly poll-of-polls percentage intending to vote Labour; BLAIR is the percentage thinking Blair would make the best prime minister; ECMAN is the percentage believing that Labour is best at handling the economy minus the percentage who think the Conservatives are best; ECON is the percentage judging that the economy, public services, and security constitute one of the three most important issues facing the country; SERVICES is the percentage who prioritize any aspect of public service provision; SECURITY is the percentage who prioritize crime, immigration/asylum, race or defence; IRAQ is a dummy variable taking the value 1 after March 2003; Δ is the difference operator; α is the adjustment parameter for the error correction mechanism; and ε_t is a stochastic error term ($\sim N(0, \sigma^2)$).[10] Parameters are estimated using ordinary least squares.

Table 3.3, Model A presents estimates for the full model. The adjusted R^2 statistic equals 0.63, indicating that the model explains a substantial portion of the variance in the dynamics of Labour support. As expected, the coefficients on the two policy competence measures – Blair as best prime minister and Labour economic management – are positive and statistically significant. However, none of the

Table 3.3 *Time series regression analyses of the dynamics of labour support, July 1997–May 2005*

	Model A	Model B
Predictor variables	β	β
ΔLabour economic management competence	0.23***	0.23***
ΔBlair's rating as best prime minister	0.28***	0.27***
Δimportance of economy as an issue	0.00	
Δimportance of public services as an issue	0.02	
Δimportance of security as an issue	−0.00	
September 2000 petrol crisis	−4.96***	−5.15***
Iraq War	−1.96***	−1.97***
Error correction mechanism (*t*–1)	−0.55***	−0.58***
Constant	−6.33***	−6.45***
Adjusted R^2	0.63	0.63
AIC	352.47	349.32

Note: dependent variable is the change in monthly 'poll of polls' average of respondents intending to vote Labour.
*** $-p \leq 0.001$; ** $-p \leq 0.01$; * $-p \leq 0.05$; one-tailed test.
Source: Gallup, MORI, ICM and YouGov (published and GPVP) monthly surveys.

coefficients for the issue-agenda terms is significant.[11] This suggests that, of the two broad sets of valence considerations in the model, the measures of the electorate's sense of Labour's policy competence clearly are the most important. Controlling for the effects of these competence assessments, changes in the issue agenda – marked as they were – did not have significant effects at the 0.05 level. However, the coefficient for the services agenda is positive and approaches significance ($p \leq 0.10$), implying that Labour may derive electoral benefit when public service provision is high on the electorate's agenda. In the event, the weakness of the economy and security issues indicates that Labour was neither helped nor hurt by changes in these aspects of the issue agenda between 1997 and 2005. This, in turn, suggests the possibility that neither Labour nor the Conservatives now 'owns' these issue areas in the way that has been traditionally thought.

Perhaps the most substantively important finding in Table 3.3 relates to the effect of the Iraq War and subsequent occupation. To obtain a more precise estimate of this effect, we re-estimate the model, using only the significant predictors in Model A. The results (Table 3.3, Model B) show that the Iraq coefficient ($\beta = -1.97$) remains negative and statistically significant ($p \leq 0.001$). The size of this coefficient suggests that, net of other considerations, Labour initially lost approximately two percentage points in its popularity because of the war. As per the model specification, the effect continued to build in subsequent months. Calculations show that the full negative effect of the occupation took about six months to develop, and that the 'cost' to Labour through the 2005 election was approximately 3.4 percentage points.[12] This is a direct effect estimate and, as we see in Chapter 4, there were additional negative effects imposed via the erosion of Blair's reputation as a competent and trustworthy leader. In the event, the negative impact of Iraq was not sufficient to deprive Labour of an election victory. However, it was a significant component in the constellation of forces that reduced the number of Labour Commons seats from 413 in 2001 to 356 in 2005. In the latter year, as analyses presented in Chapters 4 and 5 further show, Labour's declining performance was very much linked to the war and occupation.

Finally, our aggregate-level analysis tells both straightforward and ambiguous stories about the dynamics of public opinion during the course of the 2001 parliament. The straightforward story is that two key valence-based variables – the prime minister's ratings and Labour economic competence – had powerful effects on Labour support. The ambiguous story is that, although there was a dramatic change in the issue-agenda – with security-related issues becoming much more important after 9/11 – this change did not of itself either hurt or help Labour's re-election prospects. 'Security' appears to be an issue that, for the time being, is not owned by any major political party in the sense that a particular party necessarily benefits when the issue is high on the electorate's political agenda. This said, it bears reiteration that the war in Iraq damaged Labour, with the aggregate analyses suggesting that the direct effect was nearly 3.5%. In the next section, individual survey data gathered between July 2000 and April 2005 enable us to refine our analysis of the costs (to Labour) of the war and occupation, and to explore who (if anyone) benefited from Labour's 'lost' support.

Modelling individual-level party support

July 2000–April 2005

In this section, we use data from a long-running series of monthly surveys in order to examine the individual-level factors that underpinned party preferences between 2000 and 2005. The analyses enable us to assess the extent to which valence calculations varied as well as shaped voting preferences over time. In general, the analysis shows that the same factors affected party choice in more or less the same way throughout the period investigated. The only consistently significant 'time effect' relates to the period after the invasion of Iraq. Consonant with the aggregate analyses presented above, we find that people became significantly less likely to support Labour and significantly more likely to favour the Liberal Democrats.

The models in this section build directly on those that were developed and tested in *Political Choice in Britain* (Clarke *et al.*, 2004b: Chapter 4). However, there are some minor differences between the models tested earlier and those specified here. As noted previously, the inter-election survey data do not contain all of explanatory variables available in the BES data.[13] Specifically, the former do not include spatial measures of ideological and policy positions and the party considered best on a most important issue, and they use slightly simplified measures of social class and education.[14] The general specification is summarized in Equation 3.3 below. We estimate two models: (a) Labour versus other party support, and (b) Conservative, Liberal Democrat, and other party support, with Labour support as the reference category. Both models include controls for demographics and the following explanatory variables:

Party identification: Our previous work on partisanship suggests that it is best conceived, following Fiorina (1981) and others, as an ongoing cumulative tally of party performance evaluations. In this sense, party identification is a 'valenced' measure, since by implication it involves the individual's assessment of the likely performance of the party in question. We include dummy variables for

Labour, Conservative, Liberal Democrat, and 'other' party identification. The reference category is 'no party identification'. The expectation is simple; identifiers with a particular party will be more likely to vote for that party and less likely to vote for a competitor.

Leader images: As discussed earlier, voters tend to use leader images as heuristics when making their party choices. The notion of valence is central here in the sense that perceived competence is a critical component of leader images. We expect that individuals who think that Blair would make the best prime minister are more likely to vote Labour and less likely to vote Conservative or Liberal Democrat. Similarly, those who think that Hague/Duncan-Smith/Howard would make the best prime minister should opt for the Conservatives, and those thinking Kennedy would do the best job would favour the Liberal Democrats. The reference category for these dummy 'best leader' variables is 'none of the above'.

The economy – evaluations and emotions: The performance of the economy has long been regarded as a quintessential valence issue: positive economic evaluations prompt voters to support the governing party, and negative ones drive them towards the opposition. Here, we extend the traditional, cognitively oriented analyses of the impact of the economy to consider not only evaluations of economic performance but also emotional reactions to national and personal economic conditions. To do so, we construct a variable based on an exploratory factor analysis of six different measures of *economic evaluations* and *emotions*. All of these measures load on a single factor that explains over 51% of the total observed variance.[15] A high score on the resulting 'economic reactions' factor score means that an individual is very positive about the economy; a low score, that an individual is very negative. The hypothesis is that people who are positively disposed towards the economy would likely vote for the governing Labour Party, and those who are negatively disposed would choose one of the opposition parties.

Approval of the European Union: Previous research has shown that this position issue played a role in vote choice in 2001 (Clarke *et al.*, 2004b). The Conservatives have tended to take a critical position on the EU, whereas Labour and the Liberal Democrats have been more positive about it. As a result, we expect that those who score lower on a five-point 'EU approval' measure likely vote Conservative, whereas those who score higher likely vote Labour or Liberal Democrat.

Iraq: The model includes a simple dummy variable to indicate whether the respondent was interviewed before or after April 2003, the first full month of occupation following the toppling of Saddam Hussein's regime. Our expectation is that, other things being equal, those interviewed after April 2003 would be less likely to support Labour and more likely to support either the Conservatives or the Liberal Democrats. In sum, the model is:

$$\text{VOTE} = f(\text{BLAIR, HOWARD, KENNEDY, LABPID,}$$
$$\text{CONPID, LDPID, OPID, ECON, EU, IRAQ,}$$
$$\text{AGE, EDUC, GENDER, OWNER, SCOT,}$$
$$\text{WALES, CLASS)} \qquad (3.3)$$

where: VOTE is Labour, Conservative and Liberal Democrat vote intentions measured as three 0–1 dummy variables; BLAIR, HOWARD (previously Hague, Duncan-Smith) and KENNEDY respectively are 0–1 dummy variables indicating whether a respondent considers that the person would make the best prime minister; the PID variables indicate whether the person has a Labour, Conservative, Liberal Democrat or other party identification; ECON is a factor score reflecting how a respondent reacts to the economy; EU measures (dis)approval of the European Union; and IRAQ is an Iraq occupation 0–1 dummy variable. Demographic controls include age (AGE), education (EDUC), gender (GENDER), housing tenure (OWNER), region (Scotland (SCOT), Wales (WALES)), and social class (CLASS).

Table 3.4 reports the results of estimating Equation 3.3 for two dependent variables. One dependent variable (Model A) is Labour versus other party support, and the second (Model B) is Conservative, Liberal Democrat, and other party support with Labour support as the reference category. Binomial logistic regression analysis is used to estimate parameters in the first model, and multinomial logistic regression analysis is used to estimate parameters in the second model (Long, 1997). The pseudo R^2s indicate that the models have substantial explanatory power, and the effects of various predictor variables are consistent with theoretical expectations. First, the three key sets of valence terms all behave as predicted. All the leader and party identification terms are significant and correctly signed. For example, the Blair as best PM and Labour identification terms are positive and highly significant in the Labour model and negative and

Table 3.4 *Logistic regression analyses of Labour, Conservative and Liberal Democrat support, July 2000 to April 2005*

	Model A	Model B	
	Labour	Conservative	Liberal Democrat
Predictor variables	β	β	β
Best prime minister:			
Blair	2.52***	−2.22***	−2.00***
Howard	−0.54***	1.07***	−0.17*
Kennedy	−0.21***	−0.17**	1.35***
Party identification:			
Labour	1.76***	−2.37***	−1.63***
Conservative	−1.85***	2.83***	0.38***
Liberal Democrat	−1.43***	0.18	2.30***
Other party	−1.18***	−0.36***	0.09
Economic evaluations/ emotions	0.44***	−0.50***	−0.42***
EU approval	0.09***	−0.13***	0.06***
Iraq War	−0.25***	0.29***	0.71***
Gender (men)	−0.24***	0.19***	0.11**
Age	−0.00	0.01***	0.01***
Housing (owner/ occupier)	−0.19***	0.44***	0.20***
Social class (middle class)	−0.21***	0.21***	0.35***
Education	−0.09***	0.09****	0.14***
Region:			
Scotland	0.00	−0.50***	−0.61***
Wales	−0.05	−0.21*	−0.22**
Constant	−1.22***	−0.69***	−1.45***
McFadden R^2	0.55	0.50	
Per cent correctly classified	87.6	76.2	

Note: Model A is a binomial logistic regression; respondents intending to vote Labour are scored one and all others scored zero. Model B is a multinomial logistic regression; dependent variable categories are intend to vote Conservative, Liberal Democrat, other party/DK with intend to vote Labour as the reference category. Coefficients for other party/DK not shown.
*** −$p \leq 0.001$; ** −$p \leq 0.01$; * −$p \leq 0.05$; one-tailed test. N = 45,008.
Source: Gallup and GPVP monthly surveys.

significant in the Conservative and Liberal Democrat ones. Second, as also expected, the economic reactions factor-score variable is positive and significant in the Labour analysis (Model A) and negative and significant in the opposition party analysis (Model B). This pattern suggests that the consistently strong performance of the economy continued to bolster Labour support throughout the period analysed here – despite the electorate's stated conviction, from the mid-1990s onwards, that the economy was not the key problem facing the country. Third, the EU approval term is positive in both the Labour and Liberal Democrat models and negative in the Conservative one, again as predicted.

Finally, the coefficient on the Iraq War variable is negative for Labour ($\beta = -0.25$) and positive for both the Conservatives ($\beta = 0.29$) and Liberal Democrats ($\beta = 0.71$). This pattern is consistent with our aggregate time series analysis (see Table 3.3), which shows that Labour lost and the other parties gained as a result of the war and occupation. It is also not surprising that the Liberal Democrats benefited more than did the Conservatives from Labour's discomfort over Iraq, since the former party consistently questioned, whereas the Conservatives largely supported, the government's decision to join the invading force.

Calculating changes in the probability of voting for various parties, when the Iraq War variable shifts from zero to one in April 2003 (with other predictors set at their means and multiplying the resulting probability changes by 100 for ease of interpretation), indicates that participation in the war reduced the likelihood that the average respondent would vote Labour by five points. In contrast, the probability of supporting the Conservatives or the Liberal Democrats increased by three and fifteen points, respectively. These are relatively modest effects in comparison with those associated with changes in party leader images or party identification. For example, allowing feelings about Tony Blair to vary from their maximum to their minimum score, while holding other predictor variables at their means, lowers the probability of supporting Labour by fifty-two points. Similarly, abandoning a Liberal party identification and becoming a nonidentifier raises the probability of intending to vote Labour by forty-two points. Nonetheless, the effects of the war and ensuing occupation were not trivial. Reinforcing the conclusion suggested by the aggregate time series model discussed earlier, the present analysis indicates that Britain's involvement in Iraq had a significant negative impact on Labour support. As we see in Chapter 4, part of this impact was indirect – working to lower Labour support by corroding voters' views of Tony Blair.

Before proceeding, we note that a number of robustness tests were conducted on the models reported in Table 3.4. One test adds a series of monthly dummy variables – one for each month in which a survey was conducted after July 2000 – to the model of Labour support (Table 3.4, Model A). The results are clear. First, the model fit remains virtually identical to that in Table 3.4 despite the addition of forty-two independent variables. Second, the coefficients of the core explanatory variables also remain virtually identical to those reported in Table 3.4. Third, only three of the monthly dummy coefficients are statistically significant at the 0.05 level – and, in the event, two of them would be expected to be significant at this level on the basis of chance. In sum, the model in Table 3.4 explains the monthly fluctuations in Labour support very well.

An analogous test allows the coefficients of the Table 3.4 models to vary according to different phases of the election cycle. It tests whether there are distinctive variations in the impact of the different predictor variables during the three-month, pre-election, 'run-up' periods in 2001 and 2005. The test again suggests the robustness of the results in Table 3.4. Very few of the interaction terms are significant, which suggests that the effects of the predictor variables on party support are virtually identical both over the long inter-election campaign and in the short-term run-up periods immediately before elections.[16] As noted earlier, this does not mean that official short campaigns are unimportant but, rather, that the same set of factors tends to operate continuously throughout the electoral cycle.

April 2004–April 2005

In this section, we extend the analysis conducted above in two ways. First, we consider people's evaluations and emotions involving six different policy areas – the economy, crime, asylum/immigration, health, education and terrorism. We show that attitudes towards these areas cluster into four distinct groups and that they affect party support in predictable ways. Second, we include data on voters' perceptions of the most important issue facing the country. We show that, although these priorities have some effects on party support, they are not nearly as powerful as those associated with evaluations and emotions.

Table 3.5 reports the results of an exploratory factor analysis of eighteen different measures of GPVP respondents' policy evaluations and emotions. The data cover the period April 2004 to April 2005. The survey questions relating to the economy (four on evaluations, two on emotions) are identical to those used in the previous section to generate the economic reactions factor-score measure. The five other policy areas involve measures of policy evaluations (based on 0–10 scales of respondents' ratings of government performance in each area) and emotional responses (as the balance of positive versus negative emotional reactions in each policy area). Finally, there are two measures of attitudes towards the Iraq War and occupation – a 0–10 scale measuring the extent to which the respondent considers the venture to have been a success, and a five-point scale measuring approval/disapproval of it.

The factor analysis results displayed in Table 3.5 are compelling. A rotated four-factor principal components solution explains over 61% of the variance in the eighteen items. The first factor is clearly an 'economic' one, on which all six of the economic items load strongly and all of the other items load weakly. The second, public-services factor is equally clear. It shows that evaluations and emotions towards the health service and education load strongly on this factor and weakly on the others. The fourth factor is an external security factor relating to the Iraq War. Both approval/disapproval of the conflict and judgments about its success have very strong positive loadings on the factor.

The third factor is especially interesting in light of the earlier discussion of the new issue agenda in British politics. The pattern of item loadings for this factor indicates that respondents' attitudes towards crime, asylum/immigration and the risk of terrorism cluster together in the public mind, and are clearly differentiated from orientations towards other policy areas involving the economy, public services and Iraq. This important finding accords well with our earlier analysis of crime and asylum/immigration as a single 'internal security' dimension. Overall, this four-factor solution is extremely robust. Using GPVP surveys covering the April 2004 to June 2006 period produces an identical solution, as do month-by-month analyses of the data.[17]

Table 3.5 *Exploratory factor analysis of evaluations of and emotional reactions to six policy objects*

	Factors			
	Economy	Services	Security	Iraq
Personal prospective economic evaluations	**0.79**	0.09	0.12	0.06
National retrospective economic evaluations	**0.64**	0.38	0.15	0.16
National prospective economic evaluations	**0.66**	0.35	0.12	0.19
Personal retrospective economic evaluations	**0.81**	0.09	0.10	0.03
Emotional response national economy	**0.58**	0.42	0.24	0.19
Emotional response personal economic conditions	**0.72**	0.12	0.17	0.03
Evaluation of educational system	0.18	**0.78**	0.07	0.09
Evaluation of National Health Service	0.22	**0.74**	0.19	0.07
Emotional response to education system	0.14	**0.75**	0.15	0.10
Emotional response to National Health Service	0.18	**0.73**	0.18	0.08
Evaluation of crime situation	0.24	0.45	**0.52**	0.02
Evaluation of situation with asylum seekers	0.24	0.25	**0.55**	−0.22
Evaluation of risk of terrorism	0.05	0.04	**0.65**	0.26
Emotional response to crime situation	0.15	0.35	**0.64**	0.00
Emotional response to asylum seekers	0.23	0.15	**0.66**	−0.28
Emotional response to terrorism threat	0.07	0.02	**0.75**	0.20
Evaluation of Iraq War	0.13	0.13	0.03	**0.89**

Table 3.5 (*cont.*)

	Factors			
	Economy	Services	Security	Iraq
Approval/disapproval of the Iraq War	0.19	0.17	0.17	**0.86**
Per cent variance explained	18.6	17.6	14.7	10.5
Total variance explained = 61.4%				

Note: principal components analysis with varimax rotation.
Source: April 2004–April 2005 GPVP monthly surveys.

In the models of party support developed in this section, the factor analytic results are used in two ways. First, we employ the four sets of factor scores to indicate people's summary evaluative/emotional responses to the economy, public services, internal security and external security. Second, this four-fold issue classification is used to group respondents' views about the most important issue facing the country. These modifications enable us to test a more extended model of party support over the year preceding the 2005 general election, as follows:

$$\begin{aligned} \text{VOTE} = f(&B_0 + B_1\text{BLAIR} + B_2\text{HOWARD} + B_3\text{KENNEDY} \\ &+ B_4\text{LABPID} + B_5\text{CONPID} + B_6\text{LDPID} + B_7\text{OPID} \\ &+ B_8\text{ECFAC} + B_9\text{SERFAC} + B_{10}\text{ISFAC} + B_{11}\text{ESFAC} \\ &+ B_{12}\text{MIPEC} + B_{13}\text{MIPSERV} + B_{14}\text{MIPISEC} \\ &+ B_{15}\text{MIPESEC} + B_{16}\text{EU} + B_{17}\text{GENDER} + B_{18}\text{AGE} \\ &+ B_{19}\text{OWNER} + B_{20}\text{CLASS} + B_{21}\text{EDUC} + B_{22}\text{ETH} \\ &+ B_{23}\text{SCOT} + B_{24}\text{WALES}) \end{aligned} \qquad (3.4)$$

where: VOTE is vote intention, the dependent variable. In one analysis, VOTE is a dummy variable scored one if the respondent intended to vote Labour and zero, otherwise. In a second analysis, VOTE is a multiple-category variable with separate categories for Labour, Conservative, Liberal Democrat, 'Other Party', and 'Will Not Vote/Don't Know'. ECFAC, SERFAC, ISFAC and ESFAC are factor scores for the four factors shown in Table 3.5; MIPEC, MIPSERV, MIPISEC and MIPESEC are 0–1 dummy variables indicating whether a respondent, respectively, prioritized the economy, public services, internal security or Iraq as the most important problem facing the country; ethnicity is an additional demographic control variable that was unavailable in the Gallup survey data and therefore could not be specified in Model 3.3 above; and all other terms are as defined in Model 3.3. Two logistic regressions are performed. The first is a binomial logit analysis with Labour vote intentions versus all other alternatives as the dependent variable. The second, multinomial logit analysis uses the multiple category dependent variable described above, with Labour vote intentions as the reference category.

The results of the two logistic regression analyses, as presented in Table 3.6, are broadly consistent with the earlier individual-level analyses reported above, and thus reinforce our earlier observations about the importance of partisanship and leader-images as sources of party support. The models are well determined and consistent with theoretical expectations. In this regard, the most interesting findings relate to the four sets of evaluation/emotion factor scores and to the four most important issue variables. One finding is that the coefficients for the evaluation/emotion factor scores indicate that reactions to the economy are not all that counts, and that positive and negative evaluations and emotions in other policy areas matter as well for party support. The pattern of significant positive evaluation/emotion coefficients for Labour and negative coefficients for the Conservatives and Liberal Democrats extends across all four policy domains of the economy, public services, internal security, and external security.[18] Valence reactions (judgments and emotions) thus have important effects in economic and other policy domains as well.

Second, the pattern of effects exhibited by the 'most important problem' variables varies. Several coefficients associated with these variables do not exert significant effects. However, those that do work as anticipated. Thus, people who prioritized the economy were more likely to support Labour, and less likely to support either the Conservatives or the Liberal Democrats. Also as expected, people who focused on public services were less likely to support the Conservatives, and those who prioritized internal security were less likely to support the Liberal Democrats. These latter relationships may reflect Labour's success in branding the Conservatives as, at best, grudging supporters of public services, as well as an image of the Liberal Democrats as champions of civil liberties rather than citizen protection.

Table 3.6 *Logistic regression analyses of Labour, Conservative and Liberal Democrat support, April 2004 to April 2005*

	Model A	Model B	
	Labour	Conservative	Liberal Democrat
Predictor variables	β	β	β
Best prime minister:			
Blair	0.58***	−0.68***	−0.62***
Howard	−0.14***	0.82***	0.01
Kennedy	−0.24***	−0.07**	0.63***
Party identification:			
Labour	1.11***	−1.20***	−1.04***
Conservative	−1.20***	1.69***	0.26*
Liberal Democrat	−0.97***	−0.24*	1.22***
Other party	−0.62***	0.06	0.07
Services evaluations	0.36***	−0.43***	−0.38***
Economic evaluations and emotions	0.43***	−0.52***	−0.42***
Security evaluations and emotions	0.14***	−0.22***	−0.12**
Iraq evaluations and emotions	0.14***	−0.09*	−0.25***
Most important issue:			
Public services	0.16	−0.23*	−0.04
Economy	0.33**	−0.46**	−0.26*
Internal security[a]	0.06	0.10	−0.22*
Foreign policy[b]	0.07	−0.09	−0.02
EU approval	0.20***	−0.15***	−0.03
Age	0.00	−0.00	−0.00
Education	0.03	0.05	−0.01
Ethnic minority	0.16	−0.10	−0.01
Gender (men)	−0.06	0.17*	−0.05
Social class (middle class)	−0.10***	0.14***	0.12***
Region:			
Scotland	0.13	−0.48***	−0.79***
Wales	−0.09	−0.07	−0.08

Table 3.6 (*cont.*)

	Model A	Model B	
	Labour	Conservative	Liberal Democrat
Constant	−3.50***	−0.02	−0.06
McFadden R²	0.64	0.56	
Per cent correctly classified	91.0	76.9	

Note: Model A is a binomial logistic regression; respondents intending to vote Labour are scored one and all others scored zero. Model B is a multinomial logistic regression; dependent variable categories are intend to vote Conservative, Liberal Democrat, other party, will not vote/DK, with intend to vote Labour as the reference category. Coefficients for other party and will not vote/DK not shown.

[a] Respondent cites crime, asylum/immigration or terrorism as the most important issue facing the country.

[b] Respondent cites Iraq or foreign affairs as the most important issue facing the country.

***−$p \leq 0.001$; **−$p \leq 0.01$; *−$p \leq 0.05$; one-tailed test.

N = 16,161.

Source: April 2004–April 2005 GPVP surveys.

A third main result follows from the first two. The pattern of consistently significant coefficients for the evaluation/emotion variables and, the economy aside, a pattern of non-significant or marginally significant coefficients for the most important issue variables bolster the point that the impact of issues operates mainly through the cognitive and emotional reactions that voters have about party performance, rather than through the priorities that voters and parties assign to different issues per se. Both are relevant for understanding party support, but the former are more important than the latter.[19]

Personal experience and political choice

The previous section demonstrates that valence judgments, based on a combination of evaluations and emotions towards four different policy areas, play an important role in determining party support. One interesting topic related to these findings concerns the role of personal experience. For example, it frequently is argued that personal economic experience – typically measured in terms of retrospective assessments of household financial conditions – plays a role in the formation of party preferences.[20] However, there have been few, if any, studies of the extent to which personal experiences in important *non-economic* policy areas relating to public services and security affect vote choices. This is precisely the question that we explore in this section.

Starting in April 2004, the GPVP surveys asked a representative sample of British voters whether, in the previous twelve months, they or a family member had direct experience involving (a) medical treatment; (b) the education system; (c) assistance from the authorities in relation to a crime; (d) government efforts to combat terrorism; and (e) asylum seekers or immigrants. In each specified area, respondents who reported having had direct experience were then asked whether they were satisfied or dissatisfied with the experience. The overall pattern of experience/satisfaction in the April 2004–April 2005 GPVP surveys is summarized in Table 3.7. It is evident from the table that, with the exception of medical provision, most people (approximately three-quarters) had no direct experience of most policy areas. But, among those who did, there are clear variations in satisfaction by policy area. As the right-hand column of the table indicates, on balance, people tended to be more satisfied with their experience of medical provision (+48%), education (+11), and measures against terrorism (+15); and less satisfied with crime (–3) and asylum seekers/immigrants (–6).

Tables 3.8 and 3.9 focus on those respondents who had direct experience in each policy area. Table 3.8 shows the month-by-month percentages of people who were satisfied in each area. These percentages indicate that, at least in the year before the 2005 general election, people's satisfaction with their experiences in any of the five areas neither increased nor decreased. Table 3.9 provides equivalent information for eleven standard regions of Britain. Although there are some inter-regional differences (for example, satisfaction levels across areas in the East Midlands are slightly lower than the national average), most are small and not statistically significant. The only clear differences concern satisfaction in the asylum/immigration area. In this area, satisfaction levels are highest in Scotland, Wales and the 'North' (which excludes the North-West and Yorkshire/Humberside) – areas

Table 3.7 *Experiences of and satisfaction with medical treatment, crime, measures to combat terrorism, asylum seekers/immigrants, April 2004 to April 2005*

	Dissatisfied	No experience	Satisfied	Percentage satisfied minus dissatisfied
Medical treatment	21%	10	69	+48
Assistance with crime	13%	77	10	−3
Education system	8%	73	19	+11
Measures against terrorism	8%	69	23	+15
Asylum seekers/ immigrants	12%	82	6	−6

Note: cell entries are row percentages.
N = 16,168.
Source: April 2004–April 2005 GPVP surveys.

that traditionally have received the lowest numbers of asylum seekers and immigrants.

What impact might 'personal experience' have on people's political views? One obvious hypothesis is that a satisfying personal experience might dispose an individual to make a more positive evaluation of government performance in the relevant policy area. Such an experience might also encourage a more positive emotional response in that area as well. A negative experience would have the opposite effects. Some light is shed on this hypothesis by the analyses displayed in Table 3.10. These analyses involve correlating the nature of personal experiences with the evaluation/emotional reaction factor scores in various policy areas. Two sets of correlations are computed: (a) those in which people who had no experience of a particular policy area are treated as 'missing data' (see the columns headed 'with no neutral category'); and (b) correlations in which people who had no experience of a particular policy area are included by treating them as a

Table 3.8 *Over-time variations in experience satisfaction by policy area, April 2004 to April 2005*

	Policy area				
	Crime	Education	Asylum	NHS	Terrorism
2004					
April	45	74	24	79	71
May	42	68	33	79	77
June	43	72	31	77	73
July	45	74	34	76	76
August	37	67	33	76	78
September	37	71	29	77	73
October	46	73	31	77	75
November	39	70	37	77	77
December	41	75	37	77	73
2005					
January	46	72	36	78	78
February	48	72	40	75	69
March	41	68	37	74	76
April	38	72	37	75	72
Total	**42**	**72**	**34**	**77**	**75**
Average monthly N	287	328	227	1,117	383
Total N	3,736	4,262	2,959	14,525	4,892

Note: cell entries are percentages satisfied with the experience of policy dimension specified, among those with direct experience of the specified area.
Source: April 2004–April 2005 GPVP surveys.

middle 'neutral' category that assumes respondents are neither satisfied nor dissatisfied with their experience. The numbers of cases vary considerably between these two groups. Without a 'neutral' category, the number of cases is necessarily limited because the correlations are computed only for people with direct experience in a particular policy area. The decision to include or exclude the neutral category matters for multivariate analysis. Since a very small number (117) of the 16,000+ respondents directly experienced all five policy domains,

Table 3.9 *Regional variations in experience satisfaction by policy area, April 2004 to April 2005*

	Policy area					
	Crime	Education	Asylum	NHS	Terrorism	N
Region						
East Anglia	46	71	25	77	74	1,367
East Midlands	38	65	24	75	80	1,229
West Midlands	42	69	32	77	74	1,459
London	44	72	39	72	68	1,174
North	44	77	46	80	78	775
North West	42	72	37	78	81	1,657
South East	40	72	29	75	74	2,840
South West	38	70	35	78	79	1,864
Yorkshire and Humberside	45	77	33	79	76	1,421
Scotland	47	74	54	76	67	1,460
Wales	40	71	40	75	71	936

Note: cell entries are percentages satisfied with experience in the policy dimension specified.
Source: April 2004–April 2005 GPVP monthly surveys.

we need to 'recover' cases in a way that allows multivariate analysis to be done without generating false causal inferences. We explain this further below.

The results in Table 3.10 suggest three main conclusions. First, there is a very close correspondence between the satisfaction–*evaluation* correlations and the satisfaction–*emotion* correlations. For example, both with and without a neutral category, the crime, education and terrorism coefficients are identical to within 0.01 of a decimal place. This close correspondence adds weight to our earlier decision to include evaluations and emotions as part of the same factor for each policy object. Second, the rank ordering of correlations is similar whether or not the 'neutral' category is included. In both cases, the terrorism correlations are the lowest, the asylum/immigration and

Table 3.10 *Correlations between experience satisfaction and*
evaluation and emotional reaction scores, April 2004 to April 2005

	With no neutral category correlation (r) between satisfaction and:		With neutral category, correlation (r) between satisfaction and:		N with no neutral category
Policy area	Evaluations	Emotions	Evaluations	Emotions	
Crime	0.29	0.29	0.15	0.16	3,737
Education	0.35	0.34	0.18	0.18	4,265
Asylum	0.58	0.62	0.25	0.29	2,958
NHS	0.40	0.41	0.35	0.37	14,524
Terrorism	0.14	0.14	0.06	0.07	4,893

Note: coefficients are Pearson's r; all significant at $p \leq 0.01$. Average N with neutral category defined by 'no experience' in relation to the policy area in question = 16,088.
Source: April 2004–April 2005 GPVP monthly surveys.

NHS correlations are the two highest, and crime and education are in between. However, the third and key point is that the correlations are *lower* when the neutral category is included. Since we want to assess the extent to which direct experience affects other political perceptions and choices, we can be confident that inclusion of a 'neutral' category in the measures of experience may bias any estimates *downwards*, i.e. we are very unlikely to overestimate any effects that experience might have.

Effects of non-economic personal experience

In our analysis of the dynamics of the issue agenda of British politics, we distinguished among three main types of issues: the economy, public services and security. The five policy domains for which we measured personal experience and satisfaction relate to the latter two of these issue types: our measures of satisfaction with the health service and education to public service provision; and our measures of crime and asylum/immigration to (internal) security. Accordingly, we create indices of 'service satisfaction' and 'security satisfaction',[21] and we explore their explanatory power on: (1) vote intentions; (2) our

Table 3.11 *Effects of services satisfaction and security satisfaction on Labour, Conservative and Liberal Democrat vote intentions, April 2004 to April 2005*

	β	s.e.	p	Change in probability
Labour vote intentions				
Services satisfaction	+0.09	0.05	0.04	0.03
Security satisfaction	−0.05	0.08	0.55	−0.02
Conservative vote intentions				
Services satisfaction	−0.00	0.05	0.96	0.00
Security satisfaction	+0.08	0.08	0.29	0.03
Liberal Democrat vote intentions				
Services satisfaction	+0.05	0.04	0.24	0.01
Security satisfaction	+0.13	0.07	0.09	0.04

Note: binomial logistic regression analyses. Models include all independent variables specified in Equation 3.4. Values represent the change in probability of voting for the specified party given a change from the minimum to the maximum value on the independent variable. Services satisfaction and security satisfaction indices range from 1–5.
N = 15,982.
Source: April 2004–April 2005 GPVP monthly surveys.

summary (factor score) measures of issue-evaluations/emotions; and (3) voters' issue-priorities.

There is little doubt that many politicians believe that, just as 'satisfied customers' are good for business, so 'satisfied citizens' are good for votes. Other things being equal, when people have a good direct experience in a policy domain where government is active, they are more likely to take a positive view of the governing party. Similarly, negative experiences breed dissatisfaction with that party. We test this proposition by adding service satisfaction and security satisfaction variables to the models of party support specified in Equation 3.4. Table 3.11 reports only the coefficients and relevant statistics for these 'added' variables. The remaining coefficients and standard errors are all identical to those reported in Table 3.6 above.

The results shown in Table 3.11 are clear. Of the six estimated effects, the service satisfaction variable in the Labour equation is the only one that is statistically significant. Thus, although Labour benefited to a small degree electorally by satisfying some of its 'customers' in terms of public service provision,[22] for the most part satisfaction or dissatisfaction with service or security *experiences* appears to have no direct effect, either positive or negative, on party support.

But, if there is only a small direct effect of experience satisfaction on party support, then could there be significant indirect effects? We noted earlier that there are non-trivial correlations between policy domain-specific measures of evaluations/emotions and experience satisfaction. It is possible, therefore, that service satisfaction and security satisfaction could play a causal role in the determination, respectively, of service and security evaluations/emotions. With this type of relationship, problems of endogeneity and exogeneity may arise – that is, evaluations/emotions and experience satisfaction could affect each other simultaneously, and/or both could be co-determined, along with vote choice, by other factors. Moreover, the necessary statistical instruments for simultaneously estimating such relationships are often unavailable. This said, simple logic suggests that direct policy area experience is more likely to be causally prior to evaluations/emotions in that area than vice versa – an individual is more likely to evaluate services positively when s/he has good experience with them.

Here, we estimate a model that assesses the impact of four sets of factors on evaluations/emotions. The first embodies the idea suggested immediately above – that people's evaluations of and emotional responses to service provision are affected by their *experiences* of it: the more positive (negative) a person's experience in a particular policy domain, the more likely it is that her/his evaluations/emotions in that domain will also be positive (negative). The second set of causal factors relates to the use of heuristics. In this regard, we hypothesize that identifiers with the incumbent party will tend to display more positive evaluations/emotions, in any given policy area, than other respondents. By the same token, opposition party identifiers will tend to exhibit more negative evaluations/emotions in that policy domain.

The third set of causal factors relates to the impact of media exposure. In this context, we explore two possible effects. The first reflects the partisan bias of the newspapers that people read. We test the simple proposition that readers of broadly pro-Labour papers are more likely to have *positive* evaluations/emotions than readers of either broadly pro-Conservative or broadly 'neutral' papers.[23] The second reflects the distinction between 'tabloid' and 'broadsheet' newspapers. In recent years, this distinction refers more to the 'news style', rather than to the physical shape, of the various papers. 'Tabloid' generally means a more sensationalist approach to news reporting and, thus, a focus disproportionately on lurid 'bad news' stories and sensationalist accounts of 'policy failure'. 'Broadsheet' papers take different political positions but tend to be more balanced, more reflective and less 'alarmist' in their approach. Our expectation is that, over and above any 'partisan bias' effects, readers of tabloid newspapers are more likely to exhibit *negative* evaluations/emotions than people who read broadsheets or no newspaper at all.

Including controls for standard demographics, the model of *service evaluations/emotions* is:

$$
\begin{aligned}
\text{SERFAC} = {} & B_0 + B_1\text{SERVSAT} + B_2\text{LABPID} + B_3\text{CONPID} \\
& + B_4\text{LDPID} + B_5\text{OPID} + B_6\text{PROLAB} \\
& + B_7\text{TABLOID} + B_8\text{GENDER} + B_9\text{AGE} \\
& + B_{10}\text{OWNER} + B_{11}\text{CLASS} + B_{12}\text{EDUC} \\
& + B_{13}\text{ETH} + B_{14}\text{SCOT} + B_{15}\text{WALES} + \varepsilon
\end{aligned}
\tag{3.5}
$$

where: SERFAC is the public service evaluation/emotion factor scores derived from the factor analysis in Table 3.4; SERVSAT is the 'satisfaction with services' index used in Table 3.11; PROLAB measures respondents' exposure to pro-Labour versus pro-Conservative newspapers;[24] TABLOID indicates whether or not each respondent is a regular reader of a tabloid newspaper; and other variables are as defined in Equation 3.3.

Table 3.12 contains parameter estimates for Model 3.5. The table also reports the results of analysing a comparable model of 'security' evaluations/emotions, using the 'satisfaction with security' index discussed above. Since both 'services' and 'security' are continuous factor-score variables, OLS regression is used for estimation purposes. Both models are reasonably well determined, and most coefficients are statistically significant and plausibly signed. The results suggest several conclusions. First, *direct experience* plays a very important role in the formation of evaluations/emotions towards both services and security. The highly significant positive coefficients on both measures of personal experience (shown in bold) indicate that

Table 3.12 *Regression analyses of public services evaluations/emotions and security evaluations/emotions, April 2004 to April 2005*

	Satisfaction with:	
	Public services	Security
Predictor variables	β	β
Satisfaction with experiences of public services	0.40***	
Satisfaction with experiences of security		0.34***
Party identification:		
Conservative	−0.15***	−0.05***
Labour	0.25***	0.09***
Liberal Democrat	0.02	0.08***
Other party	−0.05***	0.01
Pro-Labour versus pro-Conservative newspaper readership	0.15***	0.01
Tabloid newspaper reader	−0.03*	−0.39***
Age	−0.00***	−0.00***
Education	−0.04***	0.10***
Ethnic minority	0.10***	−0.17***
Gender (men)	0.08***	0.15***
Social class (middle class)	−0.01	0.03***
Region:		
Scotland	−0.17***	0.03
Wales	−0.15***	0.00
Constant	−1.44***	−1.17***
R^2	0.26	0.23

***−p ≤ 0.001; **−p ≤ 0.01; *−p ≤ 0.05; one-tailed test.
N = 15,957.
Source: April 2004–April 2005 GPVP monthly surveys.

satisfying personal experiences with both public services and security encourage more positive evaluations of government policy.[25] Second, as anticipated, evaluations/emotions are also affected by the partisan heuristic: Labour identifiers are significantly more likely to display positive responses in both policy domains whereas identifiers with other parties are (generally) significantly less likely to do so. Finally, Table 3.12 shows that the media exposure terms behave as expected. The 'tabloid exposure' variable in the services and security equations produces strong and significant negative effects: exposure to the tabloid press is associated with negative evaluations/emotions in both policy domains. However, effects of newspaper partisan bias are more mixed. The coefficient for the 'pro-Labour newspaper bias' variable is correctly signed in both models – exposure to pro-Labour newspapers tends to produce more positive policy evaluations/emotions – but the effect is not statistically significant in the security equation. This minor anomaly aside, the key effect observed in Table 3.12 is clear. Controlling for a range of other relevant factors, direct experience strongly affects people's policy evaluations and emotions, and, as documented in earlier analyses, positive policy evaluations are associated with higher levels of support for the governing party and lower support for its opponents.

A final component of our analysis of the impact of 'experience satisfaction' is to consider possible effects on the issue agenda. The core supposition is that 'good' experiences do not necessarily help the political agenda favoured by the governing party. Recall that the marked reductions in inflation and unemployment in the 1990s and early 2000s – which represented 'good' economic performance – were associated with a reduction in the extent to which the electorate regarded 'the economy' as an important issue domain. In other words, good economic performance, in an almost self-defeating way, can reduce the salience of the economy as an issue. It may be conjectured that a similar mechanism might operate with regard to people's experiences with public services and public security. It might be the case that satisfactory experiences in a given domain simply result in people being less likely to think about that domain and therefore less likely to prioritize it as an issue. In contrast, according greater priority to an issue could be the consequence of an individual having had an unsatisfactory experience in that issue domain. If these hypotheses are correct, one would expect to find that, with the application of appropriate statistical controls, experience satisfaction with services (or security) should exert a negative effect on the extent to which people respectively prioritize services (or security) on their personal issue agendas.

We use Model 3.6 to test this hypothesis. The relative importance of services and security on the respondent's issue agenda is captured with the responses to five questions that asked respondents to rate the importance of crime, asylum/immigration, the threat of terrorism, the NHS and education on 0–10 scales. Our earlier factor analysis of evaluations and emotions shows that health and education load on a single 'services' factor, and that crime, asylum/immigration and terrorism all load on a single 'security' factor. Accordingly, we use the same clustering to produce two simple additive scales of issue-area importance, one for 'services importance' and another for 'security importance'.[26] Measures of service satisfaction and security satisfaction are the same as in Equation 3.5. Other predictor and control variables also remain the same as in Model 3.5. In sum, the model of the effect of service satisfaction on the importance of services as an issue is:

$$
\begin{aligned}
\text{SERVIM} = {} & B_0 + B_1\text{SERVSAT} + B_2\text{LABPID} + B_3\text{CONPID} \\
& + B_4\text{LDPID} + B_5\text{OPID} + B_6\text{PROLAB} \\
& + B_7\text{TABLOID} + B_8\text{GENDER} + B_9\text{AGE} \\
& + B_{10}\text{OWNER} + B_{11}\text{CLASS} + B_{12}\text{EDUC} \\
& + B_{13}\text{ETH} + B_{14}\text{SCOT} + B_{15}\text{WALES} + \varepsilon \quad (3.6)
\end{aligned}
$$

where all predictor variables other than services importance (SERVIM) are defined in Model 3.5.

Table 3.13 displays the parameter estimates for Model 3.6 and for an equivalent model for security importance. The results are compelling. Although the variance explained in service and security importance is modest, all coefficients on key predictor variables of interest are correctly signed and highly significant. The services satisfaction term in the services importance model and the security satisfaction term in the security equation are both negative and significant. People who have had negative experiences in a domain are more likely to designate the domain as an issue priority, and those who have had a positive experience are less likely to prioritize it. As with the economy, direct policy delivery has positive consequences for evaluations and emotional reactions in non-economic domains, but it can also have negative consequences by reducing the importance of these domains on the voter's issue agenda.

Table 3.13 *Regression analyses of the importance of public services and security as issues, April 2004 to April 2005*

| | Issue importance of: | |
| | Public services[a] | Security[b] |
Predictor variables	β	β
Satisfaction with experiences of public services	−0.15***	
Satisfaction with experiences of security		−0.51***
Party identification:		
Conservative	0.14***	0.18***
Labour	−0.04**	−0.12***
Liberal Democrat	0.10***	−0.15***
Other party	0.12***	0.05*
Pro-Labour versus pro-Conservative newspaper readership	−0.04*	−0.17***
Tabloid newspaper reader	0.16***	0.71***
Age	0.02***	0.01***
Education	−0.04***	−0.27***
Ethnic minority	0.04	0.39***
Gender (men)	−0.41***	−0.37***
Social class (middle class)	−0.00	−0.07***
Region:		
Scotland	0.03	−0.03
Wales	0.15**	0.01
Constant	8.47***	10.22***
R^2	0.07	0.24

Note:

[a] Public services issue importance scale constructed by averaging assessments (on 0–10 scales) of the importance of education and the NHS as policy problems.

[b] Security issue importance scale constructed by averaging assessments (on 0–10 scales) of the importance of crime, asylum seekers and terrorism as policy problems.

*** – $p \leq 0.001$; ** – $p \leq 0.01$; * – $p \leq 0.05$; one-tailed test.

N = 15,238 for public services analysis and 15,218 for security analysis.

Source: April 2004–April 2005 GPVP monthly surveys.

Conclusion: valence issues, valence politics

In this chapter, we study how events and developments between the 2001 and 2005 general elections affected the party choices that people made in May 2005. We also investigate mechanisms by which voters' valence calculations operate over the medium term. Two basic findings are especially noteworthy. One is that the sorts of valence calculations that voters have long been considered to make about economic performance also apply in other policy domains. Evaluations of, and emotional responses to, public service and security issues have similar effects on party support to those associated with the economy. A second basic finding is that, when making their party support decisions, voters engage in the same sorts of calculation at different stages of the electoral cycle. Models of party support that clearly applied in the 2001 election continued to apply, on a month-by-month basis, throughout the entire 2001–5 period. Given that voters make calculations on a continuing basis, it is hardly surprising that the outcomes of elections can depend to a considerable extent on what happens long before the contest is formally announced.

The analyses also suggest several more specific substantive and theoretical conclusions. Central components of the valence account of party support continued to be important in explaining UK party support patterns after 2001. The simple story of why Blair was able to win a third consecutive term in 2005 is that his own leader image, in comparison with that of his Conservative rival(s), remained *relatively* favourable; that the economy continued to contribute strongly to Labour's positive image of managerial competence; and that Labour's victory would have been even greater had it not lost support because of its leader's insistence in prosecuting an unpopular war.

Another finding relates to the character and role of the electorate's issue agenda. It is clear that, since 9/11, political debate has been re-focused on matters of internal and external security, combined with a marked increase in the extent to which the electorate prioritizes security-related issues. Our factor analysis of voters' evaluations of and emotional responses to a wide range of policy objects shows that there is a distinct and highly stable cluster of attitudes that now connect people's views of crime, asylum/immigration and terrorism in a global 'internal security' factor. However, at least through April 2005, none of the major parties had either benefited or suffered disproportionately as a result of the emergence of this new security agenda. One of the fascinating uncertainties in British politics over the next few years is the extent to which this new agenda might be mobilized by one party rather than another.

Finally, in terms of theoretical development, this chapter provides a more detailed account of the character of the valence assessments that voters make. Evaluations and emotions in the services and security issue domains have powerful and continuing effects on party support patterns. Positive evaluations/emotions in both domains – as well as in the economic domain – are associated with increased support for Labour and reduced support for the Conservatives and Liberal Democrats. An important innovation in this analysis is to demonstrate that people's direct experiences of policies related to public services and security have significant consequences for the way that they evaluate government performance in those domains. In essence, good experiences pay dividends because they feed through to positive evaluations and emotions and increased support for the government; bad experiences have the opposite effect. However, the 'sting in the tail' administered by personal experience concerns its consequences for issue priorities. Good personal experiences in the services and security domains appear to drive down the importance of those domains in the voters' minds. In this sense, as with the economy, policy success paradoxically carries with it the risk that voters will not prioritize the very thing that has been successfully delivered to them.

4 | *Tony's war*

Speaking before parliament in November 1945, British Foreign Minister Ernest Bevin claimed that: 'the common man is the greatest protection against war' (Holsti, 1996: 4). Although Bevin was neither the first nor the last to advance this claim – it has been a perennial topic of debate among students of international relations – in fact, ordinary citizens are not invariably united in their opposition to war. When the possibility of engaging in military conflict is salient on the political agenda, it often has positional rather than valence characteristics. Public opinion is divided, sometimes deeply. However, it also is clear that attitudes towards a war can shift, sometimes dramatically, with the typical pattern being for enthusiasm to wane as costs escalate, casualties mount, and 'light at the end of the tunnel' fades to black.[1] What had been a position issue becomes a valence one. These stylized facts aside, much remains to be learned about factors that drive public reactions to international conflicts, and how these reactions affect the dynamics of support for political parties and their leaders. In this chapter we address these topics by analysing British public opinion about the Iraq War.

The war was hotly debated for several months before it began on 20 March 2003, and those debates continued afterward. Indeed, British involvement in Iraq was a topic of controversy throughout the remainder of Tony Blair's tenure as prime minister and beyond. When first advanced, the proposal to invade Iraq split the Labour Party, and the decision to go forward ultimately required a bipartisan parliamentary coalition of Conservatives and a majority of Labour MPs loyal to the prime minister. Bipartisan support notwithstanding, Iraq was seen very much as 'Tony's war'. As discussed in the previous chapter, public reactions to the conflict had significant effects on support for the prime minister and his party in the period preceding the 2005 general election, and on the political choices voters made in that contest.

We begin this chapter by mapping the British public's support for and opposition to involvement in the Iraq War before hostilities commenced and in the crucial six-month period that followed. We also consider attitudes towards the war among various demographic and partisan groups. Next, we study factors influencing public opinion about the war. We specify rival *morality*, *benefits and costs* and *general heuristics* models, and present the distributions and dynamics of key explanatory variables. The relative explanatory power of the competing models is assessed, and the results of these analyses are used to construct a theoretically attractive composite model. Differences in attitudes towards the war between men and women are considered. Then, we map the evolution of opinion about the war in the run-up to the 2005 election, and study how Britain's involvement in the conflict influenced attitudes towards Tony Blair. The conclusion summarizes principal findings and discusses their implications for the political fortunes of Mr Blair and his party.

Divided and shifting opinions

Some observers have speculated that American President George W. Bush came into office in January 2001 determined to invade Iraq and depose Saddam Hussein. By so doing, he would finish the job that his father began over a decade earlier and fulfil the Republicans' 2000 campaign promise to oust the Iraqi dictator. Although Bush's initial predispositions are unknown, it is clear that 9/11 was the crucial precipitating event that ultimately led to the war and British participation in it. The horrific terrorist attacks causing the loss of nearly 3,000 lives in New York and Washington lent credibility to Bush's argument that rogue regimes engaged in state-sponsored terrorism had to be confronted. Bush viewed Saddam Hussein's regime in Iraq as 'Exhibit A'. The president and his advisors alleged that, in addition to sponsoring al-Qaeda, Hussein possessed weapons of mass destruction (WMDs) that he could – and likely would – employ. His arsenal supposedly included biological, chemical and, possibly, nuclear devices that could be delivered on short notice. Indeed, setting the stage for what would eventually become a topic of intense controversy, Tony Blair defended his advocacy of Britain's participation in a US-led military action against Iraq by claiming that he had intelligence indicating that Hussein could launch WMDs on forty-five-minutes' notice. Since diplomatic efforts under the auspices of the United Nations had failed repeatedly to address the threat, pre-emptive military action was required. According to Bush and Blair, the brutal Iraqi dictator was a clear and present danger; he had to go. The risks posed by leaving him in place were simply unacceptable.

Invigorated by the searing memories of 9/11, an emotional debate concerning the advisability of using military action to remove Hussein gained momentum throughout the latter half of 2002. As Bush and Blair quickly discovered, the case for war was a hard sell both abroad and at home. Even long-time allies, such as Canada, France and Germany, voiced opposition and pressed for additional diplomatic efforts. In Britain, public opinion was divided but, on balance, sceptical, with an August 2002 ICM poll showing that 50% opposed, and only 33% favoured, a military attack to remove Hussein (Figure 4.1). This distribution of opinion remained essentially unchanged as 2002 drew to a close. Then, early in 2003, as Bush and Blair voiced determination that their countries would push ahead, alone if necessary, opposition among the British public became increasingly strident. Anti-war rallies occurred in several major cities, and high-street hoardings and university campuses were covered with anti-war posters. Anti-war sentiment reached its zenith on 15 February when massive protests were held around the world. Estimates of the number of demonstrators marching in London ranged from 750,000 to two million. These events received enormous publicity in the British media, and they dramatically illustrated Blair's inability to sway public opinion to his point of view.

However, the situation soon changed again. As it became apparent that war was inevitable, support for the conflict grew. For example, when hostilities began in the third week of March, 54% of the respondents in an ICM survey said that they approved of the action and only 30% disapproved (see Figure 4.1). Approval continued to grow, with an April 2003 ICM survey showing that 63% were in favour and only 23% were opposed. As tracer bullets began to light the night sky over Baghdad on 20 March, a clear majority of the British public had rallied to the cause. Blair's deeds had succeeded – at least temporarily – where his words had not.

The impression of substantial division and volatility in public opinion about the war is bolstered by other survey data. For example, in our March, April–May, and October 2003 Participation and

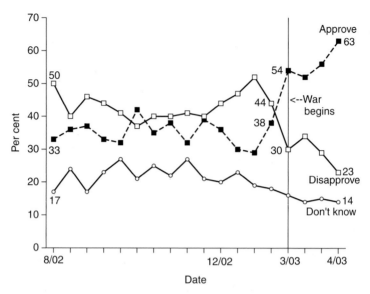

Figure 4.1 Approval/disapproval of military attack on Iraq, September 2002–April 2003 (*Note:* question asked before war began is: 'Would you approve or disapprove of a military attack on Iraq to remove Sadam Hussein?' After war began question is: 'Do you approve or disapprove of the military attack on Iraq to remove Saddam Hussein?') (*Source:* ICM monthly polls)

Democracy in Britain (PDB) surveys conducted by the Gallup organization, respondents were asked their opinions about British involvement. The question was: 'Please tell me whether you strongly approve, approve, disapprove or strongly disapprove of *Britain's involvement* [emphasis in question] in a/the[2] war with Iraq?' Echoing the ICM findings, the PDB surveys indicate that public opinion was divided, both before and after hostilities began (see Figure 4.2). Although only small minorities answered that they strongly approved of the conflict, sizable groups (ranging in size from 31% to 43%) stated that they approved. Opposition also was substantial. At the extremes of opinion, the 'strongly disapprove' group was always larger than the 'strongly approve' one, although the extent of the difference varied considerably – from nearly 18% in March before the war began to a low of just over 2% in late April and early May.

As hostilities began, who favoured the war? Who was opposed? Answers to these questions are supplied in Figure 4.3. As illustrated,

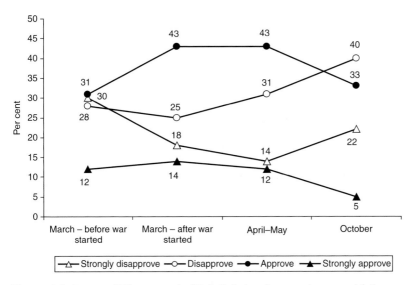

Figure 4.2 Approval/disapproval of Britain's involvement in war with Iraq (*Source*: March, April–May and October 2003 PDB surveys)

the March and April–May 2003 PDB data indicate that the war's popularity varied only marginally across social classes. *Pace* the late Mr Bevin, working-class support was no less than that among the middle and upper classes. Similarly, educational differences were modest, with people having the highest levels of formal education being somewhat less enthusiastic than those with less schooling. Again, levels of support were virtually identical in England, Scotland and Wales. Age differences were somewhat greater, with younger and older people being 8 to 10% less supportive than middle-aged ones. However, the biggest differences involved gender and partisanship. Consonant with conjectures that women are less likely than men to favour military action, Figure 4.3 shows a fourteen-point gender gap, with 56% of men, but only 42% of women, endorsing the war. Substantial partisan differences appear as well. Consistent with their parties' advocacy of the conflict, 59% of Labour identifiers and 53% of Conservative identifiers were supporters. And consistent with their party's opposition, only 32% of Liberal Democrats were in favour. Endorsements among 'other party' identifiers and nonidentifiers also were the exception, with slightly over one-third of the people in these groups voicing approval.

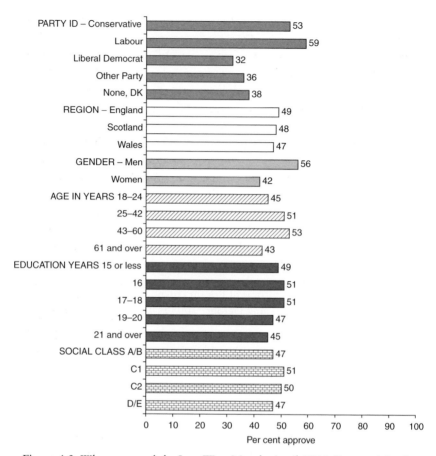

Figure 4.3 Who approved the Iraq War, March–April 2003 (*Source:* March and April–May 2003 PDB surveys)

Indicative of the overall weakness of these several relationships, a logistic regression analysis using all of the socio-demographic variables has a McFadden R^2 of merely 0.03. The analysis can correctly predict the approval or disapproval of 60% of the cases, only 6% more than could be achieved using a naive mode-guessing approach. Adding partisanship helps, but only modestly – the McFadden R^2 increases to 0.08 and 64% are correctly classified. British public opinion on the war was divided as the conflict began, but the division did not adhere closely to major socio-demographic and partisan faultlines in the electorate.

Again similar to their ICM counterparts, the PDB surveys reveal substantial temporal dynamics in opinion. As illustrated in Figure 4.2, there are two distinct shifts. Among respondents interviewed in March 2003 before the invasion began, nearly three-fifths were opposed to the war and slightly over two-fifths were in favour. However, among those interviewed immediately after the invasion, support rose by fully fourteen points to 57% and opposition fell to 43%. Although these latter figures changed only marginally in April and May, the October 2003 survey documents a second shift. In a context of mounting controversy regarding the failure to find weapons of mass destruction, intense publicity surrounding the suicide of British weapons inspector, Dr David Kelly, escalating insurgency, and mounting sectarian violence, opinion changed dramatically. In a swing of nearly seventeen points, the number supporting the war fell to 38% and the number opposing it climbed to 62%. Although opinion remained divided, the public mood was clearly more negative than it was only a few months earlier. And, as discussed later in this chapter, this negativism soon became a staple feature of British opinions about the war. However, we first investigate the explanatory power of three competing theoretical models of factors affecting those opinions.

Considering conflict

Viewed generally, there are two bodies of research on public opinion about international conflict and war. One group of studies, developed primarily by political psychologists, relies heavily on general theories of public opinion (see, for example, Alvarez and Brehm, 2002; Converse, 1964; Hurwitz and Peffley, 1987; Page and Shapiro, 1992; Zaller, 1992). A second group of studies has been developed primarily by foreign policy and international relations specialists. Although not entirely divorced from general theories of public opinion and the multi-faceted debates they have engendered, these studies focus tightly on specific factors affecting the dynamics of public opinion about major wars and other salient militarized disputes (e.g. Jentleson, 1992; Jentleson and Britton, 1998; Kull, 1995; Reilly, 1987).[3] Both types of research inform the models of attitudes towards the Iraq War tested here. And, as is more typical of the first body of research than the second, the explanatory power of the competing models is investigated using individual-level survey data, rather than aggregate-level time series data from public opinion polls.

The morality model

Echoing Ernest Bevin's claim cited at the beginning of this chapter, the morality model is motivated by the longstanding conjecture in liberal political thought that the publics of democratic polities are guardians of ethical conduct in foreign affairs. They support a war only when a convincing normative case can be made for it (Holsti, 1996). Accordingly, proponents of this model would argue that attitudes towards British involvement in war with Iraq were governed by people's judgments regarding the extent to which the conflict was morally justified. Those who believed Britain had a strong moral case for war with Iraq approved of the conflict, and those who did not believe Britain had a strong moral case opposed it. Thus, the model is specified as:

$$DAPP = f(\beta_0 + \beta_1 MORAL) \tag{4.1}$$

where: DAPP = approval/disapproval of war with Iraq; MORAL = belief that Britain has/does not have a strong moral case for going to war with Iraq; β's = parameters to be estimated.

As Figure 4.4 shows, public opinion was deeply divided over the morality of war with Iraq, and it shifted substantially over the eight months encompassed by the March and October 2003 surveys. In March, just prior to the initiation of hostilities, 45% of the PDB respondents said that they 'agree' or 'agree strongly' with the statement that Britain had a 'strong moral case' for war with Iraq.[4] This figure climbed to 58% immediately after the war began, and eroded only slightly (to 56%) in April and May. However, following the failure to find WMDs and the firestorm of adverse commentary about the war ignited by the Kelly suicide, the percentage believing Britain had a strong moral case for the war fell precipitously, and stood at only 39% in the October 2003 survey.

The benefits and costs model

This model has conceptual affinities with realist theories of the factors that propel states to take one action as opposed to another in the international political arena. Such theories stipulate that

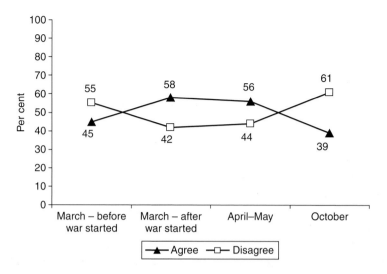

Figure 4.4 Britain has a strong moral case for war with Iraq, March–October 2003 (*Source*: March, April–May and October 2003 PDB surveys)

interests – particularly the expectation of receiving benefits in the form of greater power, security or wealth that exceed the projected costs of action – govern the decisions of state actors to initiate a war (e.g. Bueno de Mesquita, 1983; Holsti, 1996; Morrow, 2000). The benefits and costs model of public opinion on war similarly assumes that opinions about the advisability of engaging in international conflict are rooted in perceptions of likely gains and losses. Specifically, the model posits that calculations, possibly rough-and-ready, involving the perceived benefits and costs of the Iraq War explain people's support for, or opposition to, the conflict. Incorporating only four explanatory variables, the model is parsimonious. First is an interaction term comprised of two variables – the anticipated long-run benefits of the war for Britain discounted by estimates of the probability that the enterprise will be successful.[5] The third variable is perceived collective costs, i.e. costs that Britain would incur should it decide to wage war with Iraq. The fourth variable is personal costs as measured by perceived threats to the safety of oneself and one's family. Accordingly, the model is:

$$DAPP = f(\beta_0 + \beta_1 PWIN*BENWAR + \beta_2 COSTBR + \beta_3 COSTSELF) \qquad (4.2)$$

where: DAPP = approval/disapproval of war with Iraq; PWIN = probability that a war with Iraq would be successful; BENWAR = anticipated benefits of going to war with Iraq; COSTBR = belief that war with Iraq would seriously damage Britain's interests around the world; COSTSELF = belief that war with Iraq would threaten safety of self and family; β's = parameters to be estimated.

Estimates of the probability of winning the war are measured by asking the PDB respondents to use an eleven-point scale ranging from zero ('very unlikely') to ten ('very likely')[6] to estimate the likelihood of victory in a war against Iraq. Answers vary over time, with the percentage of March 2003 respondents scoring six or more on the scale increasing from 62% before the war began to 73% afterward. In the subsequent April–May survey, the comparable figure fell to 58%. Reflecting this variation, average scores in the three time periods are 6.5, 7.1 and 5.9, respectively. Given the course of the conflict, the wording of the October 2003 'success' question is necessarily different; respondents were asked to use an eleven-point scale ranging from zero ('complete failure') to ten ('complete success')[7] to judge the outcome of the war. At this time, only 29% had scores of six or greater, and less than 2% thought that the war had been completely successful. Indicative of growing reservations about British involvement, the average score is only 4.2 points, well below the mid-point (five) on the scale.

Similarly, many PDB respondents disagreed with the proposition that the war would prove beneficial. Figure 4.5 illustrates that even before the war started scepticism was common, with nearly two-thirds (65%) disagreeing with the statement that 'Britain will benefit in the long run from war with Iraq'. The percentage disagreeing fell slightly (to 59%) in April and May, before rising sharply in October when fully three-quarters (75%) rejected the idea that the war would generate long-run benefits for Britain.

Concerns about the consequences of the war are also evident in responses to questions about the war's potential collective and personal costs. Once more, there are strong temporal dynamics in the responses. Nearly 60% of those interviewed before the war began thought that it would seriously damage Britain's interests around the world (see Figure 4.6A). This percentage subsequently declined substantially (to 41%) in the April–May survey, before rebounding in October. The pattern for personal costs is somewhat different. Before

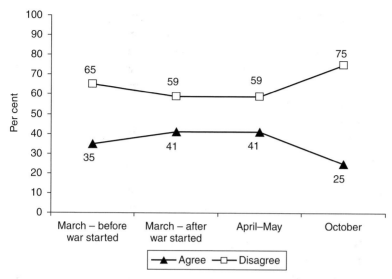

Figure 4.5 Britain will benefit in the long run from war with Iraq, March–October 2003 (*Source*: March, April–May and October 2003 PDB surveys)

hostilities began, a clear majority (56%) thought war with Iraq would threaten the safety of themselves and their families (Figure 4.6B). Perceptions of personal threat eroded thereafter – to 36% and 41% in the April–May and October surveys, respectively – as it became clear that the war per se did not pose an immediate danger to people living outside of Iraq.[8]

The general heuristics model

Similar to the discussion of factors affecting party choice in Chapter 2, the third model of opinion about the war is motivated by the observation that important political choices are often made in contexts of uncertainty. Faced with situations where stakes are high and reliable information about the consequences of alternative courses of action is in short supply, people employ various heuristic devices to guide their decisions (e.g. Chase *et al.*, 1998; Conlisk, 1996; see also Fiske and Taylor, 1984; Kahneman *et al.*, 1982). Over the past decade, political psychologists have focused on the use of heuristics in political decision-making and, depending upon the context being

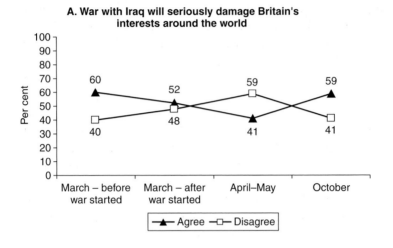

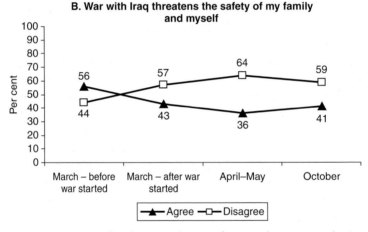

Figure 4.6 National and personal costs of war with Iraq, March–October 2003 (*Source*: March, April–May and October 2003 PDB surveys)

considered, several possibilities have been proposed (see, for example, Bowler and Donovan, 1998; Lupia and McCubbins, 1998; Lupia *et al.*, 2000; Sniderman *et al.*, 1991).

Party identification is often designated as a key heuristic. The hypothesis that political parties serve as important sources of information and cue-givers is grounded in the venerable idea that parties are objects that can be 'loved and trusted' (Wallas, 1908). People develop psychological attachments to political parties that provide guides to not only how to vote, but also who and what to believe on important political issues (e.g. Campbell *et al.*, 1960; Bowler and Donovan, 1998; Sniderman *et al.*, 1991). Consistent with their parties' positions on the war and analyses presented above, the expectation is that Conservative party identifiers endorse the conflict, and Liberal Democrat identifiers oppose it. An a priori hypothesis for Labour identifiers is more difficult to formulate because, although the party leader, Tony Blair, was the chief advocate of invading Iraq, some prominent Labour politicians, including high-ranking cabinet ministers such as Leader of the House of Commons Robin Cook, strongly opposed the idea. Also, Labour's always vocal and oftentimes influential left-wing activists maintained their record of opposing military conflicts by coming out strongly against the invasion. These intra-party clashes notwithstanding, the survey data presented above (see Figure 4.3) show that, when the war began, Labour identifiers actually were more favourably disposed towards it than any other group of party supporters.

As the principal and highly salient spokespersons for their parties, the leaders of major political parties also are important cue-givers. As discussed in Chapters 2 and 3, constant media attention helps to ensure that leaders' images can have significant cueing effects for people who seek guidance in times of political crisis and uncertainty (see also Clarke *et al.*, 2004a; Hurwitz and Peffley, 1987). Here, it is hypothesized that a positive image of Prime Minister Tony Blair, the principal architect of British involvement in the war, prompts support for it. This also should be true for Conservative leader, Iain Duncan Smith, who was another prominent supporter. In contrast, since Liberal Democrat leader Charles Kennedy opposed the war, it is expected that a positive image of him would increase the likelihood of opposing the conflict.

A variety of other heuristic devices such as the mass media, general risk orientations, 'rally effects' associated with the initiation of conflict, age and gender also may be important. Although calibrating media effects on public opinion is difficult (e.g. Norris, 1999), there is widespread consensus that the media are influential in the political process (e.g. Iyengar and Kinder, 1987; Jordan and Page, 1992; Mutz, 1992). In Britain and other mature democracies, they take proactive roles by deciding what to cover and how to cover it, and thereby shape the agenda of debate. In the British case, the print media are important because newspaper readership is widespread – fully 84% of the PDB respondents reported that they read a paper 'every day' or 'sometimes'. Major newspapers regularly articulate positions on a wide range of political topics, and a number of them have readily recognizable partisan biases. Here, we analyse the impact of readership of pro- and anti-war newspapers on support for/opposition to British involvement in the Iraq conflict.

With respect to risk orientations, the hypothesis is that people consult their generalized attitudes towards risk before making decisions in situations when stakes are high and outcomes are uncertain (e.g. Nadeau *et al.*, 1999; see also Kahneman and Tversky, 1979, 2000; Thaler, 1991, 1993). Also relevant to public opinion are rally effects that typically are engendered by a country's involvement in international crises or wars (e.g. Clarke *et al.*, 1990; Edwards and Swenson, 1997; Mueller, 1973; Norpoth, 1987). As noted above, public support for Britain's involvement in the war with Iraq increased sharply immediately after the conflict began. The hypothesis is that involvement in a war initially stimulates a sense of patriotism and/or 'we–them' thinking in people that prompts them to rally in support of the conflict and the incumbent government prosecuting it. Although previous research indicates that rally effects vary substantially in magnitude and duration, they can be substantial (e.g. Clarke *et al.*, 1990; Marra *et al.*, 1990; Mueller, 1973).

Finally, we consider whether political orientations vary by gender and age. Guided by prominent conjectures in the gender and politics and political culture literatures (e.g. Elshstain, 1987; Elshtain and Tobias, 1990; Goldstein, 2003; Inglehart 1989; Inglehart and Norris, 2003), we investigate the hypotheses that, net of other considerations, many women and younger people have political and social beliefs that military action and the use of physical force more generally are inappropriate mechanisms of conflict resolution.

In sum, the general heuristics model is:

$$\begin{aligned}
DAPP = f(\beta_0 &+ \beta_1 BLAIR + \beta_2 IDS + \beta_3 KENNEDY \\
&+ \beta_4 LABPID + \beta_5 CONPID + \beta_6 LDPID \\
&+ \beta_7 OPID + \beta_8 NEWS + \beta_9 GRISK + \beta_{10} WAR \\
&+ \beta_{11} GENDER + \beta_{12} AGE1824 + \beta_{13} AGE2542 \\
&+ \beta_{14} AGE4360)
\end{aligned} \tag{4.3}$$

where: DAPP = approval/disapproval of war with Iraq; BLAIR = feelings about Labour leader, Tony Blair; IDS = feelings about Conservative leader, Iain Duncan Smith; KENNEDY = feelings about Liberal Democrat leader, Charles Kennedy;[9] LABPID = Labour Party identification; CONPID = Conservative Party identification; LDPID = Liberal Democrat Party identification; OPID = other party identification;[10] NEWS = stand on Iraq War taken by daily newspaper;[11] GRISK = general risk orientation;[12] WAR = interviewed before/after hostilities began;[13] GENDER = gender;[14] AGE1824 = 18–24 age group; AGE2542 = 25–42 age group; AGE4360 = 43–60 age group;[15] β's = parameters to be estimated.

Comparing competing models

We first consider each of three models of opinion concerning British involvement in the Iraq War separately. Since the dependent variable has four categories ranging from 'strongly approve' to 'strongly disapprove', we use ordered probit (Long, 1997) to estimate model parameters.[16] Recognizing that the flow of causality between attitudes towards the war and feelings about Tony Blair might be bi-directional and create a simultaneity bias (e.g. Greene, 2003), we employ a set of instrumental variables for feelings about Blair in the general heuristics model.[17] The estimates reveal that the morality model behaves as anticipated; people who believe that Britain had strong moral justification for going to war with Iraq were significantly more likely ($p < 0.001$) than those who did not to approve of the conflict (see Table 4.1, Model A). The model fits the data quite well – the estimated (McFadden) R^2 is 0.24, and 61% of the cases are correctly predicted for the full four categories of the dependent variable. Fully 83% of the cases are correctly classified for the basic approve/disapprove war dichotomy.

The benefits and costs model also performs quite well; all of its parameters are statistically significant ($p < 0.05$ or better) and correctly signed (Table 4.1, Model B). As hypothesized, the likelihood of approving the war is enhanced by the interaction of perceptions that the conflict will be successful and the belief that Britain will benefit from it. As also hypothesized, both perceived collective and personal costs have negative effects, i.e. as collective and personal costs of the conflict increase, the likelihood of approving the war decreases. And,

Table 4.1 *Ordered probit analyses of attitudes towards the war in Iraq, March and April–May 2003 surveys*

Predictor variables	Model A Morality β	s.e.	Model B Benefits and costs β	s.e.	Model C Heuristics β	s.e.
Probability of winning x Benefits to Britain	xx	xx	0.06***	0.003	xx	xx
War poses personal threat	xx	xx	−0.05*	0.02	xx	xx
War damages British interests	xx	xx	−0.35***	0.03	xx	xx
Strong moral case for the war	0.78***	0.02	xx	xx	xx	xx
General risk orientation	xx	xx	xx	xx	0.06*	0.03
Party leaders:						
Tony Blair	xx	xx	xx	xx	0.19***	0.01
Iain Duncan Smith	xx	xx	xx	xx	0.04***	0.01
Charles Kennedy	xx	xx	xx	xx	−0.11***	0.01
Party identification:						
Labour	xx	xx	xx	xx	0.07	0.09
Conservative	xx	xx	xx	xx	0.31***	0.09
Liberal Democrat	xx	xx	xx	xx	0.02	0.10
Other	xx	xx	xx	xx	−0.02	0.13
Media consumption	xx	xx	xx	xx	0.07***	0.02
Age cohort:						
18–24	xx	xx	xx	xx	0.48***	0.11

Table 4.1 (*cont.*)

Predictor variables	Model A Morality β	s.e.	Model B Benefits and costs β	s.e.	Model C Heuristics β	s.e.
25–42	xx	xx	xx	xx	0.31***	0.07
43–60	xx	xx	xx	xx	0.30***	0.07
Education	xx	xx	xx	xx	−0.03	0.02
Gender	xx	xx	xx	xx	0.28***	0.05
Region:						
Scotland	xx	xx	xx	xx	0.07	0.09
Wales	xx	xx	xx	xx	0.05	0.11
Social class	xx	xx	xx	xx	−0.02	0.02
Date of interview	xx	xx	xx	xx	0.20**	0.07
Cut points:						
τ_1	−1.05***	0.07	−1.40***	0.12	0.56***	0.17
τ_2	2.31***	0.08	−0.20	0.11	1.50***	0.17
τ_3	4.06***	0.10	1.60***	0.12	2.93***	0.17
Log-likelihood	−1,938.70		−1,961.76		−2,274.23	
McFadden $R^2 =$	0.24		0.23		0.09	
Per cent correctly classified: four categories =	61.3		58.6		47.1	
two categories =	83.3		80.5		66.9	
Akaike information criterion	3,879.81		3,929.28		4,584.47	

N = 1,972.

*** –$p \leq 0.001$; ** – $p \leq 0.01$; * –$p \leq 0.05$; one-tailed tests for all parameters except cut points.

xx – variable not included in model.

as calibrated by their coefficients, the impact of collective costs is significantly stronger than that of individual costs ($\chi^2 = 65.54$, df $= 1$, $p < 0.001$). The fit of the benefits and costs model is very similar to that of the morality model; the McFadden R^2 is 0.23 and 59% of the cases can be correctly classified for the four categories of the dependent variable. Eighty-one per cent are correctly classified across the basic approve/disapprove war dichotomy.

The general heuristics model also has several statistically significant and properly signed coefficients. As anticipated given their respective stands on the war, feelings about Labour leader Tony Blair and Conservative leader Iain Duncan Smith positively influenced opinion about the war, whereas feelings about Liberal Democrat leader Charles Kennedy negatively did so. The effects of Labour and Liberal Democrat party identifications are not significant but, as hypothesized, Conservative identifiers were more likely to endorse the war than nonidentifiers or identifiers with other parties. Some other predictor variables also behave as expected – people who read newspapers that endorse the war were more likely to favour the conflict, as were risk-acceptant individuals and men. However, *ceteris paribus*, people in the oldest age cohort were less, not more, likely to favour the war than were those in all younger age groups. Viewed more generally, the general heuristics model performs reasonably well. The model's McFadden R^2 is 0.09; it correctly classifies 47% of the cases across the four categories of the dependent variable, and 67% across the approve/disapprove war dichotomy.

A tournament of models

Although the above results are suggestive, the question 'Which of the three rival models performs best?' invites closer scrutiny. A second interesting question is 'If one model outperforms its competitors, then is there additional explanatory purchase to be gained by consulting its rivals?' We use two statistical techniques to address these questions. The first focuses on the parameterization costs incurred to achieve a given level of model fit (Burnham and Anderson, 2002). As discussed above, fit may be indexed by an estimated R^2 statistic, the McFadden R^2, and the percentage of cases correctly classified. Although informative, these statistics do not account for the different number of predictor variables that the various models use to achieve a particular level of explanatory power.

To account for these differences, we employ a model selection criterion, the Akaike Information Criterion (AIC) (Burnham and Anderson, 2002). The AIC discounts the explanatory performance of models by the richness of parameterization required to achieve a given level of fit.[18] Smaller AIC values indicate better performance. AIC numbers for the three rival models of opinions on the Iraq War are presented at the bottom of Table 4.1. These statistics show that the morality model outperforms the benefits and costs model. This finding reflects the fact that, although the morality and benefits and costs models have nearly identical McFadden R^2s, the former model employs one independent variable, whereas the latter model employs three of them. The AIC statistics also indicate that the general heuristics model trails its rivals – as would be anticipated given its inferior fit statistics and inclusion of a relatively large number (fourteen) of predictor variables.

A model selection criterion, such as the AIC, provides important insights, but it does not tell us whether a particular model can make a unique contribution to explanation over and above what is provided by its competitors. In the present case, the three competing models are conceptually and operationally *non-nested* – they have different theoretical motivations and different explanatory variables. It is possible that two or more of the models are complementary, with each explaining a component of the variance in the dependent variable that is unaccounted for by its rivals. Variance encompassing tests can be used to investigate this possibility (Hendry, 1995).[19]

We use two encompassing tests – the joint nesting test and Davidson and MacKinnon's (1982) J test. These tests testify that each of the competing models of British public opinion about Iraq have something unique to say. For each pairwise comparison of the rival models, the joint nesting tests (Table 4.2, Section I) indicate that a given model does not encompass its rival, and vice versa. Thus, the morality model does not encompass either the benefits–costs or the general heuristics models. And, the latter two models do not encompass the former one. Similarly, the benefits–costs and general heuristics models do not encompass each other. J tests tell exactly the same story (see Table 4.2, Section II). Taken together, these results support the conjecture that

Table 4.2 *Encompassing tests of rival ordered probit models of attitudes towards the war in Iraq, March and April–May 2003 surveys*

I. Joint nesting tests	χ^2	df	p
A. Cost–benefit model versus morality model			
Does cost–benefit model encompass morality model?	530.74	1	0.000
Does morality model encompass cost–benefit model?	488.71	3	0.000
B. Cost–benefit model versus heuristics model			
Does cost–benefit model encompass heuristics model?	95.38	18	0.000
Does heuristics model encompass cost–benefit model?	806.77	3	0.000
C. Morality model versus heuristics model			
Does morality model encompass heuristics model?	152.35	18	0.000
Does heuristics model encompass morality model?	905.77	1	0.000

II. J tests	t	df	p
A. Cost–benefit model versus morality model			
Does cost–benefit model encompass morality model?	22.29	1	0.000
Does morality model encompass cost–benefit model?	21.17	1	0.000
B. Cost–benefit model versus heuristics model			
Does cost–benefit model encompass heuristics model?	9.30	1	0.000
Does heuristics model encompass cost–benefit model?	26.83	1	0.000
C. Morality model versus heuristics model			
Does morality model encompass heuristics model?	12.29	1	0.000
Does heuristics model encompass morality model?	28.49	1	0.000

all three models can contribute to an overall explanation of what drove British opinion about the war.

This conjecture is buttressed by theoretical work on public opinion formation by Zaller (1992) and others. As noted above, the debate over the war exposed people to an avalanche of arguments for and against the conflict. When making up their minds about invading Iraq, people were invited to think not only about the morality, but also the benefits and costs, and the likelihood of success, of the action. In the run-up to the invasion in March 2003 and throughout most of the remainder of the year, 'Iraq' dominated the mass media, with politicians and political activists attempting to make their cases in all of these terms. Anti-war protesters joined the fray, with demonstrations in London and elsewhere receiving enormous publicity. The vigorous, multi-faceted debate began months before the invasion, and continued to lead the issue agenda for months afterwards. David Kelly's suicide in July 2003 added a new, lurid dimension to media coverage, and propelled the creation of an official inquiry (the Hutton Inquiry) into events surrounding his death. Later, publication of its findings in January 2004 refuelled the controversy, with opponents of the war loudly proclaiming that the report was a 'whitewash'. Lord Hutton had studiously avoided investigating their often-repeated charges that the Blair government had 'sexed up' intelligence reports to make Saddam Hussein appear to be a much greater threat than was actually the case. The result was another inquiry (the Butler Inquiry) that was explicitly charged with investigating the quality of British intelligence leading up to the war. All of these events received great attention in the media. Such a rich and conflicting flow of information is conducive to making a variety of considerations relevant for opinion formation and change.

Estimating the parameters in a composite model that includes the predictor variables from the three rival models confirms that each contributes to explanation. As shown in Table 4.3, all variables in the morality and benefits–costs models remain statistically significant ($p < 0.05$) and properly signed in the composite model. Judgments that the moral case for war is strong increased the probability of approving the war. Perceived benefits of the war discounted by the probability of winning it also increased that probability. In contrast, perceived collective and personal costs decreased the likelihood of approval. Some variables in the general heuristics model also remain in play. Positive

Table 4.3 *Composite ordered probit model of attitudes towards the war in Iraq, March and April–May 2003 surveys*

Predictor variables	β	s.e.
Probability of winning x	0.04***	0.003
benefits to Britain		
War poses personal threat	−0.05*	0.02
War damages British interests	−0.27***	0.03
Strong moral case for the war	0.58***	0.03
General risk orientation	0.05	0.03
Party leaders:		
Tony Blair	0.06*	0.03
Iain Duncan Smith	0.01	0.01
Charles Kennedy	−0.05***	0.01
Party identification:		
Labour	−0.02	0.12
Conservative	0.09	0.10
Liberal Democrat	0.07	0.10
Other	−0.20	0.14
Media consumption:	0.04*	0.02
Age cohort:		
18–24	0.04	0.12
25–42	0.21**	0.08
43–60	0.13*	0.08
Gender	0.09	0.06
Education	0.01	0.02
Region:		
Scotland	0.12	0.10
Wales	0.04	0.12
Social class	−0.02	0.03
Date of interview	0.12	0.10
Cut points:		
τ_1	0.394	0.21
τ_2	1.926***	0.21
τ_3	4.073***	0.22
Log-likelihood	−1,634.08	
McFadden R^2 =	0.35	
Per cent correctly	65.8	
classified: four categories =	86.5	
two categories =	3,312.17	
Akaike information criterion		

***−$p \leq 0.001$; **−$p \leq 0.01$; *−$p \leq 0.05$; one-tailed tests for all parameters except cut points.

feelings about Prime Minister Tony Blair enhanced the probability of approving the war, and positive feelings about Liberal Democrat leader Charles Kennedy diminished it. People who read pro-war newspapers also were more likely to approve. Age was relevant as well, with persons in the 25–42 and 43–60 age brackets being more likely to endorse the conflict. Net of all these factors, there is also a suggestion that risk-acceptant people were more likely to approve, with the coefficient for this predictor just failing to reach significance at the 0.05 level ($t = 1.62$, $p = 0.052$, one-tailed test). Similarly, the gender coefficient approaches significance ($t = 1.51$, $p = 0.066$), hinting that men were more supportive of the war than women.

Overall, as indicated by the McFadden R^2 (0.35) and the percentage correctly classified (66% for the four-category dependent variable, and 87% for the approve/disapprove dichotomy), the composite model performs better than any of the three component models. Moreover, although the composite model is parameterized more richly than its components, it has a superior model selection statistic. Its AIC value is smaller than the AICs for any of the individual models.

We next gauge the relative impact of various predictor variables in the composite model by calculating the change in the probability of approving the war when each significant predictor is varied from its minimum to its maximum value.[20] For this exercise, other predictors are set at their mean values, or in the case of the party identification dummies at zero, thereby implicitly assuming the respondent does not identify with any party. Changes in calculated probabilities are multiplied by 100 for ease of exposition. The resulting numbers indicate that variables from each of the three rival models had sizable influences on opinion about the war. For example, *ceteris paribus*, as judgments that Britain has a strong moral case for war move from strongly negative to strongly positive, the probability of approving the conflict increases by fully seventy-four points (see Figure 4.7). Success-discounted perceived benefits and collective costs also exert large effects, with the former increasing the probability of approving the war by sixty-three points, and the latter decreasing it by forty points. Party leader heuristics are influential as well, with variations in feelings about Prime Minister Blair raising the probability of supporting the war by twenty-two points, and variations in feelings about Liberal Democrat leader Charles Kennedy lowering it by twenty points. Probabilities associated with other predictors are less

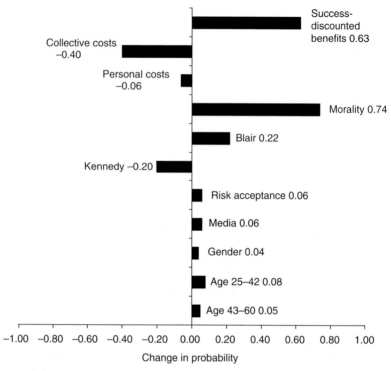

Figure 4.7 Effects of significant predictors in composite model of probability of approving war with Iraq

impressive, with their average ability to change the probability of supporting the war being slightly less than six points.

Gender and the war

As observed earlier, theorists have argued that gender differences characterize public attitudes towards war, with men being more likely than women to favour military action and other aggressive modes of conflict resolution. This interesting hypothesis merits closer scrutiny. We first investigate the extent of gender differences in approval of the war. As noted above (see Figure 4.3), there is a statistically significant ($p < 0.001$) 14% difference between the two groups in support for the war in the March and April–May PDB surveys. Examining the March, April–May and October PDB surveys separately shows that men are consistently more likely than women to approve of the war, with the difference ranging from a high of nineteen points to a low of

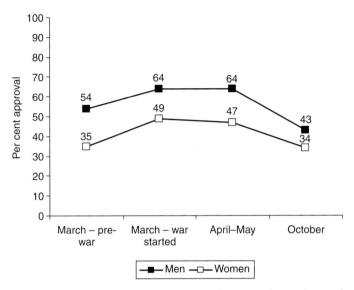

Figure 4.8 Dynamics of opinions towards war with Iraq by gender, March–October 2003 (*Source*: March, April–May and October 2003 PDB surveys)

nine points. Also, both gender groups manifest substantial dynamics in their attitudes towards the conflict. Contrary to arguments that women do not react to rally events (for a review, see Clarke *et al.*, 2005), both groups became more supportive of the war as soon as it began. In late March 2003, the percentage of men approving the war increased by over ten points immediately after hostilities commenced (see Figure 4.8). Among women the increase in support was greater – nearly fourteen points. Again, support for the war fell sharply among both groups during the period between the April–May and October 2003 surveys. Among men the decline was almost twenty-one points, and among women, almost thirteen points. In the latter survey, sizable majorities of both groups voiced their opposition.

The large differences between men and women in approval of the war, coupled with the negligible impact of gender in the multivariate models presented above (see Tables 4.1 and 4.3), suggest three possibilities. One is that gender effects are indirect, working through other independent variables. A second is that gender differences are the product of men and women placing different weights on various factors that influence their attitudes towards the war. For example, consistent with arguments in the gender and politics literature, it might be conjectured that women place greater emphasis on considerations regarding the morality of conflict, whereas men give more weight to benefits, costs and probabilities of success. A third possibility is that a gender-differentiated combination of different values and different weights on the independent variables was at work.

Table 4.4 lends considerable credence to the first possibility. Fully eighteen of twenty comparisons in the table are statistically significant and, in every case, the direction of the difference is one that would make men more likely to support the war. For example, just before hostilities began, 53% of the men, but only 39% of the women, thought that Britain had a strong moral case for war with Iraq (see Table 4.4, Panel A). The difference narrowed in the March post-invasion and April–May surveys but, in both cases, men remained approximately 10% more likely than women to endorse the moral case for the invasion. Only in October did this 'morality gap' collapse, with large majorities of both groups stating that the war lacked strong moral justification.

There are also impressive gender differences in the appraisal of benefits and costs. Across the four surveys, men were on average 17% more likely than women to say that Britain would enjoy long-run benefits because of the war, 13% less likely than women to conclude that the war would damage Britain's interests around the world, and 13% less likely to perceive that it posed a threat to self and family (see Table 4.4, Panels B, C and D). In addition, men were significantly more sanguine than women that the war would be successful (Table 4.4, Panel E). For example, when asked to rate the probability of winning, the average score for men in the March pre-war survey was 7.4 points, and the average for women was only 5.8 ($p < 0.001$). Only in October did gender differences in these probabilities collapse, with both groups becoming substantially more pessimistic about the prospects of success.

Finally, there are significant gender differences involving the general heuristics model (data not shown). As discussed above, positive feelings about Labour leader Tony Blair substantially increased the probability of approving the war, and positive feelings about Liberal Democrat leader Charles Kennedy decreased that probability. Analyses show that men consistently gave higher average scores to Blair, and women consistently gave higher average scores to Kennedy. These differences worked to enhance gender differences in attitudes towards the war.

Table 4.4 *Gender differences in attitudes towards war with Iraq, March–October 2003 (entries are percentages agreeing with statement)*

A. Britain has a strong moral case for war with Iraq

	March-Pre	March-Post	April–May	October
Men	53.4	62.8	61.1	40.4
Women	39.2	53.0	50.8	37.5
Difference	+14.2*	+9.8**	+10.3***	+2.9

B. Britain will benefit in long run from war with Iraq

	March-Pre	March-Post	April–May	October
Men	48.3	48.8	50.9	30.0
Women	24.7	31.9	32.2	21.2
Difference	+23.6***	+16.9***	+18.7***	+8.8**

C. War with Iraq threatens safety of my family and myself

	March-Pre	March-Post	April–May	October
Men	45.1	35.7	32.3	34.7
Women	63.5	49.9	38.9	46.6
Difference	−18.4**	−14.2***	−6.6*	−11.9***

D. War with Iraq will seriously damage Britain's interests around the world

	March-Pre	March-Post	April–May	October
Men	51.3	42.2	35.7	56.8
Women	66.1	61.3	46.1	61.6
Difference	−14.8*	−19.1***	−10.4***	−4.8

E. How likely Britain will be successful in Iraq War (mean scores)

	March-Pre	March-Post	April–May	October
Men	7.4	7.5	6.4	4.4
Women	5.8	6.7	5.5	4.0
Eta	0.27***	0.15***	0.19***	0.01**

*** $-p \le 0.001$; ** $-p \le 0.01$; * ≤ 0.05.
Source: March, April–May and October 2003 PDB surveys.

We investigate the second possibility, that parameters for explanatory variables in the models of attitudes towards the war varied by gender, by estimating the composite model (Table 4.3) separately for men and women. Then, we impose equality constraints on the parameters, and test whether there is a statistically significant decrease in goodness of fit.[21] These tests indicate that, with three exceptions, the twenty-one parameters are not significantly different (p < 0.05) for men and women. One exception concerns the 'success-discounted benefits' variable. The coefficient for this predictor is significantly larger (p < 0.001) for men (0.043) than women (0.035). The other two exceptions are the coefficients for the dummy variables signifying Liberal Democrat identification and Scottish residence. The former is significant for women but not for men, whereas the latter is significant for men but not for women. The overall similarity of the models for the two gender groups is also suggested by the percentages correctly classified for the men's and women's models. These differ by only 0.2% for the four-category dependent variable (65% for men and 65.2% for women) and 0.1% for the summary approve–disapprove dichotomy (86.4% for men and 86.3% for women).

In sum, the story of gender and opinion about the Iraq war is straightforward. Gender mattered largely because men and women had quite different values on important independent variables in a composite explanatory model that works well for both groups. Men and women made different judgments about the benefits, costs and morality of the conflict.

Towards consensus

Destroying Iraq's military capability and deposing Saddam Hussein and his despotic regime proved to be an easy task. Winning the peace was an entirely different matter. With Hussein's brutal dictatorship eliminated, the USA and Britain faced the difficult task of building a new democratic political system. It proved extraordinarily difficult, as Iraqi insurgents launched repeated attacks against American and British soldiers. These attacks took a bloody toll, with military casualties – especially American ones – mounting month on month. Insurgents were not content to attack troops; rather, they carried out gruesome murders of American and British civilians working as contractors to rebuild the country. The insurgency was coupled with sporadic, but serious, sectarian violence among rival ethnic and religious groups. Ordinary people suffered mightily. Between the initiation of hostilities in March 2003 and the end of 2005, it is estimated that nearly 40,000 thousand Iraqi civilians were killed. All of this violence received massive publicity in the press and, as it did, support for the war diminished.

The dynamics of attitudes towards the war are tracked in Figures 4.9, 4.10, and 4.11. Figure 4.9 maps the percentages of respondents in YouGov monthly surveys who thought that Britain and the United States were 'right or wrong to take military action against Iraq'. The figure illustrates the sharp decline in support for the war over the summer and autumn of 2003, followed by a brief and incomplete revival of support at the end of the year when Saddam Hussein was captured. The subsequent decline is substantial, such that at the time of the 2005 general election only 35% believed that the decision to invade Iraq had been 'right' and 53% believed it had been 'wrong'. These numbers were almost the opposite of what was the case when hostilities broke out two years earlier. The impression that the war became increasingly unpopular is reinforced by the data displayed in Figure 4.10. This figure shows that the percentage of GPVP respondents supporting the war declines from 44% when the survey project first began in April 2004, to 36% at the time of the 2005 election, to 24% when Tony Blair stepped

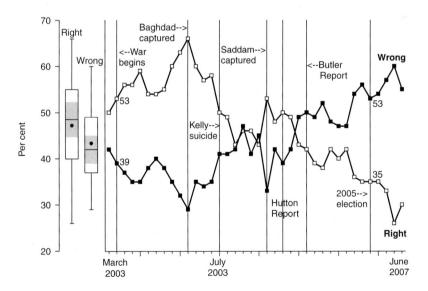

Figure 4.9 Military action against Iraq right or wrong? March 2003–June 2007 (*Note*: question is: 'Do you think the United States and Britain are/were right or wrong to take military action against Iraq? (*Source*: YouGov monthly surveys)

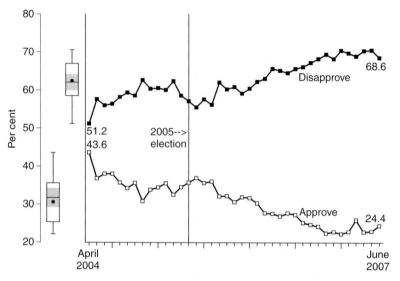

Figure 4.10 Approval of the war against Iraq, April 2004–June 2007
(*Note*: question is: 'Please tell me whether you strongly approve, approve,
disapprove, or strongly disapprove of Britain's involvement in the war with
Iraq?') (*Source*: GPVP monthly surveys)

down as Labour leader in June 2007. In contrast, the group opposing the war increased substantially – from 51% in April 2004, to
57% in May 2005, and then to 69% in June 2007.

The idea that people were moving toward consensus that the war
was a bad idea is reinforced by the data in Figure 4.11. This figure
illustrates the dynamics of GPVP respondents' judgments regarding
the success–failure of the war. Three points are noteworthy. First, the
average score on a zero (complete failure) to ten (complete success)
scale is always less than 3.8 over the April 2004–June 2007 period.
Coupled with the data on public opinion during 2003 presented
above, these numbers indicate that pessimism regarding the outcome
of the war set in quite quickly after it began. Second, as news about the
conflict continued month after month, pessimism mounted. Although
prognoses that the war would be successful increased modestly in the
run-up to the 2005 election, this mini-trend quickly evaporated in the
post-election period as the bad news continued. And, as Figure 4.11
shows, it was not just the mean 'probability of success' score that was
trending downward. This trend was closely paralleled by decreases in

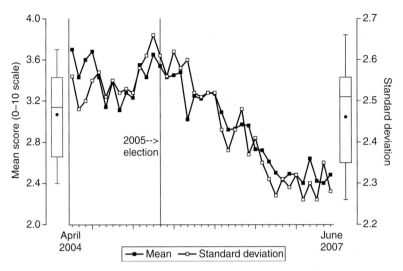

Figure 4.11 Rating the success of the war against Iraq, April 2004–June 2007 (*Note*: question is 'Using a scale from 0 to 10 where 10 means a complete success, and 0 means a complete failure, how would you rate the war against Iraq?' (*Source*: GPVP monthly surveys)

the amount of variability in public opinion. The standard deviation of the probability of success scores was becoming smaller and smaller, indicating an emerging consensus that the war could not be won.

The costs of conflict

As the 2005 general election approached, there was wide speculation that Tony Blair's insistence on involving Britain in what had become a very unpopular war had seriously tarnished his image, and would damage his party's electoral fortunes. The proposition is intuitively attractive, but not empirically obvious. Figures 4.12 and 4.13 show why. With the exception of the rally effects associated with 2001 election, 9/11, and the outbreak of the Iraq War, Blair's approval ratings had moved more or less steadily downward since he led Labour to its 1997 landslide victory (see Figure 4.12). And, as a mirror image, his disapproval ratings had trended upwards, spiking at the time of the September 2000 petrol crisis, and then again during the February 2003 protests against the war. The trend in the balance of judgments about Blair's performance is summarized in Figure 4.13, which also

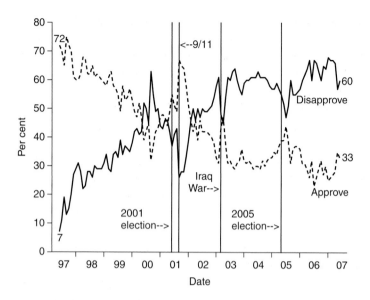

Figure 4.12 Tony Blair's prime ministerial approval ratings, June 1997–June 2007 (*Source*: Gallup and YouGov monthly polls)

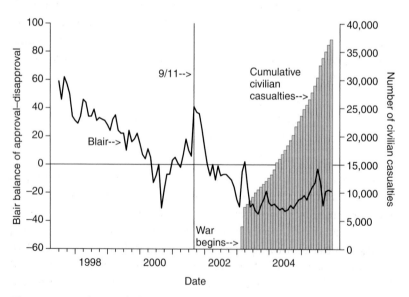

Figure 4.13 Balance of Blair's approval–disapproval ratings and cumulative civilian casualties in Iraq, July 1997–December 2005 (*Source*: Gallup and YouGov monthly polls and www.iraqbodycount.org)

displays cumulative civilian casualties in the Iraq war. This figure clearly illustrates that the negative trend in the balance of opinion about Blair long predated his decision to go to Baghdad. Hence, it is possible that much, or all, of the 'Iraq effect' on his approval ratings is more apparent than real.

We investigate this possibility using both aggregate- and individual-level data. First, we specify an aggregate time series model of the balance of Blair's approval and disapproval ratings. Conceptually akin to the time series model of Labour support in Chapter 3, the 'Blair balance' model includes an error correction term to capture a long-run co-integrating relationship between prime ministerial evaluations and judgments of Labour's competence as managers of the economy.[22] Also included is a variable to assess the short-term effects of these competence judgments, as well as several 0–1 dummy variables to measure the effects of prominent events.[23] In addition to the initiation of the Iraq War, these events include Blair's 'people's princess' speech at the time of the death of Princess Diana, the 9/11 terrorist attacks, the petrol crisis, the 7/7 terrorist attacks, and annual Labour conferences. The impact of ongoing reports of the conduct of the war is calibrated using monthly data on the number of civilian casualties (see Figure 4.13). If the war was influential net of other considerations, then this variable should have a significant negative impact on the balance of Blair's approval–disapproval ratings. In sum, the model is specified as:

$$\Delta BAL_t = \beta_0 + \beta_1 {}^* \Delta LABEC_t - \alpha_1 {}^* (BAL - c_1 {}^* LABEC)_{t-1}$$
$$+ \beta_2 {}^* \Delta DIANA_t + \beta_3 {}^* \Delta T911_t + \beta_4 {}^* \Delta PETROL_t$$
$$+ \beta_5 {}^* \Delta IRAQ_t + \beta_6 {}^* CIVIL_{t-1} + \beta_7 {}^* \Delta T77_t$$
$$+ \beta_8 {}^* LABCONF_{t-1} + \varepsilon_t \qquad (4.4a)$$

where: BAL = monthly balance (per cent approval–per cent disapproval) of Blair's performance; LABEC = monthly judgments of Labour's economic management competence; DIANA = people's princess speech; T911 = 9/11 terrorist attacks; PETROL = petrol crisis; IRAQ = initiation of Iraq War; CIVIL = monthly number of civilian casualties (logged); T77 = 7/7 terrorist attacks; LABCONF = annual Labour conference; ε = stochastic error term $\sim N(0,\sigma^2)$; Δ = differencing operator; α, β, c = model parameters.

We also include an autoregressive conditional heteroskedasticity (ARCH) component in this time series model to investigate the above mentioned possibility that the conduct of the war helped to effect a consensus in public opinion about Blair – not only did the ongoing conflict lower Blair's approval ratings, but also it made those ratings less variable (Enders, 2004: Chapter 3). This ARCH component is specified as:

$$\sigma^2_t = \omega + \lambda\varepsilon^2_{t-1} + \gamma CIVIL_{t-1} \tag{4.4b}$$

where: σ^2_t = the conditional variance of the balance of Blair (dis) approval; ω = a constant; ε^2_{t-1} = innovation variance (novel information about volatility) in the balance of Blair (dis)approval at time t–1 (lag of the squared residual from model 4.4a); CIVIL = monthly number of civilian casualties (logged); λ and γ = model parameters, with the expectation that λ will be positive and γ will be negative. The negative sign on γ will indicate that, net of other considerations, the conflict in Iraq is working to reduce the variance in public opinion about Blair. Models 4.4a and 4.4b are estimated using maximum likelihood procedures (Quantitative Micro Software, 2007: Chapter 29).

Model estimates are presented in Table 4.5. As hypothesized, evaluations of Labour's competence on the economy had a co-integrating relationship with Blair's approval ratings. As indicated by the coefficient for the error correction mechanism (α = –.16), the effect was quite weak, meaning that shocks from whatever source had considerable potential to affect Blair's approval. In this regard, the analysis reveals that several major events had sizable, if temporary, effects. Specifically, the 9/11 and 7/7 terrorist attacks had significant positive effects, driving up the balance by almost twenty points and almost sixteen points, respectively. The well-received people's princess speech had a smaller positive impact (nearly nine points), whereas the petrol crisis had a negative impact of nearly fourteen points.

As also hypothesized, Iraq had three influential effects. First, there was a classic rally, a temporary positive impact of seven points that occurred when hostilities began. A second, negative effect then kicked in as bad news about the conflict began to circulate. Parameter estimates indicate that this effect – working month after month – was ultimately quite profound. *Ceteris paribus*, over the twenty-two months separating the Kelly suicide in July 2003 and the May 2005 general election, bad news about the war (as indexed by civil casualties in Iraq) was sufficient to prompt a 27.5-point downward swing in the balance of Blair's approval ratings.[24] A third, more subtle effect reduced the variance in those ratings. The ARCH process behaves

Table 4.5 *Time series regression analysis of the dynamics of the balance of Tony Blair's approval and disapproval ratings, July 1997–December 2005*

Predictor variables: mean equation	β	s.e.
Labour economic management competence	0.60**	0.22
Error correction mechanism $(t-1)$	−0.16**	0.06
People's princess speech	8.53†	6.19
9/11 terrorist attacks	19.93***	3.98
Petrol crisis	−13.93**	5.33
Iraq War begins	7.04*	3.85
Iraq civilian casualties (logged) $(t-1)$	−0.45*	0.25
7/7 terrorist attacks	15.69***	1.82
Annual Labour conferences $(t-1)$	2.92†	1.92
Constant	−2.76	1.72
Adjusted R^2	0.30	
Durbin Watson d = 2.12, p > 0.05		
Ljung-Box Q autocorrelation (12 lags), $\chi^2 = 11.60$, p = 0.48		
Jarque-Bera normality, $\chi^2 = 1.29$, p = 0.53		
White heteroskedasticity, $\chi^2 = 40.82$, p = 0.07		

Predictor variables: ARCH 1 Process	β	s.e.
Innovation variance ε^2 $(t-1)$	0.51*	0.24
Iraq civilian casualties (logged) $(t-1)$	−4.71**	1.71
Constant	40.13***	11.33

Note: estimated via maximum likelihood, BHHH algorithm, normal distribution.
*** −p ≤ 0.001; ** −p ≤ 0.01; * −p ≤ 0.05; one-tailed test.
† −p ≤ 0.10, one-tailed test.
Source: Gallup, MORI and YouGov monthly polls, and www.iraqbodycount.org.

as expected, with civilian casualties in a given month reducing the variance in the balance of Blair's approval ratings in the subsequent month. This process can be seen graphically in Figure 4.14 where the bars, which represent the conditional variance in the balance of these ratings, are much smaller for the shaded portion of the graph that represents the period of the Iraq War up to the 2005 general election. Expressed in non-technical terms, the numbers summarized in Table 4.5 and Figure 4.14 testify that the bloody, protracted conflict in Iraq worked to build a negative consensus on Blair's performance as prime minister.

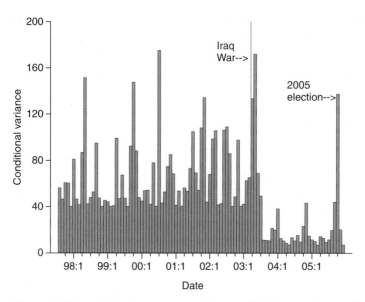

Figure 4.14 Conditional variance in balance of Blair's approval and disapproval ratings, July 1997–December 2005

The impact of the war on Blair's image at the time of the 2005 general election is assessed using data from the 2005 BES pre- and post-election panel survey. We specify a model with feelings about Tony Blair measured on a 0–10 scale as the dependent variable. Independent variables include set of predictors that are employed in the party choice analyses developed in Chapter 5, where we consider factors affecting voting behaviour in the 2005 election. These variables include an index of people's evaluations of the Iraq War as well as their emotional reactions to the conflict.[25] Also included are measures of party identification, perceptions of party best on most important issues, party–issue proximities, economic evaluations and perceptions of party best on the economy, emotional reactions to the economy and the National Health Service, and several demographic control variables (age, education, ethnicity, gender, region and social class).[26] Given the quasi-continuous nature of the dependent variable, we estimate model parameters via OLS regression.

The results, displayed in Table 4.6, reveal that feelings about Blair were affected by several variables including party identification, perceptions of parties' abilities to handle important issues, and party–issue proximities. The findings do not surprise – Labour identifiers, people thinking Labour is most capable on important issues, and people placing themselves close to Labour on position issue scales were more sanguine about Blair than those who identified with other parties, selected another party as best on their most important issue, or were closer to another party on position issues. The effects of economic evaluations, perceptions of party competence on the economy, and emotional reactions to the economy are also as expected. Those who offered positive evaluations, viewed Labour as most capable, or had positive emotional reactions tended to like Blair more than did those who offered negative evaluations, saw another party as most capable or felt negatively about the economy. Demographic characteristics were in play as well, with older people, ethnic minorities, women and working-class people being more positively disposed towards Blair, and residents of the Midlands (relative to residents of Greater London) being less positively disposed. Net of all of these effects, evaluations of the Iraq War have a significant, properly signed, impact ($\beta = 0.77$, $p < 0.001$) on feelings about Blair. People who evaluated the war positively tended to like him, and those who evaluated the war tended to dislike him. Controlling for these evaluations, emotional reactions to the conflict are not significant ($p > 0.05$).

Iraq thus had the hypothesized impact on Blair's public image when voters went to the polls in 2005. However, how large was that effect? To answer this question, we set all of the continuous predictors in the Blair affect model to their mean values and all dummy variables to zero. We then allow scores on the Iraq evaluation scale to vary from their minimum to their maximum values, and compute changes in feelings about Blair. To place the result in comparative perspective, we perform similar computations for all of the other significant predictors in the Blair affect model. The results (see Table 4.6) show that changing evaluations of the war are capable of changing feelings about Blair by 3.45 points on his 0–10 point affect scale. This is a relatively big change, being exceeded only by changing proximity to the Labour Party on position issues (4.26 points). None of the other changes exceeds two points. As we see in Chapter 5, *ceteris paribus*, a change of this magnitude in feelings about Blair is capable of effecting a large change in the probability of voting Labour in 2005. Evaluations of the war thus had sizable, but indirect, effects on party

Table 4.6 *Regression analysis of factors affecting feelings about Tony Blair at time of 2005 general election*

Predictor variables	β	Change in feelings about Blair‡
Age	0.01***	0.99
Education	−0.04x	−0.16
Ethnicity	−0.41**	−0.41
Gender	−0.38***	−0.38
Region†:		
South East	−0.10	
South West	0.01	
Midlands	−0.29*	−0.29
North	−0.09	
Wales	−0.16	
Scotland	−0.18	
Social class	−0.22**	−0.22
Party identification:		
Conservative	−0.23*	−0.23
Labour	0.63***	0.63
Liberal Democrat	0.27*	0.27
Other party	−0.29*	−0.29
Party best on most important issue:		
Conservative	−0.17x	−0.17
Labour	0.74***	0.74
Liberal Democrat	−0.43**	−0.43
Other party	−0.48**	−0.48
Party–issue proximities:		
Conservative	−0.02x	−0.51
Labour	0.17***	4.26
Liberal Democrat	−0.05*	−1.02
Economic evaluations	0.26***	1.71
Party best on economy	0.84***	0.84
Iraq evaluations	0.77***	3.45
Emotional reactions:		
Economy	0.15***	1.09
Iraq	0.04	
NHS	0.06*	0.48

Table 4.6 (*cont.*)

Predictor variables	β	Change in feelings about Blair‡
Constant		1.82***
Adjusted R² =		0.53
N = 2,906		

*** –p < 0.001; ** –p < 0.01; * –p < 0.05; x–p < 0.10; one-tailed test
† – Greater London is the reference category.
‡ – change in feelings about Blair when predictor variable is changed from its minimum to its maximum value.

choice. In the event, the large bulk of these evaluations, and hence the effects they produced, were negative.

Conclusion: conflict and consensus

In this chapter, we map the dynamics of public opinion about the Iraq War and analyse their impact on support for Tony Blair. We also investigate the effects of rival morality, benefits and costs, and general heuristics models of public opinion about the war. Key predictor variables in all three models have statistically significant effects. These results provide an empirical warrant for estimating a composite model that includes the three specific models. Model selection criteria testify that the composite model is superior to its components. Also, although there are significant differences in men's and women's scores on all key explanatory variables, the effects of most of them are statistically indistinguishable for the two gender groups. Thus, women were more negatively disposed to the war largely because they saw fewer benefits, more costs, a lower likelihood of success and a weaker moral case for the conflict.

The composite model also provides insight into understanding aggregate-level shifts in support for/opposition to it. The initial positive shift and subsequent negative shifts in public opinion were matched by parallel changes in the values of major explanatory variables. These movements are explicable given the flow of information about the conflict to which the British public was exposed. Following a classic public opinion rally when hostilities began, the

American- and British-led 'coalition of the willing' quickly dispatched Saddam Hussein's conventional forces. But, then, bad news began to accumulate. Weapons of mass destruction went undiscovered, and Iraqi insurgents began a campaign of guerilla warfare against Allied forces combined with terrorist attacks on Iraqi collaborators and Western civilians in Iraq. Bloody sectarian strife broke out. Sizable shifts in key predictor variables – judgments about the morality of the war, its benefits and costs and its likelihood of success – ensued.

Viewed generally, present findings suggest the theoretical utility of composite models for explaining the distribution and dynamics of public opinion about salient and controversial political issues such as the Iraq War. As the Iraq debate unfolded, multiple considerations were in play. Citizens were exposed to sharply contrasting arguments about the morality, benefits and costs, and likelihood of success of the conflict. Political leaders and media commentators made normatively charged, oftentimes impassioned, cases for and against the war in *all* of these terms. Politicians and pundits became part of the message – their images providing cues about who and what to believe. Given this diverse flow of information, all three types of factors – moral considerations, (success-discounted) benefits and costs, and heuristics – could be expected to influence individual opinion of the war and aggregate shifts therein. The political context encouraged the public to invoke a variety of considerations when deciding how to judge a proposed military venture, the outcome of which was very difficult to forecast. By incorporating these diverse considerations, the composite model tells a compelling story – one that should apply in political contexts characterized by vigorous debate about highly salient issues and great uncertainty about the consequences of alternative courses of action.

Evolution of public opinion about the war had important consequences for Tony Blair and for Labour. As the conflict continued and casualties mounted, opinion turned – people moved against the war, a consensus emerged that Blair was to blame, and the war became a valence issue. As the 2005 election approached, Iraq had become a distinct liability for him and, indirectly, for his party. In the next chapter, we investigate these indirect effects, and thereby calibrate the corrosive impact of 'Tony's war' on Labour fortunes in 2005.

5 | *Electoral choices*

This chapter analyses party choice and turnout in Britain's 2005 general election. As discussed in Chapters 3 and 4, the context in which this election was held differed from that of the 2001 general election. At that time, Labour was in a very strong position. The economy was vibrant, a sizable plurality of voters identified themselves as Labour partisans, and the issue agenda was dominated by public services such as the National Health Service and education, issues that Labour traditionally had claimed as its own. Labour leader Tony Blair, not especially popular, was more warmly received than his principal competitor, Conservative leader William Hague. However, by 2005, public opinion had shifted, and judgments about the performance of Prime Minister Blair and his New Labour government had become considerably more negative. In Blair's case, analyses presented in Chapter 4 have demonstrated that adverse public reactions to the continuing conflict in Iraq in the run-up to the 2005 election had done much to damage his image as a competent, trustworthy leader. Although the electoral system remained biased in Labour's favour, and most opinion polls showed the party holding a modest lead over the Conservatives, its 2005 electoral prospects were clearly more uncertain than they had been four years earlier. Labour would likely win more seats than its rivals, but a hung parliament was a real possibility.

In this chapter, we employ BES data to document the mix of public beliefs, attitudes and opinions that governed electoral choice in 2005. We then examine the explanatory power of rival models of party choice to understand the forces that affected voting behaviour in 2005. As part of this analysis, we investigate whether the effects of party leader images – a key component of the valence politics model of electoral choice – vary by voters' levels of political sophistication. Next, because the levels of support that parties receive are a function both of choices among parties and the choice to (not) participate in an election, we also study factors that affected turnout. Since it is arguably the case that the turnout decision is part and parcel of the larger party support decision people make – a 'none of the above' choice – we specify a model that explicitly incorporates turnout as an option. The chapter concludes by highlighting major findings regarding what mattered for electoral choice in 2005.

Mixed fundamentals

Economic evaluations

In discussions of forces that drive election outcomes, analysts often emphasize the importance of 'fundamentals' (e.g. Gelman and King, 1993; Wlezien and Norris, 2005). Although the set of factors designated as fundamentals is not clearly defined, there is broad agreement that a healthy economy is a *sine qua non*. In this regard, after coming to power in May 1997, Labour had presided over a prolonged economic boom characterized by a felicitous mix of strong growth coupled with low unemployment and modest price increases. To be sure, not all parts of the country had participated equally in the good times, and some sectors of the economy, such as automotive manufacturing, had struggled. And, although inflation was generally low, soaring housing prices in London, the South East and parts of East Anglia were cause for concern. Younger people worried about their ability to buy a home, and older people worried that the housing bubble might burst, leaving them in financially untenable 'negative equity' positions.

Still, the overall economic picture remained rosy in the spring of 2005, and this was reflected in public assessments of the national economy and personal economic circumstances. As the 2005 BES pre-election survey data in Figure 5.1 show, economic evaluations were quite positive, and only slightly less sanguine than in 2001.[1] Many respondents thought that good economic times would continue or get even better. When they were asked about their personal finances over the past year, 67% said they had stayed the same or improved, and only 33% that they had deteriorated. The comparable numbers for 2001 were 73% and 27%, respectively. When asked about how things would develop in the year ahead, the balance of responses in 2005, as in 2001, was tilted very much in a positive direction for both personal finances and the national economy. Differences between 2001 and 2005 are somewhat larger for evaluations of how the economy had fared over the previous year. In

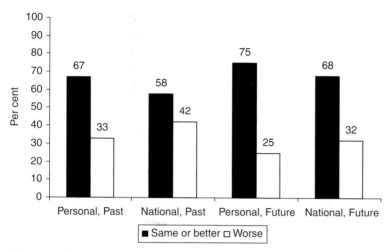

Figure 5.1 Economic evaluations, 2005 (*Source*: 2005 BES pre-election survey)

2001, 70% offered positive assessments, and 30%, negative ones. Four years later, the balance was still clearly positive, but the ratio, 58% to 42%, was less skewed. Overall, these evaluations complement objective data on the robust health of the British economy and suggest that Labour did have this fundamental secured as the 2005 election approached.

Party identification

Positive attitudes towards the economy were not mirrored in a second often-cited fundamental of partisanship. Since the development of the concept of party identification at the University of Michigan in the 1950s, political scientists have recognized that psychological attachments to political parties are important elements in the skein of forces affecting electoral choice. In its original formulation, party identification was conceptualized as a stable, long-term attachment that influenced the vote directly, and also helped to shape orientations to party leaders and currently salient issues (Campbell *et al.*, 1960). Over the past quarter century, a number of analysts have challenged this model's core claim that party identification typically is a stable feature of public political psychology. According to these critics, partisanship in the United States, Britain, and elsewhere is characterized by ongoing individual-level dynamics (e.g. Achen, 2002; Alt, 1984; Fiorina, 1981;

Franklin and Jackson, 1983; Franklin, 1992). Despite sophisticated
efforts to defend the traditional view (e.g. Green and Palmquist, 1990;
Green *et al.*, 2002), evidence from multi-wave national panel surveys
indicates the reality of partisan instability. Sizable minorities of voters change their partisan attachments between consecutive general
elections (Clarke *et al.*, 2004b). Some abandon one party and adopt
another one, whereas others move back and forth between partisanship and nonpartisanship. Partisan instability is not novel as might
be inferred from analyses documenting the aggregate dealignment of
partisan forces in many mature democracies over the past few decades
(e.g. Dalton, 2000; see also Sarlvik and Crewe, 1983). Rather, panel
surveys, including those conducted in the 1960s by Butler and Stokes,
show that large numbers of voters vary their partisan attachments.
Following Fiorina (1981) and others, we have argued that the mutabil-
ity in partisanship in Britain at any time, t, can be usefully conceptualized as the product of a dynamic process. In this process, voters use
current information about the performance of parties and their leaders
to update their partisan attachments, with previous (t–i) information
being progressively discounted over time (Clarke *et al.*, 2004b).

The finding that partisanship has dynamic properties does not neg-
ate its importance for understanding the choices that voters make at
particular points in time. In any given election, party identification
has significant effects on voting behaviour, and a party with a sizable
cohort of identifiers has an important fundamental on its side. For
example, Figure 5.2 shows that Labour held a very substantial lead over
the Conservatives and other parties at the beginning of the 2001 election campaign.[2] With a 42% share – 17% more than the Conservatives
and 33% more than the Liberal Democrats – Labour definitely had the
party identification fundamental secured when that contest began.

Four years later, as the outset of the 2005 campaign, Labour's
cohort of identifiers had fallen to 34% (Figure 5.2). A saving grace
for the party was that its competitors had made little headway. The
Conservative share stood at 25% – exactly where it was when the
2001 campaign started. The Liberal Democrats were even more dis-
advantaged; their group of identifiers stood at 12%. Nationalist and
other minor parties also had only very small groups of partisans, and
nearly one-quarter of the electorate said that they did not identify
with any party. Thus, although Labour retained a partisan edge when
the 2005 campaign began, that edge was considerably reduced, and

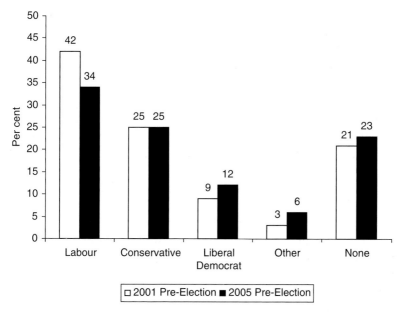

Figure 5.2 Direction of party identification, 2001 and 2005 (*Source*: 2001 and 2005 BES pre-election surveys)

a large group of nonidentifiers lent considerable potential for short-term, campaign-related forces to determine the election outcome.

Party performance

In keeping with the valence politics model of electoral choice presented in Chapter 2, we argue that party performance evaluations in a variety of areas are a third fundamental. The 2005 BES pre-election survey asked respondents to evaluate government performance in several different areas.[3] Their answers buttress the evidence presented in Chapters 3 and 4 that many people were unhappy with the job Labour had done in various policy areas. Negative evaluations outnumbered positive ones in seven of ten cases, including the National Health Service, pensions, transportation, taxes, crime, immigration and Iraq (see Figure 5.3). In some cases, the negative tilt was sizable and, in others, it was massive. Thus, only slightly over one-quarter of the BES respondents gave Labour a positive evaluation on crime, but over two-fifths gave the party a negative one. The comparable proportions for

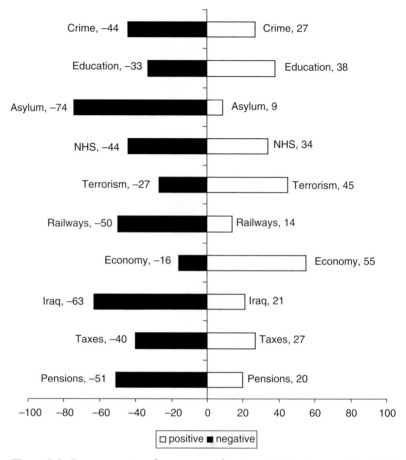

Figure 5.3 Government performance evaluations, 2005 (*Source*: 2005 BES pre-election survey)

immigration (asylum seekers) were less than one in ten (positive) and more than seven in ten (negative). The Iraq numbers were terrible as well. Also, although respondents gave Labour a very modest 'thumbs up' on education, job evaluations for other public services such as the NHS, the railways and pensions were clearly negative. There were only two 'bright' spots, the economy and terrorism. Consistent with the positive economic evaluations discussed above, a slim majority gave Labour passing marks on the economy and less than one person in five gave the party a failing grade. For terrorism, judgments also were tilted in a positive direction. Indicative of the overall problem Labour

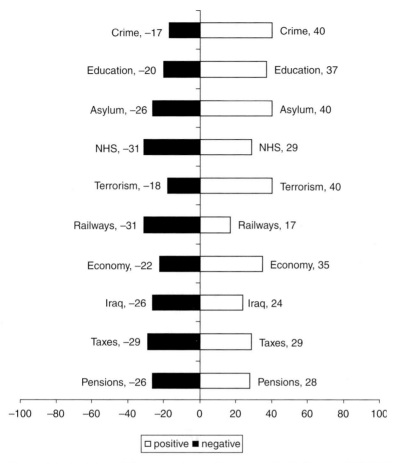

Figure 5.4 Anticipated Conservative performance, 2005 (*Source*: 2005 BES pre-election survey)

faced, its average negative evaluation score across the ten policy areas was 44%, whereas the average positive score was only 29%.

Additional perspective on these judgments can be gained by considering what kind of job the principal opposition party, the Conservatives, would do in various policy areas.[4] Expectations about likely Conservative performance, summarized in Figure 5.4, contrast with those for Labour in several respects. Although, not unexpectedly, BES respondents were more likely to say they 'didn't know' how the Conservatives – then out of power for eight years – would do, positive judgments outnumbered negative ones in six of ten areas. Also, even when negative opinions about the Conservatives were more frequent than positive ones, the differences tended to be quite small. In addition, the Tories fared well on those issues that define the core of what we have termed the 'new issue agenda' in Chapter 3. On crime, two-fifths thought the Conservatives would do a good job, and less than one-fifth thought they would do poorly. For immigration and terrorism the story was the same – positive evaluations outdistanced negative ones. Overall, the percentage of positive judgments about likely Conservative performance averaged 33%, and percentage of negative judgments averaged 24%.

The former figure is not substantially larger than Labour's average positive rating, but the latter is much smaller than that party's average negative rating. Although Tony Blair had spent nearly a decade taking every opportunity to remind the electorate about the misdeeds of previous Conservative governments, *circa* 2005 many voters seemed not to have received his message. A sizable number was unsure about the kind of job that a Conservative government would do and, of those who had opinions, positive judgments outweighed negative ones. Viewed globally, party performance judgments were a fundamental Labour did not have firmly in place on the eve of the 2005 campaign.

Emotional reactions

An important, if typically unstated, assumption in valence politics models is that party and leader performance *evaluations* are what matter for electoral choice. Emotional reactions to economic, political and social conditions and events usually are ignored. Although some political psychologists (e.g. Conover and Feldman, 1986; Marcus *et al.*, 2000; Neumann *et al.*, 2007) have questioned the wisdom of neglecting the role of emotions, the impact of emotional reactions has seldom been investigated in studies of party support in Britain, with existing research focusing on the impact of feelings about economic conditions (Clarke *et al.*, 1997; Clarke *et al.*, 2004b). In the context of the 2005 British general election, there are reasons to believe that emotions may have had significant effects. As discussed in Chapter 4, Britain's decision to join the United States in a war against Iraq triggered large protests and stimulated a storm of negative commentary about the decision and its principal proponent, Prime Minister Blair. Analyses presented in Chapter 4 indicate that this negativity had grown by the time of the 2005 election. When presented with a list of four positive (happy, hopeful, confident, proud) and four negative (angry, disgusted,

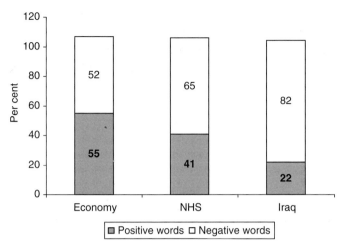

Figure 5.5 Positive and negative emotional reactions to economy, National Health Service and Iraq War (*Note*: percentages exceed 100 because multiple mentions possible (*Source*: 2005 BES pre-election survey)

uneasy, afraid) words and asked to choose which words described their feelings 'about the situation in Iraq', fully 82% of the BES pre-election survey respondents chose one or more of the negative words, and only 22% chose one or more positive words (Figure 5.5).[5]

Other issues were emotion-laden as well. The NHS is a good example. A core feature in the set of public service policies that operationally define the welfare state in Britain and most other mature democracies, prompt access to high-quality publicly funded healthcare is literally a matter of life and death for many people. The hypothesis that news about, and personal experience with, the NHS generates emotions that have potential to affect voting behaviour is certainly plausible. Finally, as in our earlier work, we believe that the economy is another intuitively attractive locus of politically consequential emotions. Economic hardship affects people's lives in many ways, and the old saying 'I'm mad as hell and not going to take it anymore!' encapsulates how voters may punish governments that have the misfortune to preside over hard times. Another such saying, 'Happy days are here again!', conveys the buoyant emotions that can lead voters to reward incumbent governments for good economic times.

In the 2005 BES pre-election survey, respondents were asked to use the eight words listed above to describe their feelings about the NHS and 'the country's general economic situation'. Paralleling evaluations of the health system discussed earlier, and indicative of the possible dangers that the issue posed for Labour, almost two-thirds of the BES respondents chose one or more negative words and only slightly over two-fifths chose one or more positive words. Reactions to the economy were different – 55% selected one or more positive words, and 52% chose one or more negative words. Thus, although Britain's strong economy predictably had generated elements of a 'feel good' factor in a majority of the electorate, many people also reported that they had negative feelings about economic conditions. Later in this chapter, we consider if, and how, these emotional reactions to the economy, the health service and the situation in Iraq influenced voting in the 2005 election.

Issues and leaders

A new issue agenda

In a seminal article published over four decades ago, Stokes (1963, see also Stokes 1992) argued that what he termed *valence issues* typically dominate national elections in mature democracies. As discussed in Chapter 2, valence issues differ from position issues such as the desirability of adopting the European Constitution. The latter have a clear 'pro–con' quality and divide public opinion, sometimes very sharply. In contrast, valence issues have very one-sided opinion distributions. Classic examples are provided by the economy; virtually everyone favours a healthy economy characterized by low levels of inflation and unemployment. And, in Britain and most other contemporary democracies, there is a strong consensus that government should provide a generous supply of public services, with universal healthcare and affordable educational opportunities being exemplars. A strong consensus also exists on the responsibility of government to protect citizens from external and internal security threats, such as those posed by hostile foreign powers, terrorists and common criminals. For valence issues, political debate centres on how best to accomplish the agreed upon goal, and which party and which leader are best able to do so.

As observed in Chapter 2, political parties often are said to 'own' certain issues (e.g. Budge and Farlie, 1983; Kiewiet, 1983). In Chapter 3, we noted that the pattern of issue ownership in British politics changed shortly after the fiasco of the September 1992 currency crisis (see also Clarke *et al.*, 2004b). Almost overnight, the crisis obliterated the Conservatives' longstanding reputation for prudent stewardship of the economy. Subsequently, Labour's ability to claim that it was the party of sound economic management was strongly reinforced by the protracted prosperity that ensued after the party came to power in 1997. Labour also continued to enjoy its historic advantage as advocate and guardian of healthcare, education and other public services.

These issue ownership differentials worked strongly in Labour's favour in 2001 when the public's issue concerns focused primarily on traditional concerns about the economy and public services. Then, the world changed. The horrific 9/11 terrorist attacks set in motion a chain of events, including the Iraq War, that dramatically reshaped the issue agenda of British politics. Issues such as crime, immigration and terrorism – mentioned by less than one respondent in ten in the 2001 BES – became highly salient. As shown in Table 5.1, almost half (49%) of the respondents in the 2005 BES pre-election survey cited crime, immigration, terrorism or the Iraq War as 'most important'[6] (see Table 5.1, Panel A). With the exception of Iraq, these issues were heavily valenced. And even opinion on the Iraq conflict was decidedly tilted in one direction – well before the 2005 campaign began, public opinion had swung against the war. Although the increased salience of these issues did not completely overshadow concerns with the economy and public services, there clearly was a 'new issue agenda' in 2005 that worked to invigorate aspects of party competition that had been only minor themes in earlier elections.

Conservative strategists recognized the new issue agenda and moved quickly to exploit it (Kavanagh and Butler, 2005). Data in Table 5.1, Panel A indicate that their success in doing so was limited. Although the Conservatives were seen as the best party on immigration and crime more often than their competitors, they trailed Labour slightly on the Iraq War, and badly on terrorism. Moreover, Labour maintained its lead on the issues that it had traditionally 'owned', such as the NHS, education and pensions. And, consonant with its image as the architect of a near decade of unbroken prosperity, Labour had a large edge over the Conservatives (36% vs 14%) as the party best able to handle economic problems. Thus, despite the negative tenor of many of the evaluations of the party's performance in office, Labour was seen as better than the Conservatives on a range of issues. The result was that, as the

Table 5.1 *Most important issue in 2005 general election and party best able to handle it*

Panel A. Pre-election survey			Best party			
Issue	Labour	Conser-vatives	Liberal Democrats	Other party	None/ DK	Total mention issue
NHS	26a	19	7	4	45	16b
Education	38	18	6	5	34	7
Pensions	32	23	11	1	33	2
Economy	36	14	7	5	39	11
Taxes	17	30	6	1	45	2
Euro, EU	30	23	12	4	32	2
Crime	22	25	9	4	40	11
Immigration	18	31	4	7	41	25
Terrorism	42	15	2	1	41	6
Iraq War	24	14	9	3	50	7
All other	22	18	10	9	41	12
Total party best	26	22	6	5	41	

Panel B. Post-election survey			Best party			
Issue	Labour	Conser-vatives	Liberal Democrats	Other party	None/ DK	Total mention issue
NHS	45a	18	6	3	29	16b
Education	46	15	18	3	19	7
Pensions	31	32	7	1	29	2
Economy	48	18	7	2	27	13
Taxes	23	26	8	1	41	2
Euro, EU	36	21	11	4	28	7
Crime	32	29	4	2	33	14
Immigration	19	32	4	6	39	21
Terrorism	54	11	2	1	32	2
Iraq War	46	8	14	4	28	5
All other	30	13	11	10	36	11
Total party best	35	22	7	4	32	

a – horizontal percentages, b – vertical percentages, sample sizes: pre-election = 3,423, post-election = 3,962.
Source: 2005 BES pre- and post-election surveys.

election campaign was about to begin, Labour held a narrow overall lead over the Conservatives (26% vs 22%) as the party best able on the most important issues. This lead was much smaller than the one Labour enjoyed in 2001, when its 'best party' issue share was 34% and the Conservative share was only 15% (see Figure 5.6). Labour's issue hegemony had largely evaporated when the 2005 campaign began.

But, this is not the end of the issue story. As Table 5.1 and Figure 5.6, Panel B show, Labour made important gains on the issues during the

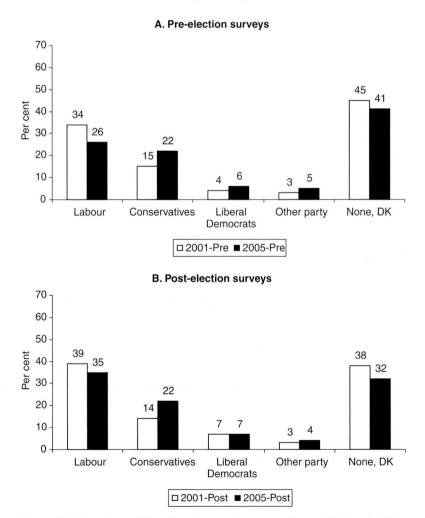

Figure 5.6 Party best able to handle most important issue, 2001 and 2005 (*Source*: 2005 BES pre- and post-election surveys)

course of the 2005 campaign. Although the mix of most important issue remained largely unchanged in the BES pre- and post-election surveys, 35% of those interviewed after the election selected Labour as best on the most important issue. This is a 9% increase over the pre-election figure. In contrast, the percentage (22%) selecting the Conservatives was unchanged, and the percentages selecting the Liberal Democrats increased by only a trivial amount (1%). The data further reveal that Labour made sizable gains on several issues, with the percentage thinking the party was best increasing by 10% or more for the NHS, the economy, crime, terrorism and even the Iraq War. Labour thus made gains on a variety of salient issues during the 2005 campaign. Given its reduced cohort of identifiers and widespread negativism about its performance in office when the campaign began, these gains helped to give Labour the momentum it needed to secure a third consecutive electoral victory.

Leaders

Historically, many commentators on British politics have claimed that party leader images have only minor effects on voting behaviour and election outcomes (e.g. Butler and Stokes, 1969; Crewe and King, 1994; King, 2002). However, a variety of aggregate- and individual-level studies have challenged this conventional wisdom (see, for example, Andersen and Evans, 2003; Clarke *et al.*, 2000; Clarke *et al.*, 2004b; Stewart and Clarke, 1992). Consonant with recent research (e.g. Lupia and McCubbins, 1998; Lupia *et al.*, 2000; Sniderman *et al.*, 1991), we argue that voters use images of the party leaders to help them make decisions in a political world where stakes are high and uncertainty abounds. In the language of cognitive psychology, leader images constitute heuristic devices that provide voters with cues about who will place a 'safe pair of hands' on the tiller of the ship of state.

Political leadership in a democracy is multi-faceted. The norms and values that undergird a democratic political regime encourage voters to judge leaders in terms of multiple criteria. Competence is an important trait, but leaders also should be trustworthy and responsive to public needs and demands. Thus, leaders should possess a felicitous combination of probity and wisdom that enables them to conduct the public's business effectively, equitably and fairly. For their part, voters should judge leaders in terms of these criteria, and these judgments should inform their party support decisions.

We asked respondents in the 2005 BES pre- and post-election surveys to rate party leaders on zero to ten-point scales using the three criteria cited above, i.e. competence, responsiveness and trust.[7] We also asked respondents to use 0–10 scales to tell us how much they (dis)liked each of the leaders.[8] The results, presented in Table 5.2, Panel A, show that no leader was especially well received by the electorate. But, in relative terms, competence was clearly Tony Blair's strong suit. Blair's competence scores were well above those of either

Table 5.2 *Party leader images, 2005*

Panel A. Mean scores on 0–10 leader image variables, pre- and post-election surveys

	Blair		Howard		Kennedy	
	Pre	Post	Pre	Post	Pre	Post
Affect	4.73	4.92	4.38	4.44	4.88	5.52
Competence	5.70	5.85	4.95	4.91	5.01	5.31
Responsiveness	4.83	4.99	5.02	5.01	5.04	5.00
Trust	4.24	4.40	4.32	4.33	4.74	5.22

Panel B. Factor loadings for 0–10 leader image variables, pre- and post-election surveys

	Blair		Howard		Kennedy	
	Pre	Post	Pre	Post	Pre	Post
Affect	0.91	0.93	0.85	0.90	0.83	0.89
Competence	0.88	0.88	0.89	0.89	0.88	0.87
Responsiveness	0.90	0.91	0.84	0.85	0.85	0.87
Trust	0.92	0.93	0.89	0.90	0.87	0.87
Eigenvalue	3.28	3.35	3.04	3.12	2.94	3.07
% item variance explained	81.9	83.7	75.9	78.1	73.6	76.6

Source: 2005 BES pre- and post-election surveys

of his major competitors, Michael Howard, the Conservative leader, and Charles Kennedy, the Liberal Democrat leader. In contrast, Blair fared relatively poorly on the responsiveness and trust scales. Indeed, he trailed Howard and Kennedy in both the pre- and post-election surveys on the responsiveness dimension, and Kennedy in both surveys on the trust dimension. He also trailed Howard on trust in the pre-election survey.

For his part, Kennedy consistently ranked first on trust and ranked first on responsiveness in the pre-election survey. On the post-election survey, he trailed Howard on responsiveness by only the narrowest of margins. Kennedy also was better liked than his rivals in both surveys, with Howard trailing in both cases. Again, it bears emphasis that these are relative comparisons. Kennedy was the only leader who managed to climb above the mid-point (five) on the 0–10 'like–dislike' scale, with a score of 5.5 in the post-election survey.

These data tell us about the *content* of leader images in 2005. But, what about the *structure* of these images? Conceptual distinctions aside, is it the case that leader images are empirically multi-dimensional, with voters clearly distinguishing between traits such as competence, responsiveness and trust? Or, alternatively, do voters have generalized images of the leaders, images that encompass various specific traits? If the latter is true, then can a general 'like–dislike' scale effectively summarize several aspects of voters' images of leader traits? To answer these questions, we conducted an exploratory factor analysis of the competence, responsiveness, trust and affect variables for each of the three British party leaders. Separate analyses were carried out for the pre- and post-election survey data. The results strongly indicate that public images of the party leaders were tightly structured in 2005 (see Table 5.2, Panel B). All six analyses summarized in the table yield single-factor solutions that explain between 73.6% and 83.7% of the item variance. Factor loadings are very impressive, ranging from a low of 0.83 to a high of 0.93. These results suggest that, for purposes of multivariate analyses of electoral choice, the like–dislike scales provide useful summaries of leader images. We employed these measures in previous work (Clarke *et al.*, 2004b), and will do so again later in this chapter.

For now, comparisons of the leader affect scores in the 2001 and 2005 BES surveys provide further evidence that Labour's situation

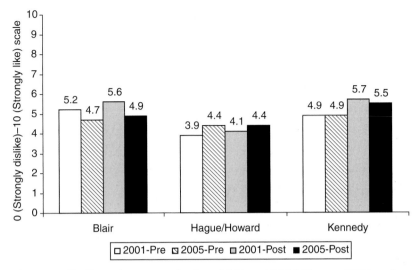

Figure 5.7 Feelings about party leaders, 2001 and 2005 (*Source*: 2001 and 2005 BES pre- and post-election surveys)

had deteriorated across the four years separating the two elections. In the 2001 pre-election survey, Tony Blair, although not highly regarded, had a considerably higher 'like–dislike' score (5.2) than Conservative leader William Hague (3.9), and a slightly higher one than Liberal Democrat leader Charles Kennedy (4.9) (see Figure 5.7). And, Blair's affect score increased to 5.6 points in the 2001 post-election survey, keeping him well ahead of Mr Hague (4.1) and only very slightly behind Mr Kennedy (5.7). Blair's 2005 pre- and post-election scores were worse than their 2001 equivalents and, unlike 2001, they did not increase over the election campaign. For his part, Michael Howard was only marginally better thought of than was his Conservative predecessor William Hague who, by all accounts, was thoroughly disliked across much of the electorate. Kennedy's scores were virtually unchanged. The overall picture, then, is similar to those depicted for party identification, government performance evaluations and perceptions of party competence on important election issues. Much of the electorate had soured on Labour leader, Tony Blair, between 2001 and 2005. Below, we document that these negative feelings had important consequences for voting behaviour in the 2005 election.

Issue proximities and spatial models

Since the publication of Anthony Downs' *An Economic Theory of Democracy* in 1957, many political scientists have adopted spatial models of party competition as the explanatory vehicle in their analyses of electoral choice (for reviews, see Adams *et al.*, 2005; Merrill and Grofman, 1999). As observed in Chapter 2, since the appearance of Downs' work, spatial models have been the principal rivals to the social psychological approach to voting behavior exemplified by the studies by Campbell *et al.*, (1954, 1960) in the United States, and adopted by Butler and Stokes (1969) in their landmark study, *Political Change in Britain*. According to Downsian spatial theory, voters discern where competing parties stand on various position issues and then calculate distances between parties' positions and personal 'ideal points'. Voters maximize utility by casting a ballot for the party closest to them. In an issue-proximity world, considerations such as party identification, leader images or competence on valence issues are irrelevant.

In the 2005 BES, we measured respondents' locations and their perceptions of parties' locations on three position issues, as well as a general left–right scale.[9] The latter scale long has been a staple concept in analyses of the ideologies of British political parties (e.g. Heath *et al.*, 2001). For issue scales, we chose tax reduction–public services spending and punish criminals–rights of the accused, as well as the desirability of Britain's continued membership in the European Union. All three issues have been salient aspects of British political discourse for many years and, hence, could be expected to be position issues that would matter to the electorate.

Figure 5.8 displays mean absolute distances between BES respondents and the Labour, Conservative and Liberal Democrat parties on the four scales. Similar to much of the data already presented, these numbers suggest that Labour was not in a particularly advantageous position at the time of the 2005 election campaign. On average, the party was closest to the electorate on only one scale, tax reduction versus increased public spending. And, even here, the average distance from the voters was only one-tenth of a point less than that of the Liberal Democrats (1.5 vs 1.6 points). On the punish criminals vs protect rights of the accused, Labour ranked last with an average distance of 2.5 points, being bested by both the Conservatives (average distance = 1.9 points) and the Liberal Democrats (average distance = 2.2 points). Labour

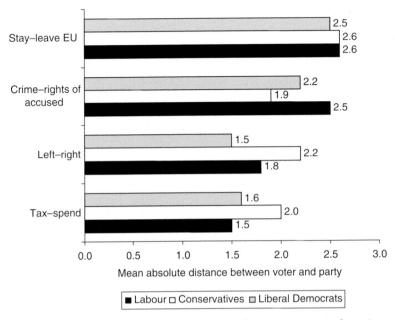

Figure 5.8 Average issue-proximity distances between voters and parties, 2005 (*Note*: stay–leave EU data from pre-election survey; crime–rights of accused, left–right and tax–spend data from post-election survey.) (*Source*: 2005 BES pre- and post-election surveys)

also ranked behind the Liberal Democrats on the general left–right and EU membership scales, although, as Figure 5.8 shows, the three parties were 'neck and neck' on the EU scale. In the next section, we will consider how issue proximities and the several other variables discussed above affected voting behaviour in the 2005 election.

Competing models of party choice

The preceding discussion suggests that a variety of considerations may have influenced the choices voters made in the 2005 election. Viewed discretely, these are: (a) economic evaluations; (b) emotional reactions to the economy, Iraq and the NHS; (c) party identification; (d) leader images; (e) party preferences on important election issues – the vast majority of which are valence issues involving judgments about actual or anticipated party performance; and (f) issue–party proximities. As discussed in

Chapter 2, party identification, party preferences on issues and leader images collectively comprise a valence politics model of electoral choice. Here, we evaluate the explanatory power of these several models.

We also consider two additional models: a social class model, and a more general demographic model which includes age, social class, ethnicity, gender and region of residence.[10] Social class traditionally has been considered the axial socio-economic faultline in British politics, and it was argued that the class cleavage could account for much of the variance in the choices voters made (Pulzer, 1968; see also Denver, 2003). In Butler and Stokes' (1969) simple formulation, social class locations shaped life-long partisan attachments which, in turn, strongly influenced voting behaviour in successive general elections.

In *Political Choice in Britain* (Clarke *et al.*, 2004b), we argued that data from the several BES surveys revealed that the claims advanced on behalf of the power of class models were unwarranted. Since at least the mid-1960s, no more than slightly over half, and typically less, of the electorate spontaneously identified with the middle or working classes. Moreover, properly calibrated, the correlation between class and voting was weaker than typically assumed and, as advocates of the class–party dealignment had argued (e.g. Dalton 2000; Sarlvik and Crewe, 1983), the correlation had declined over time. *Circa* 2001, social class models had less explanatory power than any of the other competing models of electoral choice. There is no reason to think that this situation had changed by 2005. Including several other socio-demographic variables in the analyses enables us to compare their effects with class, and to document their explanatory power in a political context where increasing attention is being paid to the political consequences of characteristics such as age, ethnicity and gender.

Tactical voting

We also consider the impact of *tactical voting* on party choice. Tactical voting occurs in multiparty systems when voters take account of the competitive situation in their constituencies. For example, consider someone living in a constituency where three parties are running. That person might prefer Party A, but conclude that a second choice, Party B, has a better chance of defeating a third choice, Party C. To help keep Party C from winning, the voter supports Party B. The sincere preference is A, but the tactical preference is B. Tactical voting fits well with rational choice theories of political behaviour. In the present example, a voter gets less utility from B than would be provided by sure loser A, but more than would accrue if C wins.

Observers have claimed that sizable numbers of voters made tactical decisions in the 1997 and 2001 elections (e.g. Curtice and Steed, 1997, 2002; see also Wlezien and Norris, 2005). In the 2001 BES, 14% of the respondents said that they had behaved tactically[11] and, net of other considerations, self-identified tactical voters did behave differently. They were significantly more likely to choose the Liberal Democrats, and significantly less likely to opt for either Labour or the Conservatives (Clarke *et al.*, 2004b).

In 2005, there was considerable speculation before the election about a possible 'unwinding' of tactical voting – people who behaved tactically in 2001 would not do so again (Fisher and Curtice, 2006). The claim was that the Conservatives had been out of power for several years and were no longer a target of intense public hostility. However, there was also discussion that 2005 might witness anti-Blair/anti-New Labour tactical voting prompted by unhappiness over the decision to invade Iraq. In the event, nearly 11% of the 2005 BES validated voters said they had behaved tactically. Down slightly from 2001, this figure remains sufficiently large to gainsay the tactical 'unwind' conjecture. Below, we will see if tactical considerations had significant effects, net of other factors that influenced the vote.

Rival models

To assess their relative explanatory power, we estimate the parameters in each of the competing models of electoral choice and compute McFadden and McKelvey R^2 statistics (Long, 1997). We also compute Akaike Information Criteria (AIC) model selection statistics (Burnham and Anderson, 2002). Rank-ordering models by their AIC values enables us to compare their relative explanatory power. The AIC imposes heavier penalties on models that are more richly parameterized than their competitors.[12] Smaller AIC values indicate superior model performance. We perform two sets of analyses. First we contrast voting for the governing Labour Party with voting for any opposition party. Since the dependent variable is a 0–1 dichotomy, binomial logit analysis is used for estimation purposes (Long, 1997). Second, we consider voting for the Conservatives, the Liberal Democrats, or other parties, with

Labour voting as the reference category. Since the dependent variable is a four-category nominal scale, multinomial logit analysis is employed.

Table 5.3 summarizes the results. The social class and 'all demographic' models have very little explanatory power.[13] This is also true for the emotional reactions model which is specified using three indicators of the balance of positive and negative feelings about the Iraq War, the health service and the economy. The economic evaluations, issue–party proximities, and party best able on most important issue models fare considerably better both in terms of their pseudo R^2 statistics and AIC values. Better still are the party identification and party leader models. Judged by its pseudo R^2 and AIC values, the party leader model outperforms all rivals in both sets of analyses.

There is also evidence that the valence politics model has strong explanatory power. Despite its rich parameterization, the valence politics model (which includes party identification variables, party best on most important issue variables, and leader image variables) has a considerably smaller AIC value than any of the models discussed thus far. However, the valence politics model does not statistically encompass all of its rivals in the sense of obviating their explanatory contributions (Charemza and Deadman, 1997). Rather, as Table 5.3 documents, a composite model which includes the variables from all of the several rivals and a tactical voting variable outperforms the valence politics model – the composite model has larger pseudo R^2 statistics, and a lower AIC value than any of its competitors. This result suggests that voting in 2005 was largely about valence considerations, but other things mattered as well. Since election campaigns put many considerations in play simultaneously – ranging from multiple valence issues to multiple position issues to leader images to partisanship – the superior performance of a composite model of voting makes sense.

Table 5.4 contains the detailed results of analyses of the composite model. Panel A shows that the valence politics variables perform as anticipated in the analysis of voting Labour vs voting for any of the opposition parties. Labour Party identification increases the probability of a Labour vote, and identification with one of the opposition parties decreases that probability. In addition, choosing Labour as the party best on the most important issue enhances the probability of a Labour ballot, and choosing the Conservatives or the Liberal Democrats reduces it. Thinking of Labour as best on the economy operates similarly – enhancing the probability of voting Labour. Party

Table 5.3 *Rival models of electoral choice in the 2005 general election*

Panel A. Dependent variable: vote Labour vs vote for another party

Model	McFadden R^2	McKelvey R^2	AIC†
Social class	0.01	0.02	2622.19
All demographics	0.04	0.07	2571.15
Emotional reactions	0.07	0.13	2471.30
Economic evaluations	0.29	0.44	1896.61
Issue–party proximities	0.24	0.46	2020.09
Party best most important issue	0.27	0.40	1943.69
Party identification	0.36	0.48	1698.23
Party leaders	0.40	0.65	1595.42
Valence politics	0.55	0.74	1215.08
Composite model‡	0.59	0.78	1145.39

Panel B. Dependent variable: vote Conservative, Liberal Democrat, other party with Labour as the reference category

Model	McFadden R^2	McKelvey R^2	AIC†
Social class	0.01	– –	4837.22
All demographics	0.07	– –	4630.24
Emotional reactions	0.05	– –	4669.76
Economic evaluations	0.23	– –	3772.71
Issue–party proximities	0.25	– –	3679.92
Party best most important issue	0.25	– –	3710.23
Party identification	0.36	– –	3183.11
Party leaders	0.39	– –	3023.69
Valence politics	0.54	– –	2317.10
Composite model‡	0.60	– –	2143.62

† – Akaike Information Criterion; smaller values indicate better model performance.
‡ – composite model includes all predictors for other models plus tactical voting.
Note: McKelvey R^2 is undefined for multinomial logit model.

Table 5.4 *Binomial and multinomial logit analyses of voting in the 2005 general election, composite specification*

Predictor variables	Panel A	Panel B		
	Labour	Conservative	Liberal Democrat	Other party
Age	−0.01**	0.02**	0.01*	0.02*
Ethnicity	−0.97***	0.43	1.02**	2.89**
Gender	−0.26	−0.18	0.27	0.77**
Region†:				
South East	−0.04	0.52	−0.15	−0.92
South West	0.16	0.15	−0.18	−1.20
Midlands	0.12	0.28	−0.55	0.33
North	0.28	0.31	−0.66*	0.06
Wales	−0.12	−0.01	−0.46	1.23*
Scotland	−0.04	0.21	−0.81*	1.19*
Social class	−0.38*	0.85***	0.25	0.06
Party identification:				
Conservative	−1.09***	1.56***	0.14	0.52
Labour	0.91***	−1.72***	−0.88***	−0.33
Liberal Democrat	−1.51***	0.25	1.69***	0.89*
Other party	−0.98**	0.51	0.40	2.77***
Party leader affect:				
Blair	0.41***	−0.50***	−0.41***	−0.38***
Howard	−0.13***	0.58***	−0.00	0.14*
Kennedy	−0.31***	0.04	0.49***	−0.01
Party best on most important issue:				
Conservative	−0.91***	1.42***	0.08	0.79*
Labour	0.80***	−0.84**	−0.72***	−0.80*
Liberal Democrat	−0.66*	−1.21*	0.84**	−0.89
Other party	−0.10	−0.84	−0.32	1.00*
Party–issue proximities:				
Conservative	−0.09***	0.20***	0.07**	0.15***
Labour	0.15***	−0.14***	−0.12***	−0.19***
Liberal Democrat	−0.12**	−0.03	0.17***	0.10
Economic evaluations	0.09	−0.55***	−0.05	0.17
Party best on economy	0.94***	−1.28***	−0.67***	−0.42
Iraq evaluations	0.02	0.05	−0.06	−0.09

Table 5.4 *(cont.)*

Predictor variables	Panel A	Panel B		
	Labour	Conservative	Liberal Democrat	Other party
Emotional reactions:				
Economy	−0.04	0.15	0.08	−0.16
Iraq	−0.06	0.22*	0.05	0.09
NHS	0.13*	−0.24**	−0.07	−0.30**
Tactical voting	−0.34x	−0.13	0.43*	0.50
Constant	2.53*	−2.95	−4.80***	−5.73**
McFadden R^2 =	0.59	0.60		
McKelvey R^2 =	0.78	−		
% Correctly classified =	87.5	81.6		
Lambda =	0.68	0.70		

*** −$p \leq 0.001$; ** −$p \leq 0.01$; * −$p \leq 0.05$; one-tailed test.
† – Greater London is the reference category; – – not defined.
Note: two analyses are presented. Panel A: binomial logit analysis of voting for Labour vs voting for any of the opposition parties; Panel B: multinomial logit analysis of Conservative, Liberal Democrat and other party voting, with Labour voting as the reference category.

leader effects are also as expected, with positive feelings about Blair increasing the likelihood of choosing Labour, and positive feelings about Michael Howard or Charles Kennedy decreasing it.

Regarding other variables in the model, the issue proximity variables work as advertised. Closer proximity to Labour increases the probability of voting for the party, and closer proximity to the Conservatives or the Liberal Democrats decreases it. Of the emotional reactions, only feelings about the NHS matter; as anticipated, people who feel positively about the health service are more likely to vote Labour. There are demographic effects as well. Consistent with conventional wisdom, working-class people are more likely to vote Labour. Younger people also are more likely to choose Labour. And, despite conjectures that Britain's involvement in the Iraq War had alienated ethnic minorities, considered as a group they were more likely than whites to support Labour. Moreover, Iraq is conspicuous by its absence – neither evaluations[14] of nor emotional reactions to the situation there have significant effects on Labour voting.

The results of the analyses of voting for specific opposition parties vs voting Labour in Table 5.4, Panel B are basically a mirror image of those just discussed. For example, positive feelings about Michael Howard and Conservative party identification increase, and positive feelings about Tony Blair and Labour identification reduce, the probability of casting a Tory vote. Similarly, choice of party as best on most important issue, belief that Labour is best on the economy, and issue proximities all have the expected effects. Emotional reactions also come into play; positive feelings about the Iraq War increase the probability of voting Conservative, and positive feelings about the NHS decrease it. Two demographics are noteworthy, with older people and middle-class people being more likely to cast a Conservative ballot.

Mutatis mutandis, most of these patterns are repeated for Liberal Democrat voting, although the emotional variables do not have significant impacts. Also, in patterns opposite to Labour, Liberal Democratic voting is more prominent among older people and the white British majority. Finally, there is evidence that the Liberal Democrats benefited from tactical voting. In 2001, decisions to behave tactically helped the Liberal Democrats and hurt both Labour and the Conservatives. In 2005, the Liberal Democrats again benefited, Labour again suffered, but the Conservatives were unaffected.

Overall, the composite model performs well. As noted, despite its elaborate parameterization, it has lower AIC values than any of its component models, and its pseudo R^2 values are larger. In the Labour vs all opposition parties analysis, the composite model correctly classifies nearly 88% of the voters. It does nearly as well in the various opposition parties versus Labour analysis, correctly classifying nearly 82%. The proportional reduction in prediction error statistics also are impressive: 0.68 and 0.70, respectively.

Party choice probabilities

Since the estimated parameters in Table 5.4 are logit coefficients, they are opaque regarding the *size* of the effects in the composite model. To see how large these are, we compute the change in probability of voting for a party when a significant predictor variable is varied over its range, holding other predictors at their means (in the case of continuous variables) or at 0 (in the case of dummy variables formed from multiple-category variables such as party identification or party best on most important issue) (Tomz *et al.*, 1999).[15] The resulting changes in probability of voting for a party (which range from zero to one) are multiplied by 100 for ease of exposition.

Performing these calculations for the Labour vs all other party voting analysis reveals that several variables had considerable potential to influence Labour voting. Most noteworthy are feelings about party leaders; as sentiment about Blair moves from the negative to the positive end of the 0–10-point affect scale, the probability of voting Labour increases by fully sixty-seven points (see Figure 5.9). The effects of feelings about opposition party leaders, Charles Kennedy and Michael Howard, are also nontrivial, having the ability to change the probability of choosing Labour by fifty-four and twenty-two points, respectively. Party identification matters as well; for example, a shift from Liberal

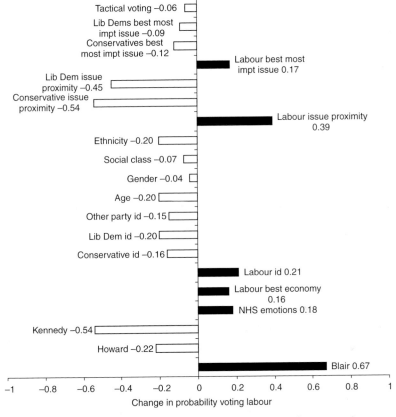

Figure 5.9 Effects of predictor variables on probability of voting Labour, composite voting model

Democrat to Labour identification enhances the likelihood of casting a Labour ballot by forty-one points. Issue effects are prominent too, with a shift from Conservative to Labour as the party best able to handle an important issue raising the probability of a Labour vote by twenty-nine points. Issue proximity effects are even larger, with proximities to Labour, the Conservatives and the Liberal Democrats altering the likelihood of choosing Labour by thirty-nine, fifty-four and forty-five points, respectively. Among the other predictors, emotions about the NHS, choosing Labour as best on the economy, age and ethnicity all shift the Labour vote probability by fifteen points or more.

Iraq and Mr Blair

Analyses presented in Chapter 4 document that evaluations of the situation in Iraq had highly significant effects on feelings about Tony Blair. This finding was not unexpected; indeed, it is now conventional wisdom that Blair's insistence on prosecuting this protracted and unresolved conflict did much to lower his standing, both in his party and in the electorate as a whole. In the run-up to the 2005 election, many observers also voiced the opinion that negative reactions to this very unpopular war would erode Labour support. However, as shown above, evaluations of and emotional reactions to the war did not have significant *direct* effects on Labour voting. Taken together, this evidence suggests that much of the negative impact of Iraq on Labour operated *indirectly* by driving down support for Blair.

We calibrate this indirect effect by using the regression analysis results from Table 4.6 to determine how much Blair's thermometer scores varied as judgments about the Iraq situation moved from the negative to the positive end of the evaluation scale. Then, that change in Blair's thermometer score is introduced into a Labour vote probability analysis to determine the change. Other variables are held at their means or at zero as described above and, once again, calculated probabilities are multiplied by 100 to facilitate interpretation. To put the findings for the indirect Iraq effect in comparative perspective, similar calculations are performed for other significant predictors of feelings about Blair.

The numbers reveal that, *ceteris paribus*, increasingly negative evaluations of Iraq operating through feelings about the prime minister could lower the likelihood of voting Labour by twenty-seven points. As Figure 5.10 illustrates, this is the second strongest of all such indirect

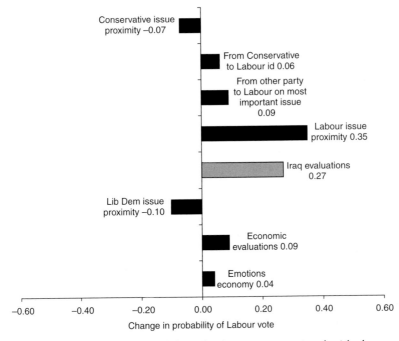

Figure 5.10 Changes in probability of Labour vote associated with changes in feelings about Tony Blair, selected effects

effects, being surpassed only by issue proximity to Labour which could indirectly alter the probability of a Labour ballot by thirty-five points. As the figure also shows, other indirect effects were much smaller, with none of them being able to shift the Labour vote probability by more than ten points. The conclusion is straightforward; Iraq mattered but, as hypothesized, it operated by affecting how people felt about Blair. Forceful chief advocate for what quickly became an unpopular war, the prime minister paid a heavy price in personal public approval. Part of that price, in turn, was passed on to his party.

Figures 5.11 and 5.12 show how various predictor variables influenced the probability of voting for the Conservative and Liberal Democrat parties, respectively. The Conservative analysis empha-sizes the importance of feelings about the party leaders, with changes in affect for Michael Howard shifting the probability of voting Conservative by fully eighty-one points (see Figure 5.11). Feelings about Blair are also noteworthy, moving the likelihood of casting a

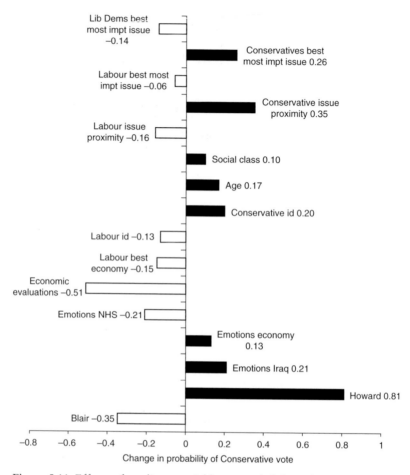

Figure 5.11 Effects of predictor variables on probability of voting Conservative, composite voting model

Conservative ballot by thirty-five points. Economic evaluations, party identification and Conservative issue–party proximities also have strong effects. Changing economic evaluations alter the likelihood of a Tory vote by fifty-one points, a shift from Labour to Conservative partisanship increases that likelihood by thirty-three points, and variations in proximity to the party on position issues does so by thirty-five points. Choosing the Conservatives, rather than the Liberal Democrats, as the party best able to handle the most important election issue boosts the Conservative vote probability by forty points.

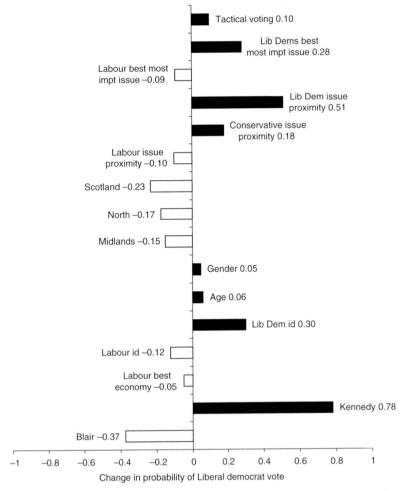

Figure 5.12 Effects of predictor variables on probability of voting Liberal Democrat, composite voting model

Emotions are influential too. Changing feelings about the NHS and Iraq each alter the probability of casting a Conservative vote by twenty-one points.

The Liberal Democrat story is again one that emphasizes leaders, issues and party identification. As illustrated in Figure 5.12, changes in feelings about Charles Kennedy alter the probability of a Liberal Democrat vote by seventy-eight points, and changes in feelings about Tony Blair by thirty-seven points. Variations in the proximity of the Liberal Democrats change the Liberal Democrat vote probability by fifty-one points, and moving from Labour to the Liberal Democrats as party best on important issues changes it by thirty-seven points. And, abandoning a Labour identification for a Liberal Democrat one boosts the likelihood of voting for the latter party by forty-two points. Other effects, including tactical voting considerations, are considerably weaker. Much discussed as a source of Liberal Democrat support, with other factors held constant, making a tactical decision increases the likelihood of voting Liberal Democrat by only ten points.

In sum, the probability of voting analyses echo the results of comparisons of rival models presented earlier. Key variables in the valence politics model, including feelings about party leaders, judgments about party competence on important issues, and partisanship, have strong effects on the probability of supporting various parties. Issue proximities are also influential and, in the Conservative case, they are joined by economic evaluations and emotional reactions to the health service and Iraq. Below, we employ a mixed logit model that provides an alternative perspective on the determinants of party choice and enables investigation of the possibility that key predictor variables, such as party leader images, have heterogeneous effects.

Political sophistication, leader images and electoral choice

The preceding analyses employ standard binomial and multinomial logit models of party choice. Like ordinary least squares regression models, these logit models assume that the parameters associated with various predictors are fixed quantities. Relaxing this assumption enables researchers to pursue theoretically interesting lines of inquiry. Here, we focus on the effects of leader images. As discussed above, until recently, it has been conventional wisdom that leader images were relatively unimportant components in the set of forces driving party choice. Given abundant evidence that this is not the case, some analysts have begun to speculate that leader image effects vary across the electorate, with more sophisticated voters being less strongly influenced by them than less sophisticated ones (e.g. Bartle, 2005). Here, we pursue this line of inquiry with a discrete choice model that allows the coefficients associated with leader image variables to vary.

These variations in the effects of leader images are hypothesized to be a function of voters' levels of political sophistication.

We use the mixed logit (MXL) model for this purpose (Glasgow, 2001, 2005; see also Train, 2003). In addition to allowing investigation of heterogeneity in the effects of predictor variables, MXL models do not require the possibly untenable assumption that the probability of choosing one party rather than another is independent of other alternatives. Analysts concerned about this 'independence of irrelevant alternatives' (IIA) assumption typically have advocated using multinomial probit models (e.g. Alvarez and Nagler, 1998; Alvarez *et al.*, 2000; but see Dow and Endersby, 2004). However, multinomial probit models do not permit the specification of random parameters. MXL has the dual advantages of allowing the analyst to relax the IIA assumption while specifying random parameters for selected predictor variables.[16]

Here, we employ this latter feature of MXL models to investigate heterogeneity in the effects of party leader images. Following the tradition of discrete choice models in fields such as transportation economics, MXL models divide predictor variables into two types – characteristics of choices and characteristics of choosers (e.g. Hensher *et al.*, 2005). An example of the former would be the proximity of a party to a voter on a position issue such as the taxation–policy services spending scale. A party's position on such a scale is a characteristic of the choice that party presents to voters. An example of the latter would be a socio-demographic characteristic such as age, gender or social class. Regardless of what choices parties offer, at any point in time a voter's socio-demographic characteristics are what they are, for example, a forty-five-year-old man working for a brokerage firm in the City or a twenty-five-year-old woman working in the grocery section at Tesco.

The MXL model permits choice set variation across individuals (Greene, 2003; see also Hensher *et al.*, 2005). The latter is useful in situations where the set of competing parties varies from one locale to the next. For example, in the British case, the SNP and Plaid Cymru compete only in Scotland and Wales, respectively, and smaller parties such as Respect, UKIP and the British National Party (BNP) run only in selected constituencies. Mixed logit models permit analysis of these country- and constituency-specific choices as part of a comprehensive analysis of voting in Great Britain as a whole.

The mixed logit model is used to extend our analyses of party choice in three ways. First, we relax the IIA assumption by treating model constants as correlated random variables. Second, we explicitly allow for varying choice sets, treating the SNP as a choice available only in Scotland, and Plaid Cymru as a choice available only in Wales. Third, we investigate the possibility of heterogeneity in party leader image effects. As per the preceding discussion, we distinguish between characteristics of choices and characteristics of choosers (voters) by considering variables that parties might be able to manipulate and variables that they cannot manipulate in the short term. Specifically, party leader images, party best on most important issues, and issue–party proximities are conceptualized as characteristics of the choices that voters make. All other variables are considered characteristics of the voters. Since SNP and Plaid Cymru are explicitly considered as choices in Scotland and Wales, respectively, we augment the set of predictor variables by including national identities.[17] We treat Labour as the reference category, and estimate parameter vectors for Conservative, Liberal Democrat, SNP and Plaid Cymru voting.

Estimates for a basic MXL model with random alternative-specific constants are summarized in Table 5.5. The story told by these numbers is very similar to that told by the simpler multinomial logit model. The predictors treated as a characteristic of the choices, i.e. leader images, party best on most important issue, and party–issue proximities, have highly statistically significant effects. Additional analyses (not shown) indicate that variations in these variables are capable of causing large changes in the likelihood that voters will opt for one of the competing parties. Several other predictors are important as well. In the case of Conservative voting, these include party identification, economic evaluations, emotional reactions to the NHS and Iraq, age, ethnicity and social class. Party identification and several other variables, including tactical voting, also have significant effects on Liberal Democrat voting. Voting for the nationalist parties is less well predicted, although party identification and ethnicity come into play. Noticeably absent is national identity, although further analyses strongly suggest that it works indirectly by encouraging SNP and Plaid Cymru partisanship. Overall, the model performs very well – 73.6% of the voters are correctly classified and the McFadden R^2 is an impressive 0.74.

Table 5.5 *Mixed logit model of party choice in the 2005 general election*

Predictor variables				

Characteristics of choices:	β			
Party leader	0.67***			
Party best most important issue	1.63***			
Party–issue proximities	0.32***			

Characteristics of choosers:

	Party vote			
	Conservative	Liberal Democrat	SNP	Plaid Cymru
	β	β	β	β
Party identification:				
Labour	−1.98***	−1.88***	−4.26*	0.10
Conservative	2.09***	0.40	−3.42	3.24
Liberal Democrat	0.85	3.20***	−1.92	1.86
Other parties	0.22	0.44	6.28x	4.40**
Economic evaluations	−0.56***	−0.08	−0.08	−0.85
Attitudes toward Iraq War	−0.02	−0.13	−0.02	0.34
Emotions – economy	0.15	0.03	−0.35	0.50
Emotions – NHS	−0.31**	−0.16	−0.49	−0.50
Emotions – Iraq War	0.28**	0.07	0.58	−0.07
National identity	−0.02	−0.25	0.77	0.29
Tactical voting	0.04	0.68*	1.68	0.54
Age	0.03***	0.03**	0.09*	0.06
Ethnicity	1.14*	1.57**	0.94	0.93
Gender	0.05	0.64*	0.64	0.75
Social class	1.29***	0.42	1.67	0.31
Constant	−3.66***	−3.73**	−6.75	−6.65
Log-likelihood = −792.08	N = 2011	McFadden	$R^2 = 0.74$	

*** – $p \leq 0.001$; ** – $p \leq 0.01$; * – $p \leq 0.05$; one-tailed test.

The testimony provided by the basic MXL model thus agrees strongly with that provided by the more familiar binomial and multi-nomial logit models discussed earlier. Differences in model specification occasioned by distinguishing between choices and choosers, including the SNP and Plaid Cymru as explicit choices, and relaxing the IIA assumption do nothing to alter the fundamental conclusions suggested by the simpler models. The stylized facts of what mattered for electoral choice in 2005 remain undisturbed. Core variables in the valence politics model, supplemented by party–issue proximities remain 'great beasts', with several other variables coming into play depending upon which party is considered.

Leader effects and political sophistication

We next specify a MXL model that enables us to determine if party leader effects are mediated by levels of political sophistication. Since theory dictates that leader image effects (with these images considered as a characteristic of choices) must be positive, we require a statistical distribution for the random leader image parameter that has support only on the positive side of the real number line (Greene, 2003). We choose the log normal.[18] A random variable X has a log normal distribution if ln(X) has a normal distribution with mean μ and standard deviation σ. An example is shown in Figure 5.13.

Variation in the random leader image parameter is hypothesized to have a log normal distribution and to be a function of political sophistication. Political sophistication is measured as the interaction between amount of available information and information-processing ability. We proxy the former using a political knowledge index, and the latter using level of formal education.[19] We consider two possible effects of sophistication on the leader image parameter. The first effect is a simple linear one – following previous research, we hypothesize that the strength of the leader image variable decreases as sophistication increases. The second possible effect is quadratic. Information about party leaders for evaluations of their performance is easily acquired because it floods the media. Hence, voters with moderate levels of political sophistication will have more information about the leaders (and more ability to process it) than unsophisticated voters, and the effect of leader images will be greater for the former group than the latter. However, voters with high levels of sophistication have a

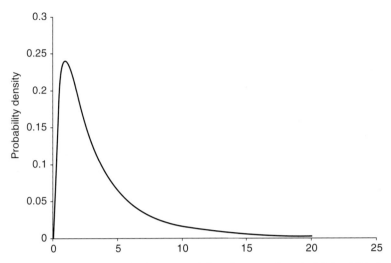

Figure 5.13 Example of a log-normal distribution where ln(X) is ~N(1,1) (definition: a random variable X has a log-normal distribution, with parameters μ and σ, if ln(X) has a normal distribution with mean μ and standard deviation σ)

broader range of political information, with leader images being only one aspect of what is at their disposal for making electoral choices. Having plentiful information and a well-developed capacity to process it, 'high cognitive' voters weigh leader images less heavily than do those with moderate levels of sophistication.

Table 5.6 summarizes how these rival models of the impact of political sophistication behave. Panel A shows that feelings about the leaders have significant effects on voting, as do party preferences on important issues and party–issue proximities. The coefficients for the latter two variables are the same order of magnitude as those estimated in the simple MXL model without a random leader effect. Note that the coefficient for the leader variable is a mean effect; it is negative because the variable is assumed to follow a log normal distribution, and the mean is less than 1.0. Also, consistent with the idea that the party leader effect varies across voters, the leader variable's coefficient has a statistically significant variance. And, as hypothesized, the impact of political sophistication, considered as a linear effect, is negative. This indicates that more sophisticated voters give less weight to leader images than do less sophisticated ones.

Table 5.6 *Summary of mixed logit models of party choice, with political sophistication effects on the impact of feelings about party leaders*

Panel A. Linear effects of political sophistication on impact of party leaders

Characteristics of choices:	β	s.e.
Feelings about party leaders	-0.27***	0.16
Party best most important issue	1.40***	0.19
Party–issue proximities	0.22***	0.05
	δ	s.e.
Standard deviation in party leader coefficient	1.12***	0.06
Impact of political sophistication on party leader coefficient	-0.22***	0.06

Log-likelihood = -800.99
N = 2,011
McFadden R^2 = 0.74
AIC = 1,755.98

Panel B. Quadratic effects of political sophistication on impact of party leaders

Characteristics of choices:	β	s.e.
Feelings about party leaders	-1.11***	0.30
Party best most important issue	1.27***	0.19
Party–issue proximities	0.21***	0.05
	δ	s.e.
Standard deviation in party leader coefficient	0.88*	0.49
Impact of political sophistication		
Party leader coefficient: linear	0.86*	0.38
Squared	-0.24**	0.10

Log-likelihood = -799.47
N = 2,011
McFadden R^2 = 0.74
AIC = 1,754.94

*** $-p \leq 0.001$; ** $-p \leq 0.01$; * $-p \leq 0.05$; one-tailed test.
Note: coefficients for party best on most important issue and party–issue proximities are fixed, not random. Political sophistication is measured as interaction of level of formal education and political knowledge.

Panel B presents results for the quadratic specification of leader effects. Again, all coefficients, including the variance for the leader variable coefficient, are statistically significant. Both coefficients for the hypothesized quadratic effects of political sophistication also are significant and, as expected, the basic term is positive and the squared term is negative. According to this model, the impact of leader images on party choice varies in a nonlinear way. The impact is greater among moderately sophisticated voters than among both unsophisticated and highly sophisticated ones.

Taken together, these MXL estimates provide interesting evidence about possible heterogeneity in the effects of leader images – key variables in the valence politics model of party choice. However, a caveat is in order. Although some analysts may find this heterogeneity to be theoretically attractive, it comes at a cost of specifying models that have more elaborate parameterizations than the basic MXL model presented earlier. In this regard, note that the AIC value for the simple MXL model is 1726.17, considerably less than either of the values for the models with leader images varying according to linear and quadratic effects of political sophistication. The AIC values for the latter two models are 1,755.98 and 1,754.94, respectively. These numbers suggest that the simpler model is preferable. As is necessarily the case, heterogeneity is purchased at the cost of parsimony. In the present instance, increases in model fit do not offset the cost. Suitably discounted, voting models with heterogeneous leader image effects caused by variations in political sophistication do not outperform a simpler model that assumes homogeneous effects across the entire electorate.

Turnout and party choice

Although party choice is an important aspect of voting behaviour, the turnout decision is also fundamental. Historically, political scientists have considered these two decisions separately. The assumption is that people do the same. They decide whether to go the polls, and they then vote for a party. But, the decisions are unrelated, and can be analysed in isolation. Our previous work (Clarke *et al.*, 2004b) followed this traditional approach by considering turnout separately. Paralleling our work on party choice, the turnout analyses were designed to test several rival models with currency in the literature on electoral participation. Specifically, these models are (a) general incentives; (b) rational choice; (c) civic voluntarism; (d) cognitive mobilization; (e) equity-fairness; and (f) social capital.

The core of the general incentives model is the well-known rational choice model of turnout proposed by Riker and Ordeshook (1968, 1973). In this model, the decision to vote is a function of a benefit–cost analysis, with (differential) benefits derived by having one's preferred party win an election discounted by the likelihood that an individual's ballot is 'pivotal', i.e. the vote that decides the contest. Since the probability that any single vote is pivotal is vanishingly small (e.g. Gelman *et al.*, 1998), costs are always greater than benefits. Accordingly, Riker and Ordeshook supplemented their model with a 'D' term that they interpret as capturing expressive benefits that individuals obtain only when they vote. These selective benefits are operationalized as sense of civic duty. Given the insuperable hurdle posed by the pivotality discount on collective benefits, the general incentives model replaces pivotality with the 'softer' concept of 'perceived personal influence'.[20] In this revised formulation, collective benefits are discounted by perceptions of one's ability to influence political outcomes. In addition, the general incentives model expands the core rational choice model to include group benefits, individual benefits and social norms.[21] Civic duty is interpreted as providing system benefits.

Key factors in the civic voluntarism model are resources (e.g. education, energy, income, physical capacity, time) that individuals possess, together with the mobilizing activities of political parties and various social groups.[22] The cognitive mobilization model views electoral participation as a consequence of knowledge of and involvement in the political process,[23] whereas the equity-fairness model sees participation as being driven by a sense of relative deprivation.[24] This feeling of relative deprivation motivates people to become politically active. Finally, the social capital model hypothesizes that turnout and other political activities are products of high levels of social trust and 'pathways to politics' provided by facilitative social networks.[25]

Analyses of these models using the 2001 BES data demonstrated that the general incentives model outperformed it rivals, but that variables from the other models also contributed to explaining turnout. Accordingly, we specify a composite model of turnout in the 2005 general election that includes variables from each of the competing models. Region of residence is added as an additional demographic control. Since the dependent variable (vote/not vote) is dichotomous, we use binomial logit to estimate model parameters.

Many of the predictors have statistically significant effects (see Table 5.7). Several variables from the general incentives model behave as expected. Thus, influence-discounted benefits, anticipated personal benefits, civic duty and social norms all have significant positive effects, and perceived costs of participation have significant negative effects. In accordance with the civic voluntarism model, variables that proxy politically relevant resources also have significant effects. These include age, disability status, education, gender and social class. Party mobilization also works as anticipated. This variable is often cited as one of the factors in the civic voluntarism model, but it also might be claimed by the social capital model. Political knowledge, a key element in the cognitive mobilization model, is significant too. Overall, the composite turnout model performs quite well, correctly classifying nearly 80% of the BES respondents as either voters or nonvoters.

We next calculate how the probability of going to the polls changes as the value of a predictor varies, with other variables held at their means. The results, displayed in Table 5.7, reveal that six predictors are capable of changing the probability of voting by twenty points or more. As in 2001, civic duty has the largest impact. As civic duty moves across its range, the probability of voting increases by forty-four points. Three other variables from the general incentives model also have large effects. Variations in influence-discounted benefits, perceived personal benefits, and social norms alter the likelihood of going to the polls by thirty-one points, thirty-five points and thirty-one points, respectively. Political knowledge, a key variable in the cognitive mobilization model also has a large influence – the probability of casting a ballot increases by thirty-six points as political knowledge moves across its range. Finally, age has a noteworthy impact; other things equal, increases in age from its minimum to its maximum value boost the likelihood of voting by twenty-six points.

The relationship between turnout and age indicates that, even with controls for a large number of important explanatory variables, younger people are less likely to go to the polls. It bears emphasis that age is strongly correlated with civic duty which, as just noted, is the strongest single predictor in the composite turnout model. As illustrated in Figure 5.14, the proportion of 2005 BES respondents

Table 5.7 *Binomial logistic regression analysis of composite model of turnout in the 2005 general election*

Predictor variables	β	Change in probability of voting
Influence-discounted benefits	0.04***	0.31
Costs	−0.04*	−0.12
Civic duty	0.13***	0.44
Political knowledge	0.22***	0.36
Perceived group benefits	−0.06**	
Perceived personal benefits	0.08***	0.35
Social norms	0.10***	0.31
Relative deprivation	0.01	
Social trust	0.74	
Political interest	0.02	
Party mobilization	0.32***	0.15
Socio-demographics:		
Age	0.02***	0.26
Disability	−0.26*	−0.05
Education	0.05x	0.04
Ethnicity	0.21	
Gender	−0.19*	−0.04
Social class	0.43***	0.08
Region†:		
South East	0.37*	0.12
South West	0.27	
Midlands	0.73***	0.14
North	0.08	
Scotland	0.36x	0.07
Wales	0.59*	0.11
Constant	−6.18***	

McFadden $R^2 = 0.26$
McKelvey $R^2 = 0.41$
% correctly classified $= 79.6$
Lambda $= 0.35$

*** $-p \leq 0.001$; ** $-p \leq 0.01$; * $-p \leq 0.05$; one-tailed test.
† – Greater London is the reference category.

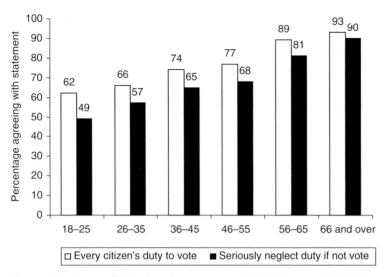

Figure 5.14 Sense of civic duty by age group, 2005 (*Source*: 2005 BES post-election survey)

who express a sense of civic duty increases strongly and monotonically across several age cohorts. For example, the percentage agreeing with the statement that they would seriously neglect their duty as a citizen if they did not vote is slightly less than 50% among eighteen to twenty-five-year olds. Among those sixty-six and older, fully 90% agree with the statement. Similarly, 62% and 93%, respectively, of these two age groups agree that it is every citizen's duty to vote in an election. Absent very long-run panel data, it is difficult to disentangle life-cycle and age cohort effects. However, analyses conducted using the 2001 BES strongly suggest that these age relationships contain a significant generational component (Clarke *et al.*, 2004b). If so, then it is very unlikely that turnout in British general elections will rebound sharply in the foreseeable future. The relationship between age and turnout and other forms of political participation is revisited in Chapter 7.

None of the above

As observed, the vast majority of studies of voting behaviour have analysed party choice and turnout separately. However, nonvoting can be viewed as an option that flows from major theories of party choice. For example, according to the logic of Downsian issue-proximity models, the expectation is that people who perceive that all parties are equally distant on issue-position scales are indifferent among the choices on offer and, hence, abstain. They have no incentive to bear the costs associated with making a trip to the polls. This line of reasoning is central to the Riker–Ordeshook model discussed above. Valence politics models also suggest that nonvoting is a sensible option for people who are nonpartisans and do not believe that any party or any leader is able to handle important problems. There is no current or past information about party or leader performance that prompts a party choice.

More simply, commentators routinely suggest that dissatisfaction with one or more of the parties encourages people to stay at home. This conjecture is often directed at people who could be expected to vote for the governing party. In 2001, for example, observers hypothesized that a combination of neo-liberal economic policies and tepid public service investment would cause Tony Blair's New Labour government to lose its socialist 'heartlands'. Discontented Labour supporters would not bolt to another party; rather, they would sit the election out. In 2005, this hypothesis was invigorated by disaffection among members of Labour's left-wing and ethnic minority communities over Blair's decision to join US President George W. Bush in the war against Iraq. Many of these traditionally strong Labour supporters would show their unhappiness with Blair and his party by choosing 'none of the above'.

Here, we test these hypotheses by specifying a unified model that includes the several predictors from both the party choice and turnout models. The dependent variable has four party choice categories (Labour, Conservative, Liberal Democrat, other parties) and a fifth, nonvoter category. Since the campaign context featured the possibility that many disgruntled Labour supporters would stay home, using Labour voting as the reference category facilitates interpretation. Thus, we can see whether factors that encouraged some voters to choose a party other than Labour prompted others not to vote at all. Multinomial logit is used to estimate model parameters.

Table 5.8 contains parameter estimates for selected predictor variables in this model. Two general observations are in order. First, all key predictor variables from the traditional composite models of party choice and turnout continue to behave as expected. For example, positive feelings about Tony Blair lessen the likelihood of voting for any of the opposition parties, and positive feelings about Michael Howard and Charles Kennedy enhance the likelihood of voting for the Conservative and Liberal Democrat parties, respectively. Similarly, key predictor variables from the turnout models such as influence-discounted benefits, costs, civic duty, political knowledge, and social norms work as anticipated. In this regard, note that the signs on the coefficients for these variables are reversed from Table 5.7 above because the unified model uses Labour *voting* as the reference category. Several other familiar findings about what drives party choice and turnout can be found in the table.

The second general observation is what constitutes the 'value added' in the unified model. This concerns the significant effects of several party choice variables on turnout. There is a very clear pattern – the Labour variables are *negatively associated* with membership in the nonvoter category. Controlling for all other considerations, people who disliked Blair, those who did not think Labour was best on important issues, those who were unimpressed with Labour's ability to manage the economy, those who were distant from Labour on position issues, and Labour identifiers were more likely to be nonvoters in 2005. All of these relationships are consistent with conjectures about the 'stay at home' behaviour of people who otherwise might have cast a Labour ballot.

Table 5.8 also shows positive relationships between key Conservative variables and nonvoting. For example, people with positive feelings about Tory leader Michael Howard were more likely to be nonvoters than Labour voters, as were people who favoured the Conservatives on the most important issue, and those who identified themselves as Conservative. Although these relationships are sensible – after all, people with pro-Conservative attitudes would be more likely to be nonvoters than Labour voters – they also hint at a failure of the party to get all of its potential supporters to the polls. This, in turn, is consistent with evidence presented in Chapter 6, indicating that the Conservatives' 2005 campaign was largely a failure. *Ceteris paribus*, having pro-Conservative attitudes on the key variables in the dominant valence politics model of party choice is associated with nonvoting. This was not good news for Mr Howard and his party in 2005. We consider this finding again in Chapter 6, which analyses party support and the 2005 election campaign.

Table 5.8 *Parameters for selected predictors in unified model of electoral choice*

	Electoral choice†			
	Conservative	Liberal Democrat	Other party	Nonvoter
Predictor variables	β	β	β	β
A. Party choice variables				
Party leader affect:				
Blair	−0.39***	−0.34***	−0.32***	−0.17***
Howard	0.44***	−0.06	0.06	0.11***
Kennedy	0.09*	0.48***	0.06	0.03
Party best on most important issue:				
Labour	−0.97***	−0.78***	−1.01***	−0.23
Conservative	0.75**	−0.12	0.59	1.11***
Liberal Democrat	−1.44**	0.78**	−1.10*	−0.10
Other party	−0.92	−0.20	0.90*	0.26
Party identification:				
Labour	−1.70***	−1.03***	−0.56	−0.53***
Conservative	1.15***	−0.01	0.22	0.47*
Liberal Democrat	−0.20	1.43***	0.44	0.75**
Other party	−0.09	0.19	2.00***	−0.05
Party–issue proximities:				
Labour	−0.13***	−0.10***	−0.16***	−0.08***
Conservative	0.18***	0.04	0.11**	0.01
Liberal Democrat	0.03	0.20***	0.12*	0.07*
Economic evaluations	−0.39***	−0.06	0.19	−0.08
Party best on economy	−1.28***	−0.71***	−0.48	−0.85***
Iraq evaluations	0.10	−0.12	−0.09	−0.08
Emotional reaction: Economy	0.14*	0.12*	−0.07	0.04
NHS	−0.22***	−0.06	−0.26**	−0.05
Iraq	0.01	−0.00	−0.02	0.07
B. Turnout variables				
Influence-discounted benefits	0.01	−0.01	−0.01	−0.02**
Costs	0.10	0.01	0.08	0.10**
Civic duty	−0.05	−0.06	−0.06	−0.23***

Table 5.8 (*cont.*)

	Electoral choice†			
	Conservative	Liberal Democrat	Other party	Nonvoter
Political knowledge	0.13*	0.04	−0.09	−0.19***
Group benefits	0.02	0.01	−0.04	0.02
Personal benefits	0.04	0.03	0.20**	−0.03
Social norms	0.02	0.01	0.01	−0.11**
Party mobilization	0.09	0.19*	0.02	−0.32***
Relative deprivation	0.13*	0.15**	0.28***	0.11*
Social trust	0.04	0.02	0.03	0.01
Age	0.01*	0.01**	0.01	−0.01*
Ethnicity	−0.05	0.90**	2.70**	0.22
Gender	−0.11	0.22	0.96***	0.38**
Social class	0.39*	0.13	−0.15	−0.35**

McFadden $R^2 = 0.45$
% correctly classified $= 68.4$
Lambda $= 0.54$

*** $-p \leq 0.001$; ** $-p \leq 0.01$; * $-p \leq 0.05$; one-tailed test.
† – Labour voting is the reference category.

Conclusion: by default

Coming into the 2005 general election, Labour was in a weaker position than it had been at the time of the 2001 election. Data presented in this chapter clearly indicate that only one of the 'fundamentals', a healthy economy, was solidly in place. Voters recognized that Labour had done a good job in managing the economy and gave the party due credit. However, other fundamentals were not in good order. Judgments about Labour's performance in several policy areas were generally unflattering and, with the exception of how it had dealt with the threat of terrorism, large majorities of voters gave the government failing grades for its handling of 'new issues' such as crime, immigration and the war in Iraq. In addition, Labour's partisan share and the percentage selecting the party as best on important election issues were both down substantially. Many voters grudgingly recognized Prime Minister Blair's competence but, in part because of his dogged insistence on pursuing an ill-advised war with Iraq, feelings about him had shifted from lukewarm to chilly. Nor could Labour take solace in its proximity to voters on important position issues – in most cases, either the Conservatives or the Liberal Democrats were closer to where voters wanted them to be.

Not everything was bad news for Labour. There were two major factors working in the party's favour. First, the electoral system had a pro-Labour bias. The distribution of party support across the constituencies was such that Labour typically required fewer votes to win seats than was the case for its rivals.[26] Second, and also very important, the electorate did not enthusiastically endorse any of the opposition parties. Although Charles Kennedy remained a popular leader of the Liberal Democrats, the number of Liberal Democrat identifiers in the electorate remained extremely meagre, and few voters believed the party would be best able to handle important issues. Similarly, the Conservatives had made only very limited headway on important issues and, although the balance of expectations about how a Tory government would perform was positive, many voters were unsure about what a Conservative future would bring. The Conservatives also had exactly the same share of identifiers as they had four years earlier, and their new leader, Michael Howard, was only slightly more liked than his decidedly unpopular predecessor, William Hague. Labour thus retained a competitive edge on the variables that mattered but, in most cases, this was largely by default.

What was very similar to 2001 was the explanatory power of rival models of electoral choice. As in 2001, social class and other demographic variables were decided non-starters. In sharp contrast, key variables in the valence model – partisanship, party preferences on important election issues and leader images – continued to have strong effects on the vote. But, and again similar to 2001, the valence model did not have the field to itself. Party–issue proximities make significant contributions to explanation, and a general composite model outperforms all of its components. These findings about the performance of rival models are robust, being endorsed not only by standard logit models, but also by a more technically sophisticated mixed logit model. Parameter estimates for this latter model suggest that the impact of leader images may vary in a nonlinear way with voters' levels of political sophistication. Although this result is consonant with recent, and not so recent, theorizing about how different groups of voters use political information, model selection criteria caution that the costs of enhanced model complexity may be a price not worth paying. Simpler party choice models perform well.

Voter turnout was up only very slightly in 2005 above its dismal 2001 level and, again, several rival models contribute to explaining who went to the polls and who did not. The general incentives model again performs best, with age-related differences in sense of civic duty suggesting the presence of possibly strong downward pressures on turnout in future elections. When considering factors that influence turnout in particular electoral contexts, it is important to recognize that the decision not to cast a ballot can be considered a 'none of the above' choice. An analysis of a unified model that incorporates both party choice and turnout provides evidence that this was the case in 2005. As numerous commentators speculated in the run-up to the election, several important factors that prompted some voters to support a party other than Labour prompted others to stay at home. The evidence also suggests that the Conservatives did not benefit fully from forces working to their advantage. Some people who should have gone to the polls to cast a Tory ballot did not bother to do so. Taken together, these two findings again indicate that, to a substantial extent, Labour won by default in 2005. In the next chapter, we consider how various factors affecting party choice and turnout were influenced by the 2005 election campaign.

6 | *The short campaign*

Election campaigns are always a time for rhetoric – sometimes very fiery and highly negative. Heated exchanges between Conservative leader Michael Howard and Prime Minister Tony Blair during the 2005 campaign provide excellent illustrations. In a speech about half-way through the campaign, the opposition leader declared:

> Mr Blair started his campaign by lying about our spending plans. When it became clear that he could not sustain these claims, he dropped them. Now he denies making them and he's resorting to false claims about our plans for hospitals ... How can anyone trust Mr Blair when his campaign is based on these lies? It's time Mr Blair started telling the truth and had an honest debate about the real challenges facing our country. (Smith, 2005: 114)

Not to be outdone, Tony Blair attacked the Conservatives, particularly on the issues of asylum and immigration:

> The Tory party have gone from being a One Nation party to being a one issue party. Afraid to talk about the economy, embarrassed by the sheer ineptitude of their economic plan, unable to defend their unfair and elitist NHS and schools policies, unable to explain how they would finance the extra police they are promising, they are left with this one issue campaign on asylum and immigration. (Smith, 2005: 150)

The leaders' caustic remarks may have reflected the fact that they believed there was more at stake in the 2005 election than was the case four years earlier. In particular, the Conservatives began the 2005 campaign with high hopes of regaining power after eight years in the political wilderness. The bloom definitely was off New Labour's rose and polls conducted at the beginning of the campaign showed the two parties running neck and neck. With victory a realistic possibility, the Conservatives campaigned intensively. Sensing the public mood, Labour took the Tory threat seriously.

This chapter investigates the impact of the official or 'short' campaign on voting in the 2005 general election. In earlier work, we presented the cases for and against the proposition that campaigns influence voting behaviour and election outcomes (Clarke *et al.*, 2004b). This presentation was motivated by the controversial claim among political scientists in Britain, the United States and elsewhere that campaigns could be influential. Now, based on mounting empirical evidence, there is a growing consensus that campaigns can, and typically do, matter (e.g. Denver and Hands, 1997; Green and Gerber, 2004; Holbrook, 1996; Johnston *et al.*, 2004; Johnston and Pattie, 1995).

Interesting questions remain regarding how much campaigns matter. Here, we start to address these questions by reviewing major events in the 2005 election campaign, and by examining trends in public opinion over the thirty-day period of the official or 'short' campaign. Next, we discuss the 'ground war' – the campaign waged at the local level by candidates and party activists. In this section, we replicate and extend analyses developed to study the 2001 campaign (Clarke *et al.*, 2004b: Chapter 5). Then, we focus on the 'air war', that is, the national campaign conducted largely by party leaders and their strategists via the national media. The conclusion of the chapter reprises major findings and discusses their implications for understanding the impact of campaigns.

The 2005 election campaign

As usual, the political parties had been gearing up for the official campaign for months prior to its formal announcement. And, as discussed in Chapter 3, the parties had been waging a 'long campaign' for years, really since the last election in 2001. So the official campaign in 2005 was the last lap of a marathon race. The start of the campaign was originally planned for Monday, 4 April, but the death of Pope John Paul II and the wedding of the Prince of Wales put politics as usual on hold for several days and delayed the election announcement until Tuesday, 5 April (Smith, 2005: 13). The campaign did not officially start until parliament was dissolved on Monday, 11 April.

The campaign began badly for Tony Blair's Labour government. On 7 April, Patricia Hewitt, the Secretary of State for Trade and Industry, announced that the car firm MG Rover was bankrupt. The company was in negotiations with the Shanghai Automotive Industry Corporation about a take-over bid, but these talks collapsed. MG Rover was Britain's last domestically owned major car manufacturer, so its bankruptcy was a totemic event. When the workers at the Longbridge factory in Birmingham left at the end of the Friday shift, many of them thought that they would never return. The government took these events very seriously and Tony Blair telephoned the Chinese premier, Hu Jintao, to try to revive the rescue process, but to no avail.

The Conservatives were the first to launch their manifesto and, in the accompanying press conference, Michael Howard held aloft a set of handwritten slogans designed to summarize key messages. They were: 'More Police; Cleaner Hospitals; Lower Taxes; School Discipline; Controlled Immigration; Accountability'. The Conservative manifesto was short and punchy, but it created immediate problems for the party over the issue of taxation. It committed the Conservatives to £12 billion savings in government expenditure to make room for tax cuts. However, the manifesto was not specific about where the savings were to come from, apart from invoking old chestnuts about cutting waste and red tape. The failure to give specifics made it easy for Labour to raise the spectre of Thatcherism – reduced taxes would be accompanied by public service cuts. Voters were invited to believe Michael Howard was Mrs T redux.

Tony Blair helped to set the tone of the campaign with his response to the Conservative launch. He told reporters 'The simple point is that you cannot, as a matter of economics, spend more, tax less and borrow less all at the same time ... It's a fraudulent prospectus' (Smith, 2005: 19–20). Labour's manifesto was launched on Wednesday, 13 April, and Blair used the opportunity to remind everyone that it was his last election as prime minister. Arguably, this was an attempt to remove the sting of his own unpopularity (see Chapters 3 and 5), although he did promise to stay on as leader for the entire parliament should Labour win the election. Gordon Brown had a prominent role in the launch, and immediately played Labour's strongest card. In his speech, he asked: 'Are you better off than eight years ago?' (Smith, 2005: 45). Polls showed that the economy was Labour's strongest issue, and the Chancellor wanted to emphasize it from the start.

Charles Kennedy's campaign for the Liberal Democrats was delayed by the birth of his son. Menzies Campbell stood in for the party leader during his forty-eight hours of paternity leave. The twenty-page Liberal Democrat manifesto was called *The Real Alternative* and it was even briefer than the Conservative manifesto. At the launch, Kennedy claimed that his party had been the real opposition to the government over issues like Iraq, student top-up fees and compulsory ID cards. Unfortunately, he had not had much sleep, and he bungled questions from reporters over the impact of local income taxes, a key Liberal Democrat promise. Kennedy appeared not to know whether the tax would be revenue neutral in comparison with council tax, and he had to be rescued by the party's treasury spokesman, Vince Cable.

Figures 6.1A–6.1D show trends in voting intentions for the three major parties over the period of the official campaign. These numbers are generated by a Bayesian state-space model that pools the results of all published surveys conducted by seven major commercial polling agencies during the campaign.[1] The agencies are BPIX, CommR, ICM, MORI, NOP, Populus and YouGov. Results indicate that Labour and the Conservatives were very close together, with the Tories being slightly ahead (see Figure 6.1A), at the start. However, this quickly changed. By the middle of April, Labour had established a clear lead over the Conservatives, a lead which it never relinquished. Indeed, the polls indicate that Conservative support trended downward throughout the campaign – the correlation (r) between Conservative vote intentions and a linear trend term for day of campaign is fully –0.94. The Tories might have fared better if the election had been held the day it was called. The Liberal Democrat pattern was basically a mirror image of the Conservative one. Although Liberal Democrat support fell slightly at the outset of the campaign, it then began to increase, with the upward trend continuing until election day. The correlation (r) with a linear trend term is an impressive +0.97.

These Bayesian 'pooling the polls' analyses can be used to help determine whether there were significant movements in aggregate party support over the course of the campaign. We do this by observing whether a party's actual vote share at the end of the campaign is inside the 97.5% boundaries of the posterior probability distribution for the first day of the campaign. These boundaries are shown as dotted lines in Figures 6.1B, 6.1C and 6.1D. For the first day of the campaign, Labour's lower and upper boundaries were 33.3% and 36.6%, respectively, and the party's actual vote share on election

A. Vote intentions – Labour, Conservatives, Liberal Democrats

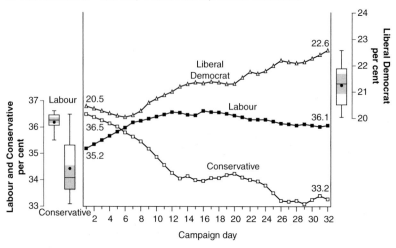

Campaign day

B. Labour vote intentions

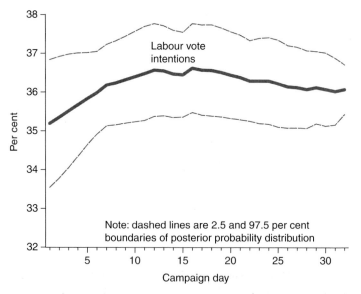

Campaign day

Figure 6.1 Dynamics of vote intentions during the 2005 general election campaign (*Source*: Bayesian pooled estimates of party support during each day of the 2005 general election. Data from BPIX, CommR, ICM, MORI, NOP, Populus and YouGov polls published during the campaign)

C. Conservative vote intentions

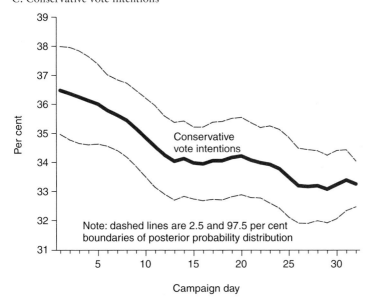

D. Liberal Democrat vote intentions

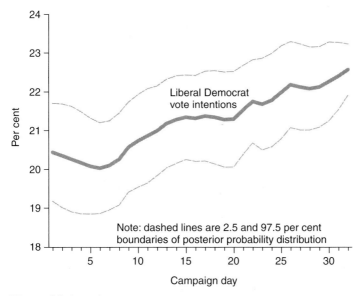

Figure 6.1 (*cont.*)

day was 36.1%. Since the vote share is inside the boundaries, the suggestion is that there may have been little, if any, real net movement in Labour support over the campaign. Conservative and Liberal Democrat results suggest significant campaign dynamics. In the Conservative case, first-day boundaries were 35% and 38.8%, and the party's actual vote total was 33.3% – well below the lower boundary. For the Liberal Democrats, the party's vote was 22.6%, above the upper boundary (21.7%) of its first-day support distribution.[2]

Figure 6.1C shows an interesting pattern in Conservative support. It appears that the initially sharp drop in the party's vote intention share was arrested by about the tenth day of the campaign. Then, on 19 April, Michael Howard launched his attack on Tony Blair as a liar, cited at the start of this chapter. Its impact was not what Mr Howard hoped. Shortly after his attack, Tory support began to slide downward again, with a comparison of Figures 6.1B and 6.1D suggesting that the Liberal Democrats, rather than Labour, benefited from the Tories' 'Bliar' attack. More attacks were on the way.

An exchange on the issue of crime, which occurred on 21 April, demonstrates how negative the 'air war' had become towards the end of the campaign. The Prime Minister announced that, 'We should get the facts straight. It is not just that crime overall has fallen. If you measure crime on the British Crime Survey violent crime has fallen too' (Smith, 2005: 139).

Michael Howard responded:

Tony Blair has quite simply lost the plot when it comes to crime. Just look at what he's been up to today – he's been patting himself on the back for the latest crime figures; trying to explain the problem away; even claiming that violent crime has fallen. Mr Blair – welcome to the real world. Violent crime has almost doubled and there are now a million violent crimes committed every year. I know: my wife Sandra and my daughter Larissa have both been mugged. (Smith, 2005: 145)

On the following day, Tony Blair attacked the Conservatives with the quote at the start of the chapter. So the negative exchanges between the party leaders had ratcheted up considerably by that stage. In this regard, we note that 85% of the 2005 BES respondents 'agreed' or 'strongly agreed' with the statement: 'Parties spend too much time bickering with each other.' This statistic clearly suggests that voters

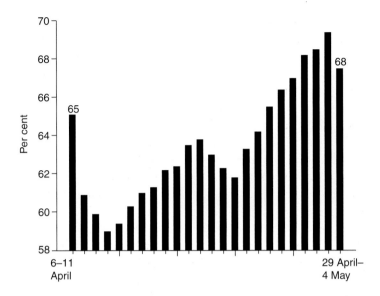

Figure 6.2 Percentages of respondents with maximum probability of voting, 2005 BES rolling campaign panel survey (*Note:* maximum probability of voting is defined as a score of 10 on a 0–10 likelihood of voting scale) (*Source:* 2005 BES rolling campaign panel survey, six-day moving averages)

dislike negative campaigning, and there is some evidence to suggest that attack politics demobilized people in 2005. Figure 6.2 displays data gathered in the 2005 BES rolling campaign panel survey (RCPS) on respondents' assessments of the probability that they would vote. The figure shows six-day moving averages over the campaign in the percentage scoring ten on a 0–10 likelihood of voting scale. The decline in this measure just after the bitter exchanges of late April is noteworthy. It subsequently bounced back but then dropped again just before polling day, which coincided with another attack on the prime minister by the Conservative leader. When Michael Howard was asked in an interview on GMTV two days before polling day if he regretted calling the Prime Minister a liar, he replied: 'What do you think is worse – calling someone a liar or taking us to war on a lie?' (Smith, 2005: 264). This answer linked the charge of lying to the Iraq War, both of which were strong negatives for Tony Blair.

The idea that negative campaigning can demobilize voters is given further credence when the BES RCPS data are employed to track

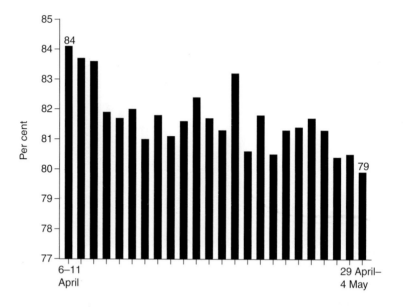

Figure 6.3 Percentages of respondents 'very' or 'somewhat' interested in election, 2005 BES rolling campaign panel survey (*Source*: 2005 BES rolling campaign panel survey, six-day moving averages)

trends in levels of public interest in the 2005 election campaign. Evolution of the daily moving averages indicates that large numbers of people were either very interested or fairly interested in the election and this remained true throughout (see Figure 6.3). However, interest declined over the month-long campaign, and there is an indication that the decline accelerated after the vituperative exchanges in late April. Despite a month of vigorous campaigning by the parties and massive media coverage, by polling day, fewer people were interested in the election than was the case at the start. This downward trend suggests that campaigns have the capacity to turn people off politics as much as to mobilize them.

Another important aspect of the 2005 campaign concerns public reactions to the party leaders. As demonstrated in Chapter 5, as is usual in British elections, leader images had important influences on voting behaviour in 2005. Figure 6.4 presents BES RCPS six-day moving averages to show how feelings about the leaders evolved over the campaign. Michael Howard and Tony Blair both began well

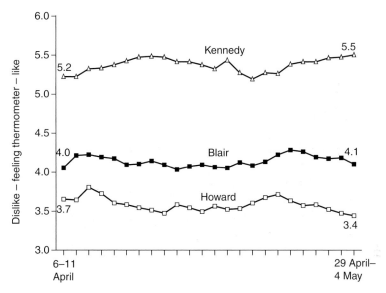

Figure 6.4 Feelings about party leaders, 2005 BES rolling campaign panel survey (*Source*: 2005 BES rolling campaign panel survey, six-day moving averages)

behind Charles Kennedy in the likeability stakes. Although Blair was marginally more popular than Howard, they were both well into the 'dislike zone' on the 0–10 'like–dislike' scale. Indeed, Howard's scores were very negative, rivalling those recorded by his predecessor, William Hague, during the 2001 campaign. As Figure 6.4 shows, neither Howard nor Blair gained in public affection as the campaign progressed. In contrast, Charles Kennedy made modest gains. Starting well ahead of his chief rivals, he remained there until polling day. Although Kennedy did not generate strong enthusiasm in the electorate, he was substantially more popular than Blair and Howard, both of whom were disliked by many voters.

An important event, which took place on 28 April, was the closest thing to a direct debate between the party leaders in the election. It was a BBC television programme in which the leaders answered questions from an invited audience. The BES rolling campaign survey conducted after the broadcast recorded that 28% of respondents saw the programme and, since it was widely reported in the media, it had the potential to influence many other voters as

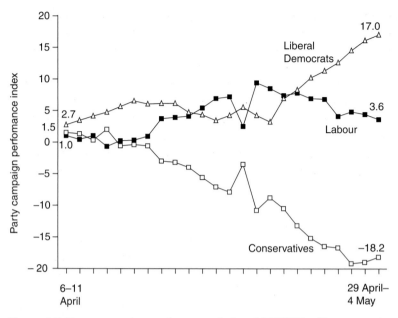

Figure 6.5 Party campaign performance index, 2005 BES rolling campaign panel survey (*Note*: index = per cent stating party is performing best in campaign minus per cent stating party is performing worst (*Source*: 2005 BES rolling campaign panel survey, six-day moving averages)

well. Tony Blair stumbled badly when a questioner claimed that doctors were refusing to make appointments more than forty-eight hours ahead of time, in order to meet government targets. 'I'm absolutely astonished at that' said the Prime Minister (Smith, 2005: 222). The idea that doctors might try to 'game the system' to satisfy bureaucratic directives evidently was not one that he had ever considered. A subsequent BES question revealed that 41% thought Charles Kennedy was most effective in the debate, 27% gave the honours to Michael Howard, and only 20% thought Tony Blair came off best.

Figure 6.5 displays the dynamics of voters' verdicts on which parties conducted the best and worst campaigns. At the outset, the three parties were level pegging, with the percentage judging that a particular party was performing best being only slightly greater than the percentage judging it was performing worst. However, things quickly changed, with the balance of opinion about the Liberal

Democrats becoming increasingly positive. In mid-campaign, the Liberal Democrats and Labour briefly traded places, with the latter party moving slightly ahead. Then, in the closing phase of the race – starting the day after Blair's dismal performance in the televised question-and-answer session – the Liberal Democrats regained momentum and surged ahead of Labour. As voters prepared to go to the polls, the Liberal Democrats were seen as clear winners in the campaign, with the percentage who thought that they had performed best outweighing the percentage who thought they had done worst by a very comfortable 17%. The comparable figure for Labour was less than 4%.

Views of the Conservative campaign were very different. As Figure 6.5 shows, public opinion about the quality of its performance trended sharply downward as the campaign progressed, with the correlation (r) between the party's campaign performance index and day of campaign being –0.97. On the eve of the election, there was a twenty percentage point difference between voters who said that the Conservatives had run the worst campaign and those saying that they had run the best one.

Figure 6.6 illustrates how the BES RCPS respondents judged the party leaders' campaign performance. As the figure shows, evaluations of the leaders were quite similar to those of the parties. For example, Liberal Democrat leader Charles Kennedy quickly established himself as the best performer, before being overtaken by Tony Blair in mid-campaign. However, very soon after the leaders' televised question-and-answer session, Kennedy regained the lead. He did not falter afterwards, with his net approval trending sharply upward as the campaign drew to a close. In contrast, the balance of opinion about Blair finished at a negative –1.8%, a number very similar to what he had at the outset. Michael Howard's numbers reinforce the idea that the campaign was a disaster for the Conservatives. His net performance ratings ramped downward, becoming increasingly worse as the election approached (r = –0.96). At the end of the campaign, his performance index score was a dismal –19.4%. Clearly, the Conservative leader, like his party, had lost the campaign in the eyes of the electorate. In the next section, we investigate these campaign dynamics in terms of which factors had important effects on party support trajectories. We begin by examining the campaign in the constituencies – the 'ground war'.

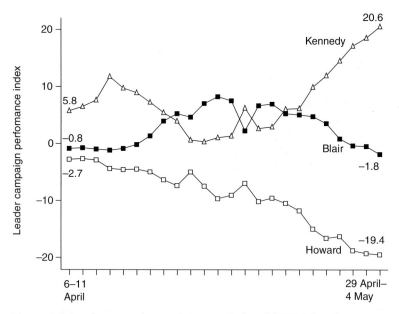

Figure 6.6 Leader campaign performance index, 2005 BES rolling campaign panel survey (*Note*: index = per cent stating leader is doing best job in campaign minus per cent stating leader is doing worst job) (*Source*: 2005 BES rolling campaign panel survey, six-day moving averages)

Local campaigns and the 'ground war' in 2005

Local election campaigns involve various activities, such as canvassing and leafleting voters, preparing and printing party manifestoes, arranging speaking events for candidates, organizing transport, setting up and running committee rooms, issuing press releases and publicity materials, and running local election-related events. Part of the funding for these activities comes from the national party organizations, and it is likely to be generous when a constituency is on a target list of winnable seats. But a substantial portion of the funds is raised and spent at the local level by party volunteers, particularly in safe seats. The legal framework that regulates spending on local elections has long been quite restrictive and spending limits are strict. In 2005, the average constituency included just under 69,000 electors and the maximum spending allowed per party was £11,359 (Electoral Commission, 2005).

A recurring theme in research on local campaigns has been the extent to which political parties focus their efforts on marginal seats.

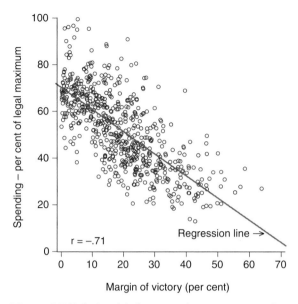

Figure 6.7 Relationship between three-party constituency-level campaign spending and marginality, 2005 general election (*Source*: Electoral Commission, 2005)

As is well known, under the first-past-the-post electoral system it pays to concentrate spending and other forms of campaigning in winnable seats. Figure 6.7 shows the relationship between constituency spending as a percentage of the maximum allowed by the three major parties and seat marginality in 2005. The correlation between these two measures is very strong (–0.71), indicating that the political parties were much more likely to spend money in marginal seats than in safe ones. Of course, the 2005 margin of victory reflects parties' 2005 campaign efforts, as well as longer-term forces acting in various constituencies. However, marginality in a particular election is strongly related to information about marginality in a preceding election that parties have available to them when a campaign begins. In this regard, the correlation between 2005 and 2001 marginality in England and Wales is fully +0.80. Scotland cannot be included in this calculation because Scottish constituency boundaries were redrawn prior to the 2005 election.

Our earlier research shows that constituency spending in the 2001 election reflected an interaction between the marginality of the seat and a party's incumbent or challenger status (Clarke *et al.*, 2004b: 157). In that election, incumbents tended to spend heavily in most seats whether they were marginal or not, whereas challengers tended to concentrate their spending in seats where competition was expected to be close. In this sense, all parties were keen to defend their territory regardless of how safe it was, but were much more selective about spending in the seats they were trying to capture.

Table 6.1 shows the relationship between campaign spending and the marginality of seats in 2005 in different types of contests. The pattern observed in 2001 of challengers spending selectively in comparison with incumbents was repeated in 2005. This is illustrated in the 114 seats where Labour challenged an incumbent Conservative. The correlation between marginality and spending by the Conservatives is −0.31 in these seats, which indicates that they spent somewhat more in their marginal seats than in their safe seats. However, the

Table 6.1 *Correlations between seat marginality and party spending by constituency battlegrounds in 2005*

Correlation (r) between seat marginality and:

Constituency battleground	Conservative spending	Labour spending	Liberal Democrat spending	N
Conservative held, Labour second	−0.31	−0.66	−0.29	114
Labour held, Conservative second	−0.77	−0.47	−0.34	221
Conservative held, Liberal Democrat second	−0.44	+0.23	−0.76	83
Liberal Democrat held, Conservative second	−0.40	+0.07	−0.19	43
Labour held, Liberal Democrat second	−0.39	−0.42	−0.72	106
Liberal Democrat held, Labour second	−0.19	−0.91	−0.80	18

Source: Electoral Commission, 2005.

correlation for Labour in these seats is −0.66, indicating that the party spent much more in marginal Conservative constituencies than in Tory strongholds. The same pattern exists in Labour-held seats where the main challenger was a Conservative or a Liberal Democrat. In the 221 Labour-held constituencies where a Conservative was the main challenger, the correlations between spending and marginality were −0.47 for Labour and −0.77 for the Conservatives. Although Labour was somewhat more willing to spend money in its marginals than in its safe seats, the Conservatives were very much more willing to do so. They knew that spending money in safe Labour seats was a waste of resources, and so they poured the money into Labour marginals.

As Table 6.1 documents, the exception to this pattern occurred in Liberal Democrat seats. In the forty-three Liberal Democrat constituencies challenged by the Conservatives, the Liberal Democrats spent relatively evenly – the correlation between marginality and spending being only −0.19. However, the equivalent correlation for the Conservatives was −0.40, indicating that their spending in Liberal Democrat marginals was higher than their spending in the safe seats, but not overwhelmingly so. There is a simple explanation for this; the Conservatives spent close to the maximum in most of these seats, because many of them were lost to the Liberal Democrats in 1997, and Tory strategists clearly thought that their party might regain them. Also noteworthy in Table 6.1 are the eighteen Liberal Democrat seats where Labour was the main challenger. Here, the Liberal Democrats spent very much less in their own safe seats than in their marginals. This reflects the fact that four of these were very safe Liberal Democrat seats in the Highlands of Scotland and in Orkney and Shetlands. The party was confident that they could retain these constituencies regardless of how much, or little, it spent on campaigning.

Thus far, we have examined party campaigning at the constituency level, but we can also examine the impact of local campaigning at the level of the individual voter. Respondents in the BES post-election survey were asked if they had been canvassed by a political party either on the doorstep or by telephone, and also if they had been reminded to vote on polling day. Percentages of respondents citing each type of contact in 2005 are presented in Figure 6.8. The percentage who reported being canvassed in 2005 was approximately the same as in 2001. In that election, 29% of those in marginal seats said that they

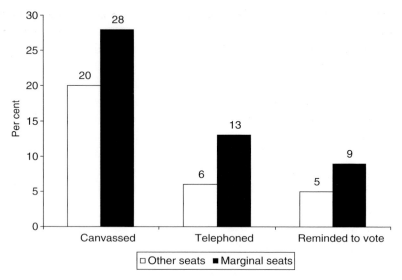

Figure 6.8 Percentages of voters contacted by parties' local campaigns in 2005 general election (*Note*: A marginal seat is defined as one in which the gap between the winning and second-place party is less than 10 per cent) (*Source*: 2005 BES post-election survey)

were canvassed on the doorstep, compared with 28% four years later. However, fewer people were reached by telephone canvassing in 2005 than in the earlier election, although the numbers reminded to vote on the day were very similar. There is also clear evidence that campaigning was more intensive in marginal seats in 2005, something which was also true in 2001. In 2005, voters in the marginals were significantly more likely to be canvassed face-to-face, about twice as likely to be phoned, and almost twice as likely to be reminded to cast a ballot than were electors in safer seats.

Table 6.2 provides information on the campaigning activities of various parties in 2005. Unlike 2001, the Conservatives were more active than Labour in 2005, since they succeeded in reaching more than half of the people who reported being canvassed, while Labour reached only four out of ten. The Liberal Democrats contacted just under a third of all those canvassed, and again this was down on their performance in 2001. The Nationalist parties also reached fewer people than they did in the earlier election.[3] As regards telephone canvassing, the Conservatives did much more than in 2001

Table 6.2 *Exposure to local campaigning in 2005 general election*

Of the 21.5 per cent canvassed face-to-face, the following were:	Percentages
Canvassed by Labour	40
Canvassed by Conservatives	52
Canvassed by Liberal Democrats	28
Canvassed by the SNP (in Scotland)	30
Canvassed by Plaid Cymru (in Wales)	28
Of the 7.5 per cent telephoned by a party, the following were:	
Telephoned by Labour	40
Telephoned by Conservatives	46
Telephoned by Liberal Democrats	13
Of the 5.5 per cent reminded to vote on polling day, the following were:	
Reminded to vote by Labour	44
Reminded to vote by the Conservatives	28
Reminded to vote by the Liberal Democrats	21

Source: 2005 BES post-election survey.

whereas Labour did less. But once again, Labour succeeded in reaching more electors on polling day to remind them to vote than did the Conservatives. Overall, this evidence suggests that the Conservatives put in a greater effort to reach individual voters than four years previously, and in this respect they out-campaigned Labour.

We have seen how the parties campaigned at the local level during the 2005 general election, but what difference did this all make? The potential for the campaign to prove decisive is suggested by the finding that over one-third of the 2005 BES respondents who voted reported making their decision during the official campaign, and another 14% said they did so shortly beforehand. As Figure 6.9 illustrates, the number of people deciding during the official campaign was 10% more than it was in 2001. The number of reported campaign deciders was also very substantial (24%) in that year, thereby reinforcing the general point that campaigns can be influential and that 2005 was not unique in this regard.

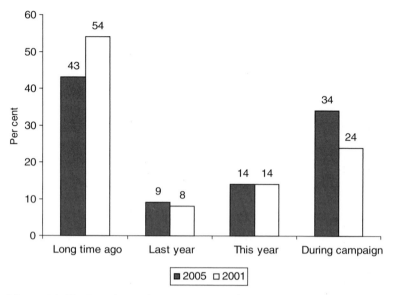

Figure 6.9 Timing of vote decision, 2001 and 2005 general elections
(*Source*: 2001 and 2005 BES post-election surveys)

The BES panel data provide additional support for this point. Comparing respondents' voting intentions in the pre-campaign survey with their reported voting behaviour in the post-election survey shows that Labour made significant advances during the campaign (see Table 6.3). Before the campaign began, slightly less than 20% said that they intended to vote Labour. In the event, almost 27% actually did so. The Liberal Democrats made sizable gains as well – although their pre-campaign vote intention share was only 6.7%, after the election 15.4% reported casting a Liberal Democrat ballot. In contrast, Conservative gains were much smaller, with the party's pre-campaign and post-election percentages being 18.2 and 22.3, respectively. This relatively modest increase, in comparison with what their competitors achieved, provides further evidence that the Tories' 2005 campaign essentially did not work.

The data in Table 6.3 emphasize the scope of campaign influence during the 2005 election. Almost half (46.7%) of those interviewed in the BES pre-campaign survey said they were undecided but, in the end, only about one-third of them (32.6%) did not vote. Labour did best among the undecideds, securing the support of 24.4% of them. Other

Table 6.3 *Pre-campaign vote intentions and voting behaviour in 2005 (vertical percentages)*

				Pre-campaign vote intentions			
	Labour	Conservative	Liberal Democrat	Other party	Undecided	Will not vote	Total vote
Actual vote							
Labour	70.5%	2.3%	6.7%	10.3%	24.4%	5.7%	26.8
Conservative	0.2	73.4	2.1	3.4	18.4	2.6	22.3
Liberal Democrat	1.8	3.4	66.0	12.1	19.7	7.8	15.4
Other party	0.9	0.6	2.6	51.7	4.9	1.6	3.9
Did not vote	26.6	20.3	22.7	22.4	32.6	82.4	31.7
Total							
Vote intention	19.7	18.2	6.7	2.0	46.7	6.7	

Source: 2005 BES pre- and post-election panel survey.

parties did not fare quite as well – the Liberal Democrats attracted 19.7% of the undecideds and the Conservatives, 18.4%. Direct transfers between the parties over the course of the campaign were rare. Only 2.3% of the pre-campaign Conservatives switched to Labour, and there was only one recorded case of a pre-campaign Labour supporter defecting to the Conservatives. In total, less than 3% of the BES panellists voted for a party other than the one they mentioned in their pre-campaign interview. This latter figure underscores the point that the campaign was mostly about persuading people who had not made up their minds before the contest officially began. There were many such people in 2005. In the next section, we analyse multivariate voting models to determine how effective the parties' campaigns were.

Modelling campaign effects: the 'ground war'

Above, we show that political parties conduct vigorous local campaigns in marginal seats, although this varies to some extent depending on the particular pattern of party competition. The classic approach to modelling campaign effects was developed by Finkel (1993, 1995) who used panel data to analyse the influence of campaigns on the vote. In the case of turnout, his approach suggests that we incorporate a likelihood of voting variable from a pre-election wave of a panel survey as a predictor in a turnout model. This likelihood of voting variable controls for factors that might explain turnout, but that operate prior to the start of the campaign. Other predictor variables are then added to the specification from the post-election wave of the panel. If a given predictor variable is statistically significant, then it means that some portion of its influence on turnout occurred during the election campaign.

Here, the campaign mobilization measures are the party campaign variables of the type discussed above (see Table 6.2) and measured after the official campaign was over.[4] They are used to model individual-level turnout and party choice together with additional predictor variables derived from the models in Chapter 5. As illustrated in Figure 6.7 above, parties campaign with different levels of intensity in different types of seats. To take these contextual effects into account, we extend and develop the Finkel approach by using a multilevel modelling strategy (Raudenbusch and Byrk, 2002; Snijders and Bosker, 1999). Multilevel models have the following general specification:

Individual level

$$Y_{ij} = \beta_{0j} + \beta 1_j \, X1_{ij} + \beta 2_j \, X2_{ij} + \ldots + \beta k_j \, Xk_{ij} + r_{ij}$$

where:
Y_{ij} is probability of individual i voting
β_{ij} are individual-level model coefficients
Xk_{ij} are individual-level predictor variables
r_{ij} is an individual-level error term

Aggregate level

$$\beta_{ij} = \gamma_{q0} + \gamma_{q1} \, W_{1j} + \gamma_{q2} \, W_{2j} + \gamma_{q3} \, W_{3j} \ldots + \gamma_{q4} \, W_{sj} + u_{qj}$$

where:
β_{ij} is the ith coefficient from the jth day of the official campaign
(For example, β_{0j} is the intercept coefficient in the individual-level model)
γ_{qj} are coefficients of the aggregate-level covariates
W_{ij} are aggregate-level covariates
u_{qj} is an aggregate-level error term

The model as shown has two levels. Additional levels also can be specified.

A multilevel modelling approach makes it possible to evaluate the effects of individual- and aggregate-level variables on turnout and party choice at the same time. In the case of the campaign ground war, the aggregate units of analysis are the constituencies that constituted the primary sampling units in the 2005 BES panel survey. This is a necessary modification of the basic Finkel approach because a key determinant of party campaigning is constituency spending which occurs and is measured at the aggregate level.

The impact of constituency spending on turnout and party choice is examined in two ways. The first uses a random intercept model in which aggregate-level constituency spending can shift the intercept of the individual-level turnout model. If, for example, there is a significant positive relationship between total constituency spending by the parties and the intercept of the individual-level turnout model, then it implies that spending directly influences the probability that an individual will vote. The second approach is a random slopes model in which a cross-level interaction between the constituency spending variable and the party campaigning variable is estimated. A positive impact of spending on the slope coefficient of the campaigning variable means that the effects of activities, such as canvassing and telephoning voters, are boosted by levels of campaign spending in a given constituency.

The multilevel turnout model is analysed using the 2005 BES RCPS data. Results are shown in Table 6.4. Model specification is guided by the results of analysing a logistic model of turnout (see Chapter 5, Table 5.7). All of the indicators in this model were included in the initial multilevel specification but then omitted if they were not statistically significant. Unlike the version in Table 5.7, the multilevel turnout model contains the probability of voting in the pre-campaign wave of the RCPS survey. This explains why many variables that are significant predictors in the earlier version are not significant in the present one. Their impact occurs prior to the start of the official campaign (when likelihood of voting is measured) and not in the

Table 6.4 *Multilevel binomial logistic regression analyses of turnout in the 2005 general election*

	Model A	Probabilities	Model B
Aggregate-level model	γ		γ
Total campaign spending	–	–	−0.001
Party mobilization *			
Campaign spending	–	–	0.01**
Individual-level model	β		β
Probability of voting	0.18***	0.41	0.18***
Party mobilization	0.29***	0.15	−0.46
Influence discounted benefits	0.03**	0.24	0.03**
Civic duty	0.28***	0.47	0.28***
Political knowledge	0.18***	0.30	0.19***
Perceived personal benefits	0.10*	0.16	0.10***
Age	0.01***	0.19	0.01***
Gender	−0.27**	−0.05	−0.28**
Social class	0.49***	0.10	0.49***
McFadden R^2		0.28	

– variable not included in model.
*** – $p \leq 0.001$, ** – $p \leq 0.01$, * – $p \leq 0.05$; one-tailed test.
Source: 2005 BES pre- and post-election panel survey.

campaign itself. In the model in Table 6.4, we focus solely on variables that influence turnout during the official campaign.

The first model in Table 6.4 (Model A) is the individual-level model with no aggregate covariates but with a random intercept specification. This allows the model intercept to vary across constituencies, which controls for contextual factors that might generate differences in individual turnout. The second column shows the impact of each of the coefficients in this model on the probability of voting.[5] Not surprisingly, the prior probability of voting had a very strong effect on turnout, but civic duty had an even stronger impact. This, in turn, suggests that sense of citizen duty was heavily influenced by the election campaign and this helps to explain why many people voted, despite the campaign's oftentimes negative tone. Other important variables were political knowledge and the influence-discounted collective benefits measure from the general incentives model. Party mobilization was important too. It has exactly the same effect on the probability of voting in this model as it does in the composite turnout model in Table 5.7. And, controlling for all of these factors, age, gender and social class also have significant effects – older people, women and middle-class people were more likely to go to the polls.

Model A recognizes contextual variation but does not identify its causes. The third column in Table 6.4 (Model B) incorporates aggregate party spending covariates into the turnout model. Since these constituency spending variables are closely related to constituency marginality, they proxy local levels of both competition and campaign effort. The aggregate level of this model contains a random intercept effect and a cross-level interaction between party mobilization and campaign spending. Estimates reveal that there were no intercept-related effects associated with campaign spending. Thus, the measure did not have a direct effect on the probability that someone would vote. However, there was a significant interaction between the party mobilization variable at the individual level and constituency spending at the aggregate level. The positive coefficient means that the mobilizing activities of parties had a bigger impact on turnout when they were accompanied by high levels of local party spending. Constituency spending and individual voter mobilization are complementary activities. The former measures capital input into campaigning in the form of spending on publicity, leaflets, meetings and the like, and the latter measures labour input into the campaign, that is, it focuses on labour-intensive activities like canvassing and tele-phoning. Both capital and labour inputs jointly enhance campaign effectiveness.

Party mobilization measures are not the only campaign-related factors that contribute to turnout. Table 6.4, Model B shows that influence-discounted collective benefits, civic duty, personal benefits and political knowledge are influential and, again, older, middle-class persons were more likely to cast a ballot. The extent to which parties affect these variables may vary, and several effects have to do with the proximity of the election which can awaken a sense of civic duty and influence potential voters in other ways. However, the official election campaign clearly works to mobilize older, higher status and politic-ally knowledgeable individuals to turn out on polling day.

We next consider how the ground war affected party choice. Table 6.5 contains parameter estimates for the multilevel logistic Labour voting model. Once again, the first column (Model A) con-tains estimates of the random intercept version and the second column identifies the effects of the predictor variables on the probability of casting a Labour ballot. Not surprisingly, pre-election Labour vote intentions have a highly significant statistical effect on actual Labour voting. As expected, key variables in the valence politics model dis-cussed in earlier chapters also were very influential. Labour identifi-cation boosted, and Conservative and Liberal Democrat identification reduced, Labour voting. With respect to leader images, there were Blair and Howard effects, but no Charles Kennedy effect. Similarly, the economy and party best able to handle a voter's most important issue influenced Labour support, as did attitudes to the National Health Service. However, only two of the party mobilization measures are significant, those for Labour and the Liberal Democrats. Conservative campaign activities did not influence the probability of Labour vot-ing. The Conservatives may have out-campaigned Labour in some respects, as the earlier analyses indicate, but this does not appear to have directly affected the likelihood of casting a Labour ballot.

The third column (Model B) in Table 6.5 incorporates the cam-paign spending measures into the model. It can be seen that Labour, Liberal Democrat and Nationalist campaign spending in Scotland and Wales all had predictable impacts on the probability of voting Labour. Unlike the turnout model of Table 6.4, there were no signifi-cant cross-level interactions between the campaign variables and the

Table 6.5 *Multilevel binomial logistic regression analyses of Labour voting in the 2005 general election*

	Model A	Probabilities	Model B
Aggregate-level model	γ		γ
Labour campaign spending	–	–	0.004*
Conservative campaign spending	–	–	0.003
Liberal Democrat campaign spending	–	–	−0.011***
Nationalist campaign spending	–	–	−0.006*
Individual-level model	β		β
Labour pre-election voting intentions	1.00***	0.13	0.98***
Labour identification	1.45***	0.18	1.45***
Conservative identification	−1.09***	−0.09	−1.00***
Liberal Democrat identification	−1.28***	−0.09	−1.23***
Blair leader affect	0.16***	0.17	0.17***
Howard leader affect	−0.10***	−0.09	−0.10***
Labour best on most important issue	0.36***	0.04	0.38***
Conservatives best on most important issue	−0.82***	−0.07	−0.85***
Emotional reactions to the NHS	0.18***	0.15	0.18***
Labour best on economy	0.68***	0.07	0.66***
Labour issue proximity	0.05*	0.10	0.05*
Tactical voting	0.71*	0.09	0.77**
Labour mobilization	0.32***	0.19	0.27***
Liberal Democrat mobilization	−0.38***	−0.11	−0.33**
Social class	0.57***	0.06	0.61***
McFadden R^2		0.45	

– variable not included in model.
*** – $p \leq 0.001$, ** – $p \leq 0.01$, * – $p \leq 0.05$; one-tailed test.
Source: 2005 BES pre- and post-election panel survey and Electoral Commission.

Table 6.6 *Multilevel binomial logistic regression analyses of Conservative voting in the 2005 general election*

	Model A	Probabilities	Model B
Aggregate-level model	γ		γ
Labour campaign spending	–	–	–0.006*
Conservative campaign spending	–	–	0.017***
Liberal Democrat campaign spending	–	–	–0.007*
Nationalist campaign spending	–	–	–0.007*
Individual-level model	β		β
Conservative pre-election voting intentions	0.77***	0.05	0.78***
Labour identification	–1.54***	–0.08	–1.50***
Conservative identification	1.87***	0.16	1.87***
Liberal Democrat identification	–0.87***	–0.04	–0.87***
Blair leader affect	–0.17***	–0.10	–0.18***
Howard leader affect	0.29***	–0.22	0.30***
Liberal Democrat best on most important issue	–1.01**	–0.04	–1.10**
Labour issue proximity	–0.05**	–0.16	–0.07**
Conservative issue proximity	0.15***	0.13	0.15***
Tactical voting	0.82***	0.03	0.85**
Labour mobilization	0.42***	0.19	0.36***
Liberal Democrat mobilization	0.02***	0.14	0.02***
Social class	0.93***	0.05	0.87***
McFadden R^2		0.58	

– variable not included in model.
*** – $p \leq 0.001$, ** – $p \leq 0.01$, * – $p \leq 0.05$; one-tailed test.
Source: 2005 BES pre- and post-election panel survey and Electoral Commission.

spending variables. So the best specification for Labour voting was the random intercept model.

Table 6.6 displays estimates for the Conservative multilevel logistic voting model. The results resemble their Labour counterparts. In Model A, the party identification variables emerge as prominent predictors with the expected signs. There are also Blair and Howard effects but, as expected, the signs are opposite to those for the Labour vote model. Although Charles Kennedy did not appear to influence the Conservative vote during the campaign, it is apparent that the anticipated performance of the Liberal Democrats on a voter's most important issue did have an influence. In addition, the Labour and Conservative issue proximity measures are significant with the expected signs. Finally, Conservative mobilization influenced the party vote, but the campaigning efforts of the other parties had little effect.

In the third column (Model B) of Table 6.6, the multilevel estimates show that all of the aggregate spending measures influenced Conservative voting. Spending by the Conservatives paid off in terms of winning votes, whereas spending by Labour, the Liberal Democrats and the Nationalist parties had the expected effects of reducing the probability of voting Conservative. Not surprisingly, the Conservative spending variable had the strongest impact, but there were no significant cross-level interactions between this variable and the Conservative party mobilization measure.

Finally, Table 6.7 contains estimates of the multilevel logistic Liberal Democrat voting model. Once again, Model A shows that partisanship and leadership variables were important predictors with the correct signs. Not surprisingly, Charles Kennedy had a big impact on the probability of voting Liberal Democrat despite his absence from the Labour and Conservative models. The most important issue indicators for all three parties played significant roles as well, as did the Liberal Democrat issue proximity measure. Tactical voting was more important in influencing the Liberal Democrat vote than it was in the models for the other parties, and this was another mechanism by which local campaigning mobilized votes. *Pace* conjectures about the 'unwinding' of tactical voting in 2005, tactical considerations worked as they did in 1997 and 2001 – favouring the Liberal Democrats. Finally, Liberal Democrat and Labour mobilization activities influenced the likelihood of supporting the Liberal Democrats, but Conservative mobilization activities had little effect.

The main difference between the Liberal Democrat model and the models for the other parties relates to the campaign spending measures. Liberal Democrat campaign spending had a very significant impact on the party vote, but the Conservative and Labour spending variables did not (Model B). It appears that the Liberal Democrats can mobilize their own voters, but these supporters are not influenced by the spending activities of the other parties, with the sole exception of the Nationalist parties. Spending by the latter in Scotland and

Table 6.7 *Multilevel binomial logistic regression analyses of Liberal Democrat voting in the 2005 general election*

	Model A	Probabilities	Model B
Aggregate-level model	γ		γ
Labour campaign spending	–	–	0.001
Conservative campaign spending	–	–	–0.001
Liberal Democrat campaign spending	–	–	0.015***
Nationalist campaign spending	–	–	–0.008**
Individual-level model	β		β
Liberal Democrat pre-election voting intentions	1.27***	0.14	1.19***
Labour identification	–0.90***	–0.05	–0.91***
Conservative identification	–1.48***	–0.07	–1.55***
Liberal Democrat identification	1.47***	0.16	1.39***
Other party identification	–0.81**	–0.04	–0.74**
Blair leader affect	–0.12***	0.07	–0.12***
Howard leader affect	–0.14***	–0.10	–0.15***
Kennedy leader affect	0.35***	0.25	0.38***
Labour best on most important issue	–0.41***	–0.02	–0.40*
Conservative best on most important issue	–0.75***	–0.04	–0.71**
Liberal Democrat best on most important issue	0.69***	0.06	0.71**
Liberal Democrat issue proximity	0.14***	0.13	0.15***
Tactical voting	1.08***	0.10	1.06***
Labour mobilization	–0.49***	–0.08	–0.42*
Liberal Democrat mobilization	0.65***	0.40	0.54***
Age	0.01***	0.08	0.01***
Ethnicity	0.89***	0.04	0.97***
McFadden R^2		0.40	

– variable not included in model.
*** – $p \leq 0.001$, ** – $p \leq 0.01$, * – $p \leq 0.05$; one-tailed test.
Source: 2005 BES pre- and post-election panel survey and Electoral Commission.

Wales reduced the probability of supporting the Liberal Democrats, suggesting that the effects of party campaign activities in these countries were rather different from England.

Overall, the results displayed in Tables 6.5, 6.6 and 6.7 indicate that there were significant campaign components in the effects of major predictors of electoral choice. Key variables in the valence politics model such as partisanship, leader images and party preferences on most important issues all exert significant effects net of controls for pre-campaign vote intentions. Party mobilization measures – operating during the campaign – were important as well, although they did not affect all parties in the same way. Party campaigns also were heavily influenced by the marginality of constituencies and this affected both spending and campaigning on the ground. Although these several results testify to the importance of the 2005 campaign, the analyses do not directly take into account the other important aspect of the election campaign – the 'air war'. We turn to this next.

Modelling campaign effects: the 'air war'

As discussed earlier, the 'air war' refers to the national campaigns in the media run by the parties' central organizations. The air war places party leaders at the centre of the political stage, and makes them the primary focal points of intense media scrutiny. Leaders' pronouncements and their comings and goings on the campaign trail are much of what constitutes election news. One important indicator of the reach of the air war is the number of electors who viewed party political broadcasts during the campaign. As shown in Figure 6.10, about seven out of ten BES respondents saw one or more of these broadcasts, the great majority seeing a Labour or Conservative broadcast. The Liberal Democrats reached significantly fewer people than their main rivals, and the minor parties reached many fewer people still, in part because they had fewer broadcasts. It is interesting to note that the Greens reached more people than UKIP, even though they ended up with a much smaller vote.[6] Only about one person in twenty saw a BNP broadcast. As for the Nationalist parties, the SNP was clearly more effective at reaching Scottish voters than Plaid Cymru was at reaching its Welsh counterparts. Still only a minority of Scottish respondents reported seeing an SNP 'party political'.

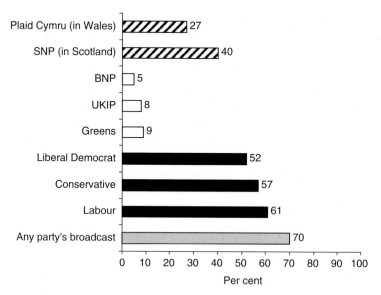

Figure 6.10 Exposure to party political broadcasts during the 2005 election campaign (*Source*: 2005 BES post-election survey)

A different strategy is needed for modelling the air war than the ground war. The air war can only be evaluated over time, since different parts of the country receive broadly the same campaign information at any one point of time. Again, the analysis can be implemented using a multilevel modelling approach, but now the aggregate-level units are not constituencies but rather days of the campaign. The BES rolling campaign panel survey (RCPS) ran from 6 April to 4 May 2005 and each day can be regarded as a unique context in which to examine turnout and party support.[7] Once again the Finkel-style model specification can be adapted to the task of identifying campaign effects. As before, we control for influences on turnout and party support which occurred prior to the campaign by including measures of the likelihood of voting and which party respondents intended to vote for taken from the first (baseline) wave of the campaign panel survey. This wave of interviewing was completed shortly before the official campaign began.

The starting point for this dynamic analysis of turnout is again the composite model from Table 5.7 in Chapter 5. It will be recalled that its key predictors are derived from the general incentives and cognitive engagement models. Once again, we replicate the composite model presented in Chapter 5 with the campaign survey data and retain statistically significant predictors. The replication is not exact because some predictor variables based on the campaign survey differ from those used in the pre/post BES face-to-face panel survey. The campaign surveys had to be shorter and more compact than the main pre/post panel survey, and so single rather than multiple indicators were used in several instances. In addition, the dependent variable for turnout in the daily campaign surveys is the probability of voting scale summarized in Figure 6.2, rather than the validated turnout measure in the face-to-face pre/post panel survey.

To estimate the effects of campaigning on turnout during the official campaign, we again use a random intercepts model. In this case, the aggregate-level covariates are used to predict variations in the model intercept across the thirty days of the campaign (Raudenbusch and Byrk, 2002: 299). The aggregate covariates included in the model are related to key events in the campaign discussed earlier in this chapter. First, a 'campaign launch' variable is included in the turnout model in the form of a dummy variable which scores one from 6 April to 12 April and zero otherwise. This variable is designed to tap the mobilizing effects associated with the start of the official campaign. It covers the days between the formal announcement of the election and the actual start of the campaign, and thereby captures the effect of the announcement rather than any specific campaign activities. The second event was the Rover car crisis which took on a value of one on 12 and 13 April, and zero otherwise. As the earlier discussion indicated, the announcement of the company's bankruptcy was made just before the start of the campaign, but it was a prominent news item, and the Longbridge car workers planned a protest rally in Downing Street when the campaign began (Smith, 2005: 24).

A third important event was Michael Howard's accusation that Tony Blair was a liar, first made on 19 April but repeated later in the campaign. The variable was scored one from 20 April through 25 April, and zero otherwise. All three of these variables are designed to capture temporary effects of events that occurred during the campaign. However, the fourth event variable is different because it occurred late in the campaign and therefore had the potential to influence the election outcome. This variable measures the impact of the leaders' 'question-and-answer' television broadcast discussed earlier.

This event occurred on 28 April, and so the variable is scored one from 29 April to 4 May, which covers the period up to polling day.

These aggregate covariates are related to specific events and so are captured by dummy variables. But an additional covariate is included in the turnout model to examine a key contextual influence on voting. This is strength of macropartisanship, or the proportion of electors with 'very strong' or 'fairly strong' partisan attachments. It might be conjectured that strength of macropartisanship moves upwards as an election approaches. The atmosphere becomes increasingly charged with partisan symbols and partisan discourse as polling day draws near. Thus, the campaign activates the latent partisanship of some people and strengthens the partisan attachments of others.[8] However, recognizing that campaign events can demobilize as well as mobilize voters, one might hypothesize that strength of macropartisanship has a more general dynamic, and can wane as well as wax depending upon the nature of particular campaigns. In the event, it is reasonable to suppose that aggregate changes in the strength of macropartisanship affect the probability that people will vote. The effect of this variable can be evaluated by adding it to the aggregate-level model, while at the same time taking into account the strength of partisanship at the individual level. In this way, we can estimate the impact of strength of macropartisanship, while controlling for the intensity of individual partisan attachments.

Parameter estimates for the random intercepts model of the probability of an individual voting appear in Table 6.8. This model explains 57% of the variance in the likelihood of voting scale. Not surprisingly, the pre-campaign probability of voting variable had a strong influence on the subsequent probability of doing so. As the estimates for Model A show, a unit increase in this variable produced a 0.64-unit increase in the probability of voting. Other parameter estimates indicate that voting was influenced by all variables in the general incentives model, except group benefits, with the most powerful effect being associated with civic duty – a key predictor in all of the turnout models. The party mobilization measures were important predictors as well, with the exception of Conservative mobilization efforts, which did not appear to influence turnout. In addition, some demographics were influential, with older people, the well educated, ethnic majorities and men more likely to vote as a result of the campaign.

Table 6.8 *Multilevel regression analyses of the probability of voting in the 2005 general election*

	Model A	Model B	Model C
Aggregate-level model	γ	γ	γ
Launch of the campaign (temporary)	–	0.17***	0.21***
Rover car crisis (temporary)	–	−0.28***	−0.28***
Blair accused of lying by Howard (temporary)	–	−0.07	–
Television debate between leaders (temporary)	–	−0.05	–
Macropartisanship	–	0.04***	0.04***
R^2	–	0.65	0.65
Individual-level model	β	β	β
Prior probability of voting	0.64***	0.62***	0.62***
Collective benefits	0.002***	0.0005	–
Personal influence costs	−0.04*	−0.02	–
Civic duty	0.19***	0.18***	0.18***
Perceived personal benefits	0.06**	0.04**	0.05**
Perceived group benefits	−0.02	−0.02	–
Social norms	−0.10***	−0.10***	−0.10***
Labour mobilization	0.12***	0.11**	0.11**
Conservative mobilization	−0.00	−0.00	–
Liberal Democrat mobilization	0.17***	0.16***	0.16***
Age	0.02**	0.03***	0.03***
Age squared	−0.0001	−0.0002*	−0.0002**
Education	0.05***	0.05***	0.006***
Ethnicity	−0.75***	−0.74***	−0.74***
Gender	0.17***	0.13**	0.13**
Social class	0.01	0.01	–
Strength of partisanship	–	0.29***	0.29***
R^2	0.57	0.57	0.57

– variable not included in model.

*** – $p \leq 0.001$, ** – $p \leq 0.01$, * – $p \leq 0.05$; one-tailed test.

Source: 2005 BES rolling campaign panel survey.

The second column (Model B) in Table 6.8 shows the results of adding the five aggregate covariates to the specification, and it can be seen that the launch of the campaign, the Rover crisis, and strength of macropartisanship had statistically significant effects on voting. Together, these variables explained 65% of the aggregate-level variation in the probability of voting. The campaign launch and the Rover crisis had temporary effects which did not endure through until polling day, but strength of macropartisanship mobilized voters throughout the whole campaign. This effect was independent of the strength of a person's own partisan attachments which were included at the individual-level part of the model. The third column (Model C) in Table 6.8 shows what happens when only the statistically significant effects in Model B are used as predictors. Coefficients in Model C do not differ from those in Model B, except for the launch of the campaign variable which has a slightly stronger impact.

In turn, the air war models of party choice replicate the models in Chapter 5 as closely as possible, but add Labour voting intentions from the baseline wave of the campaign panel survey to the specification and omit any non-significant variables. Since the dependent variable is not a probability of voting scale but, rather, a choice measure similar to that in Table 5.4, logistic regression analysis is employed. The first column in Table 6.9 contains the logistic regression coefficient estimates and the second, the effect of these variables on the probability of voting Labour. Incorporating the pre-campaign voting intention variable as a predictor produces a very high goodness-of-fit with a pseudo R-square statistic of 0.70. This has another interesting effect, since it eliminates any significant aggregate variation in the random intercept model across the campaign. The first row of Table 6.9 contains a chi-square test of the variance of the model intercepts across the campaign and it is not statistically significant. This means that there is no aggregate variation in the model intercept and, hence, no aggregate-level covariates have an effect on party choice.

Despite the control for pre-campaign voting intention, many of the variables from the party choice model in Chapter 5 have significant effects on Labour voting, indicating that part of their influence occurs during the campaign. Party identification, leader images and party preferences on most important issue are highly significant with the expected signs. In addition, Labour was helped by positive economic evaluations and also by its own campaigning. The Labour

Table 6.9 *Binomial logistic regression analyses of Labour vote intentions over the official campaign*

Chi-square test of variance of model intercept	28.79	
Individual-level model	β	Probabilities
Labour vote intentions prior to the campaign	2.41***	0.38
Labour identification	1.58***	0.22
Conservative identification	−0.51**	−0.05
Liberal Democrat identification	−1.02***	−0.09
Blair leader affect	0.25***	0.35
Howard leader affect	−0.05***	−0.05
Kennedy leader affect	−0.13***	−0.16
Labour best on most important issue	0.56***	0.07
Conservatives best on most important issue	−0.83***	−0.08
Liberal Democrats best on most important issue	−0.94***	−0.08
Other party best on most important issue	−0.76***	−0.07
Economic evaluations	0.25***	0.17
Labour best on economy	0.86***	0.11
Labour campaigning	0.45***	0.21
Liberal Democrat campaigning	−0.30***	−0.08
Gender	−0.34***	−0.04
McFadden R^2	0.70	

*** – $p \leq 0.001$, ** – $p \leq 0.01$, * – $p \leq 0.05$; one-tailed test.
Source: 2005 BES rolling campaign panel survey.

campaigning index, when varied from its minimum to its maximum values, increased the probability of voting for the party by twenty-one points. Liberal Democrat campaigning had a modest negative effect on Labour voting, and once again Conservative campaigning had no impact at all.

The Conservative logistic party choice model appears in Table 6.10. Once again, the prior voting intention variable is included to control for pre-campaign effects and the pseudo R-square statistic of the random intercept model is a very high 0.75. Similar to the Labour analysis, partisanship, leader images and party selected as best on most important issue all had significant effects on the probability of voting Conservative. As shown in the second column of the table, the effect of feelings about Michael Howard was very strong. Not many

Table 6.10 *Binomial logistic regression analyses of Conservative vote intentions over the official campaign*

Chi-square test of variance of model intercept	59.43***	
Individual-level model	β	Probabilities
Conservative vote intentions prior to the campaign	2.49***	0.29
Conservative identification	1.48***	0.14
Labour identification	−0.72***	−0.05
Liberal Democrat identification	0.61***	−0.04
Blair leader affect	−0.12***	−0.07
Howard leader affect	0.36***	0.42
Kennedy leader affect	−0.16***	−0.12
Labour best on most important issue	−0.76***	−0.04
Conservatives best on most important issue	1.60***	0.16
Liberal Democrats best on most important issue	−0.94***	−0.05
Labour best on economy	−0.63***	−0.04
McFadden R^2	0.75	

*** – $p \leq 0.001$, ** – $p \leq 0.01$, * – $p \leq 0.05$; one-tailed test.
Source: 2005 BES rolling campaign panel survey.

people thought highly of the Conservative leader in 2005 but, if they did, then it strongly increased their likelihood of voting Conservative. One clear difference between this model and the Labour model in Table 6.9 is that there are no significant party mobilization effects. Conservative voters were unmoved by the campaigning efforts of the political parties, including their own party. The chi-square test of variance of the model intercept was statistically significant indicating that the model intercept shifted across time. However, none of the covariates discussed earlier had a significant impact on Conservative voting, so other factors would have accounted for these shifts.

Table 6.11 displays the Liberal Democrat logistic party choice model. The pseudo R^2 is smaller than for the Labour and Conservative models, but remains a sizable 0.56. A chi-square test of the variance of the model intercept was not significant, so no aggregate covariates were added. Following the pattern observed for Labour and Conservative voting, partisanship, leader images and party judged best on the most

Table 6.11 *Binomial logistic regression analyses of Liberal Democrat vote intentions over the official campaign*

Chi-Square test of variance of model intercept	26.4	
Individual-level model	β	Probabilities
Liberal Democrat vote intentions prior to the campaign	2.52***	0.39
Liberal Democrat identification	1.61***	0.20
Labour identification	−0.55***	−0.04
Conservative identification	−0.72**	−0.05
Other party identification	−1.25***	−0.06
Kennedy leader affect	0.32***	0.27
Blair leader affect	−0.09***	−0.07
Howard leader affect	−0.14***	−0.09
Liberal Democrats best on most important issue	1.57***	0.20
Labour best on most important issue	−0.69***	−0.04
Conservatives best on most important issue	−0.55***	−0.04
Tactical voting	0.55***	0.05
Gender	0.21***	0.02
Education	0.08***	0.02
McFadden R²	0.56	

*** – $p \le 0.001$, ** – $p \le 0.01$, * – $p \le 0.05$; one-tailed test.
Source: 2005 BES rolling campaign panel survey.

important issue were significant predictors of Liberal Democrat voting. In every case, the signs on these variables' coefficients were in expected directions. Again, the party mobilization measures were not significant, although as a result of the campaign, men and well-educated people were more likely to vote Liberal Democrat.

Conclusion: an influential campaign

Campaigning on the ground and in the air influenced electoral choice in 2005. Campaign effects were transmitted through many variables. Key components of the valence politics model – partisan attachments, feelings about party leaders and party preferences on what voters deemed to be important issues – exerted strong effects on party choice. Party activists campaigning on the ground in the constituencies also were influential. Strength of macropartisanship had a significant mobilizing impact on turnout over the thirty days of the campaign, although its influence was not detected in the party choice models over time. Viewed generally, the analyses confirm earlier research showing that party mobilization and spending variables are two sides of the same coin, and both should be taken into account when assessing campaign effects. The evidence also suggests that campaigns can demobilize voters as well as mobilize them. In this regard, multilevel models of the dynamics of the probability of voting revealed that various campaign events affected the likelihood of electoral participation. The demobilization potential of campaigns also is suggested by the dynamics of interest in the 2005 election – dynamics that reflected the negative tone of the air war waged between Prime Minister Blair and his harsh critic, Conservative leader Michael Howard.

This completes our analysis of the 2005 general election campaign. The next chapter examines the relationship between voting and other forms of participation to assess whether the pronounced decline in voting turnout extends to other forms of citizen involvement as well.

7 | *Voting and political participation*

Britain's first fully peacetime, post-Second World War general election was held on 23 February 1950. In that contest, 84% of the eligible electorate went to the polls – a highpoint in voter turnout that has not been revisited. In twenty-first-century general elections, turnout has been dismal, with only 61.2% voting in 2005 and only 59.4 doing so in 2001. These numbers are the end-points – thus far – in a long-term decline in electoral participation in Britain. The downward trend has accelerated over the past decade, and the percentages of people taking part in the two most recent general elections are lower than at any time since 1918. This raises an important question: is the decline in turnout unique or a reflection of a more general decrease in political participation?

If voting is affected, but not other forms of involvement such as party activity, boycotting goods and services for political reasons, and protesting, then it suggests that in an increasingly complex and interconnected world citizens are finding other ways of trying to influence the political process. Although the long-term consequences of this development for British democracy will not be wholly salutatory, since making choices among governing and opposition parties traditionally has been the principal way by which the vast majority of people make their voices heard, the overall effect is unlikely to be fatal to democratic governance. Within broad limits, the percentage of people voting may not matter greatly when large numbers of citizens are availing themselves of other means of exerting political influence. In contrast, if the decline in turnout signals a wholesale withdrawal from all types of political participation, then the accountability and responsiveness features of democracy in Britain may be undermined. In this chapter, we investigate the relationship between voting and other forms of participation. In particular, we are interested in whether young people are abandoning voting, but not other political activities, or giving up on politics altogether.

We begin with the observation that declining turnout in national elections is not confined to Britain. Decreasing electoral participation has been most extensively researched in the United States, where political scientists have examined and debated this phenomenon for many years (e.g. McDonald and Popkin, 2001; Miller and Shanks, 1996; Patterson, 2002; Rosenstone and Hansen, 1992; Teixeira, 1987, 1992). Although the proposition that turnout in American national elections has trended downward is controversial, there is widespread agreement that voting rates in the USA long have been low in comparison with most other mature democracies. There is also a consensus that downward trends in electoral participation have occurred in many of these countries. Thus, voting rates have fallen in seventeen of nineteen OECD countries over a period of about forty years – 'the median change from the 1950s has been a 10% decline in turnout' (Wattenberg, 2000: 71).

Since 2002, the biennial European Social Survey project has gathered high-quality data on political participation in Britain and other European countries. This collection makes it possible to study British participation rates relative to those in a broad range of democracies, new and old alike. These comparative data have the important advantage of enabling analyses that recognize the contexts in which political activity takes place. In particular, it is possible to evaluate the extent to which institutional arrangements in Britain inhibit or stimulate participation in comparison with those in other countries.

To set the stage for this comparative analysis, we first investigate relationships between voting and other forms of participation in Britain using data gathered at the time of the 2005 general election. Then, we examine trends in participation over time drawing on data from the World Values Survey (Inglehart, 1997) for a long-run perspective, and the Government Performance and Valence Politics (GPVP) surveys for a more detailed short-run perspective. Unlike voting, reliable longitudinal data on other political activities are relatively hard to find, and measurement has been episodic and inconsistent. Nonetheless, it is possible to identify trends in some key variables. Here, we focus on age-related differences in voting and several other activities. Then, we use multilevel modelling techniques to study the dynamics of participation in Britain over the past few years. Multilevel models also are used to investigate individual- and contextual-level factors that affect various forms of political participation in Britain and other

European democracies. This is followed by an aggregate-level analysis that focuses on boycotting and buycotting activities that some
analysts contend are becoming substitutes for voting. The conclusion
reprises major findings, placing the results on political participation
in Britain in a broader comparative perspective.

Political participation in Britain, 2005

In a previous study, we employed the 2001 BES post-election survey data to develop a four-factor model of political participation
(Clarke *et al.*, 2004b: 223). The four participation factors are voting,
party activity, protesting, and voluntary or communal activities. The
2005 BES post-election survey includes a similar set of participation
indicators of voting in different types of elections, undertaking voluntary activities, taking part in demonstrations and campaigns, and
involvement in party activity.[1] Most of these variables are measured
with zero to ten scales, so that respondents identified the *likelihood*
that they would engage in various activities in the future. An example is given in Figure 7.1, which shows BES respondents' estimates
that they would take part in a protest demonstration. As the figure
indicates, more than one-third said that they would never engage in a
protest, and most of the remaining responses also were placed at the

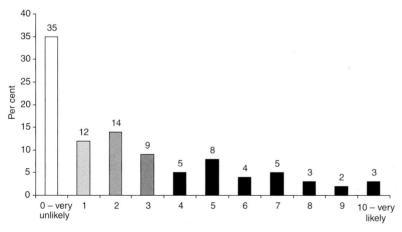

Figure 7.1 Likelihood of participating in a protest, rally or demonstration,
Britain **2005** (*Source*: 2005 BES post-election survey)

low end of the scale. The mean score was 2.6, and only 3% placed themselves at the top of the scale, thereby indicating that it is 'very likely' they will take part in a protest. These numbers confirm more casual impressions that protesting is very much a minority activity in Britain.

Descriptive statistics for several participation indicators in the 2005 post-election survey appear in Table 7.1. The largest mean scores relate to voting in European parliamentary and local government elections, but discussing politics with family and friends, being active in a voluntary organization, and boycotting goods for political reasons are all relatively frequent. Like protesting, very few people are likely to give money to a political party or to work for one. Further insights can be obtained from the correlations (r) between age and each participation measure shown in the table. All of the voting indicators are positively related to age and, thus, confirm the well-known finding that young people are less likely to vote than the middle-aged and the old. However, working with a group, protesting, and being active in a voluntary organization have negative, albeit modest, relationships

Table 7.1 *Likelihood of engaging in various forms of political participation*

Type of participation	Mean score (0–10 scale)	Correlation (r) with age
Vote in the next European parliamentary elections	6.5	0.14
Vote in the next local government elections	7.4	0.25
Work with a group on a political issue	3.4	−0.17
Take part in a protest demonstration	2.6	−0.17
Be active in a voluntary organization	4.6	−0.16
Give money to a political party	1.3	0.06
Try to convince someone how to vote	2.3	−0.07
Work for a party or candidate in an election	1.2	−0.03
Discuss politics with family or friends	5.4	−0.09
Join a boycott of products	4.2	−0.00

Source: 2005 BES post-election survey.

with age. In these cases, young people are more likely to be active, but the age biases are small. Relationships between age and the remaining forms of participation are negligible, indicating that there is no linear age gradient for these types of activity.

All of the BES participation indicators summarized in Table 7.1 are prospective in nature, but an additional set of questions was asked about activities done in the past. These include voting in the 2005 general election, volunteering to involve oneself in politics or community affairs, being active in a voluntary organization, or becoming a member of a political party. Approximately 72% claimed to have voted in the 2005 election, 14% to have volunteered, 31% to have been 'very' or 'somewhat' active in a voluntary organization, and 3% to have been a party member. The age correlations are quite strong for voting and party membership, but weak for the volunteering measures.[2] The size of the former is illustrated by the fact that only 43% of the under-twenty-fives said they had voted in the general election, compared with 80% of the over-sixty-fives. Similarly, less than 1% of the under-twenty-fives claimed to be party members compared with more than 6% of the over-sixty-fives.

This cross-sectional evidence is suggestive but says nothing about changes in levels of participation over time. Nor does it inform us about possible changes in the extent to which various age groups engage in different activities. In the next section, we consider these topics.

Trends

As observed above, attempts to examine trends in political participation encounter data availability problems. Although there are ample individual-level data on reported turnout in successive British election studies, the same is not true for other forms of participation. For example, evidence on interest group activity and protest behaviour is both limited and incomplete, and that on party membership and activism is inaccurate (Seyd and Whiteley, 1992). However, insight into trends over the past quarter century can be obtained from the BES surveys in conjunction with the World Values Surveys. The latter were first conducted in Britain in 1981.[3] Although comparisons must be made with care due to question-wording differences, the results suggest that relatively modest changes in levels of participation have

Table 7.2 *Trends in political participation in Britain, 1981 to 2005*

Form of participation	1981	1990	2001	2005
Demonstration	9.0	13.6	11.9	8.3
Boycott	6.7	14.7	30.8	21.3
Party membership	4.5	5.7	4.7	3.2
Volunteering	17.9	15.0	13.2	13.5

Source: 1981 and 1991 World Values Surveys; 2001 and 2005 BES post-election surveys.

occurred over time.[4] As Table 7.2 shows, protest behaviour has fluctuated over the years without any clear long-term trend, while party membership and volunteering have declined, and boycotting products for political reasons has increased.

There was an upsurge in protest demonstrations during the 1980s, when Margaret Thatcher was prime minister, but this has not continued. Indeed, protest numbers for 2001 and 2005 are smaller than those recorded in 1990. In contrast, boycotting goods for political reasons grew rapidly between 1981 and 2001 and, although the growth was reversed afterwards, in 2005 the level of boycotting remained significantly higher than at the beginning of the 1980s. Party membership, always a preserve of relatively fewer people, appears to have declined since the early 1990s – a pattern that is consonant with other findings on party activism in Britain (Whiteley and Seyd, 2002). Similarly, volunteering has decreased, although observed changes are modest.

Age-related changes in various types of political participation are examined in Table 7.3. Panel A focuses on electoral activity. Evidence from four BES surveys conducted since 1983 indicates a large gap in turnout rates among different age groups. At the time of the 1983 election, younger citizens were less likely to vote than their older counterparts, but the gap between age cohorts was a relatively modest 10%. By 2005, the gap between the voting rates of the eighteen to twenty-four-year olds and those sixty-five and older had become a difference of nearly 40%.

Age gradients in other forms of participation are very different, with no evidence of the development of the massive age differences

Table 7.3 *Trends in various forms of political participation by age cohort, 1981 to 2005*

Panel A. Turnout in general elections

Age cohorts	1983	1992	2001	2005
18–24	73.3	61.2	49.0	42.8
25–34	77.6	73.0	52.3	52.5
35–44	87.4	70.9	64.9	68.1
45–54	89.0	78.7	74.6	69.7
55–64	88.6	74.1	79.2	79.3
65 plus	83.9	75.7	81.0	80.4

Panel B. Protest, demonstration

Age cohorts	1981	1990	2001	2005
15–24	12.2	14.6	8.5	8.8
25–34	17.5	15.5	15.3	8.4
35–44	8.8	19.2	13.7	11.3
45–54	5.6	12.2	13.8	9.0
55–64	4.0	11.8	10.6	8.7
65 plus	2.9	8.0	7.5	3.8

Panel C. Boycott goods

Age cohorts	1981	1990	2001	2005
15–24	7.5	9.7	13.4	12.6
25–34	10.9	20.2	31.0	16.3
35–44	8.0	16.8	34.4	22.2
45–54	6.4	15.8	35.1	25.3
55–64	2.3	13.1	39.6	27.1
65 plus	3.4	10.2	25.7	21.3

Panel D. Activity in voluntary organizations

Age cohorts	1981	1990	2001	2005
15–24	9.8	10.9	8.5	10.0
25–34	17.8	17.0	10.7	11.2
35–44	28.6	28.3	14.0	14.1

Table 7.3 (*cont.*)

Panel D. Activity in voluntary organizations

Age cohorts	1981	1990	2001	2005
45–54	18.9	32.1	17.3	15.0
55–64	24.7	22.3	15.3	19.2
65 plus	12.8	23.2	12.4	11.3

Panel E. Membership of a political party

Age cohorts	1981	1990	2001	2005
15–24	1.5	1.9	1.8	0.9
25–34	3.0	4.2	1.1	0.6
35–44	5.6	6.3	2.7	2.3
45–54	6.8	8.1	5.1	2.3
55–64	4.5	6.6	6.9	5.9
65 plus	6.6	7.6	9.6	6.1

Source: 1981, 1990 World Values Surveys; 1983, 1992, 2001, 2005 BES post-election surveys.

that now characterize voting. For example, comparison of the 1981 and 2005 data reveals that the age–protest relationship has changed over time. In 1981, younger people, i.e. those aged thirty-four and under, were more likely to be protestors but, by 2005, people in the thirty-five to forty-four-year-old bracket had the highest rates of protest activity. And, *circa* 1981, people in the twenty-five to thirty-four age cohort had the highest boycotting level (10.9%; Table 7.3, Panel C) but, in 2005, boycotting had increased substantially in every age group, with those between fifty-five and sixty-four being most active. The average increase in boycotting for each of the several age cohorts is nearly 15%. As for party membership, the modest gaps between the young and the old have not changed much over the years and, in every age group but one (those aged fifty-five to sixty-four), the rate of party membership in 2005 is less than it was a quarter-century earlier. Activity rates in voluntary organizations have a similar pattern, being lower in every age group, but one, in 2005 than they were in 1981.

Taken as a whole, the evidence suggests that generational change has been taking place in political participation in Britain. Over the past quarter century, young people have become much less likely to vote. In 2005, the turnout rate among people under twenty-five was fully 31% less than it had been in 1983. For those aged twenty-five to thirty-four, the fall-off is nearly 25%. Decreases in electoral participation among older groups are much smaller, particularly among those fifty-five or older. The changed slope of the age gradient for turnout since the early 1980s indicates that simple life-cycle or period effects do not tell the whole story. The latter would show that all age groups are less likely to vote than used to be the case. A life-cycle effect refers to a pattern in which young people will have voting rates comparable to those of their elders. If a life-cycle process was underway, then the age–turnout slope would be constant over time.

Although panel data gathered over very lengthy time periods are required to disentangle life-cycle, period and generational effects, it appears that there is a *generational component* to the marked decrease in electoral participation that has occurred since the early 1990s. Our earlier analyses of relationships among age, sense of civic duty and turnout in Britain suggest the same conclusion (Clarke *et al.*, 2004b: Chapter 8). The conjecture that young people in any particular generation learn to become voters in their early adulthood also points in the same direction (Franklin, 2004). Accordingly, many young people today are learning *not* to vote and, consequently, are likely to remain abstainers in the future. The contrast with the other forms of participation is stark. For activities other than voting, age relationships are currently much weaker, and changes in these relationships over time have varied for different types of participation. Particularly salient is the rise of boycotting as a form of political activity that is favoured by sizable minorities of people in several age brackets.

These long-run data on political participation raise the question as to why these trends are occurring. To address this question, we employ data from the Government Performance and Valence Politics (GPVP) study. As discussed in Chapter 1, this project involves a series of national monthly 'continuous monitoring' surveys which started in April 2004 and are still being fielded. The surveys contain questions similar to those in the 2005 BES about the probabilities of voting, protesting and volunteering that can be used to gauge the incidence of various kinds of political involvement. Since there is not a monthly measure of party activity, we use strength of party identification as a proxy for the *likelihood* of involvement in work on behalf of a party organization.[5]

Data are employed from the April 2004 to December 2007 GPVP surveys, a total of forty-four months overall.[6] The 2005 general election occurred just over a year after these surveys first were conducted, so it is possible to examine contextual effects of the election on different forms of political participation over this period. Data on the participation variables are displayed in Figure 7.2. The three indicators in the figure are measures of the likelihood of voting in the next general election, attending a protest demonstration and volunteering in the community. These eleven-point scales show that, not surprisingly, voting is the most frequent activity with a mean score of 8.3. However, the mean scores for volunteering and protesting of 4.7 and 2.8, respectively, indicate that these are activities that many people are likely to eschew.

Figure 7.3 displays the GPVP data on strength of partisanship. Only slightly over one in ten of the GPVP respondents interviewed between April 2004 and December 2007 reported being 'very strong' party identifiers, and nearly half (47%) said that they either did not identify with a party or did so only weakly. The

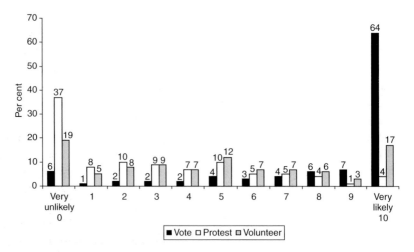

Figure 7.2 Likelihood of voting in next general election, protesting or volunteering, Britain, April 2004–December 2007 (*Source*: April 2004–December 2007 GPVP surveys)

average strength of party identification of a four-point scale is 1.5. This figure is very similar to that for respondents in the 2005 BES post-election survey. Their mean strength of party identification is 1.4, nearly a full point below that recorded when the first BES post-election survey was conducted in 1964. As Figure 7.4 illustrates, strength of partisanship in Britain has manifested an almost perfectly linear downward trend (r = +0.95) since that time. This long-term decline is consistent with the decrease in party organizational activity discussed above.

Understanding forces that account for these different forms of political involvement requires a well-specified general model of political participation. This model should incorporate contextual factors likely to influence responses over time. For example, when people are queried about their vote intentions immediately prior to an election, they are being asked about a decision they are about to make in the context of a particular campaign. In contrast, when they are asked the same question at the mid-point in the life of a four- or five-year parliament, campaign stimuli, such as those discussed in Chapter 6, and other factors that may eventually prompt them to vote for a given party, or perhaps not to vote at all, may not yet be in play. Similarly, the extent of party activity can be expected to manifest a cyclical

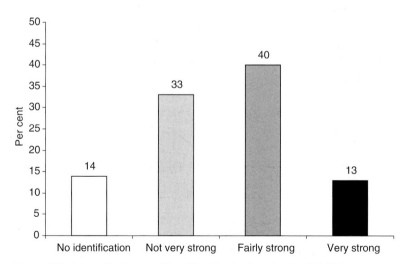

Figure 7.3 Strength of party identification in Britain, April 2004–December 2007 (*Source*: April 2004–December 2007 GPVP surveys)

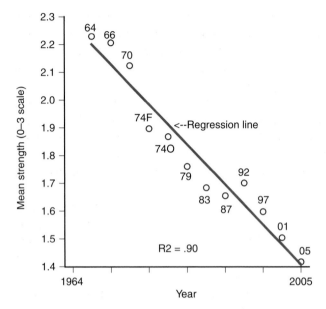

Figure 7.4 Trend in strength of party identification in Britain, 1964–2005 (*Source*: 1964–2005 BES post-election surveys)

'surge and decline' pattern across successive elections since much party organizational work occurs during election campaigns.

Context may also matter for other forms of participation, although the connection with the electoral cycle per se may be less evident. Protests, for example, typically are stimulated by highly controversial issues, such as Margaret Thatcher's 1990 proposal to implement a community charge (poll tax), or Tony Blair's insistence in 2003 that Britain join the US-led war against Iraq. To analyse individual-level participation within a specific temporal context requires a multilevel modelling approach (Goldstein, 1995; Raudenbush and Bryk, 2002) similar to that employed in Chapter 6. The next section discusses this and the individual-level model of participation.

Individual-level influences

We first develop an individual-level model of political participation that builds on the turnout analysis discussed in previous chapters of this book and in *Political Choice in Britain* (Clarke et al., 2004b).

The latter specifies several rival models of electoral participation and, although all contribute to explaining turnout, the cognitive engagement and general incentives models were dominant. Here, we briefly review these two models and then employ them to analyse citizen involvement in British politics.

The cognitive engagement model has 'model citizen' overtones that have a distinguished lineage in normative political thought. The core idea is that an individual's ability to acquire and process information fosters political participation (Norris, 2000; Dalton, 2006). More specifically, educational attainment, political information and attention to elections and to politics more generally are key factors that affect the likelihood that a person will participate. Thus, the argument is that growth of mass circulation newspapers and current affairs journals, television and radio broadcasts, and, most recently, access to the internet has greatly enhanced the supply of information people need to play the role of 'critical citizens' (Norris, 2000). Education is particularly important since it increases the capacity to gather and process information. Supplied with relevant information and the ability to process it, cognitively engaged individuals evaluate the performance and promises of incumbent parties and their adversaries with the aim of making informed political choices.

Highly educated, attentive and policy-informed people are more likely to be politically involved than are uneducated, inattentive ones. These elements of the cognitive engagement model are captured by four variables in the GPVP surveys. These are formal education level, attention to politics, media consumption and evaluations of government performance in delivering on key policies such as health, crime and education.[7] Educational level is an important indicator of the ability to make sense of political information, and attention to politics is a measure of interest in gathering and using such information. Daily newspaper readership captures extent of exposure to current affairs in the media and it also proxies, at least roughly, the possession of politically relevant information. Finally, policy performance evaluations tap the 'critical citizen' dimension of the model. Policy evaluations are incorporated with a quadratic specification, on the hypothesis that the mobilizing effects of improved policy delivery are subject to diminishing returns.

In turn, the general incentives model was originally developed to explain high-intensity forms of participation undertaken by party activists, that is, activities such as organizing election campaigns, canvassing voters or selecting candidates that require a lot of time and energy (Seyd and Whiteley, 1992, 2002; Whiteley and Seyd, 2002; Whiteley *et al.*, 2006). The core idea of the general incentives model is rooted in both rational choice and social-psychological claims that individuals participate when the benefits to themselves *and* to the wider society outweigh the costs. The model goes beyond the conventional egocentric rational choice account of participation (e.g. Riker and Ordeshook 1968, 1973) by taking account of altruistic motives and social norms as explanatory factors.

As specified here, the general incentives model has four variables. These are collective benefits weighted by perceived personal political influence, costs of participating, and individual and group benefits of participating.[8] Influence-discounted collective benefits and perceived costs are at the core of the traditional rational choice model of voting (Riker and Ordeshook, 1968, 1973). Following the discussions in earlier chapters, collective benefits are measured using respondents' perceptions of utilities provided by major political parties. If people think that there is very little difference among parties, then they have little incentive to support any of them. In contrast, if they perceive big differences in what various parties will deliver, then they should participate. The collective benefits variable in the model is the sum of the perceived differences between pairs of parties weighted by an individual's sense of political efficacy, since people only have an incentive to get involved if they believe that they can influence outcomes.

Other variables in the general incentives model assess the perceived costs of participation and the private and group incentives for getting involved. Individuals will be deterred from participating as perceived costs rise. However, they are more likely to become involved when they think that it will benefit themselves or groups with which they sympathize.

Analyses presented in Chapters 3, 5 and 6 attest to the importance of valence politics considerations in influencing party choice. These considerations are also relevant to an individual's decision to participate, and they are incorporated into the present analysis using four different variables. These are leader images, economic evaluations, party competence on important issues and satisfaction with democracy.[9] In the context of political participation, the core idea of the valence model is that citizen involvement will vary according to levels of (dis)satisfaction with the performance of political leaders, the incumbent government and the wider political system. The leadership variable in the model is constructed similar to the collective benefits measure. If someone sees no differences among the party leaders, then s/he has no incentive to vote for any of them. But, if a leader is judged superior to his/her competitors, then this provides an incentive to vote and to do so for the party with the best leader. Economic perform- ance is linked to valence evaluations of leaders and of political par- ties. For example, a citizen who thinks that one of the parties can effectively manage the economy has a particular incentive to get out and vote for that party. However, a person who thinks that no party can manage the economy effectively has little incentive to do so. The same logic applies to the effects of perceptions of which party is best able to handle important issues facing the country. An individual who thinks that one of the parties can handle a most important issue well is more likely to vote for that party. However, participation can be diminished when no party is judged to be able to address the issue.

In addition, it is conjectured that citizens who are satisfied with the way that democracy works in Britain are encouraged to get involved. Such satisfied citizens express their support for the political com- munity and regime via voting and other forms of participation. On the other hand, dissatisfaction with the practice of democracy can prompt involvement. For voting per se, this form of political activ- ity is closely associated with passing judgments on political actors (parties and their leaders), the principal groups of which are closely associated with the existing regime. Dissatisfaction with leaders and parties spills over to affect judgments about the way the system as a whole works. This dissatisfaction can be expressed by going to the polls and voting for change. The claim that extremist parties thrive on public discontent may be a cliché, but that does not mean that it is empirically vacuous.

The argument that dissatisfaction prompts involvement can be applied to other types of participation. For example, research on feel- ings of relative deprivation and political protest (e.g. Muller, 1979; Walker and Smith, 2002) suggests that citizens are likely to engage in protest behaviour when they are discontented with the perform- ance of parties and leaders or with the political system as a whole. Of course, it is also possible that valence judgments work differently for different types of participation. Judgments that prompt citizens to abandon the ballot box may simultaneously encourage them to take to the streets.

Another difference relates to voluntary activity. Citizens who become involved in community politics are likely to weigh the costs and benefits of such involvement, but it is less clear that these evaluations are influenced by national-level valence judgments. In this respect, the voluntary activity model may very well differ from the turnout model. Equally, one may expect differences in how the general incentives model works when applied to different modes of participation. One example relates to perceived costs of participation. Since the costs of voting are relatively trivial, one might anticipate that this variable will have only a marginal impact on voting (e.g. Aldrich, 1993). But this may not be true of protesting or volunteering, both of which involve considerable time, effort and, possibly, foregone income. In these cases, it is plausible that perceived costs will have sizable effects on the decision to participate.

Parameter estimates for the multilevel participation models are displayed in Table 7.4. The models have random intercept specifications which mean that the intercepts fluctuate across the thirty-three months encompassed by the GPVP surveys. This has the effect of controlling for any time-related contextual influences on various types of participation not captured explicitly by the predictor variables. A chi-square test of the variance of the intercepts identifies any time-dependent contextual effects at work. In the event, these tests are significant for all four models, highlighting the point that, net of individual-level characteristics, context influences various forms of participation.

The dependent variable for Model A in Table 7.4 is likelihood of voting in the next general election. Coefficients are standardized to facilitate comparisons of relative effects of the predictor variables. The model explains about one-fifth of the variance and all the coefficients are highly significant with the expected signs, except for newspaper readership and perceptions of costs which are not significant ($p > 0.05$). Attention to politics and age have the strongest effects. It is also clear that leadership evaluations and party performance on the economy together with the other valence measures are important predictors. The policy evaluation measure shows that policy success stimulates voting, but with diminishing returns to performance. Equally, variables from the general incentives model – influence-discounted collective benefits, individual benefits and group benefits – are all

Table 7.4 *Multilevel regression analyses of political participation in Britain, April 2004 to December 2007*

	Model A Voting	Model B Protesting	Model C Volunteering	Model D Partisanship
Chi-square test of intercept variance	277.6***	123.5***	97.1***	118.9**
	β	β	β	β
Newspaper readership	−0.01	0.02***	0.03***	0.02***
Attention to politics	0.28***	0.24***	0.12***	0.21***
Policy evaluations	0.02***	0.03***	0.03***	−0.01
Policy evaluations squared	−0.04***	0.02***	−0.01	0.03***
Party best on economy	0.10***	−0.04***	−0.01***	0.14***
Leader evaluations	0.12***	−0.07***	−0.05***	0.18***
Party best on most important issue	0.06***	0.01	−0.01*	0.15***
Personal influence collective benefits	0.02***	0.16***	0.13***	0.15***
Perceived costs	−0.01	−0.13***	−0.18***	−0.00
Individual benefits	0.03***	0.04***	0.01***	0.00
Group benefits	0.09***	0.08***	0.10***	0.03***
Democratic satisfaction	0.06***	−0.13***	−0.01***	0.03***
Occupational status	0.04***	−0.01	0.09***	−0.02***
Education	0.04***	0.08***	0.12***	−0.01

Table 7.4 (*cont.*)

	Model A Voting	Model B Protesting	Model C Volunteering	Model D Partisanship
Gender	−0.04***	−0.03***	−0.04***	−0.01
Age	0.22***	0.08***	0.09***	0.17***
Age squared	−0.14***	−0.13***	−0.11***	−0.07***
Ethnicity	−0.07***	0.04***	0.00	−0.02**
Individual-level R^2	0.20	0.20	0.16	0.36

*** − $p < 0.001$; ** − $p < 0.01$; * − $p < 0.05$.
Note: entries are standardized coefficients.
Source: April 2004–December 2007 GPVP monthly surveys.

highly significant with the expected signs. Among the demographic variables, occupational status has a positive impact on likelihood of voting, and ethnic minorities and men are less likely to vote than are members of the ethnic majority and women. And, as anticipated by our earlier discussion, controlling for all other factors, younger people are less likely to vote than are older ones. However, the negative sign on the squared age term indicates that, net of other considerations, electoral participation tends to be highest among middle-aged people and lower among the young and the elderly.

The protest model (Table 7.4, Model B) also explains about one-fifth of the variance. In this case, attention to politics is the strongest predictor. Considering the three theoretical models, it appears that the cognitive engagement model has a more prominent role in explaining protesting than voting. Education has a stronger effect on protesting than do newspaper readership and policy evaluations. The impact of influence-discounted collective benefits from the general incentives model is particularly significant. And, whereas perceptions of costs have no significant influence on voting turnout, they do have a significant negative influence on protesting. This finding is consonant with the fact that the costs of voting are relatively small in comparison with protesting.

The biggest difference between the voting and protesting models relates to the valence variables. Most of these have negative effects in the protest model, implying that poor performance by leaders and parties serves to encourage, rather than to discourage, protest behaviour. A similar point can be made regarding satisfaction with democracy – those who are satisfied are less likely to protest than their dissatisfied counterparts. Demographic variables also have effects in the protest model, with well-educated people, women and members of ethnic minorities being more likely to protest. Age also plays a role – similar to voting turnout, the likelihood of protesting is highest among middle-aged people and lower among both the young and the elderly. This similarity aside, many of the determinants of protesting are different from voting, either in their strength relative to other significant predictors, or in the direction of their effects, or both.

The volunteering model (Table 7.4, Model C) is generally similar to the protest model. Many of the valence variables have the same signs as in the protest model and collective benefits and costs play relatively more important roles in explaining volunteering than voting. One difference between the protest and volunteering models relates to attention to politics, which is relatively stronger in the former than in the latter. Age again has a curvilinear effect – *ceteris paribus*, volunteering is most likely among middle-aged people, and less likely among younger and older ones. Other demographic variables also behave in a similar way as in the protest model, except that occupational status has a significant impact on volunteering and ethnicity has no impact at all.

Results for the strength of partisanship model (Table 7.4, Model D) reveal that influence-discounted collective benefits have the expected significant positive impact. However, costs are not significant, which is also true in the voting turnout model. The valence variables have positive effects in much the same way as they do in that model. Thus, differential leadership evaluations, thinking that a particular party is best on an important issue, and (squared) policy evaluations are positively associated with the strength of partisanship variable. Relatively speaking, age is the second most important variable in the turnout and partisanship model – again, this is consistent with the findings in Table 7.3. And, once more, the relationship between age and strength of partisanship is curvilinear; *pace* arguments by Converse (1969) and others, in contemporary Britain at least, younger and older people tend to have weaker partisan attachments than do middle-aged people. In contrast, there are no significant effects of education or gender in the partisanship model. There are also differences involving gender, education and individual benefits. Neither of the demographic variables has a significant impact on partisanship, whereas they do in the voting model. Similarly, anticipated individual benefits do not influence the strength of partisan attachments, although they do have the predicted positive effect on likelihood of voting.

Viewed globally, these analyses demonstrate several similarities in the factors that drive different forms of participation in Britain. The overall story is that individuals have to be engaged to participate, but they also have to believe that the benefits of political action outweigh the costs in situations where the latter are non-trivial. In addition, valence variables are important for all types of participation, but they have different effects on protesting and volunteering than on voting and partisanship. Broadly speaking, good performance stimulates voting and strengthens partisanship, whereas poor performance tends to enhance the probability of protesting and, to a lesser extent, of volunteering. Age also plays a prominent role in every model, and the effects are consistently nonlinear. In all cases, controlling for other effects, the likelihood of political involvement increases among the middle-aged, and then diminishes among the elderly. These relationships are relatively much stronger in the voting and partisanship models than in the volunteering and protesting models.

This evidence raises the interesting question of whether the factors influencing participation in Britain also occur in other countries. It is particularly useful to explore this issue, because it then becomes possible to examine the role of different institutional and constitutional arrangements on participation in Britain and elsewhere.

Comparative perspectives

The European Social Survey (ESS) provides a useful vehicle for cross-national examination of political participation. Important institutional differences exist among various European countries, but they are not so large as to undermine the validity of comparative analysis, since the countries are democracies and, broadly speaking, have a common cultural heritage. The ESS conducts biennial surveys in more than twenty countries. The project is jointly funded by the European Commission, the European Science Foundation and academic funding bodies in each participating country.[10] The first round of surveys occurred in 2002, included twenty-one European countries and Israel, and focused, *inter alia*, on political participation.

The ESS includes an extensive set of questions about political participation, with respondents being asked about various activities they had engaged in over the previous twelve months. Here, we select ESS variables that most closely approximate the four participation items discussed earlier. They are turnout in the most recent national election, working for a political party or action group, working in a voluntary organization and taking part in a demonstration.[11] The pooled responses to these items are displayed in Figure 7.5. As shown, over 79% of the ESS respondents reported voting in the last national election, whereas just under 16% said they worked in a voluntary organization. Between 7% and 8% took part in a demonstration, and just under 5% worked for a political party or action group.

Similar to the analyses discussed above, we first specify individual-level models of various forms of participation in the several European countries using the theoretical perspectives provided by the cognitive engagement, general incentives and valence politics models.

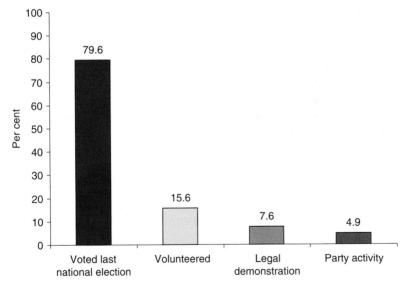

Figure 7.5 Selected political activities in twenty-one European democracies, 2002 (*Source*: 2002 ESS, Israel excluded; respondents stating they were ineligible to vote excluded in calculation of vote percentage)

To investigate possible contextual effects, we permit the intercepts for the participation models to vary across countries. A further, related step includes aggregate-level variables that measure institutional differences among the countries. These variables enable us to study contextual influences on individual-level participation. The specification replicates the British models in Table 7.4 as closely as possible. However, many of the indicators in the European Social Survey differ from those in the GPVP monthly surveys, although they are all designed to measure the same basic concepts. It is useful to note some key differences between ESS and GPVP measures.

One difference concerns media consumption which is rather more extensively measured in the ESS than in the GPVP surveys. The ESS variable is an index based on responses to questions about respondents' use of television, radio and newspapers to acquire political information.[12] Similarly, interest in politics is a more elaborate measure based on a principal components analysis of three indicators.[13] Although the policy evaluation scale is more restricted and focuses only on education and health, it can still be used to capture the 'critical citizen' aspect of cognitive engagement.[14] The leadership variable in the ESS is constructed using a question about levels of trust in politicians.[15] This is not as comprehensive a measure as in the GPVP surveys, but it focuses on a key feature of public judgments about leaders. Judgments about economic performance and democracy satisfaction are tapped using eleven-point scales.[16] The former is included with a quadratic specification in the same way as the policy evaluation scale, on the grounds that there are likely to be diminishing returns to economic satisfaction. The collective benefits variable is proxied by closeness to a party[17] – a respondent who feels close to a party expects collective benefits if it is elected, and this acts as an incentive to participate. This variable is weighted by personal political efficacy which is measured by a question that asks respondents whether they think that politics is too complicated for them to understand.[18] There are no attitudinal measures of perceived costs of participation in the ESS, but a proxy measure is provided by the number of hours the respondent works in the average week.[19] Other components of the general incentive model are captured by a set of indicators of civic norms regarding voting and attitudes towards volunteering.[20]

Table 7.5 contains parameter estimates for the individual-level models of various forms of political participation in the several

Table 7.5 *Multilevel binomial logistic regression analyses of political participation in European democracies*

	Model A Voting	Model B Protesting	Model C Volunteering	Model D Partisanship
Chi-square test of intercept variance	1,823.4***	1,870.3***	1,452.1***	347.8***
	β	β	β	β
Attention to political information in media	0.02	−0.00	0.00	−0.02
Interest in politics	0.28***	0.13***	0.33***	0.87***
Policy evaluations	0.06***	0.07***	−0.02	0.01
Policy evaluations squared	−0.0003***	−0.003**	0.00	−0.00
Leader evaluations	0.05***	−0.04**	−0.02	0.02
Satisfaction with democracy	0.00	−0.08***	−0.02	−0.06**
Approval of economy	0.07***	−0.07	−0.01	−0.12***
Approval of economy squared	−0.01***	0.007	0.00	0.01***
Personal influence collective benefits	0.19***	0.13***	0.09***	0.25***
Perceived costs	−0.00	−0.005***	−0.005**	0.01*
Civic norms	0.32***	0.00	0.08***	0.03
Volunteering norms	0.13***	0.26***	0.43***	0.45***

Table 7.5 (*cont.*)

	Model A Voting	Model B Protesting	Model C Volunteering	Model D Partisanship
Occupational status	0.13***	0.02*	0.09***	0.01
Education	0.09***	0.13***	0.17***	0.11***
Age	0.17***	−0.04***	0.02***	−0.00
Age squared	−0.001***	0.00	−0.0002***	−0.00
Gender	−0.04	0.10***	0.37***	0.17
Ethnicity	−1.03***	0.41**	−0.11	0.42**
McFadden R^2	0.20	0.17	0.10	0.10

*** − $p < 0.001$; ** − $p < 0.01$; * − $p < 0.05$.
Source: 2002 ESS.

European countries. As noted above, we employ a multilevel random intercept specification. Since the dependent variables are dichotomies, logistic regression is used for estimation purposes. As shown, model intercepts vary significantly across the twenty-two countries, indicating that there are additional aggregate-level influences at work – influences not captured by the individual-level variables. Despite the measurement differences discussed above, most results are quite similar to those for the British analyses reported earlier. For example, of the cognitive engagement variables, interest in politics and education are significant predictors in all four models. In addition, policy evaluations influence voting and protesting, but not volunteering or party activity. These findings echo those in the British analyses, except that policy evaluations also have a weak influence on volunteering in the British case.

Regarding the general incentives model, influence-discounted collective benefits are important in all of the European models, whereas costs are important for protesting and volunteering, but not for voting. This is also very similar to the British findings. Civic norms and volunteering norms play rather similar roles in the European analysis as selective and group benefits do in the British case. Another common feature of the two analyses is that valence judgments such as economic evaluations, democratic satisfaction and leader evaluations have positive effects on voting, but negative ones on protesting.

Although there are several similarities between the British and the European analyses, there are also differences. It is apparent that the valence variables play very little role in explaining volunteering in the European model, whereas they play a significant role in the comparable British one. Equally, the valence variables do little to explain party activity – cognitive engagement and general incentives variables are what matter in the European case. Finally, although the effects of age on turnout and volunteering are similar in the British and European analyses, there are no age effects associated with party activity in the European case, and the effects on protesting are negative. Across European democracies as a whole, younger people are more likely to protest than are their older counterparts.

Aggregate-level effects

The European participation models have intercepts that vary significantly from one country to the next. To explain these cross-national differences, we incorporate aggregate-level variables in the multivariate participation models. The number of such variables that can be examined is limited by the fact that there are only twenty-two countries. This makes it necessary to concentrate on a few key institutional differences. With that caveat in mind, our theoretical perspective focuses on factors that serve to widen political choices available to individual citizens. For example, it is frequently observed that Britain's single-member plurality electoral system restricts choice, produces a lot of wasted votes and thus discourages participation. This idea has been frequently discussed in the voting literature (e.g. Lijphart, 1994), but it might be relevant for other types of participation as well.

Party systems vary substantially across countries, and these differing 'electoral choice sets' may affect participation rates. For example, large numbers of political parties contesting national elections appear to reduce turnout (Cox and Amorim, 1997). The explanation for this is that information costs of voting rise significantly as the number of parties increases, since citizens must know more about the many choices on offer in the electoral arena. This effect works to offset any additional benefits which might accrue from expanding the set of alternatives. As we see below, this has implications for voting in countries with proportional electoral systems.

The first aggregate-level variable that we use is the Vanhanen index of democratization,[21] which is based on two key measures of effective democracy – competition and participation (Vanhanen, 1997). In Vanhanen's view, a thriving democratic polity should have both a competitive party system and high levels of citizen participation. The former is measured by the percentage of votes won by parties other than the largest party, so that democratic competition implies strong support for opposition parties, or minor parties in governing coalitions. The latter is measured by the percentage of the population who turn out to vote, so that aggregate turnout appears in the model as part of the index. The Vanhanen index correlates highly with other measures of democratic effectiveness such as the Freedom House ratings of political rights and civil liberties, and the Bollen index of political democracy (Vanhanen, 1997). Our expectation is that a high score by a country on the Vanhanen index is associated positively with individual participation. The mechanisms posited involve the existence of relatively vigorous inter-party competition and the existence of social norms favouring citizen involvement.

A second dimension of electoral choice relates to the ideological diversity of the party system. Relatively small ideological distances among the parties are likely to restrict effective choice and thereby to inhibit participation. In contrast, a wider ideological spectrum gives people a greater chance of finding a party with which they agree on important issues, and this should encourage their participation. This effect may be partly offset by the additional costs of information processing in an ideologically diverse party system, but the sign of the coefficient would reveal the balance of these potentially offsetting effects. One approach to the measurement of ideological diversity across countries is based on data gathered in surveys asking experts where they place parties on ideological scales. Here, we use the Laver–Benoit index (Laver, 2001) which measures ideological differences between parties on the basis of such surveys.[22] The specific indicator measures the ideological difference between the major party and the third party in a country.

A third aggregate-level variable focuses on the electoral system. We mentioned the restrictive character of the single-member plurality electoral system earlier, and it would be desirable to test the effects of such a system in a comparative analysis. A well-known measure of electoral distortion is the Gallagher Least Squares index[23] (Gallagher and Mitchell, 2005). This index assesses the accuracy with which electoral systems translate vote shares in elections into seat shares in legislatures. We would expect electoral participation to be inhibited in countries with high levels of distortion, but this may very well carry over to other types of participation as well. For example, electoral distortion is likely to promote protest behaviour when citizens believe that they are disenfranchised by their electoral institutions.

A fourth variable is the effective number of political parties. This can be measured in different ways, but one accepted approach is the Laakso and Taagepera index (1979).[24] This index measures the degree of fragmentation of a party system. The earlier discussion indicates that a multiparty system has the effect of inhibiting electoral participation, but it may stimulate other activities such as protesting and party work. These possibilities are examined in the analysis. Finally, a dummy variable is added to indicate which countries formerly had communist regimes. The expectation is that political participation in general will be inhibited by the nearly half-century experience of communism with its corrosive legacy of suppressing political rights and freedoms while amplifying levels of political and social mistrust.

Estimated coefficients for aggregate-level variables are displayed in Table 7.6. These coefficients measure the effects of aggregate-level variables on the intercepts of the logistic regression models of various types of political participation (see Table 7.5). None of the aggregate variables has a significant impact on volunteering, and only party system ideological diversity has an influence on party activity – as expected, increases in ideological diversity are associated with involvement in party work. However, there are several significant effects on voting and protesting. In the former case, a high score on the Vanhanen democratization index is associated with higher levels of individual-level turnout. In countries where electoral competition is vigorous and where voting norms are strong, people are more likely to go to the polls. In contrast, the effective number of parties inhibits individual-level turnout, a finding consonant with the point that information-processing costs are high in multiparty systems. High costs discourage participation. However, *ceteris paribus*, when the range of ideological alternatives is expanded, this encourages electoral participation, even though it might impose additional information-processing costs. It also appears that electoral

Table 7.6 *Aggregate-level predictors of political participation in European democracies*

Predictor variable	Model A Voting	Model B Protest	Model C Volunteering	Model D Party activity
Effective number of parties	−0.12*	−0.04	0.08	−0.00
Vanhanen democratiza- tion index	0.05***	0.02	−0.00	−0.02
Gallagher electoral distortion index	−0.02*	0.05*	0.01	0.01
Laver–Benoit ideological diversity index	0.09*	0.21**	−0.08	0.10*
Former communist state	−0.07	−1.07*	−0.79	−0.17
Aggregate R^2	0.70	0.44	0.00	0.00

*** – $p \leq 0.001$; ** – $p \leq 0.01$; * – $p \leq 0.05$; one-tailed test.
Source: 2002 ESS.

distortion inhibits turnout, an effect which is explained by the large numbers of wasted votes which occur when distortion is high, as it is in Britain.

Aggregate-level covariates also influence the likelihood of pro- testing. Not surprisingly, high levels of electoral distortion stimu- late protest behaviour. Since such distortions bias public inputs to the policy-making process, it is not surprising that a high score on the Gallagher index is associated with additional protesting. People tend to engage in demonstrations and other forms of protest activ- ity when the ballot box is judged to be an ineffective way of voicing their concerns. The strongest aggregate effect on protesting is associ- ated with the Laver–Benoit ideological diversity index. The effect is positive, indicating that people in countries with high levels of ideo- logical diversity are more likely to protest. *Ceteris paribus*, the extent of ideological diversity in a party system indexes the severity of policy conflicts that can mobilize citizens to engage in rallies, demonstra- tions and other types of direct political action.

From ballot box to marketplace politics?

Interest in the incidence of and inter-relationships among various forms of political participation is longstanding (e.g. Barnes and Kaase, 1979; Marsh, 1977; Perry *et al.*, 1992; Verba and Nie, 1972; Verba *et al.*, 1971). Barnes and Kaase's (1979) pathbreaking comparative study catalogued how the repertoire of political action in Western democracies had expanded in the 1960s and 1970s to encompass a variety of 'unconventional' activities ranging from marches and rallies, to 'sit-ins' and other forms of civil disobedience, to violence against persons and property. Above, we investigated the frequency of public involvement in several such activities in Britain and other European democracies. Here, we focus more closely on two closely related forms of political action – 'boycotting' and 'buycotting'.

Writing in the late 1970s, Barnes and Kaase (1979) included boycotting goods and services in their political action inventory. Some three decades later, boycotting has been joined by 'buycotting' which occurs when concerned citizens purchase products such as 'fair-trade' coffee, 'fair-wage' clothing and shoes, genetically unmodified foods, and 'green goods' ranging from energy-conserving light bulbs to hybrid automobiles to make political statements and advance causes they care about. Unlike the chance to vote in national elections, boycotting and buycotting opportunities occur on an ongoing basis as millions of citizens go about their quotidian market activities. Because the total volume of such opportunities is enormous, and the amount of money involved is staggering, boycotting and buycotting activities can be powerful political tools. Not requiring the intermediation of politicians or parties, these activities may appeal strongly to people who are disaffected with traditional forms of political action. Recognizing this, some analysts have contended that declining turnout in many mature democracies is linked to the rise of politically motivated marketplace activities. Quite simply, increasing numbers of citizens are substituting purchasing power for ballots (e.g. Thomassen, 2005: 6–7).

The 2002 ESS data enable us to compare the incidence of boycotting and buycotting in Britain and other European democracies, and how these activities are related to other, more traditional forms of political participation. We begin by considering how boycotting and buycotting are correlated with other activities measured in the ESS

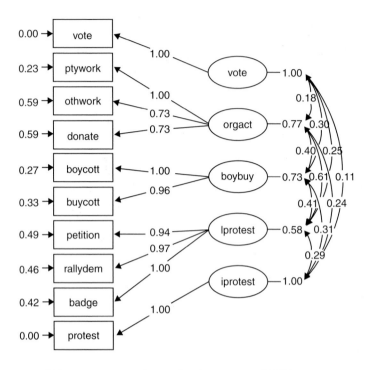

Chi-square = 66.20, df = 28, P-value = 0.0006, RMSEA = 0.026

Figure 7.6 Structure of political participation in Britain, 2002

surveys. For this purpose, we employ confirmatory factor analysis (CFA) (e.g. Bollen, 1989), and specify a five-factor model of political participation with separate, but inter-related factors for voting turn-out, organizational activities, legal protests, illegal protests and boy-cotting/buycotting. Unlike conventional exploratory factor analysis (EFA), the inter-factor correlations in a CFA are parameter estimates of relationships between latent-level variables purged of random measurement error. These inter-factor correlations calibrate relation-ships between boycotting/buycotting, on the one hand, and other, more traditional forms of political participation, such as voting and party and interest group activities. The implication of the substitution argument is that these correlations are negative. As people abandon the ballot box, they opt for other modes of political involvement. In the contemporary era, becoming boycotters and buycotters may be a favoured alternative.

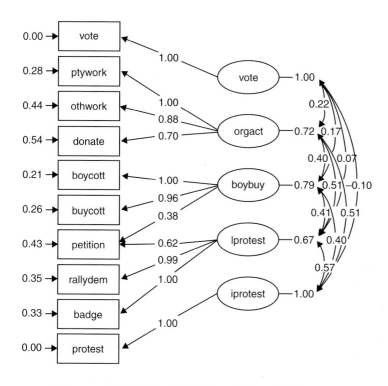

Chi-square = 724.08, df = 27, P-value = 0.00000, RMSEA = 0.026

Figure 7.7 Structure of political participation in European democracies excluding Britain, 2002

Figures 7.6 and 7.7 summarize key results of the confirmatory factor analyses of ten political activities for Britain and twenty-one other European countries. The first point to note is that the models fit extremely well in both cases. Although the chi-square 'badness-of-fit' statistics are significant, this is virtually guaranteed by the large ESS sample sizes. In contrast, the RMSEA fit statistics are very small, 0.026 in both the British and the pan-European analyses, with values of this statistic significantly below 0.05, as is the case here, indicating a good fit (Browne and Cudeck, 1993). Also impressive are the many strong, statistically significant factor loadings, which average 0.87 for the British CFA and 0.77 for the European one. These results testify that – as measured by the ESS data gathered via a common survey instrument – the *structure* of political participation is invariant between Britain and other European countries considered as a group.

The other big story told by these analyses is that all of the correlations between the boycotting/buycotting factor and the other participation factors are *positive*. For Britain, these correlations, all of which are statistically significant, range from a low of 0.35 with the voting factor to a high of 0.71 with the legal protest factor (Table 7.7, Panel A). The comparable numbers for the European CFA model are 0.19 for the voting factor and 0.56 for the legal protest factor (Table 7.7, Panel B). These positive correlations between voting and the boycotting/buycotting factor indicate that there is no *individual-level* evidence of a substitution effect whereby people are abandoning the ballot box for marketplace politics. More generally, the array of significant inter-factor correlations – several of which are quite strong – in the British and European confirmatory factor models testifies that people who are politically active in one way tend to be active in other ways as well.

Next, we extend the search for possible substitution effects between voting and boycotting and buycotting activities in two ways. First, we investigate whether correlations between the two types of political participation differ for younger and older people. It is the former who may be doing the substituting, frequenting fair-trade coffee houses rather than polling places. As shown earlier, younger people do vote at substantially lower rates than do older ones; perhaps, they also do *relatively* more boycotting and buycotting. If so, then there may be negative correlations between these activities among younger people, correlations that cannot be observed in global analyses such as those summarized in Table 7.7.

To pursue this hypothesis, we divide the British and all of the European ESS country samples into two age groups – those under thirty-five years of age and those thirty-five and over. We then compute the correlations (r) between voting turnout in the last general election and boycotting and buycotting activities. The results, summarized in Table 7.8, fail to indicate individual-level tradeoffs between the two types of participation. Across Britain and twenty-one other European countries, there are forty-seven statistically significant correlations. All are positive, with twenty-two occurring for the under-thirty-five age groups and twenty-five occurring for the thirty-five-and-older groups. These correlations tend to be quite modest in magnitude, but

Table 7.7 *The structure of political participation in Britain and other European democracies, inter-factor correlations*

Panel A. Great Britain

	Factors				
	Voting	Organizational activity	Boycotting, buycotting	Legal protests	Illegal protests
Organizational activity	0.20				
Boycotting, buycotting	0.35	0.60			
Legal protests	0.33	0.91	0.71		
Illegal protests	0.11	0.27	0.36	0.38	1.00

Panel B. Other European democracies

	Factors				
	Voting	Organizational activity	Boycotting, buycotting	Legal protests	Illegal protests
Organizational activity	0.25				
Boycotting, buycotting	0.19	0.54			
Legal protests	0.09	0.84	0.56		
Illegal protests	−0.10	0.60	0.44	0.70	1.00

Note: inter-factor correlations are generated by confirmatory factor analyses summarized in Figures 7.6 and 7.7.
Source: 2002 ESS.

no more so for the younger people than for the older ones. Thus, there is no individual-level evidence of substitution effects among young people in Britain or any of the other twenty-one European countries in the 2002 ESS data set.

Table 7.8 *Correlations between boycotting, buycotting and turnout by age group in twenty-one European democracies, 2002*

	Age group			
	Under 35		35 and older	
	Boycott	Buycott	Boycott	Buycott
Country				
United Kingdom	0.17*	0.17*	0.12*	0.13*
Austria	0.05	0.13*	0.05*	0.04
Belgium	−0.03	0.13*	0.00	0.07*
Czech Republic	0.05	0.01	0.08*	0.14*
Denmark	0.08*	0.16*	0.02	0.08*
Finland	0.09	0.08	0.04	0.12*
France	0.12*	0.02	0.13*	0.08*
Germany	0.11*	0.18*	0.07*	0.10*
Greece	0.02	0.04	0.03	0.02
Hungary	0.10*	0.07	0.07*	0.11*
Ireland	0.11*	0.17*	0.07*	0.04
Italy	0.03	0.04	0.06	0.03
Luxembourg	−0.05	0.14*	0.01	0.19*
Netherlands	−0.01	0.07	0.02	0.10*
Norway	0.10*	0.14*	0.08*	0.09*
Poland	0.09*	0.04	0.07*	0.06*
Portugal	0.16*	0.16*	0.01	0.03
Slovenia	0.01	0.08	0.01	0.04
Spain	0.02	0.12*	0.00	0.02
Sweden	0.09*	0.08	0.06*	0.10*
Switzerland	0.20*	0.22*	0.11*	0.14*

* – $p \leq 0.05$.
Source: 2002 ESS.

A second way of searching for possible substitution effects involving voting and boycotting/buycotting is to shift to the aggregate level of analysis. It is possible for individual-level correlations between these two types of activities to remain positive while their aggregate balance in particular countries shifts away from voting and towards

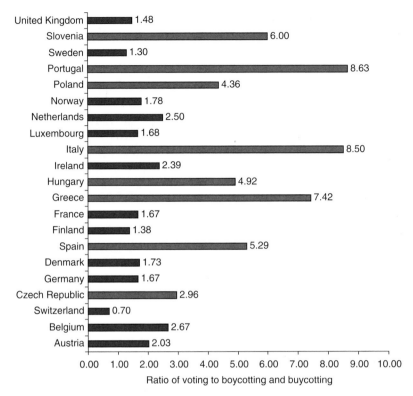

Figure 7.8 Ratios of voting to boycotting and buycotting in European democracies, 2002 (*Source*: 2002 ESS)

boycotting and buycotting. Consonant with the CFA results presented above and their aggregate-level correlation of +0.91 in the 2002 ESS surveys, we treat boycotting and buycotting as a single phenomenon. Figure 7.8 displays ratios of the percentages of voters in the most recent national election (using official turnout figures) to boycotters plus buycotters in the 2002 ESS surveys. These ratios vary markedly across the twenty-one countries. Although voters outnumber boycott-ers/buycotters everywhere but in Switzerland, differences between the relative sizes of the two groups tend to be much smaller in Britain and elsewhere in northern Europe than in southern and eastern Europe. Illustratively, the British voting and boycotting/buycotting figures are 59% and 40% for a ratio of 1.48 to one. For Sweden, they are 78% (voting) and 60% (boycotting/buycotting) for a ratio of 1.30 to one.

In contrast, the equivalent numbers for Portugal are 69% and 8% for a ratio of 8.63 to one. The figures for Slovenia are 72% (voters) and 12% (boy/buycotters) for a ratio of 6.0 to one. Overall, although turnout rates in southern and eastern European countries are very similar to those in the northern countries, the incidence of boycotting and buycotting tends to be much lower. Specifically, average turnout is 68% for the northern countries and 71% for the southern and eastern countries. However, in the northern countries, boycotting/buycotting averages 40%, whereas in the southern and eastern countries, the average is only 12%. The average ratio of turnout to boycotting and buycotting is less than two to one in northern Europe, but fully six to one in southern and eastern Europe.

These patterns prompt us to consider three hypotheses about the aggregate incidence of boycotting and buycotting in Britain and elsewhere. First, as discussed above, there is a negative relationship between the frequency of these activities and turnout. Country-level correlations (r) support this conjecture, but only very weakly – the correlations are −0.20 for voting and boycotting, and −0.13 for voting and buycotting. Second, the finding that levels of boycotting and buycotting are very much the preserve of northern European countries is suggestive. One may conjecture that boycotting and buycotting are relatively popular in these countries because many of their citizens can afford to use the marketplace as an arena of political action. Fair-trade coffees, fair-wage running shoes and green goods cost more, but the tariff is bearable. Viewed this way, what drives boycotting and buycotting is the ability of citizens in wealthy countries to buy politically attractive goods – goods that are unaffordable luxuries for much larger proportions of people in poorer countries. Consistent with this hypothesis, the correlations (r) between boycotting and buycotting, on the one hand, and GDP per capita (in 2002 US dollars), on the other, are substantial, +0.63 in the former case, and +0.69 in the latter one. In the logged metric, these correlations are stronger still: +0.75 for boycotting and +0.70 for buycotting.

The importance of national wealth as an aggregate correlate of boycotting and buycotting is sustained in multivariate regression analyses that use turnout and GDP per capita as predictor variables. In these analyses, a dummy variable for status as a former communist state is added to ensure that a significant wealth coefficient is not a spurious

Table 7.9 *Regression analyses of aggregate-level boycotting and buycotting, twenty-one European democracies*

Predictor variables	Model A		Model B	
	Boycotting		Buycotting	
	β	s.e.	β	s.e.
Constant	−3.31	3.20	−2.13	3.31
Turnout last election (log)	−0.28	0.52	−0.51	0.54
GDP per capita (log)	0.72**	0.24	0.74**	0.24
Former communist state	−0.36	0.37	−0.04	0.38
R^2 =		0.59		0.51
Adjusted R^2 =		0.52		0.43

** − $p \leq 0.01$, * − $p \leq 0.05$; one-tailed test.
Note: boycotting and buycotting are measured as natural logs of percentages calculated from 2002 ESS data.
Source: 2002 ESS and International IDEA website: www.idea.int/vt.

artefact of the negative effects of communist regimes on both economic and political development. The regression results, displayed in Table 7.9, confirm the importance of national wealth; GDP per capita is the only predictor with a statistically significant impact ($p \leq 0.01$) on the incidence of boycotting (Model A) and buycotting (Model B) in the twenty-one European countries. Neither being a former communist state nor turnout in the most recent national election has a significant effect. However, the sign on the latter variable is negative, thereby quietly hinting − nothing more − that aggregate-level substitution processes may be afoot.

The third hypothesis serves as a caveat about the second one. Some three decades ago, Barnes and Kaase (1979) observed that the incidence of hitherto 'unconventional' political activities had increased in the prosperous and secure mature democracies they studied. The repertoire of political action had expanded beyond voting along multiple dimensions. This, in turn, suggests that a wide variety of activities, not just boycotting and buycotting, are correlated strongly and positively with national wealth. If so, we should observe such a correlation

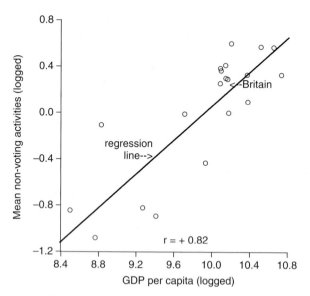

Figure 7.9 Mean number of nonvoting political activities by GDP per capita, twenty-one European democracies, 2002 (*Source*: 2002 ESS and World Bank)

between a summary measure of non-electoral forms of participation and GDP per capita. And, we do. As Figure 7.9 illustrates, across the twenty-one ESS countries, the correlation between the logged versions of GDP per capita and the average number of non-electoral political activities is fully +0.82. As the figure also shows, regressing mean number of nonvoting activities on GDP per capita produces a regression line that passes very close to the British point on the graph. The analysis describes the British case very well.

The regression analysis summarized in Table 7.10, Model A reveals that this strong relationship persists with controls for turnout in the previous general election and former communist state status, both of which fail to exert significant effects. Model B extends the analysis to a dependent variable that does not include boycotting and buycotting. The results are substantially unchanged. In both analyses, the turnout coefficient is negative, but far from statistical significance. Substitution processes involving voting turnout, on the one hand, and boycotting/buycotting and other forms of citizen politics, on the other, may be afoot but, as yet, they are not in play.

Table 7.10 *Regression analyses of average levels of engagement in various forms of political participation, twenty-one European democracies*

Predictor variables	Model A		Model B	
	All activities but voting		All activities but voting and boy/buycotting	
	β	s.e.	β	s.e.
Constant	−5.55**	2.12	−6.04**	1.97
Turnout last election (log)	−0.20	0.35	−0.09	0.32
GDP per capita (log)	0.65***	0.15	0.60***	0.15
Former communist state	−0.20	0.25	−0.22	0.23
R^2 =	0.70		0.71	
Adjusted R^2 =	0.64		0.65	

*** −p ≤ 0.001, ** −p ≤ 0.01; one-tailed test.
Note: activities include voting, boycotting, buycotting, donating money, party work, work for other organizations, wearing a badge, signing petitions, taking part in rallies or demonstrations, taking part in illegal protests.
Source: 2002 ESS.

Conclusion: citizen politics in Britain and elsewhere

When it comes to citizen political participation, Britain is not unique. Rather, the British structure of political activity closely resembles that of other European democracies considered as a group. In addition to voting, the contemporary European repertoire of political action includes party work, volunteering, boycotting and buycotting, rallies, demonstrations and, for very small minorities, illegal protests. There also are many similarities in the factors that drive various forms of political participation in Britain and elsewhere. In this regard, the pan-European analyses presented in the chapter identify institutional factors which influence political participation in Britain, but can be studied only in a comparative context.

One such factor is the ideological diversity of a party system. The manifesto research programme shows that British political parties have moved quite close together in the ideological spectrum over the past decade (Budge *et al.* 2001; Klingemann *et al.*, 2006). Echoing findings on the determinants of turnout presented in *Political Choice in Britain* (Clarke *et al.*, 2004b), the institutional analyses in this chapter indicate that ideological convergence reduces both electoral participation and protest behaviour and, in effect, creates apathy. In addition, Britain's adherence to a single-member plurality electoral system, unique among European countries studied here, inhibits turnout and promotes protest behaviour. However, a change in the national electoral system to some form of proportional representation would not necessarily be a 'good thing'. PR is likely to stimulate the growth of new parties, and this, in turn, would work to reduce turnout as information-processing costs rise for average citizens. At the same time, analyses suggest that inter-party competition can also have a positive impact on electoral participation, so this may offset problems associated with multiparty politics. Institutions can have multiple, offsetting, effects on levels of turnout and other forms of political activity.

We know that electoral participation in Britain, as in many other mature democracies, is in long-term decline. Present evidence locates a key source of this decline in the fact that many in the current generation of young people are abandoning voting. Political action via the ballot box no longer attracts young people in the same way as it did a generation ago. Age gradients in other forms of political activity are not nearly as steep, although the multivariate British analyses clearly suggest a general pattern of increasing participation through middle age, with decreasing activity among the elderly.

The British and pan-European analyses show that several variables in the cognitive engagement and general incentives models have significant and properly signed effects on voting turnout. A number of these predictors also influence other forms of political participation such as protesting, volunteering and party work. In addition, valence politics variables are very much in play. Evaluations of the performance of political parties on the economy and other policy areas, judgments about the performance of party leaders, as well as more broad-gauged reactions to the performance of the political system have a variety of significant effects. Again, these effects are not confined to turnout but, rather, extend in predictable ways to other political activities.

The British analyses also tell an interesting story about increasingly popular boycotting and buycotting activities. Some observers have proposed that the enhanced popularity of these activities signifies that marketplace politics is emerging as a substitute for electoral participation. This conjecture has little empirical support. At the individual level, all of the significant correlations between boy/buycotting and voting turnout in twenty-one European democracies – new and old alike – are positive, not negative. This is true for both younger people as well as older ones. At the aggregate level, there is a very mild hint of a substitution pattern, but only that. Correlations are negative, but very weak and statistically insignificant.

What matters is national wealth. Across the twenty-one European democracies included in the 2002 European Social Survey, relationships between boy/buycotting and GDP per capita are positive and very strong. However, this is true for other non-electoral activities as well. Viewed globally, the big difference between Britain and other wealthy northern European democracies, versus their counterparts in southern and eastern Europe, is not lower turnout but higher levels of engagement in other forms of political participation. In the context of democratic politics, national wealth, and what accompanies it in terms of educational opportunities, dense communication networks, and access to politically relevant information, help to boost citizen involvement in a diverse range of political activities – some system supportive, and others system challenging.

8 | *Performance, people and the political system*

In previous chapters, we show that valence judgments have powerful effects on party choice and electoral participation. In this chapter, we consider how these judgments affect people's orientations towards themselves as political actors and their orientations towards various institutions of the British political system. A focus on people's sense of themselves as political actors enables us to explore the sources of several key independent variables that drive electoral turnout and other forms of political participation. Specifically, we develop and test models that explain why some people are more interested in politics, feel more politically efficacious, or have a stronger sense of civic duty than do others. In turn, a focus on orientations towards political institutions – on support for the 'political regime' (Easton, 1965) – enables us to study the extent to which effective government performance affects trust in major political institutions, attitudes towards parties and elections, and extent of satisfaction with the practice of democracy in Britain.

The first section develops a typology of citizens' orientations towards the political system and describes operational measures of key concepts. The second section outlines the theoretical reasoning motivating our argument that valence considerations affect people's orientations towards politics in general just as they affect electoral choice in particular. Our core claim is that people are more likely to respond positively towards political institutions and processes when they think that those institutions and processes have delivered, or are likely to deliver, valued goods and services. They are more likely to respond negatively when institutions and processes have failed to deliver (or are seen as unlikely to deliver) them. Although we emphasize the importance of valence judgments, we also recognize that other factors could influence citizens' political orientations. Accordingly, we develop a set of operational measures of ideology and values, and of personal and social orientations, to consider their competing or complementary effects.

In the third section, we specify and estimate explanatory models of various political orientations. Analyses of these models indicate that valence considerations play the most important role in determining people's attitudes towards state-level institutions and processes, with secondary roles played by ideology and values. However, the determinants of individual-level orientations such as political interest, efficacy and civic duty include a complex mix of valence judgments, ideology, personal orientations and demographic characteristics.

Describing political orientations

Personal political orientations

Analyses of voting turnout in Chapter 5 reveal that people's orientations towards, or engagement with, politics have an important impact on the extent to which they participate in the electoral process. Individuals are more likely to vote, inter alia, when they are interested in politics, have a sense of political efficacy, or have a strong sense that voting is a civic duty. But these analyses do not tell us *why* people vary in their levels of interest, efficacy or duty.

In *Political Choice in Britain*, we show that *levels* of political interest and political efficacy have not changed much since the 1970s. In that decade, BES surveys document that, on average, 62% of the electorate had at least some interest in politics (Clarke *et al.*, 2004b: Chapter 9). In 2001 and 2005, the equivalent figures were 64% and 71%, respectively, suggesting that political interest has increased over time (see Table 8.1). A similar pattern obtains for long-term trends in sense of political efficacy. Levels of efficacy in Britain have not changed much in the past four decades. Large numbers of people have always thought that they had little or no ability to influence the political process (Clarke *et al.*, 2004b: Chapter 9). Data gathered in the 2005 BES reaffirm this finding. When asked: 'on a scale from 0 to 10, where 10 means a great deal of influence and 0 means no influence, how much influence do *you* have on politics and public affairs?' a large majority of respondents indicated that they did not feel very politically efficacious. Specifically, 25% gave themselves a score of zero, 75% scores of four or lower, and the average was only 2.7 points (see Figure 8.1). Although low, the latter figure constitutes an increase from 2001 when the mean on

Table 8.1 *Interest in politics, Britain 2005*

A. *'How much interest do you generally have in what in going on in politics?'*

	%	
A great deal	7	
Quite a lot	26	
Some	38	% with at least some interest = 71
Not very much	24	
None at all	5	
(N)	(4,159)	

B. *'How interested were you in the general election that was held on May 5th?'*

	%	
Very interested	30	
Somewhat interested	43	% at least somewhat interested = 73
Not very interested	19	
Not at all interested	8	
(N)	(4,158)	

C. *'On a scale of 0 to 10 how much attention do you generally pay to politics?'*

	%	
Pay no attention 0	5	
1	3	
2	6	
3	9	
4	9	
5	16	Mean score = 5.4
6	15	
7	17	
8	13	
9	5	
Pay a great deal of attention 10	3	
(N)	(4,158)	

Source: 2005 BES post-election survey.

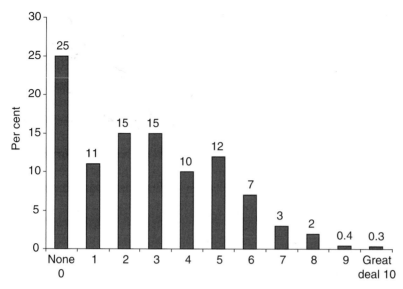

Figure 8.1 Perceived personal political influence, 2005 (*Source*: 2005 BES post-election survey)

the perceived political influence scale was only 1.8. More generally, time series data from the BES and other national surveys indicate that there has been no secular decline in either political interest or political efficacy.

Measures of sense of civic duty do not have as extensive a lineage as do measures of political interest and efficacy. However, the former have been asked in several surveys conducted since the mid-1990s. The results indicate that the percentage of respondents expressing a belief that voting is a duty is always substantial (see Figure 8.2). For example, the 1997 and 2001 BES surveys asked respondents whether they agreed with the statement that 'it is every citizen's duty to vote'. In 1997, 79% agreed, a figure that was almost exactly replicated in 2001. Four years later, agreement fell slightly to 75% in the 2005 pre-campaign survey and then increased to 77% in the 2005 post-election survey. The 2001 and 2005 BES surveys also asked respondents whether they agreed or disagreed with the statement that nonvoting was a 'serious neglect' of their duty as a citizen. Levels of agreement were 65% in the 2001 post-election survey, and 66% and 69% in the 2005 pre- and post-election surveys, respectively. These numbers are very similar to those generated by questions asked periodically in

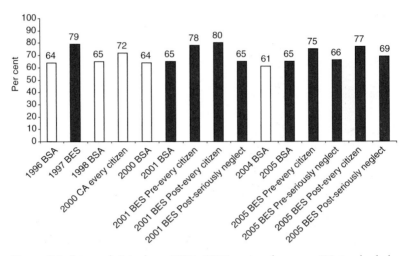

Figure 8.2 Sense of civic duty, 1996–2005 national surveys (*Note*: shaded bars represent election years. *Source*: BSA, CA and BES national surveys)

the annual British Social Attitudes (BSA) surveys.[1] Since 1996, from 61% to 65% of the BSA respondents have indicated that they believe 'it's everyone's duty to vote in a general election'. Viewed generally, the survey data suggest that the idea of voting as a civic duty is widespread, but not ubiquitous, in contemporary Britain. And, as we know from analyses presented in Chapter 5, there are very large age-related differences, with younger people being much less likely to view voting as an important part of citizenship.

Overall, the survey data on individual political orientations do not suggest any distinctive patterns. However, it is equally clear that at any point in time people exhibit very different individual orientations towards politics. Some are very interested, highly efficacious and/or strongly feel a sense of civic duty that impels them to participate in the political process. Others are not. To explain these individual-level variations, we treat interest, efficacy and duty as related but distinct aspects of individual political orientations.

We measure political interest using answers to three questions asked in the 2005 BES. These questions involve general interest in politics, interest in the general election, and the amount of attention (on a 0–10 scale) paid to politics and public affairs. Responses are displayed in Table 8.1. An exploratory factor analysis reveals that

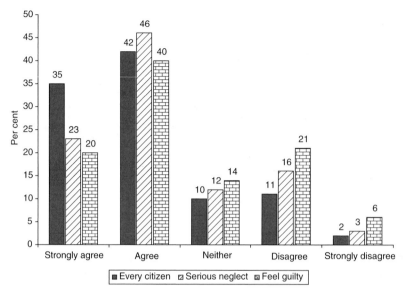

Figure 8.3 Three measures of sense of civic duty, 2005 (*Source*: 2005 BES post-election survey)

the variables load strongly on a single factor.[2] Accordingly, we use the factor scores produced by this analysis in our investigation of the sources of political interest.

As per the preceding discussion, we measure political efficacy by asking BES respondents to use a 0–10 scale to assess the amount of influence they have on politics and public affairs. As Figure 8.1 shows, the modal category is zero (which represents 25% of the respondents), with only very small proportions registering scores of either nine (0.4%) or ten (0.3%). This pattern of most people thinking that they have little or no political influence is consistent with results produced by traditional Likert-based measures of efficacy (e.g. Clarke *et al.*, 2004b: Chapter 8). We measure civic duty using responses to the three Likert statements depicted in Figure 8.3.[3] As per the preceding discussion, there are relatively high levels of agreement with all three statements, indicating that many people believe that voting is a duty of citizenship. The three correlations (r) between these three variables are all above +0.6. An index of civic duty is constructed by computing respondents' average scores for the three items.

Political system orientations

In addition to having different views of themselves as political actors, people also differ in their orientations towards, or support for, the political system. Following Easton (1965; see also Kornberg and Clarke, 1992), we distinguish between support for *political authorities* – the government of the day – and support for the *political regime* – the system of rules, practices, institutions and processes that provides the 'authoritative allocation of values' in a society. We consider four aspects of regime support. The first is the extent to which citizens trust major institutions of the state. The 2005 BES included a series of 0–10 scales to measure how much respondents trusted the Westminster parliament, the civil service, the police and local government.[4] Mean scores show that the police received the highest levels of trust (average trust score = 5.9), although other institutions were not far behind (see Figure 8.4). An exploratory factor analysis reveals that these orientations towards various institutions load on a single underlying factor that explains almost 64% of their item variance. We use factor scores generated by this analysis as a summary measure of institutional trust.

A second aspect of regime support involves attitudes towards political parties as organizations that play important roles in linking citizens to the system of governance in a democratic polity. The 2005 BES asked respondents to indicate whether they agreed or disagreed with several statements about the performance of Britain's political parties in general, rather than views of particular parties. The responses indicate that many people are displeased with how parties operate.[5] As Figure 8.5 shows, over four of five BES respondents agreed that 'there is a big difference between what parties say and what they do' and that 'parties spend too much time bickering', and nearly two-thirds agreed that parties 'are more interested in winning elections than governing'. In addition, slightly over half thought that 'the main parties offer no choice', and over two-fifths, that parties do more to divide people rather than to unite them. Attitudes towards Britain's parties as measured by these statements can be summarized effectively by a single underlying factor that explains almost half the variance in the item responses (see Figure 8.5).

A third aspect of regime support pertains to attitudes towards the electoral process. Providing periodic opportunities for people to

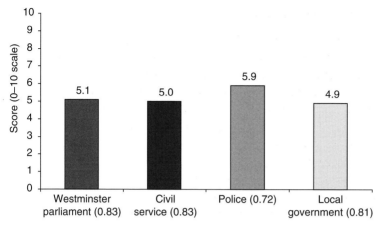

Figure 8.4 Trust in political institutions, 2005 (*Note*: numbers in parentheses are factor loadings. Exploratory factor analysis generates one factor that explains 63.8% of the item variance. *Source*: 2005 BES post-election survey self-completion questionnaire)

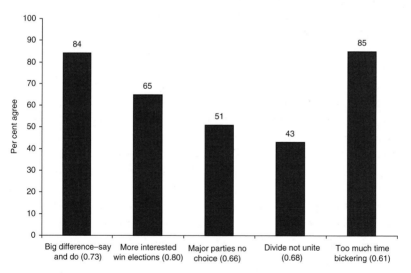

Figure 8.5 Evaluations of the party system, 2005 (*Note*: numbers in parentheses are factor loadings. Exploratory factor analysis generates one factor that explains 48.9% of the item variance. *Source*: 2005 BES post-election survey self-completion questionnaire)

choose among competing political parties, elections long have been a
focal point of Britain's democratic process. The data summarized in
Figure 8.6 indicate that public evaluations of how elections perform
are mixed. For example, many people do not think that elections provide opportunities to make meaningful political choices – less than
30% of the 2005 BES respondents believed that parties 'offer real
choices in elections' and almost half thought that 'elections don't
change anything'.[6] Nevertheless, elections are not seen as shams;
almost 70% concurred that 'elections hold politicians accountable',
and fully 84% rejected the view that elections are 'a waste of time and
money'. These variegated reactions notwithstanding, an exploratory
factor analysis reveals that judgments about elections load strongly on
a single factor. Factor scores from this analysis provide our measure
of electoral process evaluations.

In addition to attitudes towards governmental institutions, parties and elections, we are interested in citizens' overall assessments of the operation of Britain's democratic political system. A
convenient summary measure of these assessments is provided by
answers to a question about satisfaction with democracy in Britain.
Data presented in *Political Choice in Britain* (Clarke *et al.*, 2004b:

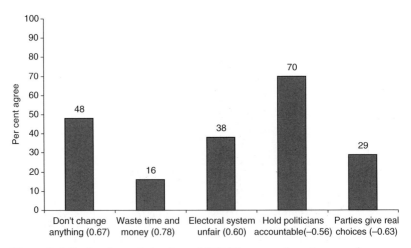

Figure 8.6 Evaluations of elections, 2005 (*Note*: numbers in parentheses
are factor loadings. Exploratory factor analysis generates one factor that
explains 42.7% of the item variance. *Source*: 2005 BES post-election survey self-completion questionnaire)

Chapter 9) document that satisfaction with British democracy has increased gradually, but irregularly, since the early 1970s. Consistent with this pattern, Figure 8.7 illustrates that approximately two-thirds of those interviewed in the 2001 BES were at least fairly satisfied with 'democracy in Britain today'. By 2005, nearly seven in ten expressed this opinion. However, as in earlier surveys, ringing endorsements are few and far between. In both 2001 and 2005, less than one person in ten said that they were 'very satisfied' with how British democracy was working. Later in this chapter we examine the individual-level determinants of the four aspects of support for the British political system.

Explaining political orientations

People vary both in the ways in which they think about themselves as political actors and in their levels of support for the political system. How can we account for these variations? In this section, we develop three broad theoretical answers to this question. These answers focus on valence judgments, ideology and values, and what we term 'personal and social orientations'. Our general theoretical schema is summarized in Figure 8.8.

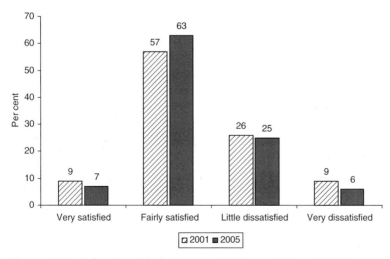

Figure 8.7 Satisfaction with democracy in Britain, 2001 and 2005 (*Source*: 2001 and 2005 BES post-election surveys)

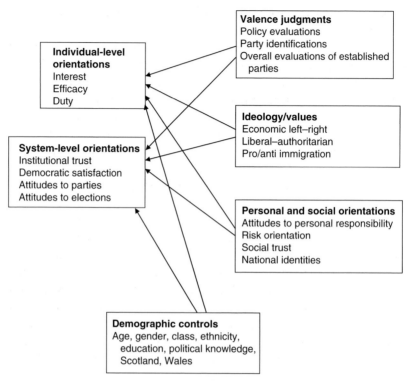

Figure 8.8 Pathways to political orientations

Valence judgments

As discussed in previous chapters, valence judgments involve evaluations of the competence of rival political parties and their leaders to solve major problems that the country faces. When forming these judgments, people use their own direct experiences as well as their more general assessments of how well (or badly) policy is being delivered across a range of areas. Analyses in Chapters 5 and 6 show that valence considerations play key roles in determining the political choices that voters make. At the core of valence judgments is the idea that rational citizens will support a party deemed best able to deliver desired policy outcomes. As discussed in Chapter 2, citizens make these assessments by comparing the past and projected record of an incumbent party with their estimates of the likely performance of opposition parties. Operating in a world where reliable information on policy outcomes is difficult to come by, voters employ party leader images as cost-effective cues that help them to decide which party will do the best job.

The consequences of valence calculations can extend beyond party choice. People who conclude that the incumbent government is performing well also may be more positively disposed towards other aspects of the political system. To see how such effects might work, we first need to distinguish among three types of valence calculations. Thus far, we have described these calculations in terms of judgments about the policy competence of rival parties and leaders. Although these comparative *policy judgments* about projected performance are central to valence politics, there are two other possible dimensions of valence judgments. One relates to party identification or partisanship. As discussed in earlier chapters, we regard partisanship as a summary of an individual's accumulated evaluations of the performance of parties and their leaders. A 'running tally' of party and leader performance (Fiorina, 1981), partisanship is continually updated in the light of new information, with earlier information being progressively discounted. Viewed this way, partisanship is linked to, but distinct from, contemporaneous policy judgments. At any time t, someone may identify with one party because of what it has done in the past, but simultaneously think that another party now stands a better chance of delivering policy in key areas.

A third dimension is what might be termed generic valence judgments. These involve evaluations of parties and leaders in general, rather than voters' evaluations of particular parties or leaders. For example, a voter who prefers party or leader X to party or leader Y may think quite highly of both X and Y. This person's views are clearly different from someone who prefers X to Y but who has a very low opinion of both X and Y. The person who thinks well of both X and Y would have high generic valence judgments; the person with a low opinion of both would have low generic valence judgments.

Is there evidence to support the idea that the British electorate's performance judgments are structured in this way? Table 8.2 summarizes an exploratory factor analysis of several variables that reflect various aspects of the valence calculations outlined above. The analysis yields a distinct three-factor solution, which explains over 60% of the variance in the component variables.[7] The solution distinguishes sharply among policy judgments, partisanship and generic judgments. The health of the economy is a key valence issue, and the first factor

Table 8.2 *Exploratory factor analysis of dimensions of valence assessments*

Valence variables	Factor		
	Policy	Partisanship	Generic
Emotional responses to national economy	**0.69**	0.18	0.27
Emotional responses to personal economy	**0.81**	−0.05	0.03
Economic evaluations/cognitions	**0.75**	0.28	0.09
Labour party identifier	0.15	**0.87**	0.17
Opposition party identifier	−0.11	**−0.91**	0.07
Overall evaluations of Iraq War	0.08	0.30	**0.52**
Average evaluation of party leaders*	0.14	0.04	**0.74**
Party can handle most important problem	−0.02	0.02	**0.58**
Mean evaluation Labour and Conservative competence	0.34	−0.15	**0.71**

Note: principal component analysis, total item variance explained = 60.5%.
* – average scores on 0–10 leader affect scores; Conservative, Labour and Liberal Democrat leaders for England; Conservative, Labour, Liberal Democrat and SNP for Scotland; Conservative, Labour, Liberal Democrat and Plaid Cymru leaders for Wales.
Source: 2005 BES post-election survey.

clearly captures reactions to economic conditions. It shows that emotional responses to the economy and economic evaluations all load highly on the same underlying economic policy judgment dimension. High loadings on the second factor (which are positive for incumbent Labour identifiers and negative for opposition identifiers) suggest that there is a distinct and separate dimension that represents incumbent versus opposition partisanship.

The four remaining variables load strongly on a third factor, which closely corresponds to the generic judgments concept articulated above. This factor combines overall evaluations of what was, in effect, a bipartisan Labour/Conservative pro-war policy towards Iraq; individual-level average evaluations of the Labour, Conservative and Liberal Democrat leaders (ratings for the leaders of the SNP and

Plaid Cymru are also included in Scotland and Wales, respectively); an evaluation that the most important problem facing the country can be best handled by one of the three parties; and a combined assessment of the degree of competence of Labour and Conservatives to deal with several salient policy areas including asylum, crime, the economy, health, taxation and terrorism. The three-factor structure reported in Table 8.2 thus provides empirical support for the theoretical distinctions that we have drawn among the dimensions of valence calculation. The critical question is whether these types of valence assessment influence either individual political orientations or regime support. There are good theoretical reasons to think that they do.

Regarding orientations towards the self as a political actor, people who make positive judgments about either government or regime performance also should tend to think that the political system responds to their needs precisely as it delivers what they think it should deliver. As a result, they will be more likely to experience a sense of political efficacy than will those who view the incumbent government's or the regime's performance and, by implication, responsiveness more negatively. In a similar vein, positive performance judgments represent a form of 'positive feedback' that is likely to reinforce citizens' sense of engagement and involvement with the political system. As a result, such judgments will strengthen both people's interest in politics and their sense of civic duty. In contrast, negative performance judgments will reduce the sense of involvement, leading to lower levels of political interest and duty. Taken together, these considerations suggest a simple hypothesis:

$H_{8.1a}$: Political efficacy, political interest and civic duty should vary positively with citizens' policy judgments, with incumbent *versus* opposition partisanship, and with generic judgments about the performance of the major parties and their leaders.

Just as valence assessments will affect levels of political engagement, they also will affect how people think about the political system more generally, i.e. valence assessments will influence regime support. As noted, we regard institutional trust, positive evaluations of parties and elections, and democracy satisfaction as indicators of regime support. The key idea for establishing a linkage between valence judgments and regime support is rooted in democratic theory. Democracies are political systems '*for* the people', i.e. they are charged with delivering the goods and services that their citizens need and want. To the extent that a political regime is seen to do so – the more satisfactory its performance – the more likely it is that people will support it and hold positive views of its various component institutions and processes (e.g. Dahl, 1971; Easton, 1965). By the same token, perceived non-delivery constitutes grounds for a withdrawal of support. Thus, we hypothesize:

$H_{8.1b}$: Institutional trust, pro-party attitudes, pro-election attitudes and democracy satisfaction should vary positively with citizens' policy judgments, with incumbent *versus* opposition partisanship, and with generic judgments about the performance of the major parties and their leaders.

Ideology and values

Although democratic theory provides good reasons for hypothesizing that valence considerations will have significant effects on individual and system orientations, there are other possible sources of such orientations. As Figure 8.8 anticipates, one source is ideology and values. We regard an individual's ideology as a core set of political beliefs and values that a person holds and that underpins her/his view of the political world. Although the ideological beliefs held by citizens in advanced industrial societies have been summarized by locations on a left–right continuum, it is clear that a single dimension does not adequately capture the range of values and beliefs that many people espouse. In this regard, British researchers have recognized that an economic left–right ideological dimension, where left represents a preference for state intervention and redistribution and right is a preference for a minimalist state and free markets, needs to be supplemented by a liberal–authoritarian dimension. On this second dimension, liberal is associated with a compassionate, understanding and tolerant approach to dealing with criminals, those with unconventional lifestyles, and various socially marginalized groups, whereas authoritarian connotes a more judgmental, intolerant and punitive approach to those who 'break the rules' and 'stretch the boundaries' established by law and prevailing social norms.

In our view, this second, liberal–authoritarian dimension needs to be disaggregated into two separate sub-dimensions that distinguish between people's attitudes towards criminals on the one hand and towards socially excluded groups on the other. Criminals and marginalized minorities seem to be two very different groups. Criminals, by definition, have *chosen* to break the law. Members of excluded groups have clearly made no such choices. Accordingly, we hypothesize that the ideology of the British electorate can be usefully characterized in terms of positions in a three-dimensional space. The first dimension corresponds to the traditional economic left–right continuum. The second dimension relates exclusively to how law-breakers should be dealt with – whether a tolerant, liberal approach, or a punitive, authoritarian one, should be adopted. The third dimension focuses on treatment of ethnic minorities, the disabled, the poor and other groups that may suffer because of social, economic or political exclusion. We tap people's positions on this latter dimension using attitudes towards asylum-seeking and immigration – an issue cluster that has become markedly more salient over the past decade.

Table 8.3 reports the results of an exploratory factor analysis of fifteen survey items in the 2005 BES designed to measure value positions along these three dimensions.[8] Also shown is the percentage of respondents who agreed with each statement or, where appropriate, the mean score on a 0–10 self-location scale. Over 40% of the 2005 BES respondents consistently adopted negative positions towards immigrants and asylum seekers and clear majorities took punitive, 'authoritarian' positions with regard to criminal behaviour. For example, fully 82% believed that 'violent criminals should lose their human rights'. Similarly, the mean score on a 0–10 scale measuring a tradeoff between punishing criminals (0) and protecting the rights of the accused (10) was 3.7 – clearly on the punishment side of the scale. In contrast, positions on a left–right scale are much more moderate, with the mean score (5.4) being very close to the centre (five) of the zero (left) to ten (right) continuum.

Regarding the factor analysis, the fifteen items load cleanly on the three hypothesized dimensions (see Table 8.3). The first factor is a pro–anti immigrant dimension; the second is an authoritarian–liberal dimension concerning the treatment of criminals; and the third is a traditional economic left–right dimension. The left–right self-placement scale, which permits respondents to interpret the meanings of left and right, loads strongly on this third dimension. However, it loads only weakly on the other two dimensions. Factor scores

Table 8.3 *Exploratory factor analysis of dimensions of ideology/values*

	Percent agree	Factor		
		Anti-immigrant	Liberal–authoritatrian	Economic left–right
Ideology and values variables				
Immigrants – increase crime rate	47	**0.71**	0.33	0.13
Immigrants – good for the economy	30	**−0.78**	−0.13	0.11
Send asylum seekers home	42	**0.74**	0.29	0.06
Immigrants bring new ideas	49	**−0.70**	−0.12	0.02
Immigrants take jobs	41	**0.76**	0.06	0.04
Death penalty is never justified	37	−0.17	**−0.62**	−0.05
Violent criminals should lose human rights	82	0.08	**0.61**	0.09
Convicted criminals rehabilitated	26	−0.29	**−0.57**	0.03
Lawbreakers – longer prison sentences	63	0.27	**0.56**	0.03
Suspected terrorists – jail without trial	49	0.41	**0.45**	0.22
Reduce crime versus protect rights*	3.7	0.02	**−0.59**	0.11
Ordinary people – fair share of wealth	14	−0.11	−0.14	**0.57**
No need for strong trade unions	12	0.09	−0.05	**0.70**

Table 8.3 (*cont.*)

		Factor		
	Percent agree	Anti-immigrant	Liberal–authoritatrian	Economic left–right
Private enterprise best for economy	28	−0.06	0.10	0.70
Left–right self-placement*	5.4	0.21	0.24	0.53

Note: principal components analysis; total item variance explained = 47.5 per cent.
* – mean score on 0–10 scale.
Source: 2005 BES post-election survey and self-completion questionnaire.

produced by the analysis are used to measure respondents' locations on the three dimensions.

How might people's positions on each of these three dimensions affect their individual or system orientations? With respect to the impact of left–right ideology on individual-level orientations, it seems unlikely that economic left–right position would have a linear effect on political interest, efficacy or duty. There is no obvious a priori reason why either being in favour of or opposed to state intervention should increase an individual's sense of political interest, political efficacy or civic duty. However, it is plausible that people located at the *extremes*, rather than towards the centre, of the economic left–right spectrum might be especially involved. We hypothesize that:

$H_{8.2a}$: Political efficacy, political interest and civic duty should display curvilinear relationships with positions on the economic left–right scale, being highest among ideological 'extremists' and lowest among 'centrists'.

Such curvilinear relationships are less likely in the context of the liberal–authoritarian and pro–anti immigrant dimensions. On both dimensions, the average British voter seems to be considerably removed from the positions adopted by the major political parties. As noted, the mean position for respondents on the 0–10 'reducing crime' vs 'protecting the rights of the accused' scale was 3.7. Respondents were also asked to place the three major parties on the same scale. The mean score position for Labour was 5.1; for the Conservatives, 4.1; and for the Liberal Democrats, 5.0. Thus, respondents generally thought all three major parties were more in sympathy with rights of the accused, and less in sympathy with the need to reduce crime, than they themselves were.

A similar lack of correspondence between people's values and positions adopted by the major parties can be seen with regard to immigration and asylum. As discussed in Chapters 3 and 4, when respondents in the 2005 BES survey were asked an open-ended question involving their views about 'the single most important issue facing the country at the present time', 20% identified immigration/asylum as the most important issues – ahead of the NHS (15%), law and order (12%), the economy (9%) and education (6%) (see Figure 3.1). In contrast, an examination of the 2005 party manifestos reveals an almost studied avoidance of the issues of asylum and immigration. The Labour manifesto mentions these topics on pages fifty-two and fifty-three, amounting in total to about one page of coverage in a 112-page document. The Conservative manifesto devotes a single page (page nineteen) out of twenty-nine to these issues. For their part, the Liberal Democrats offer a single sentence on 'economic migration' in their discussion of 'the economy and business'. In sum, none of the major parties emphasized a 'reduce crime/protect rights' position close to the average voter. And none of the parties accorded prominence to immigration/asylum – the leading 'most important issue' for the 2005 BES respondents. In these circumstances, it might be expected that both 'authoritarians' and those more critical of immigration would feel 'let down' by conventional party politics. It also might be expected that such people would be less interested in politics, less politically efficacious and less bound by a sense of civic duty than their more liberal and more 'pro-immigrant' counterparts. These expectations can be stated summarily as:

$H_{8.2b}$: Political efficacy, political interest and civic duty should vary negatively with positions on the liberal–authoritarian and pro–anti immigration scales.

The potential impact of ideology extends beyond orientations to the self as a political actor. As with valence calculations, ideological positions also may affect people's system-level orientations. Indeed, we argue that for the same reasons that 'authoritarians' and 'anti-immigrants' are less likely to be politically interested, efficacious or dutiful – because they think that their views are not well represented in mainstream party politics – they also are less likely to exhibit strong support for the regime as a whole. In short, the system-level corollary to $H_{8.2b}$ can be stated as:

$H_{8.2c}$: Institutional trust, pro-party attitudes, pro-election attitudes and democracy satisfaction should vary negatively with positions on the liberal–authoritarian and pro–anti immigration scales.

We argue above that economic left–right position should have a curvilinear effect on individual-level orientations such as interest, efficacy and duty. However, in terms of system-level orientations, two rival hypotheses can be proposed. The first is based on the idea that, since the Thatcher government's market reforms of the 1980s, the broad status quo economic position in Britain has been located towards the 'free market' end of the 'state intervention vs free market' continuum. It follows that people who are located on the 'economic right' are more likely to support the current regime that preserves this status quo position than are those on the 'economic left'. In turn, this suggests a simple linear hypothesis about the effects of economic left–right on regime support:

$H_{8.2d}$: Institutional trust, pro-party attitudes, pro-election attitudes and democracy satisfaction should vary positively with positions on the economic left–right scale.

A rival, curvilinear hypothesis involves the possibility that people on the *extremes* of the left–right scale are more likely to engage in ideological critiques of (and thus less likely to support) the existing political regime than are those located closer to the centre of the scale. The accompanying hypothesis is:

$H_{8.2e}$: Institutional trust, pro-party attitudes, pro-election attitudes and democracy satisfaction should display curvilinear relationships with positions on the economic left–right scale; regime support should be lowest among ideological 'extremists' and highest among 'centrists'.

Personal and social orientations

As depicted in Figure 8.8, a third set of influences on people's individual- and system-level political orientations derive from their personal and social values and identities. There are a number of possible values and identities that could be important in this context. Here, we concentrate on four of them.

The first relates to sense of personal responsibility. The 2005 BES survey asked respondents to indicate the extent to which they agreed or disagreed with three statements about the need for people to keep promises, to help others even if their personal safety is threatened, and to take responsibility for themselves.[9] Large numbers of respondents expressed a sense of personal responsibility – 71% said they would never break a promise, 70% would help someone even if there was a threat to their personal safety, and fully 83% wanted people to take more responsibility to provide for themselves (see Figure 8.9). These answers load on a single factor, which we interpret as a measure of the extent to which people prioritize 'personal responsibility' as a general value in everyday life.

A second personal orientation is trust in others, which is an important component of social capital (e.g. Putnam, 2000). We measure

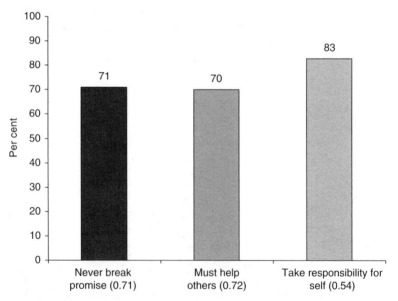

Figure 8.9 Sense of personal responsibility, 2005 (*Note*: numbers in parentheses are factor loadings. Exploratory factor analysis generates one factor that explains 42.8% of the item variance. *Source*: 2005 BES post-election survey)

sense of social trust using two questions (0–10 scales) that asked BES respondents about the extent to which most people can be trusted and the extent to which people try to be fair rather than taking advantage of others.[10] As Figure 8.10 illustrates, social trust is widespread, albeit not ubiquitous, in contemporary Britain. The mean scores on the two 0–10 trust scales are 6.2 in both cases. For purposes of our analyses of political orientations, we average scores on the two scales.

The third personal orientation is an individual's *propensity to accept risk*. For this measure, we use a four-point self-placement scale.[11] Placements on this scale indicate that attitudes towards risk vary widely. Just over one person in ten is 'very willing' to accept risks, over five in ten are 'somewhat willing', nearly three in ten are 'somewhat unwilling' and slightly less than one in ten is 'very unwilling' to do so. Finally, we construct a measure of *national/regional identity* which shows that 22% of the 2005 BES respondents thought of themselves primarily as English, 5% as Scottish, 2% as Welsh and 18% as British. The remainder thought of themselves as being equally British and English/Scottish/Welsh or having some other or no identity.

How might these personal and social characteristics affect political orientations? In the case of personal responsibility and social trust, we argue that people who score highly on such measures are likely to be engaged in their communities (and vice versa). Given the permeability

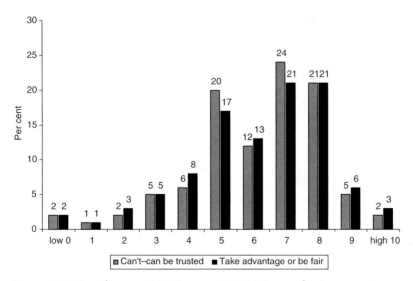

Figure 8.10 Social trust, 2005 (*Source*: 2005 BES post-election survey)

between social and political networks, high levels of individual social engagement, in turn, are likely to spill over and influence individual political engagement. Accordingly, we expect that those who with high levels of responsibility and trust will be more likely to be politically interested, efficacious and dutiful:

$H_{8.3a}$: Political efficacy, political interest and civic duty should vary positively with personal responsibility and social trust.

It also can be argued that the effects of social trust go further. The 'spill over' effects of social trust on political engagement could extend to trust and confidence in national political institutions. The expectation is that high levels of social trust will be associated with higher levels of regime support:

$H_{8.3b}$: Institutional trust, pro-party attitudes, pro-election attitudes and democracy satisfaction should vary positively with social trust.

The effects of risk orientations may be more variegated. People who incline to risk acceptance are likely to be more outgoing individuals than those who are risk averse. We hypothesize that a preparedness to accept risk will be associated with a general sense of personal efficacy and interest in others that, in turn, extends to the political realm. In short, risk-acceptant people, although they may be no more dutiful than their risk-averse counterparts, are likely to exhibit relatively high levels of both political interest and efficacy:

$H_{8.3c}$: Political efficacy and political interest, but not civic duty, should vary positively with risk acceptance.

Finally, we consider the effects of national/regional identity. The British state has long contended with the question of how to reconcile the sometimes competing, and sometimes complementary, notions of British, English, Scots and Welsh identity. The devolution process initiated by the Blair government after 1997, which saw the creation of a Scottish parliament and a Welsh assembly in 1999, gave added impetus to efforts by nationalists in Scotland and Wales to strengthen the sense of national/regional identity in their respective countries. The new assemblies have also created new opportunities for another meaningful area of citizen involvement while possibly making Westminster politics more remote. Accordingly, in the new 'variable geometry' of Britain's post-devolution parliamentary system, there is no compelling a priori argument for thinking that the individual political engagement of national/regional identifiers should differ from that of others.

But if regional identities carry no obvious implication for individual engagement, the same is not necessarily true for regime support. For example, it might be anticipated that strong Scottish or Welsh identifiers would feel less attachment to the institutions of the British state than would 'English' or 'British' identifiers or those who feel 'equally' British and English, Scottish or Welsh. Therefore, we expect that Scottish and Welsh identifiers will exhibit lower levels of regime support than do other identity groups:

$H_{8.3d}$: Institutional trust, pro-party attitudes, pro-election attitudes and democracy satisfaction should all vary negatively with Scottish and Welsh identity.

The hypotheses developed in this section can be regarded, for the most part, as both potentially competing and complementary. In principle, there is no reason why valence, ideology and personal orientations should not influence patterns of individual political engagement and regime support. At the same time, it is important to assess the relative strength of the alternative explanations.

Modelling political orientations

We consider seven models. Three focus on individual political orientations (interest, efficacy, civic duty) and four deal with system orientations or regime support (institutional trust, party attitudes, election attitudes, democracy satisfaction). The general form of the seven models is identical. Following the logic outlined in Figure 8.8 and the hypotheses stated in the previous section, the general specification is:

Political Orientation $= \beta_0 + \beta_1$ Policy Judgments $+ \beta_2$ Incumbent/ Opposition Partisan Identification $+ \beta_3$ Generic Judgements $+$ β_4 Economic Left–Right $+ \beta_5$ Economic Left–Right Squared $+$ β_6 Liberal–Authoritarian $+ \beta_7$ Pro-Anti Immigration $+ \beta_8$ Personal Responsibility $+ \beta_9$ Risk Acceptance $+ \beta_{10}$ Social Trust $+$ β_{11} Scottish Identity $+ \beta_{12}$ Welsh Identity $\Sigma \beta_{13\text{-}k}$ Demographic and Other Controls $+ \varepsilon$ (8.1) where: economic left–right squared is the square of the economic left–right scale, designed to capture non-linear effects of left–right ideology; demographic and other controls include age, education, ethnicity, gender, political knowledge, social class and residence in Scotland or Wales; ε is a stochastic error term ($\sim N(0,\sigma^2)$); and all other variables are as defined previously in the text. Since almost all the political orientation measures, whether they refer to individual or system orientations, are interval-level measures, we use OLS regression to estimate model parameters. Democracy satisfaction is an exception. Since it is measured as a four-category ordinal scale, we use ordered logit (Long, 1997) to estimate parameters in its model.

Models of individual orientations

Table 8.4 reports estimates of the parameters in equation 8.1 for individual orientations, with separate analyses for political interest, political

Table 8.4 *Regression analyses of individual political orientations*

	Model A	Model B	Model C
	Political interest	Political efficacy	Civic duty
Predictor variables	β	β	β
Valence judgments Hypothesis: $H_{8.1a}$			
Policy judgments	0.02	0.15***	0.06***
Partisanship	−0.04**	0.15***	−0.01
Generic judgments	0.20***	0.57***	0.17***
Ideology and values Hypothesis: $H_{8.2a}$			
Left–right scale position	−0.52***	−0.41*	−0.23***
Left–right scale squared	0.07***	0.05*	0.03***
Hypothesis: $H_{8.2b}$			
Liberal–authoritarian scale	0.02	−0.16***	0.07***
Pro–anti immigration scale	−0.20***	−0.11*	−0.09***
Personal orientations Hypothesis: $H_{8.3a}$			
Personal responsibility scale	0.04*	0.13***	0.15***

Table 8.4 (*cont.*)

	Model A	Model B	Model C
Social trust scale	0.01	0.04	0.04***
Risk scale	0.07***	0.17***	−0.01
Demographics/controls			
National identity:			
Scottish	−0.22*	−0.02	−0.04
Welsh	−0.06	−0.10	−0.00
Age	0.01***	−0.01**	0.01***
Education (post-A level)	0.18***	0.30***	0.09**
Ethnic minority	0.17**	0.78***	0.25***
Gender (male)	0.12***	−0.35***	−0.19***
Political knowledge scale	0.16***	0.11***	0.11***
Region:			
Scotland	0.04	−0.12	0.11
Wales	−0.09	−0.09	0.00
Social class (middle class)	0.01	−0.02	0.09**
Constant	−1.20***	−0.53	1.36***
Total R^2	0.30	0.13	0.24
R^2 valence only	0.09	0.08	0.07
R^2 ideology only	0.12	0.04	0.06
R^2 personal orientations only	0.05	0.02	0.10
R^2 demographics only	0.24	0.04	0.19
N	3,173	3,173	3,173

*** – $p \leq 0.001$; ** – $p \leq 0.01$; * – $p \leq 0.05$; one-tailed test.

efficacy and civic duty. The results broadly support the hypotheses advanced earlier, although there are some anomalies. Consider, first, $H_{8.1a}$, which suggests that valence calculations should affect all three individual orientations. With regard to political interest, the evidence is mixed. Although the policy judgments variable is correctly signed ($\beta = +0.02$), the coefficient is insignificant. Worse, the coefficient for the (incumbent versus opposition) partisanship term is significant ($p < 0.01$) but negatively signed ($\beta = -0.04$). This suggests that positive policy evaluations of the governing party vis-à-vis the opposition (as expressed in our partisanship measure) reduce, rather than increase, interest in politics. Interest, in short, is stimulated more by negative evaluations of past performance than by positive ones. This said, by far the largest valence effect on interest is the 'generic judgments' term, which measures the effects of respondents' overall assessments of the main parties and their leaders taken together as a group. Here, the coefficient ($\beta = +0.20$) is both positive and significant, indicating that generic valence judgments work as anticipated to determine political interest – increasingly positive assessments of the major parties are associated with increasing levels of political interest.

$H_{8.1a}$ receives stronger support in relation to political efficacy and civic duty. With regard to efficacy, all three valence effects are positive and significant, with the largest effect ($\beta = +0.57$) again being associated with the generic judgments term. In the civic duty model, partisanship is not significant but, as expected, both policy judgments and generic judgments are positive and significant ($p < 0.05$). The overall pattern of valence effects in Table 8.4, then, is generally in line with $H_{8.1a}$, although there is some difference. Positive valence assessments consistently increase people's sense of political efficacy, contribute to their sense of civic duty and, on balance, increase their interest in politics.

Hypothesis $H_{8.2a}$ concerns the effects of economic left–right ideology on individual political engagement. According to the hypothesis, this relationship should be curvilinear, with those in the political 'centre' being the least engaged. Parameter estimates bear out this expectation (see Table 8.4). Coefficients for the left–right terms in all three equations are significant and negative (e.g. $\beta = -0.52$ in the interest equation) and the coefficients for the squared terms (e.g. $\beta = +0.07$ in the interest equation) are significant and positive. This pattern clearly indicates that interest, efficacy and duty are highest among people at either extreme of the economic left–right spectrum. $H_{8.2a}$ is supported by the data.

Hypothesis $H_{8.2b}$ states that 'authoritarians' and those unsympathetic to immigrants will exhibit lower levels of political engagement on the grounds that their views have tended to be ignored by the British political establishment in recent years. The coefficients in Table 8.4 suggest that, although this is the case for people opposed to immigration, it does not apply to those taking authoritarian positions. In all three models, the immigration variable has a significant negative coefficient, indicating that people who score relatively highly on the scale are less likely to be political interested, efficacious or dutiful. However, taking an authoritarian position produces a more inconsistent reaction. Authoritarians are not significantly different from liberals in terms of political interest, although they do feel less politically efficacious. However, authoritarians also have a stronger sense of civic duty than do their more liberal counterparts. Overall, then, $H_{8.2b}$ is 'partially supported' by the evidence.

Hypothesis $H_{8.3a}$ refers to the effects of personal responsibility and social trust on individual political engagement. The conjecture is that such effects should be positive because the socially engaged should also tend to be politically engaged. Again, the hypothesis is broadly, though not invariably, supported by the data. Personal responsibility has a significant positive effect in all three equations; social trust is consistently signed correctly, although it is significant only for civic duty. In sum, a sense of personal responsibility has more general consequences for individual political engagement than does a high level of social trust.

Hypothesis $H_{8.3c}$ addresses the impact of risk orientations on political engagement. Our expectation is that risk-averse individuals will be less interested in politics and feel less efficacious than risk-acceptant individuals. However, we saw no reason why risk orientation should be connected to civic duty. These predictions are borne out by the results in Table 8.5. Risk orientations do indeed have positive effects on both interest and efficacy, but not on duty.

Finally, Table 8.4 reports the effects of the various demographic control variables. *Ceteris paribus*, age is associated positively with political interest and sense of civic duty but negatively with political efficacy. Older people are more likely to be politically interested and dutiful, but they are less likely to think that their efforts are influential. Gender effects also vary – men are more politically interested, but less efficacious and dutiful, than women. In addition to these patterns, three demographic effects stand out. Ethnic minority status, education and political knowledge consistently exert positive and significant effects on each personal political orientation.

The overall picture of individual engagement is perhaps best summarized by the R^2 values reported in Table 8.4. These include the R^2 values for the full models, as well as the R^2 values obtained for the subsets of the 'valence', 'ideology' and 'personal orientations' predictors. For the political interest and civic duty models, demographics explain more variance than do any of the three clusters of explanatory variables. For example, the valence and ideology variables explain only

Table 8.5 OLS *and ordered logistic regression analyses of system-level political orientations*

	Model A	Model B	Model C	Model D
	Institutional trust	Parties	Elections	Democracy satisfaction
Predictor variables	β	β	β	β
Valence judgments				
Hypothesis: $H_{8.1b}$				
Policy judgments	0.20***	0.14***	0.15***	0.67***
Partisanship	0.11***	0.19***	0.10***	0.36***
Generic judgments	0.38***	0.29***	0.30***	0.68***
Ideology and values				
Hypothesis: $H_{8.2d}$ and $H_{8.2e}$				
Left–right scale position	0.22**	0.10	−0.13	0.69***
Left–right scale squared	−0.02	−0.01	0.03*	−0.06**
Hypothesis: $H_{8.2c}$				
Liberal–authoritarian scale	−0.10***	−0.13***	−0.04*	0.01
Pro–anti immigration scale	−0.13***	−0.15***	−0.17***	−0.04
Personal responsibility scale	0.02	−0.06***	0.04**	−0.00
Personal orientations				
Hypothesis: $H_{8.3b}$				
Social trust scale	0.06***	0.02*	0.04***	0.01
Risk scale	−0.02	−0.02	−0.01	−0.03
Demographics/controls				
Hypothesis $_{8.3d}$				
National identity:				
Scottish	−0.06	−0.01	−0.05	0.37
Welsh	−0.22	−0.08	−0.13	0.01
Age	0.00*	−0.00*	0.00**	0.01***
Education (post-A level)	0.03	0.13***	0.09*	−0.15

Table 8.5 (*cont.*)

	Model A	Model B	Model C	Model D
	Institutional trust	Parties	Elections	Democracy satisfaction
Ethnic minority	−0.20**	−0.08**	−0.19**	0.08
Gender (male)	−0.03	−0.08**	−0.05	0.12
Political know-ledge scale	−0.00	0.01	0.06***	0.03
Region:				
Scotland	−0.07	−0.09	−0.10	−0.08
Wales	0.06	−0.08	−0.02	−0.01
Constant	−2.90***	−1.42***	−2.21***	
Social class (middle class)	−0.01	0.05	0.02	−0.10
Total R^2	0.33	0.26	0.25	0.13
R^2 valence only	0.26	0.17	0.17	0.10
R^2 ideology only	0.11	0.12	0.10	0.02
R^2 personal orientations only	0.06	0.03	0.05	0.01
R^2 demographics only	0.02	0.03	0.05	0.01
N	3,173	3,173	3,173	3,173

*** – $p \leq 0.001$; ** – $p \leq 0.01$; * – $p \leq 0.05$; one-tailed test.
Note: parameters in models A, B, and C are estimated using OLS regression, and parameters in model D are estimated using ordered logistic regression. R^2 values for democracy satisfaction are McFadden R^2.

7% and 6%, respectively, of the variance in civic duty; the equivalent figure for the demographic controls is 19%. It is only in the efficacy model that valence ($R^2 = 0.08$) explains more than do the demographics ($R^2 = 0.04$) – and even here the overall explained variance in the full model ($R^2 = 0.13$) is not particularly impressive. Thus, although the findings document that valence, ideology and personal orientations exert significant and, for the most part, theoretically plausible effects, none of them considered alone offers a compelling explanatory account of personal political attitudes.

Models of system-level orientations

Table 8.5 contains parameter estimates for Model 8.1 applied to four system-level orientations: institutional trust, attitudes towards parties, attitudes towards elections and democracy satisfaction. The results are clearer than are those reported for individual political orientations. For example, $H_{8.1b}$ states that all three types of valence judgments should have positive effects on all aspects of regime support. The results in Table 8.5 support this conjecture. In each of the four equations, the three valence measures have positive and highly significant coefficients. As valence theory predicts, to the extent that governments, parties and leaders are judged to deliver, citizens increase their support for the political regime.

The two hypotheses relating to the role of economic left–right ideology fare less well. $H_{8.2d}$ posits a positive linear effect of left–right ideology on regime support; $H_{8.2e}$ posits a curvilinear effect, with support highest among centrists. In the institutional trust model, the significant positive coefficient for left–right supports the positive linear effect postulated in $H_{8.2d}$. Similarly, in the democracy satisfaction equation, the combination of significant positive (for left–right) and negative (for left–right squared) coefficients supports the curvilinear claims of $H_{8.2e}$. However, these are the *only* significant left–right ideology effects observed out of a total of eight possible effects. Other hypothesized effects of left–right ideology are contradicted by null findings.

Although economic left–right ideology appears to have little impact on regime support, the same is not true for the liberal–authoritarian and pro–anti immigration dimensions. $H_{8.2c}$ says that these two variables should negatively affect regime support, reflecting the inability of the major parties to address either the law and order or the immigration concerns of many citizens. Results in Table 8.5 consistently support $H_{8.2c}$. As predicted, in all three models – for institutional trust, parties and elections – both the liberal–authoritarian and pro–anti immigration scales have significant *negative* effects. Although these effects do not extend to democracy satisfaction, the overall pattern of results clearly favours $H_{8.2c}$: authoritarians and those critical of immigration are significantly less likely to support the regime than are their more liberal or pro-immigration counterparts.

We advance two hypotheses about the impact of personal and social orientations on regime support; social trust should be associated positively ($H_{8.3b}$), and Scots and Welsh identities should be related negatively ($H_{8.3d}$) to system-level political orientations. The findings are unambiguous – social trust exerts a significant, positive effect on all four orientations, thereby providing strong support for $H_{8.3b}$. Although Scottish and Welsh identities are undoubtedly important in continuing debates over the future of devolution (and Scottish and Welsh national independence) in the UK, these identities currently do not have significant effects in any of the models and, thus, do not translate into lower levels of support for the political system as a whole.

Regarding the models of individual engagement, we observe that demographic factors are as – if not more – important than are predictors involving valence judgments, ideology and personal characteristics. However, it is clear from Table 8.5 that demographics explain very little variance in the regime support variables. Age has an inconsistent effect (positive for institutional trust, election attitudes and democracy satisfaction, but negative for party attitudes), and education and knowledge are both positively associated with party and election attitudes. Beyond these minor effects, with one exception, the demographic variables have null effects on the four dimensions of regime support. The exception is ethnicity – ethnic minority status is associated with lower levels of institutional trust and with more negative attitudes towards parties and elections. Taking account of our earlier findings about ethnicity, it appears that Britain's ethnic minorities are more politically engaged but feel less attached to the system's political institutions than does the white British majority.

The weak demographic effects in the system-level orientation models are confirmed by the R^2 values for the subset models. For example, the R^2 for the full institutional trust model is a respectable $R^2 = 0.33$. The R^2 for a model including only the demographic variables is $R^2 = 0.02$, suggesting that demographics explain very little of the variance in institutional trust. Note how this contrasts with the valence subset model, which yields an $R^2 = 0.26$, or with the ideology model, which produces an $R^2 = 0.11$. This pattern of greater explanatory power for valence judgments and, to a lesser degree, for ideology is replicated in the models for parties and elections (see Table 8.5). The key point is that valence judgments not only have a wide variety of significant effects, but they also make the largest contributions to explaining variance, in all four regime support variables. Valence judgments, ideological positions and personal orientations may contribute modestly to explaining people's political engagement, but they play prominent roles in determining their reactions to the political system as a whole. And of the three clusters of explanatory variables, valence considerations are most important.

Conclusion: political performance and political orientations

This chapter assesses the rival claims of valence politics, ideology and personal orientations as explanations for why people engage with politics and/or support the political regime. With regard to individual-level political engagement, no one set of explanatory factors clearly outweighs the others. Demographics, valence, ideology and personal orientations, such as social trust and sense of personal responsibility, all affect the way that people approach politics. The mix of determining factors varies according to which dimension of engagement is being analysed. For example, valence judgments matter more for political efficacy and civic duty than they do for political interest. Ideological factors, particularly economic left–right positions and attitudes towards immigration, as well as an individual's sense of personal responsibility, consistently affect engagement. However, these effects are relatively modest when compared with the explanatory power of demographic variables such as age, ethnicity and education.

Thus, our analysis of individual political engagement suggests that a complex mix of explanatory factors is at work. In contrast, analyses of regime support yield less equivocal conclusions. We are able to identify three robust sets of factors that consistently affect all aspects of regime support. The strongest effects involve valence, which are operationalized in terms of policy judgments, incumbent vs opposition party identifications, and generic judgments about the major British parties and party leaders. There are consistent secondary effects for two of the three dimensions of ideology, with regime support being highest among liberals and those sympathetic to immigration. However, economic left–right ideological position does not have a consistent impact on regime support. Finally, there is also an important, but subordinate, role for social trust – those who trust others more appear to support the regime more as well. Crucially, support for the democratic process in Britain lies very much in the hands of the politicians themselves. The key driver of regime support is citizens' views of the overall policy and managerial competence of the main political parties. To the extent that the parties and party leaders can convey a sense of their collective competence to deliver goods and services to the electorate, citizens will respond by increasing their support for the regime. In this sense, then, regime support is a renewable resource.

In addition to the several hypotheses evaluated in this chapter, our analysis provides additional evidence about the sources of some major drivers of voter turnout. We now know that political interest, efficacy and duty vary positively with generic valence judgments about the overall competence of parties and party leaders. We know that these attitudes vary in a curvilinear way with economic left–right positions and that they are likely to be significantly lower among people who take a negative view of immigration. We also know that interest, efficacy and civic duty are higher among people who express a strong sense of personal responsibility. The implications of these findings are clear. Politicians can do more to convince people of their own policy and managerial competence; to address effectively the vexed question of immigration, which has been collectively de-prioritized in recent years, and to devise policies that encourage people to develop a greater sense of personal responsibility. Their success in doing so may go far to affect the factors that have contributed to declining levels of citizen political engagement in contemporary Britain.

9 | *Performance politics reconsidered*

The story of this book is a story of performance politics. What counts most – not exclusively – when voters make their choices are judgments about how well the competing political parties and their leaders perform on issues that matter. These typically are what Donald Stokes (1963, 1992) called 'valence issues'. As discussed in earlier chapters, valence issues are ones upon which there is strong agreement. The quintessential example is the economy – virtually everybody wants a buoyant economy characterized by vigorous, sustainable growth, coupled with low rates of inflation and unemployment. But, economic well-being is not all. Healthcare, education and other public services are also important. In Britain and other mature democracies, effective delivery of these public services long has been a key aspect of performance politics. Judgments about party performance on valence issues have multiple sources, but they are not simply reflections of what people read in the newspaper and see on television. Personal experience counts as well.

In recent years, the traditional valence issue agenda that defined the battleground of party competition since the end of the Second World War has been transformed to include concerns about crime, immigration and terrorism. Although overwhelming majorities always have been opposed to criminal and terrorist activities, opinion about immigration has followed a different course. Historically, although some people have been opposed to an expansive immigration policy, others have looked favourably on it, arguing that large-scale immigration fuels economic growth and is consistent with principles of diversity and tolerance that are central tenets of a democratic political culture. However, in Britain and elsewhere, immigration now has become a valence issue. Many people want to reduce immigration rates, and attitudes towards asylum seekers are especially negative. These attitudes do not stand alone; rather, analyses presented in Chapter 3 show that they are closely intertwined in the public mind with threats of crime and terrorism. In the wake of the 9/11 and 7/7 terrorist attacks, immigration has become a salient item on the political agenda. That agenda remains dominated by valence politics concerns but, as we see in Chapter 3, the mix of issues has changed.

In the world of valence politics, nearly everyone holds the same opinion on issues that matter for electoral choice. In the language of the spatial theories of party competition discussed in Chapter 2, voters have the same 'ideal point'. Performance, actual and anticipated, in achieving consensually agreed-upon policy goals is how parties and their leaders are judged. When making political judgments, voters are acting in an environment of high stakes and abundant uncertainty. Reliable information about who can best deliver desired policy outcomes is hard to come by. Endowed with agency, not omniscience, voters rationally rely heavily on cues provided by party leader images and partisan attachments. Rating leaders in terms of characteristics such as competence, responsiveness and trustworthiness enables voters to choose a party whose leader will be a 'safe pair of hands' – someone who will manage the affairs of state effectively and make consequential decisions with prudence and sagacity.

Some analysts have claimed that the impact of leader images on electoral choice varies over the electorate, with more politically sophisticated voters relying less on leader cues than unsophisticated voters do. Analyses presented in Chapter 5 provide some support for this conjecture. These analyses also support an interesting rival hypothesis whereby political sophistication, as indexed by the interaction of formal education and political knowledge, has a curvilinear impact on the nexus between leader images and electoral choice. Leader effects are greatest among people with modest levels of political sophistication, and less among both the least and the most sophisticated. Although theoretically interesting, neither of the models that incorporate political sophistication interaction effects outperforms a simpler model that posits constant leader effects across the electorate. In fact, the simpler model performs slightly better. Given its parsimony and statistical power, the simpler model remains attractive.

Partisan attachments also provide valuable cues. As storehouses of information about past performance, these attachments summarize political knowledge relevant for electoral choice. To be useful, partisanship must be updated, and voters oblige. Contrary to the model of stable party identification extolled by 'Michigan' social psychologists, British voters have partisan attachments that are potentially mutable (see Appendix C). Voters make ongoing judgments about party and leader performance, and incorporate these judgments into an accumulated stream of performance information, with earlier judgments being progressively discounted over time. When current evaluations strongly contradict information about past performance, voters are willing to change their partisanship. By updating their partisan attachments in light of novel information, voters maximize the effectiveness of party cues as guides to electoral choice.

The world of valence politics thus is populated by voters who are 'smart enough' to know that they 'are not smart enough'. A psephological anthropologist visiting this world will encounter voters who try to make the best of the difficult choice situations they confront. Sharing major policy goals and lacking a large fund of reliable information about what the future will bring, they make performance judgments about competing parties – which party will do best on the valence issues they care most about is the crucial question they pose. When making their decisions, voters supplement these performance evaluations with cues provided by leader images and partisan attachments. Borrowing a metaphor from the philosophy of science, one may view these 'valence voters' as 'ruthless Popperians' for whom party support, at any given point in time, is a experientially based conjecture about which party is most likely to facilitate the achievement of desirable states of the world. If refuted by experience, then the conjecture is abandoned and another one is offered.

This metaphor does not automatically imply a valence politics model of electoral choice. 'Downsian' voters concerned about maximizing their utilities by supporting a party that is closest to them in a uni- or multi-dimensional position issue space would behave in exactly the same way. However, the case for the valence politics model is strongly buttressed by empirical evidence. Whether one is analysing vote intentions in the 'long campaign' between successive elections or actual voting behaviour, the valence politics model statistically dominates its Downsian competitor. Downsian issue-proximity variables have 'bite', but their effects are substantially less than those of the combined valence politics troika of party performance judgments on valence issues, leader images and partisanship.

The valence model also dominates various sociological models, a finding that does not surprise. In a world characterized by ongoing, sometimes large-scale dynamics in party support over relatively brief time horizons, models featuring social class or other largely static sociological characteristics are 'non-starters' both logically and empirically. The inability of sociological models to account for political change was appreciated nearly half a century ago by Campbell *et al.* (1960) when they grappled with the 'puzzle of '52' – if social location shapes political preference, then abrupt changes in parties' political fortunes, such as the landslide victory by Dwight Eisenhower, the Republican candidate in the 1952 US presidential election, should not happen. But they do. Campbell *et al.*'s conclusion that sociological accounts cannot accommodate the fast pace of political change remains valid today. Sociological variables are simply too slow moving and too far back in the famed 'funnel of causality' to provide a satisfactory account of electoral choice.

Note that we say 'dominate', not 'encompass', when describing the statistical performance of the valence politics model, versus its rivals. Other models, principally the Downsian spatial model are not statistically irrelevant; rather, they make significant contributions to explaining variation in voting behaviour. Hence, even with a discount imposed for richer parameterization, model selection criteria repeatedly testify that a composite model including both valence and spatial variables is preferable to a pure valence model. Ones gains little by adding non-valence variables, but one does gain something.

Why? We believe that the explanation for the statistical superiority of the composite model is rooted in the nature of election campaigning in particular, and political communication more generally. When attempting to attract voters, parties do not confine themselves to making performance claims, however powerful these may be. Rather, they also invoke any arguments and symbols that they think might help. Some arguments concern position issues, and some symbols invoke ancient mythologies of class and other group loyalties and antagonisms. In their attempts to maximize the number who salute, parties are willing to run many flags up the poll. Parties' campaign efforts and intensive media coverage ensure that these messages are communicated throughout the electorate. Exposed to a rich variety of information, voters have – in Zaller's (1992) language – many 'considerations' at their disposal when they make electoral choices. The result is that composite models outperform, if only marginally, the core valence politics model that dominates the explanation of electoral choice.

The analyses presented in this book provide strong support for the valence politics model. As in earlier elections, the issues that British voters cared about in 2005 were heavily valenced. As observed, the issue mix was different from what it had been in 2001, with topics such as crime, immigration and terrorism supplementing traditional concerns with the economy and core public services such as healthcare and education. But nearly all of these issues – new and old alike – were valence issues of the kind described by Stokes (1963, 1992), not the 'pro–con' position issues emphasized by Downs (1957) and the many spatial theorists who have taken his lead.

Even the Iraq War, which was a highly contentious position issue when it first achieved salience in the autumn of 2002, had evolved into a valence issue by the time that the 2005 election was held. Opinions about the war were driven by a combination of moral and prudential considerations, supplemented by cues provided by political parties, leaders, the media and personal psychology. Although pro-war sentiment increased among both men and women when the conflict first began, women were significantly less enthusiastic. This gender difference reflected differences in distributions on key explanatory variables, rather than differences in the impact of these variables. Women were less likely to believe that the war had a strong moral justification, less likely to appreciate its collective or personal benefits, and more likely to conclude that it entailed significant costs.

As the war dragged on, opinion continued to evolve. Enthusiasm for the conflict dissipated, and the emergent consensus was that Prime Minister Tony Blair had made a very significant mistake in supporting the US-led invasion and subsequent occupation. Fueled by seemingly endless media speculation and the results of the Butler Inquiry, some people concluded that Blair had deliberately exaggerated the threat posed by Iraqi dictator Saddam Hussein to build public support for the conflict. Political spin went dangerously out of control and the prime minister was responsible – or so the argument ran. Blair's image suffered substantial damage as a result of Iraq, and that damage translated into a significant reduction in Labour support in the 2005 election.

The issues that mattered in that election were a mix of 'old' and 'new' valence issues, with most voters judging that Labour had not done a particularly good job on them. The major exceptions were the economy and terrorism, with substantial majorities giving Labour high grades. Labour strategists, recognizing that many voters were favourably impressed by the healthy economy, quickly moved to have their party take credit. The pitch was that New Labour's Blair–Brown team had repeatedly demonstrated their competence – they knew how to generate the economic well-being that was a necessary prerequisite for funding cherished public services. Over the course of the campaign, this claim was made repeatedly – it was the key reason why voters should give Labour another term in office.

The economy, then, was one 'fundamental' that Labour had firmly in place when the 2005 campaign began. Two other fundamentals from the valence politics model also were on Labour's side. One of these was leader image. Despite the corrosive effects of Iraq, Tony Blair's image was *relatively* favourable compared to that of his chief rival, Conservative leader Michael Howard. Similar to his immediate predecessors, William Hague and Iain Duncan-Smith, Howard was not warmly received. Blair was fortunate that the Conservatives repeatedly demonstrated an uncanny ability to select leaders who were heartily disliked by many voters. Also, Howard was a newly minted leader of an opposition party. Being such, he was not able to gain voters' respect, let alone their affection, by demonstrating his ability to handle major domestic and foreign policy issues. True enough, Howard was a former cabinet minister, but that was long ago. Serious problems with Iraq notwithstanding, Tony Blair remained the people's choice for competence.

Partisanship was Labour's other favourable fundamental in 2005. Much like leadership, the party's edge on partisanship diminished substantially between 2001 and 2005. However, voters abandoning Labour had not moved en masse to the Conservatives or anywhere else for that matter. When the campaign opened, Labour's percentage of partisans was in the mid-30s, but Conservatives were stuck in the mid-20s, exactly where they had been four years earlier. The Liberal Democrats, with 12%, were up 3% from where they were in 2001, but they were still very far behind. In fact, their partisan share was exactly what it was four decades earlier.

Despite having advantages on a key valence issue, leader image and partisanship, Labour and the Conservatives were running 'neck and neck' when the 2005 campaign began. Slightly over one-third of the voters were undecided, so the campaign would be very important. In the event, Labour at least held their own, the Liberal Democrats did very well, and the Conservatives did very poorly. Indeed, analyses indicate that Mr Howard and his party would have been better off if a campaign had not occurred. But, it did, and the Conservatives lost it. Evidence presented in Chapter 6 indicates that both the national campaign and the local campaign – the 'air war' and the 'ground war' – were influential. In addition to affecting party choice, there is also a suggestion that negative outbursts by the party leaders during the campaign worked to diminish the likelihood that voters would go to the polls.

Voter turnout in 2005 was 61.2%, only slightly above the post-Second World War low of 59.4% recorded in 2001. Analyses in Chapters 5 and 6 indicate that a general incentives model that combines benefit–cost considerations with social norms provides a stronger explanation of turnout than do rival models motivated by civic voluntarism and cognitive engagement theories. Sense of civic duty, one of the key variables in the general incentives model, varies strongly across age groups, and it appears that this relationship reflects generational as well as life-cycle differences. Although a generational component in civic duty cannot be established with certainty absent very long-range panel data, such a component – if it exists – would work to diminish electoral participation across a series of future elections. The incidence of other political activities varies across age groups, but the differences are especially pronounced for turnout.

Electoral participation is also affected by key variables in the valence politics model. Students of voting and elections typically have performed completely separate analyses of party choice and turnout. However, the decision not to vote can be usefully viewed as a 'none of the above' choice by people considering the alternatives on offer by the competing parties. Analysing nonvoting in this way reveals that feelings about Tony Blair worked exactly as some observers had speculated before the election. In addition to exerting powerful effects on choosing Labour or one of the opposition parties, feelings about Blair affected turnout. All else equal, people who felt negatively about him were more likely than others to desert Labour and become nonvoters. These analyses also indirectly reflect the failure of the Conservatives' campaign efforts. People who were favourably disposed towards the Tories on what they considered to be the most important issue, those who had a relatively favourable image of Michael Howard and Conservative identifiers all were less likely to cast a ballot. This means that there were potential Conservative votes that went unharvested. These valence effects on turnout would remain hidden by conventional analyses that treat party choice and turnout as separate phenomena and, as is typical, omit valence politics variables from consideration when studying who votes.

Some factors affecting turnout at the aggregate level can be revealed only by cross-national comparative analyses. Accordingly, we merged survey data gathered in Britain and twenty-one other European democracies with aggregate indicators of the nature of the electoral and party systems of these countries. Multilevel analyses reveal that, controlling for several important individual-level variables, turnout reflects cross-national variations in the effective number of parties, the extent to which the electoral system distorts parties' vote shares when allocating parliamentary seats, and the extent of ideological diversity in the party system. Consonant with expectations generated by the rational choice part of our general incentives model, turnout is lower when there are more effective parties and when electoral distortion is high. More parties mean higher information-processing costs and more distortion obfuscates the translation of votes into seats. As also expected, enhanced ideological diversity positively influences turnout. Here, the argument is that ideological diversity is an indicator of collective benefit differentials when one party or party coalition rather than another wins an election. Again, these aggregate-level effects on electoral participation necessarily remain hidden in single-country analyses.

The decrease in turnout in recent British elections is not atypical. Rather, declining turnout has been a prominent feature of electoral politics in many mature democracies over the past two decades. Some observers have speculated that the decline is part of a substitution process whereby people, particularly young people, are abandoning voting and adopting other political activities. Especially salient in this regard are buycotting and boycotting, whereby people purchase some products and avoid purchasing others to further worthy causes. To achieve fair trade, fair wages and a 'green future', concerned citizens are abandoning the voting booth in favour of the marketplace. Increasingly, people are seeing marketplace decisions as political choices.

This interesting hypothesis is not supported at either the individual or the aggregate level, at least not yet. At the individual level, the structure of political participation is very similar in Britain and other European democracies considered as a group, and, in both cases, correlations between voting turnout, on the one hand, and buycotting and boycotting, on the other, are positive. Analyses of national samples of the electorates of these countries one at a time show that positive correlations obtain both for older and younger groups in every case. More generally, all types of political participation are positively, not negatively, correlated.

Nor is it the case that significant substitution effects can be found at the aggregate level. Rather, the dominant pattern is for citizens in Britain and other wealthy northern European countries to participate more in all types of non-electoral activities than do people in poorer southern and eastern European countries. As Barnes *et al.*, (1979) observed nearly three decades ago, an expansive political action repertoire tends to be the preserve of citizens in wealthy democracies. Since then, turnout rates have declined, but voting remains the dominant form of political activity for citizens young and old alike.

Results of our analyses also emphasize that the impact of valence judgments is not confined to the electoral arena. Rather, their effects extend to people's views of themselves as political actors and their orientations towards the institutions and processes of Britain's democratic political regime. Analyses of the 2005 BES data reveal that valence calculations positively influence people's sense of political efficacy. Also, regime-level effects are strong and consistent. People's judgments about the performance of political parties and party leaders influence more general orientations towards the electoral and party systems, levels of trust in key political institutions such as parliament, the civil service, local government and police, and summary assessments of the performance of British democracy. Political support at the level of authorities and regime is a renewable resource. Support flows and ebbs in response to the political performance judgments that people make. Performance politics is at the heart of contemporary British democracy.

After Tony

The world of valence politics neither began with Tony Blair's arrival nor ended with his departure. The dominant figure in British politics for over a decade, Mr Blair turned over leadership of the Labour

Party and the reins of government to his long-time colleague and rival, Gordon Brown, on 27 June 2007. At first, it appeared that 'turning Brown' was exactly what Labour needed to revive its political fortunes. Risking a mixed metaphor, Figure 9.1 shows that throughout the summer and into early autumn the party enjoyed a 'Brown bounce' in the polls, and opened up a substantial lead over the Conservatives. Journalists, politicos and others began talking incessantly about a snap election to capitalize on Labour's rejuvenated popularity. Brown did not deny the possibility and momentum built. Some of his younger aides acted decidedly bullish and talked up a forthcoming election call. But a decision to go was not announced. September came and went, and Brown continued to hesitate. After reviewing polling data showing Labour weakness in key marginal constituencies and listening to fears expressed by MPs who would lose their seats if things did not go well, he climbed down. In a BBC interview on 6 October, he announced that there would not be an election.

The result was a firestorm of criticism, with some observers openly accusing the prime minister of weakness, indecision and political

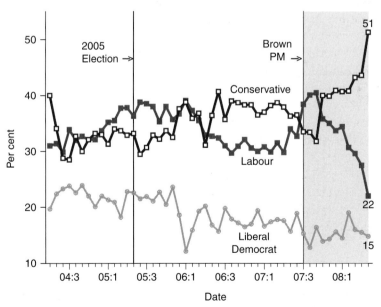

Figure 9.1 The dynamics of party support, April 2004–May 2008
Source: April 2004–May 2008 GPVP monthly surveys

cowardice. Conservative leader David Cameron said it was a 'humiliating retreat'. It did not help that Brown had authored a book entitled *Courage*. As illustrated in Figure 9.2, since his decision not to go to the people, Brown's image has suffered greatly. It is not just that voters do not like him as much as they once did – likeability has never been his strong suit – but, his reputation for responsiveness and trustworthiness has deteriorated markedly. And, most important, after spending a decade presiding over a healthy economy and establishing a record of effectiveness as Chancellor of the Exchequer, his competence rating has declined from a robust 5.8 in September 2007 to a meagre 3.3 in May 2008. At least for now, Brown has lost his ace card.

Saddled with an economic downturn, and lumbered with an avalanche of negative publicity about the failure to hold a referendum on the EU Treaty of Lisbon, a controversial plan to detain terrorist suspects for forty-two days without charging them, and a widely criticized U-turn on tax policy, Mr Brown and his party have crashed together in the polls. Figure 9.3 shows that shortly after Labour's crushing by-election defeat in Crewe, the May 2008 GPVP survey gave the party only a 22% vote intention share compared to 51% for the surging Conservatives. And, only 16% thought Brown would do the best job as prime minister, compared to 38% for Conservative

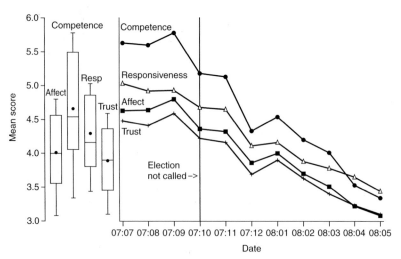

Figure 9.2 The dynamics of Gordon Brown's image, July 2007–May 2008
Source: July 2007–May 2008 GPVP monthly surveys

leader David Cameron. That 16% is Iain Duncan-Smith territory, and that 51% is enough to give the Conservatives a landslide majority government.

Of course, the probability of an early election is now very small. Labour has a comfortable parliamentary majority and – unless he is ousted as party leader – Brown, like Mr Micawber, can wait for something to turn up. That something can work in various ways, but a very important one is by restoring his image as a competent, responsive and trustworthy leader. As Figure 9.3 testifies, there is an extremely close correlation ($r = +0.90$) between how people have rated first Blair, and now Brown, on the one hand, and Labour vote intentions, on the other. In the language of time series analysis, this close relationship is one whereby the dynamics of prime ministerial performance evaluations and governing party support co-integrate – they travel together in a dynamic equilibrium. The powerful effect of leader image on party support has been documented throughout this study. It is one that will do much to hurt, or help, the closely inter-twined fortunes of Labour and Gordon Brown as they move towards

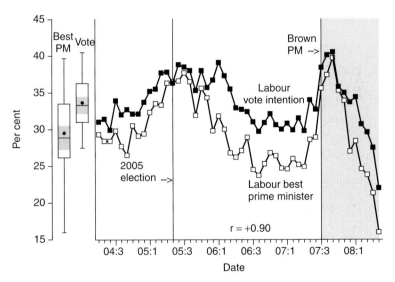

Figure 9.3 The dynamics of Labour support and Labour leader as best prime minister, April 2004–May 2008
Source: April 2004–May 2008 GPVP monthly surveys

a forthcoming general election. Performance politics forces acting on valence voters will determine the result of the next election, but what their configuration will be remains to be seen.

❋ ❋ ❋ ❋

It was dark when Charles and Isabella Frost left Sudbury. The weekly adult education class on twentieth-century British history had just finished, and they were driving home in Isabella's new Mini Cooper. After retiring last spring, Charles had been complaining to Isabella that he was bored, and she suggested taking an extension course offered by the local uni. Reluctant at first, Charles now found it rather enjoyable. Isabella was home for a bank holiday, and thought it would be interesting to hear what the professor had to say. He was glad to have her along.

This evening's class focused on the period after World War Two, starting with Labour's historic victory in the 1945 general election. The lecture started with a discussion of the Beveridge Report and the foundation of the British welfare state. Waxing enthusiastic, the professor, a member of Militant in his younger days, described how the Report, with its call to slay the five 'evil giants' of 'want', 'disease', 'ignorance', 'squalor' and 'idleness,' had defined the post-war political agenda. Security – physical, economic, social – was the overriding theme of that agenda, and it resonated strongly with an electorate which had endured nearly two decades of privation and war. Recognizing the powerful appeal of Labour's new programmes, the Conservatives – prodded by Rab Butler – had endorsed many of them. A decade later, prosperity was fuelling a Conservative government's ability to implement what had become a consensual policy agenda. When Prime Minister Harold Macmillan claimed, 'You never had it so good!', many voters believed him.

Driving along the back roads, Charles tried to think back to the 1950s. He didn't remember much, but one memory that always came to mind was that day when his aunt Agnes took him to the corner shop the day sweets came off ration. The queue was long, but it had been an exciting outing for a lad of six. Of course, Agnes had left years ago, moving to Toronto after she married an RCAF captain, Ernie Woolhaven. Although Agnes was getting well on in years, she still kept in touch. Always up for the latest, she had learned how to use the internet, emailed regularly, and even did online opinion polls.

Remarkable for someone in their mid-80s, and certainly a sign of how times were changing, Charles thought.

Drifting back to tonight's lecture, Charles reflected that elements of this policy agenda were still very much at the core of British politics. Tony Blair and New Labour had promised to deliver the economic prosperity needed to make real improvements in healthcare, education and other public services after nearly two decades of Conservative neglect. Everybody's lot would be better. For a long time, Charles had believed the story, but now things had changed. Blair had finally departed and his successor, Gordon Brown, seemed to be making a hash. Although he had done an admirable job as Chancellor of the Exchequer, the economy was now faltering badly. Brown's persistent claim that Labour was the only party that could keep the good times going was just not as persuasive as it once was.

Moreover, and contrary to what Charles had expected, Brown was not demonstrating the leadership qualities that many people had expected. The aborted election call last October had shown badly. Holding an election only two years on from the last one seemed to be nothing but political opportunism. Then, the story that Brown had decided not to go because the polls were unfavourable reinforced this impression, while adding more than a hint of cowardice. At the time, one of the patrons of Charles' local had quipped that 'Brown just turned yellow'. Uncharitable, but maybe spot on, Charles thought. More recently, the weakening economy and the U-turn over the 10p tax again suggested that Brown might not be up to the job. Untrustworthy, unresponsive – and yes – incompetent, were words that came to mind. It was time to give the Conservatives another chance.

Rounding a curve on the narrow road, Charles swerved to avoid a hedgehog. 'Don't see many of those anymore', he commented to Isabella. She too was thinking about the evening class. Isabella agreed with the professor that security was the overriding policy goal in post-Second World War British politics, but thought that the mix of issues that mattered now was very different. Crime, immigration and terrorism were what many people were talking about nowadays. It seemed they were all tangled up in people's minds, and what should be done wasn't at all clear.

As Isabella mused, her mobile phone made a familiar faint chirping sound, telling her that she had text message. It was Annie with a reminder to meet her tomorrow at the fair-trade boutique that their friend Rama was managing. Strange how the message came just when she was considering these issues, Isabella thought. She flashed back to July 2005 when Annie had narrowly missed being on the bus that was bombed by terrorists. Only Isabella and Annie's chance meeting on that street in London and ensuing brief chat had kept her off that bus. Having a friend come so close to disaster was a personal experience that convinced Isabella that her political priorities had to change.

But, what to do? Isabella supported the Liberal Democrats in 2005, but the Iraq War was now mostly off the table, and the new party leader, Nick Clegg, seemed pleasant but very inexperienced. And there was something to Annie's argument that voting for the Lib Dems or some other minor party might make you feel good for a few minutes, but was not a way to get anything done. As for Labour, Prime Minister Brown was calling for tough action against criminals and suspected terrorists, but Isabella worried that innocent people's civil rights and liberties would be trampled. Moreover, her dad was a pretty good judge of character, and his conclusion that Brown was showing himself to be indecisive and ineffective carried weight.

That left the Conservatives. All that stuff about voting blue to get green seemed so vague, but they definitely had a reputation for taking tough action, and now they were also showing their concern about not going overboard and creating a police state. David Cameron might be a bit of a toff with that Eton background and all, but he was very articulate and not afraid to face down Brown in parliament. Maybe dad was right and the Conservatives would be the answer next time around ... maybe. There was still a lot of time to decide.

Charles took Isabella's Mini around the bend, making the gentle right turn seem like a straight shot. A road sign pointed to Great Yeldham. The Frosts were almost home.

Appendix A: Vote in 2005 by socio-demographic characteristics (validated voters, horizontal percentages)

Socio-demographic characteristics	Vote			
	Labour	Conservative	Liberal Democrat	Other
Age:				
18–25	47	15	32	7
26–35	44	25	25	6
36–45	48	24	20	8
46–55	34	34	26	6
56–65	31	42	21	6
66 and older	35	41	29	5
V = 0.12, p ≤ 0.001				
Education (age completed)				
Still in school	40	7	48	5
15 or younger	41	34	18	7
16	41	33	19	7
17	37	37	19	7
18	39	34	21	6
19 or older	36	31	28	5
V = 0.11, p ≤ 0.001				
Ethnicity				
White British	38	33	23	7
Other	61	19	19	2
V = 0.11, p ≤ 0.001				
Gender				
Men	39	29	24	8
Women	39	35	22	5
V = 0.08, p ≤ 0.01				

(*cont.*)

Socio-demographic characteristics	Vote			
	Labour	Conservative	Liberal Democrat	Other
Housing tenure				
Own outright	29	45	21	6
Mortgage	42	28	23	7
Rent	53	15	26	6
V = 0.18, p ≤ 0.001				
Occupational sector				
Public	39	28	26	7
Private	40	35	19	6
Other	33	34	28	5
V = 0.07, p ≤ 0.001				
Social class (Registrar General)				
Non-manual				
I	30	32	30	8
II	37	36	22	5
III.1	32	39	23	5
Manual				
III.2	47	28	18	7
IV	49	19	23	10
V	67	17	9	7
V = 0.12, p ≤ 0.001				
Social class (Heath-Goldthorpe)				
Salariat	35	35	25	5
Routine non-manual	34	36	25	6
Petty bourgeoisie	23	56	15	6
Foremen and technicians	51	25	18	8
Working class	52	22	18	9
V = 0.13, p ≤ 0.001				

(*cont.*)

Socio-demographic characteristics	Vote			
	Labour	Conservative	Liberal Democrat	Other
Region				
East Anglia	30	43	22	5
East Midlands	39	37	19	6
London	39	32	22	7
North	50	20	23	4
North West	46	29	21	5
South East	26	43	26	6
South West	23	39	33	6
West Midlands	39	35	19	8
Yorkside and The Humber	44	29	21	7
Scotland	40	16	23	22
Wales	43	21	18	18
Great Britain (total)	36	33	23	8
United Kingdom (total)	35	32	22	10

Sources: 2005 BES post-election survey for all variables but region. Regional voting data are from Kavanagh and Butler (2005: Appendix 1).

Appendix B: Turnout by socio-demographic characteristics

	Voted 2005 general election	Votes 'all' or 'most' general elections
	%	%
Age:		
18–25	43	47
26–35	56	58
36–45	70	75
46–55	72	78
56–65	83	92
66 and older	82	94
Cramer's V, p ≤	0.29, 0.001	0.37, 0.001
Education (age completed)		
15 or younger	71	79
16	60	69
17	69	75
18	73	74
19 or older	76	80
Still in school	58	60
Cramer's V, p ≤	0.14, 0.001	0.13, 0.001
Ethnicity		
White British	69	76
Other	56	58
Cramer's V, p ≤	0.07, 0.001	0.11, 0.001
Gender		
Men	66	74
Women	70	76
Cramer's V, p ≤	0.04, 0.01	0.02, p = 0.30

(cont.)

	Voted 2005 general election	Votes 'all' or 'most' general elections
	%	%
Housing tenure		
Own outright	80	89
Mortgage	71	75
Rent	50	58
Cramer's V, p ≤	0.25, 0.001	0.28, 0.001
Occupational sector		
Private	64	71
Public	78	85
Other	68	74
Cramer's V, p ≤	0.14, 0.001	0.15, 0.001
Social class (Registrar General)		
Non-manual		
I	81	89
II	77	84
III.1	71	74
Manual		
III.2	58	70
IV	60	67
V	56	62
Cramer's V, p ≤	0.18, 0.001	0.18, 0.001
Social class (Heath-Goldthorpe)		
Salariat	80	85
Routine non-manual	69	73
Petty bourgeoisie	72	71
Foremen and technicians	61	74
Working class	57	66
Cramer's V, p ≤	0.20, 0.001	0.18, 0.001
Trade union membership		
Trade union member	76	83
Staff association member	68	80
Not member	67	73
Cramer's V, p ≤	0.07, 0.001	0.09, 0.001

(cont.)

	Voted 2005 general election	Votes 'all' or 'most' general elections
	%	%
Region		
East Anglia	64	70
East Midlands	62	81
London	58	71
North	58	72
North West	57	71
South East	64	81
South West	66	70
West Midlands	60	77
Yorkside and The Humber	59	73
Scotland	61	78
Wales	62	80
Cramer's V, p ≤	NA	0.10, 0.001
Great Britain (total)	61	75
United Kingdom (total)	61	NA

NA – not available.

Sources: 2005 BES post-election survey for all variables but region. Regional turnout data are from Kavanagh and Butler (2005: Appendix 1). Turnout in 2005 is computed using validated voting data.

Appendix C: Dynamics of party identification

The valence politics view of party identification differs in crucial respects from the original social psychological conceptualization. In its classic 'Michigan' formulation, party identification is a long-term psychological attachment between a voter and a political party similar to identifications people form with ethnic, religious or other social groups (Campbell *et al.*, 1960; see also Butler and Stokes, 1969). Michigan-style party identifications typically develop early in the life-cycle as a result of childhood and adolescent socialization processes and, except in periods of realignment, they tend to be directionally stable, strengthening in intensity as people age (Converse, 1969). Party identification is an 'unmoved mover' in the funnel of causal forces determining the vote – it exerts powerful direct effects and acts as a 'perceptual screen' that shapes images of candidates, issues and party leaders.

The valence politics model accepts the idea that partisan attachments have important direct and indirect effects on electoral choice. However, the model claims that these attachments have dynamic qualities, and are subject to change in response to ongoing evaluations of actual or anticipated performance of political parties and their leaders. This notion of partisanship as a 'running tally' of current and discounted past performance evaluations was originally developed by Fiorina (1981), and over the past quarter-century it has been featured in a number of studies (e.g. Achen, 1992, 2002; Franklin, 1984, 1992; Franklin and Jackson, 1983; Stewart and Clarke, 1998). However, the conjecture that partisan attachments manifest dynamic properties remains controversial (e.g. Green *et al.*, 2002).

Panel data gathered since the 1960s provide strong prima facie evidence that party identification in Britain exhibits substantial individual-level change over relatively modest time intervals. This evidence from panel surveys has been analysed in detail in Chapter 6 of *Political Choice in Britain* (Clarke *et al.*, 2004b). Here, we

327

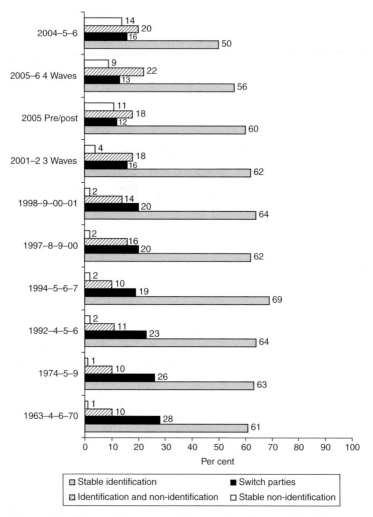

Figure A.1 Observed dynamics of party identification, British panel surveys
Source: 1963–2006 BES, 1994–2001 BEPS and 2004–6 GPVP panel surveys

summarize and update key findings. As illustrated in Figure A.1, the percentages of people in national multi-wave panels reporting that they have switched (one or more times) from one party to another is always substantial, varying from a high of 28% across the seven-year 1963–70 panel to a low of 13% across the two-year 2005–6 panel. Other groups, varying in size from 10% to 22%, have moved from

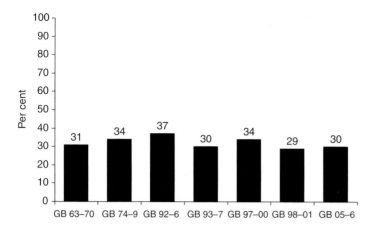

Figure A.2 Mover groups in mixed Markov latent class analyses of the dynamics of party identification in British panel surveys
Source: 1963–2006 BES, 1994–2001 BEPS and 2004–6 GPVP panel surveys

being party identifiers to nonidentifiers or vice versa. Even over the brief period encompassed by the 2005 pre-campaign and post-election BES surveys, 30% either switched parties or moved between identification and non-identification. It bears emphasis that these impressive levels of observed partisan instability are not unique to a particular historical period such as the dealignment era of the 1970s (Dalton, 2000; Sarlvik and Crewe, 1983). Rather, substantial partisan instability is evident in all of the BES and related panel data gathered over the past forty years.

Reacting to this turnover table evidence, Green and his colleagues (2002) have claimed that observed partisan instability is largely an artefact of random measurement error. They hypothesize that once this measurement error is controlled, party identification typically displays the very high levels of stability claimed by Michigan social psychologists. We test this interesting hypothesis using rival mixed Markov latent class (MMLC) models (Hagenaars and McCutcheon, 2002; van der Pol *et al.*, 1999). The results (see Clarke *et al.*, 2004b, Chapter 6 for details) show that, allowing for random measurement error, a generalized 'mover–stayer' model consistently outperforms an 'all stayer' model, as well as the famous 'black–white' mover–stayer model proposed by Converse (1964).[1] In addition, as shown in Figure A.2, the proportion of people in the mover chain is always sizable, ranging from a low of 29% to a high of 37% in seven four-wave panels. There is no suggestion of trends in these data – 30% were in the mover chain for the most recent (2005–6) panel, and 31% were in the mover chain for the very first (1963–70) panel. Partisan instability has been a prominent feature of British political psychology since at least the 1960s.

Strong evidence of substantial individual-level dynamics in British voters' partisan attachments is an important empirical finding in support of the valence politics model of electoral choice. The longstanding nature of these dynamics is consonant with the conjecture that the explanatory power of the model is itself longstanding. That similar dynamics may be found in Canada and the United States (e.g. Clarke and McCutcheon, 2009; Clarke *et al.*, 2009) suggests that the valence model travels well in space as well as time.

Notes

3 Valence politics and the long campaign

1 The economy variable includes references to unemployment, inflation or the economy in general, and the services variable includes references to the NHS, education, housing, pensions or the public services generally. The security measure includes references to crime/law and order, race and defence issues. When data are not available in a given month, linear interpolation is used to supply missing observations.

2 The relationship observed here reproduces almost exactly a longer-term trend relationship that was found using Gallup-based measures of issue priorities over the period 1974–2000.

3 Caution is required in drawing inferences from such data because governments frequently revise the basis upon which various indicators are calculated. Such revisions make it difficult to assemble long-run performance measures of objective policy performance outside the economic sphere, and even in the latter changes in the way key indicators are computed are common. Economic performance measures also are periodically recalibrated. The Thatcher government was notorious for having changed the algorithm for calculating the unemployment rate no less than eleven times.

4 Note that there are also upward 'spikes' in the series at the time of the first Gulf War in 1990 and at the time of the invasion of Iraq in March 2003. These essentially ephemeral effects can easily be modelled using single-month dummies. However, for clarity of exposition, we do not include further dummy terms in the model specified here.

5 The impact of 9/11 grows at a rate determined by the coefficient on the lagged endogenous variable ($\beta = 0.59$). As measured by its impact (October 2001 = time t) parameter, the initial effect of 9/11 was 22.2 points. The effect in November was $22.2 + 22.2^*.59 = 35.3$. In December, the total effect was $22.21 + 22.2^*.59 + 22.2^*.59^2 = 43.0$ points. The long-term (asymptotic) effect is $22.2/(1-0.59) = 54.1$ points.

6 A third measure of valence assessments, party identification, is not included in the model because time series data for party identification are not available for the November 2003–March 2004 period.

7 We use this indirect competence indicator as it is the only suitable measure available in this particular dataset.

8 Previous research has established that leader images are weakly exogenous to party choice (Clarke *et al.*, 2004). As a result, we can be confident that our estimates of the effects of party leader image on Labour support are not distorted by simultaneity bias.

9 As shown in Figure 3.12, Labour's economic competence ratings were well ahead of those of the Conservatives for most of the 1997–2005 period.

10 Note that this specification does not include variables for changes in the economy. This is because the Labour economic management variable picks up the effects of the economy on party support. If we add variables for changes in inflation, unemployment and interest rates (all at either time t or t–1) to model 3.2, none of them achieves statistical significance.

11 Although results are not reported here, we also estimated models that considered the separate effects of the 'internal security' (i.e. crime, asylum/immigration and race) and 'external security' (defence) agendas. Using these measures separately or together fails to produce a significant effect on Labour support.

12 As in Table 3.1, the form of the model means that the precise cost to Labour cannot be inferred directly from the magnitude of the coefficient itself, since the impact (a) occurs every month between April 2003 and the election in May 2005 and (b) discounts each month at the rate indicated by the adjustment parameter associated with the error correction mechanism.

13 The 2000–5 dataset employed merges the results of two separate survey research projects, which used different modes of data collection. For the period July 2000 to October 2003, the surveys were conducted by telephone by Gallup. There was then a five-month break in the series (November 2003 to March 2004), followed by a resumption of data collection in April 2004, using internet surveys conducted by YouGov. (The Gallup survey series was funded by ESRC. The US National Science Foundation funded the YouGov series.) We have made extensive comparisons of the consequences of using internet versus other survey modes. Our key findings, which compare internet with face-to-face surveys *collected at the same time*, show conclusively that estimating identical vote choice models across the two modes produces no significant differences in coefficient magnitudes. Given that the telephone and internet data used here were collected *at different points in time*, we have no way of assessing formally if there was a mode effect in terms of the measured levels of party support. This matters, potentially, for

our efforts to estimate the effects on party support of the occupation of Iraq. We therefore conducted formal tests *using only the Gallup data*–which continue through to October 2003, some six months after the invasion–to determine if there was a clear 'war effect' on support for all three parties. There was. After the invasion, net of all other individual level effects, the probability of voting Labour was lower (logistic regression $\beta = -0.32$) and the probability of voting either Conservative ($\beta = +0.20$) or Liberal Democrat ($\beta = +0.14$) higher. Given that the war effect was evident even before our internet data series begins, we can be confident that we can estimate a set of 'war effects' using the combined telephone/internet dataset, without those estimates being contaminated by a mode shift effect.

14 The social class variable distinguishes between manual (value = 0) and non-manual (value = 1) occupations. Education is measured on a 1–5 scale based on number of years in education.

15 The six measures are prospective personal financial evaluations; retrospective personal financial evaluations; prospective national economic evaluations; retrospective national economic evaluations; the balance of positive versus negative emotions towards personal economic conditions; and the balance of positive versus negative emotions towards national economic conditions. One factor, explaining 51.5 per cent of the item value, has an eigenvalue greater than 1.0.

16 The only substantive interesting interaction effects relate to the impact that Blair's image had on both Labour and Conservative support. His role was of considerable importance outside of the election run-up periods. The significant interaction terms for the Blair variable (positive in the Labour equation, negative in the Conservative one) suggest that his impact was even more important in the election run-up periods. Details are available upon request.

17 We also performed separate factor analyses for all of the monthly data gathered between May 2004 and April 2005. Factors structures are identical in each analysis and the item loadings are very similar. These results indicate that the factor structure is very robust. Details are available upon request.

18 In the Labour model, the coefficients for economy ($\beta = 0.44$), services ($\beta = 0.36$), internal security ($\beta = 0.14$), and external security ($\beta = 0.14$) are all positive and significant. This contrasts with the Conservative and Liberal Democrat models where all effects are either negative or not significant.

19 We also estimated models that contained interaction terms between most important issue and the evaluation/emotion measures. Adding these variables generally produced non-significant results and invariably

failed to increase the models' explanatory power. Details are available upon request.

20 The literature is voluminous. In the British context, see, for example, Clarke *et al.* (1997); Sanders (1991, 2005).

21 The former involves additively aggregating our 'with neutral category' NHS and education satisfaction measures to form a single services satisfaction index. The latter performs an analogous operation with our 'with neutral category' crime, asylum/immigration and terrorism satisfaction measures, to form the security satisfaction measure.

22 The change in probability for the service variable in the Labour equation is +0.03. This suggests that an individual who was 'very satisfied' with her/his public service experience was 0.03 more likely to vote Labour than a similar person who was 'very dissatisfied'.

23 Partisan stances of the major UK newspapers vary over time. In the run-up to the 2005 election, the positions adopted were: broadly pro-Labour – *Guardian, Mirror*; broadly pro-Conservative – *Mail, Express, Telegraph*; broadly neutral – all others.

24 The index is scored one if a pro-Conservative paper is read, two if a neutral paper or no paper at all is read, and three if a pro-Labour paper is read.

25 Specifically, the coefficient for 'service satisfaction' in the 'service evaluations/emotions' equation is $\beta = +0.40$. The equivalent coefficient for 'security satisfaction' in the 'security evaluations/emotions' model is $\beta = +0.34$.

26 The services importance scale is constructed by adding together the NHS and education 'importance' scores (and dividing by two). The security importance scale is constructed by adding together the crime, asylum/immigration, and terrorism 'importance' scores (and dividing by three).

4 Tony's war

1 See, for example, Almond (1950); Alvarez and Brehm (2002); Chittick *et al.* (1995); Holsti (1996); Hurwitz and Peffley (1987); Jentleson (1992); Jentleson and Britton (1998); Jordan and Page (1992); Kull (1995); Marra *et al.* (1990); Meernik and Ault (2001); Mueller (1973); Ostrom and Job (1986); Page and Shapiro (1992); Peffley and Hurwitz (1992); Reilly (1987); Richman *et al.* (1997); Zaller (1992).

2 The phrase 'a war with Iraq' was used in interviews conducted before the war began. Then, the phrase was changed to 'the war with Iraq'.

3 For example, Jentleson (1992) argues that the American public is more likely to support the use of military force when the principal policy

objective is to restrain aggression rather than to change a political regime. Assessments of the legitimacy of the action, perceptions of its likelihood of success, and a general sense of risk aversion are the principal reasons. These three variables are incorporated in the models tested below.

4 The question used to measure opinions regarding the morality, benefits, and costs of the war reads: 'Next, I'm going to read you some statements. Please tell me whether you strongly agree, agree, disagree, or strongly disagree with each of them. How about: (a) "Britain will benefit in the long run from going to war with Iraq"; (b) "War with Iraq threatens the safety of my family and myself"; (c) "There is a strong moral case for Britain going to war with Iraq"; (d) "War with Iraq will seriously damage Britain's interests around the world"'. The order of presentation of the statements was randomized across interviews. Statement (a) measures perceptions of collective benefits of the war; statement (b) measures perceptions of personal threats posed by the war; statement (c) measures opinions regarding morality of the war; statement (d) measures perceptions of the collective costs of going to war. For purposes of multivariate analysis of approval/disapproval of the war (see below), responses to (a) to (d) are coded: (i) 'strongly agree' = four; (ii) 'agree' = three; (iii) 'disagree' = two; (iv) 'strongly disagree' = one.

5 Discounting benefits by the probability of attaining them is fundamental to the structure of expected utility models (e.g. Schoemaker, 1982). A similar discount is also a feature of the Ajzen and Fishbein (1980) model of attitude formation.

6 The question wording is: 'Now please think of a scale from 0 to 10 where 10 means *very likely* and 0 means *very unlikely* ... (a) How likely do you think it is that a [the] *war against Iraq* will be successful?' Again, the phrase 'a war against Iraq' was changed to 'the war against Iraq' once hostilities began.

7 The question re: probability of winning the war was changed in the October 2003 survey to read: 'Using a scale from 0 to 10 where 10 means a *complete success* and 0 means a *complete failure*, how would you rate the war against Iraq?' For purposes of the multivariate analyses, missing data were recoded to mean values.

8 Although many people did not believe the war posed a threat to their personal safety, they also believed that it was unlikely that the 'war on terrorism' would be won in the foreseeable future. On a zero ('very unlikely') to ten ('very likely') scale indicating 'how likely it is that the war against terrorism will be won in the next few years?', average scores in the March pre-war, March post-war, and April–May surveys were quite low – 3.9, 4.0 and 3.7, respectively. The average score then fell to 2.8 in October ($F = 34.69$, $p < 0.001$).

9 Feelings about party leaders are measured using 0–10 feeling thermometer scales. The question is: 'Using the 0 to 10 scale, where 10 means *strongly like* and 0 means *strongly dislike*, how do you feel about … (a) Tony Blair; (b) Iain Duncan Smith; (c) Charles Kennedy'. For purposes of the multivariate analyses, missing data were recoded to mean values.

10 Party identification is measured using the standard BES question, 'Generally speaking, do you think of yourself as Conservative, Labour, Liberal Democrat or what?' Responses are converted into a series of 0–1 dummy variables, with nonidentifiers as the reference category.

11 Respondents who read a daily newspaper taking a pro-war stand were coded +1; those who read a daily newspaper taking an anti-war stand were coded –1, and all other respondents were coded zero. Pro-war newspapers included the *Daily Mail* and the *Scottish Daily Mail*, *Express*, *Scotsman*, *Sun*, *Telegraph* and *The Times*. Anti-war newspapers included the *Daily Record*, *Guardian*, *Independent*, *Mirror* and *Scottish Mirror*.

12 The general risk orientation question is: 'Generally speaking, how willing are you take risks? Are you very willing, somewhat willing, somewhat unwilling, or very unwilling to take risks?' For purposes of the multivariate analyses, the responses were coded: 'very willing' = four; 'somewhat willing' = three; 'somewhat unwilling' = two; 'very unwilling' = one.

13 The war rally variable is coded zero for March 2003 respondents interviewed before hostilities began. All other respondents are coded one.

14 Men are coded one, women zero.

15 Age group variables are 0–1 dummies for those aged 18–24, 25–42 and 43–60. These groups are designed to capture different socialization experiences corresponding to whether a person first entered the electorate during the 'Blair era', the 'Thatcher–Major era' or the 'Wilson–Callaghan era', respectively. People aged sixty-one or older constitute the reference category.

16 The dependent variable is scored: 'strongly approve' = four, 'approve' = three, 'disapprove' = two, 'strongly disapprove' = one. Model parameters are estimated using STATA 10MP's OPROBIT procedure. Given that the October survey was conducted several months after conventional warfare had ceased, and that it uses an alternative, retrospective question about the success of the conflict, parameters are estimated using the March and April–May data.

17 Instrumental variables include party identification, feelings about Charles Kennedy and Iain Duncan-Smith, national and personal economic evaluations, emotional reactions to national and personal economic conditions, general risk orientations, newspaper readership,

timing of interview (pre/post start of Iraq War), age cohorts, education, gender and social class.

18 $AIC = -2\log(L(\theta|y)) + 2K$, $\log(L(\theta|y))$ is the natural log of the likelihood function, and K is number of parameters. See Burnham and Anderson (2002).

19 In general, when considering two models A and B, there are four possibilities: (i) A encompasses B, but B does not encompass A; (ii) B encompasses A, but A does not encompass B; (iii) A encompasses B and B encompasses A; (iv) neither A nor B encompass each other. Cases (i) and (ii) indicate that one of the encompassed models is redundant, case (iii) indicates that the empirical information at hand cannot distinguish between the models, and case (iv) indicates that both models make unique contributions to explanation.

20 Probabilities are calculated using the CLARIFY program for STATA (Tomz *et al.*, 1999).

21 Parameter equality tests are performed using STATA's 'TEST' procedure.

22 Labour's economic managerial competence is measured as the percentage citing Labour in response to the question: 'If Britain were in economic difficulties, which party do you think could handle the problem best – the Conservative Party or the Labour Party?' in the monthly PDB and GPVP surveys.

23 The dummy variables are scored one for the month in which the event occurred, and zero otherwise.

24 There were 9,973 civilian casualties when the Kelly suicide occurred in July 2003 and 27,802 at the time of the 2005 general election. The natural log of the difference of these numbers is 9.79. The total effect of this increased number of casualties is $-0.45/(1-0.84) * 9.79 = 27.5$ where -0.45 is the short-term impact of civilian casualties and 0.84 is the computed coefficient for the lagged endogenous variable in the rearranged Blair approval error correction model.

25 Evaluations of the Iraq War were measured using the results of an exploratory factor analysis of responses to the following questions: (a) 'How well do you think the present government has handled the situation in Iraq?' Responses to (a) were scored 'very well' = five, 'fairly well' = four, 'neither well nor badly' or 'don't know' = three, 'fairly badly' = two, 'very badly' = one; (b) 'Using a scale from 0 to 10 where 0 means a complete failure and 10 means a complete success, how would you rate the war in Iraq?' (c) 'Please tell me whether you strongly approve, approve, disapprove, or strongly disapprove of *Britain's involvement* in Iraq?' (emphasis in original). Responses to (c) were scored 'strongly approve' = five, 'approve' = four, 'don't know' = three,

'disapprove' = two, 'strongly disapprove' = one. Item (a) is from the pre-election survey, and (b) and (c) are from the post-election survey. The factor analysis yielded one factor with an eigenvalue greater than one, and a factor score variable was computed. Emotional reactions to the war were measured by giving respondents a list of four positive (happy, hopeful, confident, proud) and four negative (angry, disgusted, uneasy, afraid) words and asked to choose which words described their feelings 'about the situation in Iraq'. The emotional reaction to Iraq variable is the number of positive words minus the number of negative words designated. Similar variables are constructed for emotional reactions to the economy and the NHS.

26 Other predictor variables in the model are constructed as follows: (i) *issue-proximities*–respondents were asked to place themselves and Labour, Conservative and Liberal Democrat parties on 0–10 scales for the following dimensions: (a) left–right, (b) tax–spend, (c) EU membership, (d) crime-rights of the accused. The issue-proximity variables are the average absolute distances between the respondent and each of the parties on the four dimensions; (ii) *party best on most important issue*–respondents were asked: 'As far as you're concerned, what is the *single most important issue* facing the country at the present time?' (emphasis in original). Respondents supplying an issue were then asked: 'Which party is best able to handle this issue?' 0–1 dummy variables are created for Labour, the Conservatives, the Liberal Democrats and all other parties. Respondents not designating a most important issue, those stating that no party was best able to handle the most important issue, and those stating they did not know which party is best are the reference category; (iii) *party identification*–see note 10 above; (iv) *economic evaluations* were measured using the results of an exploratory factor analysis of responses to these questions: (a) 'How does the financial situation of your household now compare with what it was 12 months ago?' (b) How do you think the general economic situation in this country has changed over the last 12 months?' (c) 'How do you think the financial situation of your household will change over the next 12 months?' (d) 'How do you think the general economic situation in this country will develop over the next 12 months?' Responses were scored: 'lot worse' = –2, 'little worse' = –1, 'don't know' = zero, 'little better' = one, 'lot better' = two. The analysis yielded one factor with an eigenvalue greater than one, and a factor score variable is computed; (v) *emotional reactions to the NHS and the economy*–respondents were given a list of four positive (happy, hopeful, confident, proud) and four negative (angry, disgusted, uneasy, afraid) words and asked to choose which words described their feelings about the NHS (the economy). The

emotional reactions variables are the number of positive words minus the number of negative words designated; (vi) *socio-demographics*–age in years; ethnicity is a 0–1 dummy variable with respondents designating themselves as 'white British' scored one, and all others scored zero; gender is scored male = one, female = zero; region of residence is a series of 0–1 dummy variables with Greater London as the reference category; social class is the six-category Registrar General (RG) classification. Respondents not able to be classified using the RG scheme who have a spouse/partner are given the spouse/partner's RG classification.

5 Electoral choices

1 Economic evaluations were measured using the results of an exploratory factor analysis of responses to the following questions: (a) 'How does the financial situation of your household now compare with what it was 12 months ago?'; (b) 'How do you think the general economic situation in this country has changed over the last 12 months?'; (c) 'How do you think the financial situation of your household will change over the next 12 months?'; (d) 'How do you think the general economic situation in this country will develop over the next 12 months?'. Responses were scored: 'lot worse' = –2, 'little worse' = –1, 'don't know' = zero, 'little better' = one, 'lot better' = two. The factor analysis yielded one factor with an eigenvalue greater than one, and a factor score variable was computed.

2 Party identification was measured using responses to the standard BES question: 'Generally speaking, do you think of yourself as Labour, Conservative, Liberal Democrat, [Scottish National (Scotland)/Plaid Cymru (Wales)] or what?'. 0–1 dummy variables were created for Labour, Conservative, Liberal Democrat and miscellaneous other parties. Respondents stating 'none', 'no party', or 'don't know' were treated as the reference category.

3 The question wording is: 'How well do you think the present government has handled each of the following issues?'. The numbers designated 'positive' in Figure 5.3 are the percentage of respondents judging that the government has handled a particular issue 'very well' or 'fairly well' and the numbers designated 'negative' are the percentage judging that the government has handled that issue 'fairly badly' or 'very badly'. The order of presentation of issues was randomized.

4 The question wording is: 'How well do you think a Conservative government would handle each of the following issues?'. The order of presentation of issues was randomized. The numbers in Figure 5.4 are computed as described in note 3 above.

5 The questions are: (a) 'Which, if any, of the following words describe your feelings about the country's general economic situation?'; (b) 'Which, if any, of the following words describe your feelings about the National Health Service?'; (c) 'And which of them describes your feelings about the situation in Iraq?'. Respondents could choose from one to eight words, or state that none of the words applied. Since multiple responses were possible, percentages total to more than 100.

6 The question wording is: 'As far as you're concerned, what is the *single most important issue* facing the country at the present time?' (emphasis in original). Respondents supplying an issue were then asked: 'Which party is best able to handle this issue?'. For purposes of the multivariate analyses, 0–1 dummy variables are created for Labour, the Conservatives, the Liberal Democrats and miscellaneous other parties. Respondents not designating a most important issue, those stating that no party was best able to handle the most important issue, and those stating they did not know which party is best, were treated as the reference category.

7 The questions are: (a) 'Now, some questions about the party leaders. Using a scale that runs from 0 to 10, where 0 means a very incompetent leader and 10 means a very competent leader, how would you describe [Tony Blair, Michael Howard, Charles Kennedy]?'; (b) 'Now please use the 0 to 10 scale to indicate the extent to which the different leaders respond to voters' concerns. How would you describe [Tony Blair, Michael Howard, Charles Kennedy]?'; (c) 'Now please use the 0 to 10 scale to indicate how much trust you have for each of the party leaders, where 0 means no trust and 10 means a great deal of trust. How much do you trust [Tony Blair, Michael Howard, Charles Kennedy]?'. The order of (a), (b) and (c) was rotated, and the order of the leaders was rotated within that rotation.

8 The question wording is: 'Now, let's think more generally about the party leaders. Using a scale that runs from 0 to 10, where 0 means strongly dislike and 10 means strongly like, how to you feel about [Tony Blair, Michael Howard, Charles Kennedy]?'. The order of the names of the leaders was randomized.

9 Respondents were asked to place themselves and Labour, Conservative and Liberal Democrat parties on 0–10 scales for the following dimensions: (a) left–right, (b) tax–spend, (c) EU membership, (d) crime–rights of the accused. The issue-proximity variables were the average absolute distances between the respondent and each of the parties on the four dimensions.

10 Age is years; ethnicity is a 0–1 dummy variable with respondents designating themselves as 'white British' scored one, and all others scored

zero; gender is scored male = one, female = zero; region of residence is a series of 0–1 dummy variables with Greater London as the reference category; social class is the six-category Registrar General (RG) classification. For respondents not able to be classified using the RG scheme who have a spouse/partner, we use the spouse/partner's RG classification.

11 Tactical voting is measured using responses to the following question: 'People give different reasons for why they vote for one party rather than another. Which of the following best describes your reasons?' (a) 'the party had the best policies'; (b) 'the party had the best leader'; (c) 'I really preferred another party but it stood no chance of winning in my constituency'. Respondents choosing (c) are considered tactical voters and scored one; all other voters are scored zero.

12 The $AIC = -2*(\ln L(\theta|x)) + 2*K$ where $\ln L(\theta|x)$ is the value of the likelihood for a model K is the number of estimated parameters in the model (Burnham and Anderson, 2002).

13 The social class–voting relationship remains very weak if one uses the Heath-Goldthorpe class measure rather than the Registrar General's measure. Using the Heath-Goldthorpe measure in the Labour vs opposition binomial logit analysis yields a McFadden $R^2 = 0.02$. The model correctly classifies 61.4% of the respondents, less than 1% more than could be done using a naive mode-guessing procedure. For the multinomial logit analysis of voting for specific opposition parties with Labour as the reference category, the McFadden $R^2 = 0.02$, and the model correctly classifies 41.1%, 2.1% better than mode guessing.

14 Orientations towards the Iraq War were measured using the results of an exploratory factor analysis of responses to the following questions: (a) 'How well do you think the present government has handled the situation in Iraq?' Responses to (a) were scored 'very well' = five, 'fairly well' = four, 'neither well nor badly' or 'don't know' = three, 'fairly badly' = two, 'very badly' = one; (b) 'Using a scale from 0 to 10 where 0 means a complete failure and 10 means a complete success, how would you rate the war in Iraq?'; (c) 'Please tell me whether you strongly approve, approve, disapprove, or strongly disapprove of *Britain's involvement* in Iraq?' (emphasis in original). Responses to (c) were scored 'strongly approve' = five, 'approve' = four, 'don't know' = three, 'disapprove' = two, 'strongly disapprove' = one. Item (a) is from the pre-election survey, and (b) and (c) are from the post-election survey. The factor analysis yielded one factor with an eigenvalue greater than one, and a factor score variable was computed.

15 In a binomial or multinomial logit model, the size the effect of any predictor variable depends on the values of all other predictor variables

(Long, 1997). Here, we illustrate what such effects are for each predictor, given plausible values for other predictors.

16 Formally, the mixed logit model is described as: $P(j|vi) = \exp(U_{ji})/\Sigma \exp(U_{ji})$. In this setup, the utility of party choice j for voter i: $U_{ji} = \alpha_{ji} + B_j X_i + \Phi_j Z_{ji} + \Theta_{ji} W_{ji}$, where: α_{ji} = alternative-specific constant (fixed or varying); B_j = vector of fixed coefficients; X_i = fixed individual char-acteristics; Φ_j = vector of fixed coefficients; Θ_j = vector of varying coef-ficients; Z_{ji} & W_{ji} = choice-varying attributes of choices. The randomly varying coefficients are modelled as: $\Theta_{ji} = \rho_{jk} + \delta_{jk}\xi_i + \sigma_k\psi_{ki}$ where: ρ_{jk} = constant term; δ_{jk} = coefficient for individual-specific mean; ξ_i = set of individual characteristics; σ_k = standard deviation of marginal dis-tribution of ρ_{jk}; ψ_{ki} = individual, choice specific random disturbances. To ensure identification in the MXL model, we follow the same rules used to establish necessary conditions for identification in a multino-mial probit model (see, for example, Glasgow 2001).

17 The national identity question is 'Which, if any, of the following best describes how you see yourself?' Response categories differ in England, Scotland and Wales. For example, in Wales, the response categories are: (a) 'Welsh not British', (b) 'More Welsh than British', (c) 'Equally Welsh and British', (d) 'More British than Welsh', (e) 'British not Welsh', (f) 'None of the above', (g) 'Other [Write In]'. In Scotland substitute 'Scottish' for 'Welsh', and in England, substitute 'English' for 'Welsh'. For purposes of the multivariate analyses, the variable is coded as a five-point ordinal scale with (a) = five and (e) = one. Respondents in cat-egories (f) and (g) are coded three.

18 The log normal distribution has support only on the positive side of the real line. The log normal distribution is defined as $f(x) = 1/[x\sigma(2)^{1/2}] * e^{-[\log(x)-\mu]**2/2\sigma**2]}$ and $0 < x < \infty$, $\mu > 0$, $\sigma > 0$, where: μ is the scale parameter, σ is the shape parameter, and e is the base of the natural logarithm. See www.statsoft.com/textbook/stdisfit.html.

19 Political knowledge was measured as the number of correct answers to the following 'true–false' statements: (a) 'Polling stations close at 10 pm on election day'; (b) 'The Liberal Democrats favour a system of pro-portional representation for Westminster elections'; (c) 'The minimum voting age is 16'; (d) 'The standard rate of income tax payable is 26p in the pound'; (e) 'The Chancellor of the Exchequer is responsible for setting interest rates in the UK'; (f) 'Labour wants university students to pay a fee of up to £3,000 each year for their education'; (g) 'The Conservative Party favours imposing strict limits on the number of asy-lum seekers who can enter Britain each year'; (h) 'Any registered voter can obtain a postal vote if they want one–by ringing their local council and asking for a postal vote'. The order in which (a)–(f) was asked was

randomized. Age completing formal education is used to measure level of education.

20 Differential benefits are measured using data from 0–10 'dislike–like' scales for various parties, missing data recoded to mean values for each scale. These data are used to calculate mean absolute distances. For example, suppose that person A rates the Conservatives at nine, Labour at three and the Liberal Democrats at five. The absolute gaps between these three numbers are $9-3=6$ for the Conservative/Labour comparison; $9-5=4$ for the Conservative/Liberal Democrat comparison; and $5-3=2$ for the Liberal Democrat/Labour comparison. The average differential benefits gap for person A is $(6+4+2)/3=4$. Now consider person B, who dislikes all three parties and rates them all the same, at two. Each pair-wise party comparison is now $(2-2=0)$ and the average differential benefits gap is zero. Political influence is measured using a 0–10 scale: 'On a scale from 0 to 10 where 10 means a great deal of influence and 0 means no influence, how much influence do *you* have on politics and public affairs?' (emphasis in original). Missing data were coded to the mean of the response distribution. Costs of voting are measured by asking respondents if they 'strongly agree', 'agree', 'neither agree nor disagree', 'disagree' or 'strongly disagree' with the following statements: (a) 'It takes too much time and effort to be active in politics and public affairs'; (b) 'People are so busy that they don't have time to vote'. Responses are recoded from one ('strongly disagree') to five ('strongly agree') with 'don't know' responses coded three. Recoded responses to (a) and (b) are summed to form an additive index. Sense of civic duty is measured using the following questions: (a) 'It is every citizen's duty to vote in an election'; (b) 'I would be *seriously* neglecting my duty as a citizen if I didn't vote' (emphasis in original). Responses to (a) and (b) were scored: 'strongly agree' = five, 'agree' = four, 'neither agree nor disagree' or 'don't know' = three, 'disagree' = two, 'strongly disagree' = one. Responses to (a) and (b) were summed to form a civic duty index.

21 The group benefit questions are: (a) 'Being active in politics is a good way to get benefits for groups that people care about like pensioners or the disabled'; (b) 'When people like me vote, they can really change the way that Britain is governed'. Responses are scored from 'strongly agree' = five to 'strongly disagree' = one, with 'don't know' scored three. Responses to (a) and (b) are summed to form a group benefits index. Responses to the following 'agree–disagree' statements were used to measure the perceived personal benefits of voting: (d) 'Being active in politics is a good way to get benefits for me and my family'; (e) 'I feel a sense of satisfaction when I vote'; (f) 'I would feel very guilty if I didn't vote in a general

election'. Responses are scored: 'strongly agree' = five, 'agree' = four, 'neither agree nor disagree' or 'don't know' = three, 'disagree' = two, 'strongly disagree' = one. Responses to (d), (e) and (f) are summed to form a personal benefits index. Social norms are measured using responses to the following statements: (g) 'Most of my family and friends think that voting is a waste of time'; and (h) 'Most people around here usually vote in general elections'. Responses to (g) were scored: 'strongly agree' = one, 'agree' = two, 'neither agree nor disagree' or 'don't know' = three, 'disagree' = four, 'strongly disagree' = five. Responses to (h) are scored: 'strongly agree' = five, 'agree' = four, 'neither agree nor disagree' or 'don't know' = three, 'disagree' = two, 'strongly disagree' = one. Responses to (g) and (h) are summed to form a social norms index.

22 Party mobilization was measured using four dichotomous items (scored 0–1) concerning whether: (a) someone tried to convince the respondent to vote for a party; (b) a party canvasser visited the respondent's home and talked to him/her; (c) someone from a party telephoned the respondent to ask them how they would vote; (d) someone from a party contacted the respondent on election day to see if they had voted or intended to vote. The party mobilization variable is sum of (a)–(d). Level of education is age completing formal education, and disability status is scored: have disability = one, do not have disability = zero.

23 The political knowledge index is described in note 19 above. Political involvement is measured using the following question: 'How much interest do you generally have in what is going on in politics?' Response categories are: 'a great deal' (scored four), 'quite a lot' (scored three), 'some' (scored two), 'not very much', 'don't know' (scored one).

24 The relative deprivation variable was measured using: (a) 'The government generally treats people like me fairly'; (b) 'There is often a big gap between what people like me expect out of life and what we actually get'. Responses to (a) are scored: 'strongly agree' = one, 'agree' = two, 'neither agree nor disagree' or 'don't know' = three, 'disagree' = four, 'strongly disagree' = five. Responses to (b) are scored from 'strongly agree' = five to 'strongly disagree' = one. The relative deprivation variable is the sum of (a) and (b).

25 Two questions with 0–10 scales were used to measure social trust: (a) 'On balance, would you say that most people can't be trusted or that most people can be trusted?'. End-points on the scale are: zero 'most people can't be trusted' and ten 'most people can be trusted.' (b) 'Do you think that most people you come into contact with would try to take advantage of you if they got the chance or would they try to be fair?' End-points on the scale are: zero 'try to take advantage' and ten 'try to be fair'. The social trust variable is the average score on (a) and (b).

26 The average size of the electorate in Labour-held seats in 2005 was 66,857, the average for Conservative seats was 72,956, and the average for Liberal Democrat seats was 69,431. See Johnston *et al.* (2006).

6 The short campaign

1 The model was originally developed by Jackman (2005) to gauge the dynamics of party support in the 2004 Australian election. A measured party intention share in a poll conducted by a particular polling agency on a particular day is assumed to be a draw from a normal distribution. The mean of that distribution on a given day reflects the underlying 'true' state of support for a party plus a 'house' effect due to the survey procedures used by a polling agency. Parties' underlying support is assumed to evolve as a random walk with shocks drawn from a normal distribution over the course of the campaign. Initial state values for party support are drawn from a uniform distribution, with support boundaries chosen by the analyst. For purposes of identifying the model, party support evolves towards fixed values at the end of the campaign. In the present analysis, these values are parties' actual vote shares in Britain in the 2005 election. Daily posterior probabilities are generated using Markov Chain Monte Carlo procedures implemented by Winbugs 1.4, interfacing with Andrew Gelman's R4Winbugs program.

2 Party vote shares for Britain were 36.1% for Labour, 33.2% for the Conservatives and 22.6% for the Liberal Democrats. Across the UK, the shares were 35.3% for Labour, 32.3% for the Conservatives, and 22.1% for the Liberal Democrats.

3 There are too few cases to generate reliable estimates of the effects of Nationalist party telephone canvassing or reminders to vote on election day.

4 They include exposure to a party political broadcast. See Figure 6.8.

5 Probabilities were calculated using the Clarify software package. This is done by varying the predictors from their minimum to maximum values to identify their impact on the probability of voting, while holding other variables constant at their mean values. See Tomz *et al.* (2003).

6 In 2005, the Greens received 283,447 votes in Great Britain and UKIP received 605,173 (Kavanagh and Butler, 2005: 204).

7 The 2005 BES RCPS survey started on 4 April and ran until 4 May. Every day, a random sub-sample of the pre-campaign baseline survey respondents (total N = 7,793) were contacted and requested to complete the campaign survey. The average achieved N for these 'daily replicates' was 209 cases. Although this figure is not as large as one would like for estimating quantities of interest, it has the advantage of being

an independent random sample of the RCPS panelists, thus enhancing its value for modelling purposes.

8 The BES RCPS data indicate that there was very little net movement in the strength of macropartisanship over the 2005 campaign. The mean score on a 0–3 strength of party identification scale was 1.59 for day one (6 April) and 1.61 for day twenty-nine (4 May). The scale is scored nonidentifier or 'don't know' = zero, 'not very strong' = one, 'fairly strong' = two, 'very strong' = three.

7 Voting and political participation

1 Variables from the 2005 BES survey on participation in Britain include: vote in the next European parliamentary elections (SPSS variable name = bq49a); vote in the next local government elections (bq49c); work with a group on a political issue (bq49d); take part in a protest or demonstration (bq49e); be active in a voluntary organization (bq49f); give money to a political party (bq49g); try to convince someone how to vote (bq49h); work for a party or candidate in an election (bq49i); discuss politics with family or friends (bq49j); join a boycott of products (bq49k).

2 The Cramer's V statistic for age and voting is 0.21, for volunteering and voluntary activity 0.07 in both cases, and for party membership 0.12.

3 See http://worldvaluesurvey.org and Inglehart (1997).

4 The World Values Surveys ask if respondents have ever joined in a boycott (e026), participated in a demonstration (e027), or belonged to a political party (e028). In relation to voluntary activity, there are questions in the surveys that ask respondents if they have actively volunteered for 15 different types of organization (excluding political parties) (e081 to e095). The percentages in Table 7.3 relate to the number of people who have actively participated in one or more of these. The BES surveys have eleven-point scales asking if people are likely to undertake these activities in the future in the case of demonstrating, boycotting, and volunteering. The percentages in Table 7.3 refer to those respondents who give a score of eight or more on these scales. Finally, party membership is measured by a question that asks if they belong to a political party.

5 The utility of strength of partisanship for this purpose is suggested by the fact that 92 per cent of the party members in the 2005 BES post-election survey were either 'very strong' or 'fairly strong' partisans.

6 A survey was not conducted in September 2006.

7 The cognitive engagement model contains four variables: (a) Age-completed education has six categories: 14 years or under, 15, 16, 17 and 18, 19 and 20, 21 and over (q112); (b) Newspaper readership question

is: 'How often do you read a daily morning newspaper?' Response categories are: every day, sometimes, not at all (q106); (c) Attention to politics—the question is: 'On a scale from 0 to 10, how much attention do you pay to politics and public affairs?' 0 means no attention at all and 10 means a great deal of attention (q35); (d) Policy performance evaluations are factor scores from a principal components analysis of respondent evaluations of five policy areas. These are crime (q55), education (q56), asylum seekers (q57), the National Health Service (q58), and terrorism (q59). For example, in the case of crime respondents were asked: 'Do you think that the crime situation in Britain has … got a lot better, got a little better, the same, got a little worse, got a lot worse?'

8 The general incentives model contains the following measures: (a) Personal Efficacy times Collective Benefits—personal efficacy is measured with a scale asking if politics is too complicated for the respondent to understand. Response categories are: never, seldom, occasionally, regularly and frequently (polcmpl). Collective benefits are measured with a question asking if the respondent feels close to a political party. Response categories are yes and no (clsprty): (b) Costs—number of hours the respondent works in the average week (workhrs); (c) Civic and volunteering norms—a factor analysis of a set of five indicators of the importance of various civic duties to the respondent produced a two factor solution. The eleven-point indicators measured the importance of voting in elections (impvote), having independent opinions (impopin), being active in a voluntary organization (impavo), obeying the law (impoblw), and being active in politics (impapol). The analysis explained 63 per cent of the variance and the civic norms factor loaded on voting, independent opinions and obeying the law. The volunteering norms factor loaded on being active in a voluntary organization and in politics.

9 The valence model contains the following indicators: (a) Party best on the economy is a dummy variable where one—one of the parties is perceived as best at handling the economy; zero—none of the parties are (q17); (b) Leadership evaluations measure the absolute differences between respondent affective evaluations of the three major party leaders, identified using eleven-point scales (q24—Tony Blair; q25—Michael Howard, q26—Charles Kennedy); (c) Party best on most important issue is a dummy variable where 1—the respondent thinks that a party is best at handling his or her most important issue; 0—the respondent does not think this (q46); (d) Strength of partisanship is measured by responses to the following question: 'Would you call yourself very strongly, fairly strongly, not very strongly [Party Named]', the scale contains a fourth category, 'don't know' (q34); (e) Democratic

satisfaction measures responses to the following question: 'Thinking about how well democracy works in this country, on the whole are you very satisfied, fairly satisfied, a little dissatisfied or very dissatisfied with the way that democracy works in this country?' Response categories run from one to five, where don't know is category three (q53).

10 See http://ess.nsd.uib.no.

11 The set of ESS participation measures include: (a) voted in the last national election (vote); (b) worked in a political party or action group (wrkpty); (c) worked in another organization or association (wrkorg); (d) donated money to a political organization (dntmny); (e) boycotted certain products (bctprd); (f) bought products for political/ethical/environmental reasons (bghtprd); (g) signed a petition (sgnptit); (h) taken part in a lawful demonstration (pbldmn); (i) worn or displayed a badge/sticker (badge); (j) participated in an illegal protest (ilglpst).

12 Media consumption of political news is the sum of three variables measuring the use of television, radio and newspapers for political information. Each variable is measured with an eight-point scale of hours spent using the media in a typical weekday (tvpol, rdpol, nwsppol).

13 Interest in politics is measured using factor scores from an analysis of three variables. These were an eleven-point scale measuring how important politics is to the respondent (imppol), a four-category scale measuring interest in politics: very, quite, hardly and not at all interested (polintr), and a seven-category scale measuring how much discussion of politics takes place with friends and family: every day, several times a week, once a week, several times a month, once a month, less often than once a month, never (discpol). The analysis explained 68 per cent of the variance in the three indicators and all loadings exceeded 0.78.

14 Policy evaluations are measured as the sum of two eleven-point satisfaction scales relating to education (stfedu) and health (stfhlth).

15 Leadership evaluations are measures using an eleven-point trust in politicians scale (trstplt).

16 These variables are measured as eleven-point scales that measure satisfaction with the economy (stfeco) and the practice of democracy in the respondent's country (stfdem).

17 Collective benefits are measured using responses to a question asking if the respondent feels close to a political party. Response categories are 'yes' and 'no' (clsprty).

18 Political efficacy is measured with a question asking how often politics is too complicated for the respondent to understand. Response categories are: 'never', 'seldom', 'occasionally', 'regularly' and 'frequently' (polcmpl).

19 The variable name is 'workhrs'.

20 Civic and volunteering norms are measured using a factor analysis
   of a set of five indicators of the importance of various civic duties
   to the respondent. The analysis produced a two-factor solution. The
   eleven-point indicators measured the importance of voting in elections
   (impvote), having independent opinions (impopin), being active in a
   voluntary organization (impavo), obeying the law (impoblw) and being
   active in politics (impapol). The factor analysis explained 63 per cent
   of the variance and voting, independent opinions and obeying the law
   loaded on the 'civic norms' factor. Being active in a voluntary organization and being active in politics loaded on 'volunteering norms' factor.
      Demographic variables also were included in the model. These were:
   (a) occupational status: recoded ISCOCO scale−2,000 to 2,470 = six
   (professionals), 1,000 to 1,319 = five (managers), 3,000 to 3,480 = four
   (technicians), 4,000 to 4,223 = three (routine white-collar workers),
   5,000 to 8,340 = two (skilled manual workers), 9,000 to 9,330 = one
   (semi and unskilled manual workers); (b) age: transformation of
   year born variable (yrbrn); (c) gender−men = 1, women = 0 (gndr);
   (d) ethnicity−respondent belongs to an ethnic minority group = 1, otherwise = 0 (blgetmg).

21 This is the index for the year 2000 obtained from the Global Indicators
   shared dataset, 2005 taken from www.pippanorris.com.

22 See www.politics.tcd.ie/ppmd/.

23 This is defined by the following formula:
   $LsQ = [(\Sigma(s_i - v_i)^2)/2]$ where s_i is the share of seats captured by party i,
   and v_i is the share of votes. For a full discussion of the properties of this
   measure see Gallagher and Mitchell (2005: 602–5).

24 This is defined by the following expression: $N_v = 1 / \Sigma(P_v)^2$ where P_v is
   each party's proportion of the total votes.

8 Performance, people and the political system

1 The British Social Attitudes civic duty data are generated by the following question: 'Which of these statements comes *closest* to your
  view about general elections? (i) It's not really worth voting, (ii) People
  should vote only if they care who wins, (iii) It's everyone's duty to vote.'
  The wording of the Citizen Audit (CA) civic duty question is the same
  as (i) in note 3 below.

2 The factor loadings for the three variables are: (i) general political interest = 0.90, (ii) interest in the 2005 general election = 0.85, (iii) attention
  to politics = 0.90.

3 The BES civic duty statements are: (i) 'It is every citizen's duty to vote
  in an election', (ii) 'I would be seriously neglecting my duty as a citizen

if I didn't vote', (iii) 'I would feel very guilty if I didn't vote in a general election'.

4 The question sequence begins: 'Now, thinking about British political institutions like parliament, please use the scale of 0 to 10 to indicate how much trust you have for each of the following, where 0 is no trust and 10 is a great deal of trust'. Respondents then were asked about their levels of trust for: (i) 'the parliament at Westminster', (ii) 'the civil service', (iii) 'the police', (iv) 'local government in your area'.

5 The question sequence begins: 'Now some questions about political parties in Britain, not any particular party, but political parties generally. Please tick *one* box on each line to show how much you agree or disagree with each of these statements.' The statement wordings are: (i) 'There is often a big difference between what a party promises it will do and what it actually does when it wins an election'; (ii) 'Political parties are more interested in winning elections than in governing afterwards'; (iii) 'The main political parties in Britain don't offer voters real choices in elections because their policies are pretty much the same'; (iv) 'Political parties do more to divide the country than to unite it'; (v) 'Political parties spend too much time bickering with each other'.

6 The question sequence begins: 'Please indicate how you feel about general elections in Britain – not a particular election but elections in general. Please tick *one* box on each line to show how much you agree or disagree with each of these statements.' The statement wordings are: (i) 'Elections allow voters to express their opinions but don't really change anything'; (ii) 'All things considered, most elections are just a big waste of time and money'; (iii) 'The electoral system in Britain is unfair because only Labour or the Conservatives can ever win an election'; (iv) 'Elections help to keep politicians accountable'; (v) 'In elections, the political parties give people real choices'.

7 Wording of the valence judgment questions is presented in the endnotes to Chapter Five.

8 The wording of these agree–disagree statements is: (i) 'Immigrants increase crime rates'; (ii) 'Immigrants generally are good for Britain's economy'; (iii) 'Most asylum seekers who come to Britain should be sent home immediately'; (iv) 'Immigrants make Britain more open to new ideas and cultures'; (v) 'Immigrants take jobs away from people who were born in Britain'; (vi) 'The death penalty, even for very serious crimes, is never justified'; (vii) 'Violent criminals deserve to be deprived of some of their human rights'; (viii) 'Convicted criminals need to be rehabilitated rather than be punished'; (ix) 'People who break the law should be given longer prison sentences'; (x) 'The government has the right to put people suspected of terrorism in prison without trial'; (xi)

'Ordinary working people get their fair share of the nation's wealth'; (xii) 'There is no need for strong trade unions to protect employees' working conditions and wages'; (xiii) 'Private enterprise is the best way to solve Britain's economic problems'.

The wording of the 'crime versus rights' question is: 'Some people think that *reducing crime* is more important than *protecting the rights of people accused* of committing crimes. Other people think that protecting the rights of accused people is more important than reducing crime. On a 0–10 scale, where would you place yourself on this scale?' Zero is identified as 'reducing crime is more important' and ten is identified as 'rights of accused more important'. The 'left–right' question is: 'In politics, people sometimes talk about parties and politicians as being on the *left* or *right*. Using the 0 to 10 scale on this card, where the end marked 0 means *left* and the end marked 10 means *right*, where would you place yourself on this scale?'.

9 The question wording is: 'Do you agree strongly, agree, neither agree nor disagree, disagree, or disagree strongly with the following statement? (i) No matter what, I would *never* break a promise that I made to someone else; (ii) Even when their personal safety is *seriously threatened*, people must be willing to help others; (iii) People should take more responsibility to provide for themselves.'

10 The wording of the trust questions is: (i) 'Now I'd like to ask you about another topic. On balance, would you say that most people can't be trusted or that most people can be trusted? Please use the 0 to 10 scale to indicate your view'; (ii) 'Do you think that most people you come into contact with would try to take advantage of you it they got the chance or would they try to be fair? Please use the 0 to 10 scale again, where 0 means would try to take advantage and 10 means would try to be fair'.

11 The question wording is: 'Generally speaking, how willing are you to take risks?' Response categories are: 'very willing', 'somewhat willing', 'somewhat unwilling', and 'very unwilling'.

Appendix C: Dynamics of party identification

[1] Clarke and McCutcheon (2009) discuss why Green *et al.* (2002) find high levels of partisan stability in their multi-wave panel models.

Bibliography

Achen, Christopher. 1992. 'Social Psychology, Demographic Variables, and Linear Regression: Breaking the Iron Triangle in Voting Research', *Political Behavior*, **14**: 195–211.

2002. 'Parental Socialization and Rational Party Identification', *Political Behavior*, **24**: 151–70.

Adams, James, Samuel Merrill and Bernard Grofman. 2005. *A Unified Theory of Party Competition*. New York: Cambridge University Press.

Ajzen, Icek and Martin Fishbein. 1980. *Understanding Attitudes and Predicting Social Behavior*. Englewood Cliffs, NJ: Prentice-Hall.

Aldrich, John H. 1993. 'Rational Choice and Turnout', *American Journal of Political Science*, **37**: 246–78.

Almond, Gabriel A. 1950. *The American People and Foreign Policy*. New York: Harcourt, Brace & Company.

Almond, Gabriel A. and Sidney Verba. 1963. *The Civic Culture: Political Attitudes and Democracy in Five Nations*. Princeton: Princeton University Press.

Alt, James E. 1984. 'Dealignment and the Dynamics of Partisanship in Britain', in Russell J. Dalton, Paul Beck and Scott Flanagan (eds), *Electoral Change in Advanced Industrial Democracies*. Princeton: Princeton University Press.

Alvarez, R. Michael and John Brehm. 2002. *Hard Choices, Easy Answers*. Princeton: Princeton University Press.

Alvarez, R. Michael and Jonathan Nagler. 1998. 'When Politics and Models Collide: Estimating Models of Multi-Party Elections', *American Journal of Political Science*, **42**: 55–96.

Alvarez, R. Michael, Jonathan Nagler and Shaun Bowler. 2000. 'Issues, Economics and The Dynamics of Multi-Party Elections: The British 1987 General Election', *American Political Science Review*, **94**: 131–49.

Andersen, Robert and Geoffrey Evans. 2003. 'Who Blairs Wins? Leadership and Voting in the 2001 Election', *British Elections and Parties Review*, **13**: 229–47.

Ansolabehere, Stephen and James M. Snyder. 2000. 'Valence Politics and Equilibrium in Spatial Election Models', *Public Choice*, **103**: 327–36.

Banks, Jeffrey S., John Duggan and Michel LeBreton. 2002. 'Bounds for Mixed Strategy Equilibria and the Spatial Model of Elections', *Journal of Economic Theory*, **103**: 88–105.

Barnes, Samuel H. and Max Kaase. 1979. *Political Action: Mass Participation in Five Western Democracies*. Beverly Hills: Sage Publications.

Bartle, John. 2005. 'Homogeneous Models and Heterogeneous Voters', *Political Studies*, **53**: 653–75.

Beer, Samuel. 1965. *British Politics in the Collectivist Age*. New York: Alfred A. Knopf.

1982. *Britain Against Itself: The Political Contradictions of Collectivism*. New York: W. W. Norton.

Berelson, Bernard, Paul F. Lazarsfeld and W. McPhee. 1954. *Voting*. Chicago: University of Chicago Press.

Black, Duncan. 1948. 'On the Rationale of Group Decision-Making', *Journal of Political Economy*, **56**: 23–34.

1958. *The Theory of Committees and Elections*. Cambridge: Cambridge University Press.

Bollen, Kenneth A. 1989. *Structural Equations with Latent Variables*. New York: Wiley-Interscience.

Bowler, Shaun and Todd Donovan. 1998. *Demanding Choices: Opinion, Voting and Direct Democracy*. Ann Arbor: University of Michigan Press.

Brady, Henry and Paul M. Sniderman. 1985. 'Attitude Attribution: A Group Basis for Political Reasoning', *American Political Science Review*, **79**: 1061–78.

Browne, M. W. and R. Cudeck. 1993. 'Alternative Ways of Assessing Model Fit', in Kenneth A. Bollen and J. Scott Long (eds.), *Testing Structural Equation Models*. Beverly Hills, CA: Sage Publications.

Budge, Ian and Dennis Farlie. 1977. *Voting and Party Competition*. London and New York: John Wiley & Sons.

1983. *Explaining and Predicting Elections: Issue Effects and Party Strategies in Twenty-Three Democracies*. London: Allen and Unwin.

Budge, Ian, Hans-Dieter Klingemann, Andrea Vollens, Judith Bara and Eric Tanenbaum. 2001. *Mapping Policy Preferences: Estimates for Parties, Electors, and Governments, 1945–1998*. Oxford: Oxford University Press.

Bueno de Mesquita, Bruce. 1983. *The War Trap*. New Haven: Yale University Press.

Burnham, Kenneth P. and David R. Anderson. 2002. *Model Selection and Multimodel Inference: A Practical Information-theoretic Approach*, 2nd edn. New York: Springer-Verlag.

Butler, David and Donald Stokes. 1969. *Political Change in Britain: Forces Shaping Electoral Choice*. New York: St. Martin's Press.

Calvert, Randall. 1985. 'Robustness of The Multidimensional Voting Model: Candidates, Motivations, Uncertainty and Convergence', *American Journal of Political Science*, **29**: 69–85.

Camerer, Colin F. 2003. *Behavioral Game Theory: Experiments in Strategic Interaction*. New York: Russell Sage Foundation.

Campbell, Angus, Philip Converse, Warren Miller and Donald Stokes. 1960. *The American Voter*. New York: John Wiley & Sons.

Campbell, Angus, Gerald Gurin and Warren Miller. 1954. *The Voter Decides*. Evanston, IL: Row, Peterson.

Charemza, Wojciech W. and Derek F. Deadman. 1997. *New Directions in Econometric Practice*, 2nd edn. Aldershot: Edward Elgar.

Chase, Valerie M., Ralph Hertwig and Gerd Gigerenzer. 1998. 'Visions of Rationality', *Trends in Cognitive Sciences*, **2**: 206–14.

Chittick, William O., Keith R. Billingsley and Rick Travis. 1995. 'A Three-Dimensional Model of American Foreign Policy Beliefs', *International Studies Quarterly*, **39**: 313–31.

Clarke, Harold D. and Allan McCutcheon. 2009. 'The Dynamics of Party Identification Reconsidered', *Public Opinion Quarterly*, **73**: forthcoming.

Clarke, Harold D., Euel E. Elliott, William Mishler, Marianne C. Stewart, Paul Whiteley and Gary Zuk. 1992. *Controversies in Political Economy: Canada, Great Britain, the United States*. Boulder, CO: Westview Press.

Clarke, Harold D., Karl Ho and Marianne C. Stewart. 2000. 'Major's Lesser (Not Minor) Effects: Prime Ministerial Approval and Governing Party Support in Britain Since 1979', *Electoral Studies*, **18**: 255–74.

Clarke, Harold D., Allan Kornberg and Thomas J. Scotto. 2009. *Making Political Choices: Canada and the United States*. Toronto: University of Toronto Press.

Clarke, Harold D., Allan Kornberg and Marianne C. Stewart. 2004a. 'Referendum Voting as Political Choice: The Case of Quebec', *British Journal of Political Science*, **34**: 345–55.

Clarke, Harold D., William Mishler and Paul Whiteley. 1990. 'Recapturing the Falklands: Models of Conservative Popularity, 1979–83', *British Journal of Political Science*, **20**: 63–81.

Clarke, Harold D., David Sanders, Marianne C. Stewart and Paul Whiteley. 2004b. *Political Choice in Britain*. Oxford: Oxford University Press.

Clarke, Harold D., Marianne C. Stewart, Michael Ault and Euel Elliott. 2005. 'Men, Women and The Political Economy of Presidential Approval', *British Journal of Political Science*, **35**: 31–51.

Clarke, Harold D., Marianne C. Stewart and Paul F. Whiteley. 1997. 'Tory Trends: Party Identification and the Dynamics of Conservative Support Since 1992', *British Journal of Political Science*, **26**: 299–318.

    1998. 'New Models for New Labour: The Political Economy of Labour Party Support, January 1992–April 1997', *American Political Science Review*, **92**: 559–75.

Conlisk, John. 1996. 'Why Bounded Rationality?', *Journal of Economic Literature*, **34**: 669–700.

Conover, Pamela and Stanley Feldman. 1986. 'Emotional Reactions to the Economy: I'm Mad as Hell and I'm Not Going to Take It Any More', *American Journal of Political Science*, **30**: 50–78.

Converse, Philip E. 1964. 'The Nature of Belief Systems in Mass Publics', in David E. Apter (ed.), *Ideology and Discontent*. Glencoe, IL: The Free Press.

    1969. 'Of Time and Partisan Stability', *Comparative Political Studies*, **2**: 139–72.

Cox, Gary and Octavio Amorim. 1997. 'Electoral Institutions, Cleavage Structures and the Number of Parties', *American Journal of Political Science*, **41**: 149–74.

Crawford, Vincent and Joel Sobel. 1982. 'Strategic Information Transmission', *Econometrica*, **50**: 1431–51.

Crewe, Ivor. 1974. 'Do Butler and Stokes Really Explain Political Change in Britain?', *European Journal of Political Research*, **2**: 47–92.

Crewe, Ivor and Anthony King. 1994. 'Did Major Win? Did Kinnock Lose? Leadership Effects in the 1992 Election', in Anthony Heath et al. (eds), *Labour's Last Chance? The 1992 Election and Beyond*. Dartmouth: Aldershot.

Curtice, John and Michael Steed. 1997. 'The Results Analysed', in David Butler and Dennis Kavanagh (eds), *The British General Election of 1997*. London: Palgrave Macmillan.

    2002. 'The Results Analysed', in David Butler and Dennis Kavanagh (eds), *The British General Election of 2001*. London: Palgrave Macmillan.

Dahl, Robert A. 1971. *Polyarchy: Participation and Opposition*. New Haven: Yale University Press.

Dalton, Russell J. 2000. 'The Decline of Party Identification', in Russell J. Dalton and Martin P. Wattenberg (eds), *Parties Without Partisans: Political Change in Advanced Industrial Democracies*. Oxford: Oxford University Press.

2006. *Citizen Politics: Public Opinion and Political Parties in Advanced Industrial Democracies*, 4th edn. Washington, DC: Congressional Quarterly Press.

Davidson, Russell and James G. MacKinnon. 1982. 'Some Non-nested Hypothesis Tests and The Relations Among Them', *Review of Economic Studies*, **49**: 551–65.

Denver, David. 2003. *Elections and Voters in Britain*. London: Palgrave Macmillan.

Denver, David and Gordon Hands. 1997. *Modern Constituency Electioneering*. London: Frank Cass.

Denzau, Arthur and Kevin Grier. 1984. 'Determinants of Local School Spending: Some Consistent Estimates', *Public Choice*, **44**: 375–83.

Dorussen, Han and Michaell Taylor (eds). 2002. *Economic Voting*. London: Routledge.

Dow, Jay and James W. Endersby. 2004. 'Multinominal Probit and Multinomial Logit: A Comparison of Choice Models for Voting Research', *Electoral Studies*, **23**: 107–22.

Downs, Anthony. 1957. *An Economic Theory of Democracy*. New York: Harper and Row.

Duch, Raymond M. and Randolph T. Stevenson. 2008. *The Economic Vote: How Political and Economics Institutions Condition Election Results*. New York: Cambridge University Press.

Easton, David. 1965. *A Systems Analysis of Political Life*. New York: John Wiley & Sons.

Edwards, George C. and Tami Swenson. 1997. 'Who Rallies? The Anatomy of a Rally Event', *Journal of Politics*, **59**: 200–12.

Electoral Commission. 2005. *Election 2005: The Results*. London: The Electoral Commission.

Elshtain, Jean Bethke. 1987. *Women and War*. New York: Basic Books.

Elshtain, Jean Bethke and Sheila Tobias (eds). 1990. *Women, Militarism and War: Essays in History, Politics and Social Theory*. Lanham: Rowman and Littlefield.

Enders, Walter. 2004. *Applied Econometric Time-Series*, 2nd edn. New York: John Wiley & Sons.

Enelow, James M. and Melvin Hinich. 1984. *The Spatial Theory of Voting*. New York: Cambridge University Press.

Finkel, Steven E. 1993 'Reexamining the "Minimal Effects" Model in Recent Presidential Campaigns', *Journal of Politics*, **55**: 1–21.

1995. *Causal Analysis With Panel Data*. Thousand Oaks, CA: Sage Publications.

Fiorina, Morris P. 1981. *Retrospective Voting in American National Elections*. New Haven: Yale University Press.

Fisher, Stephen D. and John Curtice. 2006. 'Tactical Unwind? Changes in Party Preference Structure and Tactical Voting from 2001 to 2005', *Journal of Elections, Public Opinion and Parties*, 16: 55–76.

Fiske, Susan T. and Shelley E. Taylor. 1984/2007. *Social Cognition*, 3rd edn. New York: McGraw-Hill.

Franklin, Charles H. 1984. 'Issue Preferences, Socialization, and the Evolution of Party Identification', *American Journal of Political Science*, 28: 459–78.

  1992. 'Measurement and the Dynamics of Party Identification', *Political Behavior*, 14: 297–309.

Franklin, Charles H. and John E. Jackson. 1983. 'The Dynamics of Party Identification', *American Political Science Review*, 77: 957–73.

Franklin, Mark N. 2004. *Voter Turnout and the Dynamics of Electoral Competition*. New York: Cambridge University Press.

Gallagher, Michael and Paul Mitchell (eds). 2005. *The Politics of Electoral Systems*. Oxford: Oxford University Press.

Gelman, Andrew and Gary King. 1993. 'Why are American Presidential Election Campaign Polls so Variable When Votes are so Predictable?', *British Journal of Political Science*, 23: 409–51.

Gelman, Andrew, Gary King and W.J. Boscardin. 1998. 'Estimating the Probability of Events That Have Never Occurred: When Is Your Vote Decisive?', *Journal of The American Statistical Association*, 93: 1–9.

Glasgow, Garrett. 2001. 'Mixed Logit Models for Multiparty Elections', *Political Analysis*, 9: 116–36.

  2005. 'Evidence of Group-Based Economic Voting: NAFTA and Union Households in the 1992 U.S. Presidential Election', *Political Research Quarterly*, 58: 427–34.

Glazer, Amihai and Suzanne Lohmann. 1999. 'Setting the Agenda: Electoral Competition, Commitment of Policy, and Issue Salience', *Public Choice*, 99: 377–94.

Goldstein, Harvey. 1995. *Multilevel Statistical Models*. New York: John Wiley.

Goldstein, Joshua. 2003. *War and Gender: How Gender Shapes the War System and Vice Versa*. New York: Cambridge University Press.

Green, Donald P. and Alan S. Gerber. 2004. *Get Out the Vote: How to Increase Voter Turnout*. Washington: The Brookings Institution.

Green, Donald P. and Bradley Palmquist. 1990. 'Of Artifacts and Partisan Instability', *American Journal of Political Science*, 34: 872–902.

Green, Donald P., Bradley Palmquist and Eric Schickler. 2002. *Partisan Hearts & Minds: Political Parties and the Social Identities of Voters*. New Haven: Yale University Press.

Greene, William H. 2003. *Econometric Analysis*, 5th edn. New York: Prentice-Hall.

Grofman, Bernard. 1985. 'The Neglected Role of the Status Quo in Models of Issue Voting', *Journal of Politics*, 47: 230–7.

Hagenaars, Jacques A. and Allan L. McCutcheon (eds). 2002. *Applied Latent Class Analysis*. Cambridge: Cambridge University Press.

Heath, Anthony F., Roger M. Jowell and John K Curtice. 1985. *How Britain Votes*. Oxford: Pergamon Press.

2001. *The Rise of New Labour: Party Policies and Voter Choices*. Oxford: Oxford University Press.

Hendry, David. 1995. *Dynamic Econometrics*. Oxford: Oxford University Press.

Hensher, David A., John M. Rose and William H. Greene. 2005. *Applied Choice Analysis: A Primer*. Cambridge: Cambridge University Press.

Hinich, Melvin J. 1977. 'Equilibrium in Spatial Voting: The Median Voter Theorem is an Artifact', *Journal of Economic Theory*, 16: 208–19.

Holbrook, Thomas M. 1996. *Do Campaigns Matter?* Thousand Oaks, CA: Sage Publications.

Holsti, Ole R. 1996/2004 (revised). *Public Opinion and American Foreign Policy*. Ann Arbor: University of Michigan Press.

Hotelling, Harold. 1929. 'Stability in Competition', *Economic Journal*, 39: 41–57.

Hurwitz, Jon and Mark Peffley. 1987. 'The Means and Ends of Foreign Policy as Determinants of Presidential Support', *American Journal of Political Science*, 31: 236–58.

Inglehart, Ronald. 1989. *Culture Shift in Advanced Industrial Society*. Princeton: Princeton University Press.

1997. *Modernization and Post-Modernization*. Princeton: Princeton University Press.

Inglehart, Ronald and Pippa Norris. 2003. *Rising Tide: Gender Equality and Cultural Change Around the World*. New York: Cambridge University Press.

Iyengar, Shanto and Donald Kinder. 1987. *News That Matters: Television and American Opinion*. Chicago: University of Chicago Press.

Jackman, Simon. 2005. 'Pooling The Pools Over an Election Campaign', *Australian Journal of Political Science*, 40: 499–517.

Jentleson, Bruce W. 1992. 'The Pretty Prudent Public: Post Post-Vietnam American Opinion on the Use of Military Force', *International Studies Quarterly*, 36: 49–74.

Jentleson, Bruce W. and Rebecca C. Britton. 1998. 'Still Pretty Prudent: Post-Cold War American Public Opinion on the Use of Military Force', *Journal of Conflict Resolution*, 42: 395–417.

Johnston, Richard and Henry E. Brady. 2002. 'The Rolling Cross-Section Design', in Mark N. Franklin and Christopher Wlezien (eds), *The Future of Election Studies*. Amsterdam: Pergamon Press.

Johnston, Richard, Michael G. Hagen and Kathleen Hall Jamieson. 2004. *The 2000 Presidential Election and the Foundations of Party Politics*. New York: Cambridge University Press.

Johnston, Ron and Charles Pattie. 1995. 'The Impact of Spending on Party Constituency Campaigns in Recent British General Elections', *Party Politics*, **1**: 261–73.

Johnston, Ron, David J. Rossiter and Charles J. Pattie. 2006. 'Disproportionality and Bias in the Results of the 2005 General Election in Great Britain: Evaluating the Electoral System's Impact', *Journal of Elections, Public Opinion and Parties*, **16**: 37–54.

Jordan, Donald L. and Benjamin I. Page. 1992. 'Shaping Foreign Policy Opinions', *Journal of Conflict Resolution*, **36**: 227–41.

Kahneman, Daniel and Amos Tversky. 1979. 'Prospect Theory: An Analysis of Decision Under Risk', *Econometrica*, **47**: 313–27.

(eds) 2000. *Choices, Values and Frames*. New York: Cambridge University Press and Russell Sage Foundation.

Kahneman, Daniel, Paul Slovic and Amos Tversky (eds). 1982. *Judgment Under Uncertainty: Heuristics and Biases*. Cambridge: Cambridge University Press.

Kavanagh, Dennis and David Butler. 2005. *The British General Election of 2005*. Basingstoke: Palgrave Macmillan.

Key, V.O. 1968. *The Responsible Electorate: Rationality in Presidential Voting, 1936–1960*. New York: Vintage Books.

Kiewiet, D. Roderick. 1983. *Macroeconomics & Micropolitics: The Electoral Effects of Economic Issues*. Chicago: University of Chicago Press.

King, Anthony (ed.). 2002. *Leaders' Personalities and the Outcome of Democratic Elections*. Oxford: Oxford University Press.

Klingemann, Hans-Dieter, Andrea Voskens, Judith Barr, Ian Budge and Michael McDonald. 2006. *Mapping Policy Preferences II: Estimates for Parties, Electors and Governments in Eastern Europe, European Union and OECD, 1990–2003*. Oxford: Oxford University Press.

Kollman, Kenneth, John Miller and Scott Page. 1992. 'Adaptive Parties in Spatial Elections', *American Political Science Review*, **86**: 929–37.

Kornberg, Allan and Harold D. Clarke. 1992. *Citizens and Community: Political Support in a Democratic Society*. New York: Cambridge University Press.

Koutsoyiannis, A. 1975. *Modern Microeconomics*. London: Macmillan.

Kull, Steven. 1995. 'What the Public Knows That Washington Doesn't', *Foreign Policy*, **101**: 102–15.

Laakso, Marku and Rein Taagepera. 1979. 'Effective Number of Parties: A Measure with Application to West Europe', *Comparative Political Studies*, **12**: 3–27.

Laver, Michael (ed.). 2001. *Estimating The Policy Positions of Political Actors*. London: Routledge.

Lewis-Beck, Michael S. 1988. *Economics and Elections: The Major Western Democracies*. Ann Arbor: University of Michigan Press.

Lewis-Beck, Michael S., William Jacoby, Helmut Norpoth and Herbert Weisberg. 2008. *The American Voter Revisited*. Ann Arbor: University of Michigan Press.

Lijphart, Arend. 1994. *Electoral Systems and Party Systems: A Study of Twenty-Seven Democracies, 1945–1990*. New York: Oxford University Press.

Lin, Tse-min, James M. Enelow and Han Dorussen. 1999. 'Equilibrium in Multicandidate Probablistic Spatial Voting', *Public Choice*, **98**: 59–82.

Lodge, Milton, Marco Steenbergen and Shawn Brau. 1995. 'The Responsive Voter: Campaign Information and the Dynamics of Candidate Evaluation', *American Political Science Review*, **89**: 309–26.

Long, J. Scott. 1997. *Regression Models for Categorical and Limited Dependent Variables*. Thousand Oaks, CA: Sage Publications.

Lupia, Arthur and Mathew D. McCubbins. 1998. *The Democratic Dilemma: Can Citizens Learn What They Really Need to Know?* Cambridge: Cambridge University Press.

Lupia, Arthur, Mathew D. McCubbins and Samuel L. Popkin (eds). 2000. *Elements of Reason: Cognition, Choice, and the Bounds of Rationality*. New York: Cambridge University Press.

Macdonald, Stuart Elaine and George Rabinowitz. 1998. 'Solving the Paradox of Nonconvergence: Valence, Position and Direction in Democratic Politics', *Electoral Studies*, **17**: 281–300.

Marcus, George E., W. Russell Neumann and Michael MacKuen. 2000. *Affective Intelligence and Political Judgement*. Chicago: University of Chicago Press.

Marra, Robin F., Charles Ostrom and Dennis Simon. 1990. 'Foreign Policy and Presidential Popularity', *Journal of Conflict Resolution*, **34**: 588–623.

Marsh, Alan. 1977. *Protest and Political Consciousness*. London: Sage Publications.

Matthews, Steven. 1979. 'A Simple Directional Model of Electoral Competition', *Public Choice*, **34**: 141–56.

McDonald, Michael P. and Samuel L. Popkin. 2001. 'The Myth of the Vanishing Voter', *American Political Science Review*, **95**: 963–74.

McKelvey, Richard D. 1976. 'Intransitivities in Multi-dimensional Voting Models and Some Implications for Agenda Control', *Journal of Economic Theory*, **12**: 472–82.

McKelvey, Richard D. and Peter C. Ordeshook. 1990. 'A Decade of Experimental Research on Spatial Models of Elections and Committees', in James Enelow and Melvin J. Hinich (eds), *Advances in The Spatial Theory of Voting*. New York: Cambridge University Press.

Meernik, James and Michael Ault. 2001. 'Public Opinion and Support for U.S. Presidents' Foreign Policies', *American Politics Research*, **29**: 352–73.

Merrill, Samuel III and Bernard Grofman. 1999. *A Unified Theory of Voting: Directional and Proximity Spatial Models*. Cambridge: Cambridge University Press.

Miller, Warren E. and J. Merrill Shanks. 1996. *The New American Voter*. Cambridge, MA: Harvard University Press.

Morrow, James D. 2000. 'Alliances: Why Write Them Down?', in Nelson W. Polsby (ed.), *Annual Review of Political Science*, vol. 3. Palo Alto, CA: Annual Reviews.

Mueller, Dennis. 2003. *Public Choice III*. New York: Cambridge University Press.

Mueller, John E. 1973. *War, Presidents and Public Opinion*. New York: John Wiley.

Muller, Edward N. 1979. *Aggressive Political Participation*. Princeton: Princeton University Press.

Mutz, Diana. 1992. 'Mass Media and Depoliticization of Personal Experience', *American Journal of Political Science*, **36**: 483–508.

1998. *Impersonal Influence: How Perceptions of Mass Collectives Affect Political Attitudes*. Cambridge: Cambridge University Press.

Nadeau, Richard, Pierre Martin and Andre Blais. 1999. 'Attitudes Towards Risk-Taking and Individual Choice in the Quebec Referendum on Sovereignty', *British Journal of Political Science*, **29**: 523–39.

Neumann, W. Russell, George E. Marcus, Ann N. Crigler and Michael MacKuen (eds). 2007. *The Affect Effect*. Chicago: University of Chicago Press.

Norpoth, Helmut. 1987. 'Guns and Butter and Government Popularity in Britain', *American Political Science Review*, **81**: 949–59.

1997. *Confidence Regained: Economics, Mrs. Thatcher, and the British Voter*. Ann Arbor: University of Michigan Press.

Norpoth, Helmut, Michael S. Lewis-Beck and Jean Dominique Lafay (eds) 1991. *Economics and Politics: The Calculus of Support*. Ann Arbor: University of Michigan Press.

Norris, Pippa (ed.). 1999. *On Message: Communicating the Campaign*. London: Sage Publications.

2000. *A Virtuous Circle: Political Communication in Postindustrial Societies*. Cambridge: Cambridge University Press.

Ostrom, Jr, Charles W. and Brian L. Job. 1986. 'The President and the Political Use of Force', *American Political Science Review*, 80: 541–66.

Page, Benjamin I. and Robert Y. Shapiro. 1992. *The Rational Public: Fifty Years of Trends in Americans' Policy Preferences*. Chicago: University of Chicago Press.

Parry, Geraint, George Moyser and Neil Day. 1992. *Political Participation and Democracy in Britain*. Cambridge: Cambridge University Press.

Patterson, Thomas E. 2002. *The Vanishing Voter: Civic Involvement in An Age of Uncertainty*. New York: Knopf.

Pattie, Charles, Patrick Seyd and Paul Whiteley. 2004. *Citizenship in Britain: Values, Participation and Democracy*. Cambridge: Cambridge University Press.

Peffley, Mark and Jon Hurwitz. 1992. 'International Events and Foreign Policy Beliefs: Public Response to Changing Soviet–U.S. Relations', *American Journal of Political Science*, 36: 431–61.

Plott, Charles. 1967. 'A Notion of Equilibrium and Its Possibility under Majority Rule', *American Economic Review*, 57: 787–806.

Pommerehne, Werner and Bruno S. Frey. 1976. 'Two Approaches to Estimating Public Expenditures', *Public Finance Quarterly*, 4: 395–407.

Popkin, Samuel L. 1991. *The Reasoning Voter: Communication and Persuasion in Presidential Campaigns*. Chicago: University of Chicago Press.

Pulzer, Peter. 1968. *Political Elections and Representation in Britain*. London: Allen and Unwin.

Putnam, Robert. 2000. *Bowling Alone: The Collapse and Revival of American Community*. New York: Simon & Schuster.

Quantitative Micro Software. 2007. *Eviews 6, User's Guide II*. Irvine, CA: Quantitative Micro Software.

Rabinowitz, George and Stuart Elaine Macdonald. 1989. 'A Directional Theory of Issue Voting', *American Political Science Review*, 83: 93–121.

Raudenbush, Stephen W. and Anthony S. Bryk. 2002. *Hierarchical Linear Models: Applications and Data Analysis Methods*, 2nd edn. Thousand Oaks, CA: Sage Publications.

Reilly, John (ed.). 1987. *American Public Opinion and U.S. Foreign Policy, 1987.* Chicago: Chicago Council on Foreign Relations.

Richman, Alvin, Eloise Malone and David B. Nolle. 1997. 'Testing Foreign Policy Belief Structures of the American Public in the Post-Cold War Period: Gross Validations from Two National Surveys', *Political Research Quarterly*, 50: 939–55.

Riker, William. 1980. 'Implications from the Disequilibrium of Majority Rule for the Study of Institutions', *American Political Science Review*, 74: 432–46.

Riker, William and Peter C. Ordeshook. 1968. 'A Theory of the Calculus of Voting', *American Political Science Review*, 62: 25–42.

1973. *An Introduction to Positive Political Theory.* Englewood Cliffs, NJ: Prentice-Hall.

Rosenstone, Steven J. and John Mark Hansen. 1993. *Mobilization, Participation and Democracy in America.* New York: Macmillan.

Sanders, David. 1991. 'Government Popularity and the Next General Election', *Political Studies*, 62: 235–61.

2005. 'The Political Economy of Party Support, 1997–2004: Forecasts for the 2005 General Election', *Journal of Elections, Public Opinion and Parties*, 15: 47–71.

Sanders, David, Harold D. Clarke, Marianne C. Stewart and Paul Whiteley. 2007. 'Does Mode Matter for Modeling Political Choice?: Evidence from The 2005 British Election Study', *Political Analysis*, 15: 257–85.

2008. 'The Endogeneity of Preferences in Spatial Models: Evidence from The 2005 British Election Study', *Journal of Elections, Public Opinion and Parties*: Special Issue on Internet Surveys and National Elections Studies, 18: 413–31.

Sarlvik, Bo and Ivor Crewe. 1983. *Decade of Dealignment: The Conservative Victory of 1970 and Electoral Trends in the 1970s.* Cambridge: Cambridge University Press.

Schoemaker, Paul J.H. 1982. 'The Expected Utility Model: Its Variants, Purposes, Evidence and Limitations', *Journal of Economic Literature*, 20: 529–63.

Schofield, Norman. 1978. 'Instability of Simple Dynamic Games', *Review of Economic Studies*, 45: 575–94.

1985. *Social Choice and Democracy.* Berlin: Springer-Verlag.

2003. 'Valence Competition in the Spatial Stochastic Model', *Journal of Theoretical Politics*, 15: 371–83.

2005. 'A Valence Model of Political Competition in Britain: 1992–1997', *Electoral Studies*, 24: 347–70.

Seyd, Patrick and Paul Whiteley. 1992. *Labour's Grassroots: The Politics of Party Membership.* Oxford: Clarendon Press.

2002. *New Labour's Grassroots: The Transformation of the Labour Party Membership*. London: Palgrave Macmillan.

Smith, Jon. 2005. *Election 2005*. London: The Press Association/Politico's.

Sniderman, Paul M., Richard A. Brody and James Kuklinski. 1984. 'Policy Reasoning on Political Issues: The Problem of Racial Equality', *American Journal of Political Science*, **28**: 75–94.

Sniderman, Paul M., Richard A. Brody and Phillip E. Tetlock (eds). 1991. *Reasoning and Choice: Explorations in Political Psychology*. Cambridge: Cambridge University Press.

Snijders, T. A. B. and Roel J. Bosker. 1999. *Multilevel Analysis: An Introduction to Basic and Advanced Multilevel Modeling*. London: Sage Publications.

Stewart, Marianne C. and Harold D. Clarke. 1992. 'The (Un)Importance of Party Leaders: Leader Images and Party Choice in the 1987 British Election', *Journal of Politics*, **54**: 447–70.

1998. 'The Dynamics of Party Identification in Federal Systems: The Canadian Case', *American Journal of Political Sciences*, **42**: 97–116.

Stokes, Donald E. 1963. 'Spatial Models of Party Competition', *American Political Science Review*, **57**: 368–77.

1992. 'Valence Politics', in Dennis Kavanagh (ed.), *Electoral Politics*. Oxford: Clarendon Press.

Texeira, Ruy A. 1987. *Why Americans Don't Vote: Turnout Decline in the United States 1960–1984*. New York: Greenwood Press.

1992. *The Disappearing American Voter*. Washington: The Brookings Institution.

Thaler, Richard. 1991/1994. *Quasi Rational Economics*. New York: Russell Sage Foundation.

(ed.). 1993. *Advances in Behavioral Finance*. New York: Russell Sage Foundation.

Thomassen, Jacques (ed.). 2005. *The European Voter: A Comparative Study of Modern Democracies*. Oxford: Oxford University Press.

Tomz, Michael, Jason Wittenberg and Gary King. 1999. *CLARIFY: Software for Interpreting and Presenting Statistical Results*. Cambridge, MA: Harvard University, Department of Government.

2003. *CLARIFY: Software for Interpreting and Presenting Statistical Results*. Cambridge, MA: Harvard University, Department of Government.

Tourangeau, Roger, Lance Rips and Kenneth Rasinski. 2000. *The Psychology of Survey Response*. New York: Cambridge University Press.

Train, K. 2003. *Discrete Choice Methods with Simulation*. Cambridge: Cambridge University Press.

van der Brug, Wouter, Cees van der Eijk and Mark N. Franklin. 2007. *The Economy and the Vote: Economic Conditions and Elections in Fifteen Countries.* Cambridge: Cambridge University Press.

van der Pol, Frank, Rolf Langeheine and Wil de Jong. 1999. *PANMARK 3 User's Manual,* 2nd version. The Netherlands: Voorburg.

Vanhanen, Tatu. 1997. *Prospects of Democracy: A Study of 172 Countries.* London: Routledge.

Verba, Sidney and Norman H. Nie. 1972. *Participation in America.* New York: Harper & Row.

Verba, Sidney, Norman H. Nie and Jae-on Kim. 1971. *The Modes of Democratic Participation: A Cross-national Comparison.* New York: Sage Publications.

Walker, Iain and Heather J. Smith. 2002. 'Fifty Years of Relative Deprivation Research', in Iain Walker and Heather J. Smith (eds), *Relative Deprivation: Specification, Development and Integration.* Cambridge: Cambridge University Press.

Wallas, Graham. 1908. *Human Nature in Politics.* London: Archibald Constable and Company.

Wattenberg, Martin P. 2000. 'The Decline of Party Mobilization', in Russell J. Dalton and Martin P. Wattenberg (eds), *Parties without Partisans: Political Change in Advanced Industrial Democracies.* Oxford: Oxford University Press.

Whiteley, Paul. 1995. 'Rational Choice and Political Participation – Evaluating The Debate', *Political Research Quarterly,* **48**: 211–34.

Whiteley, Paul and Patrick Seyd. 1994. 'Local Party Campaigning and Voting Behaviour in Britain', *Journal of Politics,* **56**: 242–52.

2002. *High-Intensity Participation – The Dynamics of Party Activism in Britain.* Ann Arbor: University of Michigan Press.

Whiteley, Paul, Patrick Seyd and Anthony Billinghurst. 2006. *Third Force Politics: Liberal Democrats at the Grassroots.* Oxford: Oxford University Press.

Whiteley, Paul, Marianne C. Stewart, David Sanders and Harold D. Clarke. 2005. 'The Issue Agenda and Voting in 2005', in Pippa Norris and Christopher Wlezien (eds), *Britain Votes 2005.* Oxford: Oxford University Press.

Wittman, Donald. 1973. 'Parties as Utility Maximizers', *American Political Science Review,* **67**: 490–8.

1977. 'Candidates with Policy Preferences: A Dynamic Model', *Journal of Economic Theory,* **14**: 180–9.

Wlezien, Christopher and Pippa Norris. 2005. 'Conclusion: Whether the Campaign Mattered and How', in Pippa Norris and Christopher Wlezien (eds), *Britain Votes 2005.* Oxford: Oxford University Press.

Zaller, John. 1992. *The Nature and Origins of Mass Opinion.* New York: Cambridge University Press.

Zaller, John and Stanley Feldman. 1992. 'A Simple Model of the Survey Response: Answering Questions versus Revealing Preferences', *American Journal of Political Science,* **36**: 579–616.

Index

1992 currency crisis, 152–3
2005 British Election Study (BES), 20–2
2005 election, 143, 189–91, 192
  competing models, 163–8
  economic evaluations, 144–5
  emotional reactions, 150–2, 168
  issue agenda, 55–64, 152–6
  leaders, 156–9, 200–1
  local campaign/ 'ground war', 204–12
  official campaign, 193–203, 229–30
  party identification, 146–7, 170
  party performance, 147–50
  result, 9–10
  spatial models, 160–1
  tactical voting, 163
  turnout and party choice, 186–7
9/11, *see* September 11, 2001 (terrorist attack)
'affect' heuristics, 42–3
age, *see also* Conservatives, older issues
  and public opinion on British participation in Iraq War, 107, 120, 125
  political participation and, 234–5, 236–8, 248
air war, 193
Annie, decision not to vote, 6
Ansolabehere, Stephen, 45
asylum/immigration, 55, 61–2, 62–4, *see also* new security agenda
  evaluation of 2005 Labour party, 147
authoritarians, 298–9

benefits and costs model, 110–3, 117–20

BES (2005 British Election Study), 20–2
Bevin, Ernest, 103
bias, inherent in electoral system, 14
Black, Duncan, 30
Blair, Tony
  2005 campaign remarks, 192, 194
  2005 election success, 101
  advocacy for Iraq war, 104–5
  'Bliar' attack, 198, 223
  claims of crime reduction, 198
  damage from Iraq War, 7, 13–14, 53–4, 133–41, 170–4
  ineffectual call to Chinese premier, 193–4
  leadership ratings, 70, 157–8, 159, 200–1, 203
  party leader image, 11–12, 54
  'people's princess' speech, 135, 136
  stumbled in tv debate, 201–2
  voter view of Blair's response to September 11, 2001 (terrorist attack), 3
  voters' perception of, 2–3
BNP
  2005 campaign broadcasts, 221
  running only in selected constituencies, 175
Bosnian War, 2, 9
boycotting, 234, 236, 238, 239, *see also* marketplace politics
Brown, Gordon
  as Chancellor
    economic judgment trusted, 3–4
    efficient running of the economy, 2
    operating within 'golden rule', 10
  as Prime Minister, 314–18, 319, 320
  choice as replacement for Blair, 15